Refining Composition Skills

Refining Composition Skills

Rhetoric and Grammar for ESL Students

THIRD EDITION

REGINA L. SMALLEY

MARY K. RUETTEN

University of New Orleans

Maxwell Macmillan
International Publishing Group

Library of Congress Cataloging-in-Publication Data

Smalley, Regina L.
Refining composition skills : rhetoric and grammar for ESL students / Regina L. Smalley, Mary K. Ruetten. —3rd ed.
p. cm.
Includes index.
ISBN 0-02-411825-7
1. English language—Rhetoric. 2. English language—Textbooks for foreign speakers. I. Ruetten, Mary K. II. Title.
PE1408.S577 1990
808′.042—dc20 89-27101
CIP

Collier Macmillan Canada, Inc.

Credits appear at the back of the book, which constitutes an extension of the copyright page.

Editor: Maggie Barbieri
Production Manager: Nick Sklitsis
Text Designer: Jane Edelstein
Cover Designer: Jane Edelstein
Cover photograph: The Image Bank

This book was set in Garamond by Digitype, Inc., and printed and bound by Von Hoffman Press, Inc. The cover was printed by Von Hoffman Press, Inc.

Printing: 2 3 4 5 6 7 Year: 0 1 2 3 4 5 6
Maxwell Macmillan International Publishing Group
ESL/EFL Department
866 Third Avenue
New York, NY 10022

Printed in the U.S.A.

ISBN 0-02-411825-7

Preface

The third edition of *Refining Composition Skills* presents an integrated program of writing for high-intermediate and advanced students of English as a second language. It combines extensive practice in rhetorical strategies and techniques with a review of appropriate grammatical structures and verb tenses. With its extensive appendixes, the text can further serve as a handbook for writing, grammar, and mechanics. The primary audience is the academically oriented ESL student; however, the text also can be useful in developmental writing courses for native speakers who could benefit from more guidance in writing compositions.

Refining Composition Skills can accommodate the needs of students of varying degrees of experience and levels of writing skills. Inexperienced writers will build a solid foundation in writing beginning with Unit One, which presents the basic paragraph patterns useful for high school- or college-level writing: narrative, descriptive, and expository. This unit covers developing and restricting topic sentences; organizing and developing effective, detailed support of the controlling idea; and outlining. Students who have had considerable practice composing the types of paragraphs presented in this unit may consider the chapters in Unit One a review. More experienced writers might begin the text with Unit Two, which focuses on the multiparagraph essay. This unit introduces the common patterns of exposition along with argumentation. Here the emphasis is on a strong thesis statement and appropriate and well-organized support.

Except for Chapters 1 and 5, which provide introductions to the paragraph and essay, respectively, each chapter in *Refining Composition Skills* focuses on a rhetorical mode of development and the conventions associated with that mode. Each chapter contains four basic components: reading selections, an introduction to the rhetorical pattern, the relevant composition skills (devices for achieving coherence), and a grammar review. The rhetorical patterns are carefully and clearly explained and illustrated, often with student samples that can be used as models early in the chapter. The section on composition skills introduces techniques for achieving coherence, such as the use of adverbial clauses and transitional expressions, and encourages the application of those skills in the writing of compositions, thus emphasizing the necessity for revision in the writing process. In addition, each chapter includes exercises for mastery of the composition skills. The grammar review section is designed to reinforce the rhetoric. Therefore, the grammatical structures reviewed are generally those that are particularly appropriate for the rhetorical pattern. Although the grammar review is not intended to be comprehensive, an attempt has been made to include those common problem areas for ESL students. The grammar is presented in the context of the rhetorical mode—or pattern—and the exercises are often designed to generate further writing practice of that pattern. To conclude the writing and grammar components, additional writing assignments of varying difficulty are provided.

One of the major changes in the third edition of *Refining Composition Skills* is an expanded and improved reading component. Each chapter (except Chapters 1 and 5) begins with several thematically chosen readings with topics geared toward the interests of academically oriented ESL students. The readings are followed by comprehension/discussion questions intended to generate lively class discussions and provocative essay topics. In addition, each chapter topic is reinforced in the examples and exercises throughout the chapter. The reading passages also function as examples of the rhetorical modes and of professional writing, providing evidence that the principles of rhetoric apply in writing both outside and inside the classroom. The expanded reading component allows for greater flexibility in teaching: teachers who wish to focus on the academic content of the essays can begin with the introductory essays, whereas teachers who prefer the developmental approach can begin with the sections on rhetoric.

Other revisions in this edition include a checklist at the end of each chapter and an appendix on proofreading. The checklists, which summarize the important aspects of the particular type of paragraph or essay under consideration in each chapter, provide students with a handy way to check the rhetorical effectiveness of their essays. The proofreading exercises in Appendix VII give additional practice in this important skill. Finally, many of the student models, exercises, and examples have been improved in this edition. In short, *Refining Composition Skills* retains its developmental, step-by-step approach to writing while providing greater emphasis on reading and academic content.

Acknowledgments

We would like to thank our reviewers, our colleagues, and our students for offering their valuable suggestions during the preparation of the third edition. We are especially grateful to Cooper R. Mackin, Mary's husband, who provided help and abiding encouragement; to Maggie Barbieri, ESL editor at Macmillan, who urged us to undertake this revision; and to Kathy Niemczyk, college production managing editor, who saw this edition through production with care and efficiency.

R. L. S.
M. K. R.

Contents

Unit One THE PARAGRAPH

Refining Composition Skills

Unit One

THE PARAGRAPH

Chapter 1

Introduction to the Paragraph

WHAT is a paragraph? You probably know that a paragraph is a group of sentences and that the first sentence of this group is indented; that is, it begins a little bit more to the right of the margin than the rest of the sentences in this group. But it is not enough to say that a paragraph is a group of sentences. How do these sentences relate to each other? How does a paragraph begin and where does it end? What constitutes a good paragraph? These are the questions we answer in this first unit.

The Topic of a Paragraph

To begin with, a *paragraph* is defined as a group of sentences that develops one main idea; in other words, a paragraph develops a topic. A *topic* is the subject of the paragraph; it is what the paragraph is about. Read the following paragraph, which is *about* the habit of smoking cigarettes.

> Smoking cigarettes can be an expensive habit. Considering that the average price per pack of cigarettes is about one dollar, people who smoke two packs of cigarettes a day spend $2.00 per day on their habit. At the end of one year, these smokers have spent at least $730.00. But the price of cigarettes is not the only expense cigarette smokers incur. Since cigarette smoke has an offensive odor that permeates clothing, stuffed furniture, and carpet, smokers often find that these items must be cleaned more frequently than nonsmokers do. Although it is difficult to estimate the cost of this additional expense, one can see that this hidden expense does contribute to making smoking an expensive habit.

EXERCISE 1-1

Study the following paragraphs to find their topics. Write the topic for each paragraph in the space provided.

1. A final examination in a course will give a student the initiative to do his or her best work throughout the course. Students who are only taking notes and attending classes in order to pass a few short tests will not put forth their best effort. For instance, some of my friends in drama, in which there is no final examination, take poor notes, which they throw away after each short test. Skipping classes also becomes popular. Imagine the incredible change a final examination would produce. Students would have to take good notes and attend all classes in order to be prepared for the final examination. —*Suzanne Gremillion*

This paragraph is about ______________________________.

2. Another reason why I like the beach is its solitary atmosphere. At the beach I have no witness but the beach, and I can speak and think with pleasure. No one can interrupt me, and the beach will always be there to listen to everything I want to say. In addition, it is a quiet place to go to meditate. Meditation requires solitude. Many times when I am confused about something, I go to the beach by myself, and I find that this is the best place to resolve my conflicts, solve problems, and to think. —*M. Veronica Porta*

This paragraph is about ______________________________.

3. Some seeming English-Spanish equivalents are deceptive. Their forms are similar, but they have developed different shades of meaning in the two languages. These are sure to cause trouble for Spanish speakers learning English. The Spanish word *asistir* looks like the English word *assist* but has none of the latter's meaning of "help." Instead, *asistir* means "to attend" or "to be present." Thus, Spanish English speakers will say that they assisted a class when they mean that they were present at it. *Actual* in Spanish means "present," not English "actual"; *desgracia* means "misfortune" not "disgrace," *ignorar* means "not to know" instead of "to ignore." —Jean Malmstrom, *Language in Society* (New York: Hayden, 1965), pp. 108–9.

This paragraph is about ______________________________.

4. When we make attributions about ourselves or about others, we tend to attribute the behavior in question to either *internal* or *external* forces. When you see someone crash his car into a telephone pole, you can attribute that unfortunate piece of behavior either to internal or external causes. You might conclude that the person is a terrible driver or emotionally upset (internal causes), or you might conclude that another car forced the driver off the road

(external cause). If you fail an exam, you can attribute it to internal causes such as stupidity or a failure to study, or you can attribute it to external causes such as an unfair test or an overheated room. —John P. Houston, *Motivation* (New York: Macmillan, 1985), p. 255.

This paragraph is about ______________________________.
____

Although usually you are assigned topics to write about, often these topics are too general to be developed adequately in one paragraph. After all, for most practical purposes your paragraphs will range in length from about seven to fifteen sentences. Therefore, you will need to *restrict* your topic; that is, you will need to narrow down your topic to a more specific one. Suppose, for example, that you are asked to write about your favorite place and you choose a country such as Mexico. Although you could easily write several sentences naming all the things you like about Mexico, it would be more interesting for your reader if you narrowed down the topic *Mexico* to a particular place in Mexico, such as the Great Temple in the Aztec ruins. Your topic should be narrowed down as much as possible. Look at how the topic *Mexico* is narrowed here:

Of course, there are many other ways to narrow the same topic. For example:

Now let us suppose that you are asked to write a paragraph about drugs. Obviously, the topic *drugs* is far too broad for specific development in one paragraph; the topic needs to be narrowed down, restricted. Observe here how the topic *drugs* can be restricted:

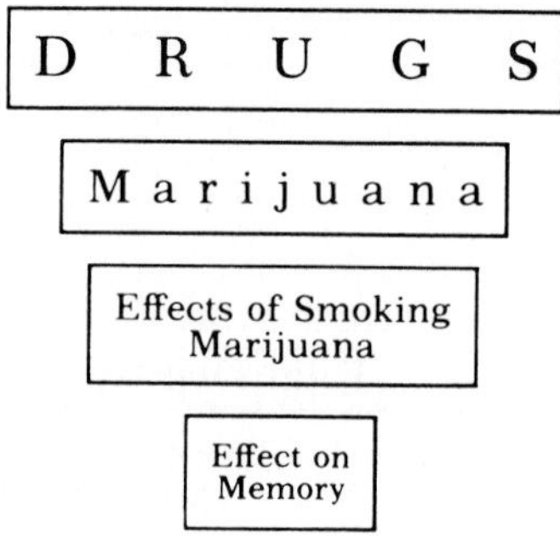

This paragraph, then, will discuss *one* of the effects of smoking marijuana: memory loss. Like most topics, this one can be narrowed down in several ways. Observe:

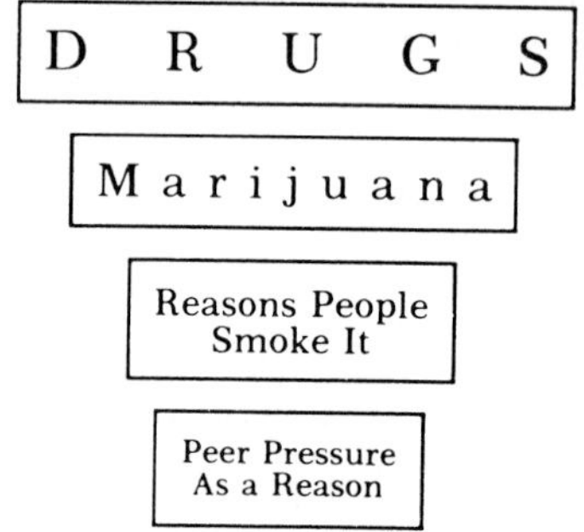

This paragraph will discuss one of the reasons people smoke marijuana: peer pressure.

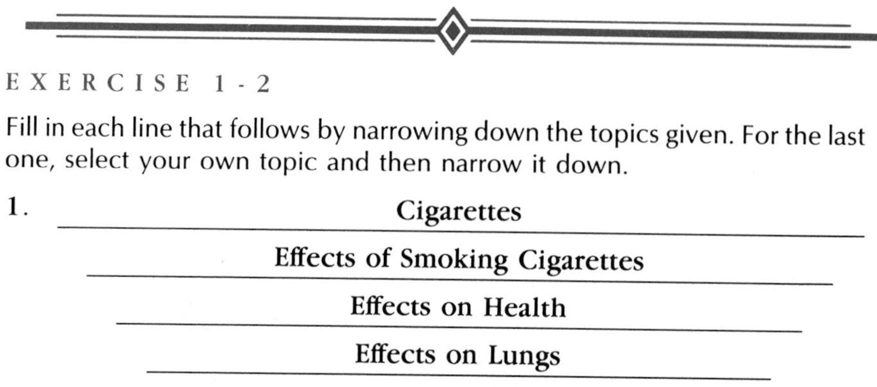

EXERCISE 1-2

Fill in each line that follows by narrowing down the topics given. For the last one, select your own topic and then narrow it down.

1. Cigarettes
   Effects of Smoking Cigarettes
   Effects on Health
   Effects on Lungs
2. Cigarettes

Cigarette Smokers
___
Types of Cigarette Smokers
___

___

3. Technology
___
Computers
___
Three Uses of Computers
___

___

4. Fatal Diseases
___
Cancer
___

___

___

5. My Hometown
___

___

___

___

6. ___

___

___

___

The Topic Sentence

The topic of a paragraph is usually introduced in a sentence; this sentence is called the *topic sentence*. However, the topic sentence can do more than introduce the subject of the paragraph. A good topic sentence also serves to state an idea or an attitude about the topic. This idea or attitude about the topic is called the *controlling idea*; it controls what the sentences in the paragraph will discuss. All sentences in the paragraph should relate to and develop the controlling idea. To illustrate, let us look at the following topic sentence to identify the topic and the controlling idea:

Smoking cigarettes can be an expensive habit.

In this sentence, the topic is the ***habit of smoking cigarettes***; the controlling idea is that smoking can be *expensive*. A paragraph that develops this topic sentence should demonstrate that smoking cigarettes can indeed be an expensive habit. Reread the paragraph on page 3 and see if it develops the idea of *expensive*.

Of course, there are many other controlling ideas one could have about the topic of smoking cigarettes. Indeed, one of the most popular is that it is hazardous to health. See how this idea is developed in the following paragraph:

> Smoking cigarettes is hazardous to your health. Several years ago, a United States government study was released that linked the intake of tar and nicotine, found in cigarettes, with the development of cancer in laboratory animals. The evidence was so overwhelming that the United States government required cigarette manufacturers to put a warning on the outside of each package of cigarettes, which says, "Warning: The Surgeon General has determined that cigarette smoking is hazardous to your health." Aside from the most serious and dreaded disease, cancer, cigarette smoking also can aggravate or promote other health problems. For example, smoking can increase the discomfort for people with asthma and emphysema. It can give one a "smoker's cough" and contribute to bronchitis. Finally, recent studies have shown that cigarette smokers are more susceptible to common colds and flu. Whether you get an insignificant cold or the major killer, cancer, smoking cigarettes is hazardous. Is it worth it?

EXERCISE 1-3

Study the topic sentences that follow. Circle the controlling idea and underline the topic in each sentence. *Note*: The controlling idea and the topic may be expressed in more than one word. The first one is done for you.

1. Another way to reduce the rate of inflation is to balance the federal budget.
2. Einstein's unsuccessful attempt to get nuclear weapons banned was disappointing to him.
3. Savings bonds are also a safe investment.
4. Another problem for students is finding a part-time job.
5. A properly planned science fiction course should include a unit on political implications.
6. Some seeming English-Spanish equivalents are deceptive.
7. Another reason air pollution is hazardous is that it damages the earth's ozone layer.
8. Although bright, Maria is a very shy girl.
9. A final advantage Martina Navratilova has on the court is her constant aggressiveness.
10. One of the biggest problems with athletic scholarships is that more attention is paid to sports than to education.

Improving the Topic Sentence

As indicated, a topic sentence introduces the topic and the controlling idea about that topic. However, it is not enough merely to have a topic and a controlling idea. The controlling idea should be clear and focused on a particular aspect. For example, consider the following topic sentence:

Drinking coffee is bad.

This sentence has a topic—*drinking coffee*—and a controlling idea—*bad*—but they are vague. In what way is coffee bad? For whom or what is it bad? Is drinking only a little coffee bad, or is drinking a lot of coffee bad? As you can see, this topic sentence leaves a lot of questions that probably cannot be answered effectively in one paragraph. The sentence needs more focus, and that focus can come from the controlling idea:

Drinking over four cups of coffee a day can be harmful to pregnant women.

In this version, the topic itself is narrowed down some more, and the controlling idea is more precise.

EXERCISE 1-4

Study the following groups of sentences. Circle the number of the better topic sentence in each pair. The first one is done for you.

1. There are many things that make learning the English language difficult.
2. (circled) What makes English particularly difficult to learn is pronunciation.

3. Enrolling in college is not an easy task.
4. Registration at State College is a painful process.

5. *Gone with the Wind* may be an old movie, but it is still a good movie.
6. The acting in *Gone with the Wind* was superb.

7. The wide variety of merchandise makes Sears convenient.
8. The home-repair department in Sears is convenient.

9. The architecture in Chicago reflects trends in modern design.
10. Chicago is an interesting city because of its history, architecture, and sports activities.

EXERCISE 1-5

Read the following weak topic sentences. Rewrite each one to make it more specific. You can narrow down the topic and/or the controlling idea. The first one is done for you.

1. The Honda Civic is an excellent automobile.
   The Honda Civic is economical to maintain.
2. My hometown is a wonderful place.
3. Many improvements are needed at this school.
4. Exercise is good for you.
5. Driving a car can be hazardous.
6. Computers are useful.
7. There are many interesting things to do at the park.
8. Watching television is bad for you.

Recognizing the Topic Sentence

A topic sentence, then, serves to introduce the topic and the controlling idea. But where should the topic sentence be placed in the paragraph? Generally, because the topic sentence does introduce, it is a good idea to place it at or near the beginning of the paragraph. However, depending on the kind of paragraph it is in, the topic sentence may be placed near the middle or even at the end of the paragraph. Sometimes neither the topic nor the controlling idea is explicitly stated in one sentence; this does not mean, however, that a topic and controlling idea are not present. In this kind of paragraph, the topic and controlling idea are implied; that is, they are clearly suggested in the development of the paragraph. However, it is usually a good idea to state topic sentences clearly, not only to be certain that the idea is clear but also to help control the development of the paragraph.

EXERCISE 1-6

Study the following paragraphs. In the space provided, write out the topic sentence for each paragraph, underlining the topic and circling the controlling idea. If the topic sentence is implied, write one out.

1. Another interesting area of research has to do with the distinction between intrinsic and extrinsic motivation. We are intrinsically motivated when we do something "for the fun of it," or for no

other reason than to perform the behavior. We sing in the shower, not because we expect applause, or because we are trying to earn money, but merely because we like to do it. We do crossword puzzles, paint pictures, and look at the sunset because it is intrinsically rewarding to do so. We don't expect any external reward. Extrinsic motivation, on the other hand, refers to situations in which we do act because we expect some external reward. We may only show up at the office because we need the money. We may only go to school to please our parents. We may be exceptionally polite to a particular individual because we want something from her. —John P. Houston, *Motivation* (New York: Macmillan, 1985), p. 268.

Topic Sentence: ____

____

2. In 1944 the United States signed a treaty with Mexico guaranteeing that country 1.5 million acre-feet of Colorado River water a year. But the big division of the Colorado's precious water had occurred in 1922 under the Colorado River Compact, signed by the seven states along the river and the federal government. What makes the agreement shaky—some describe it as "a house of cards"—is that it is based on an overly optimistic estimate of the river's average flow. About 15 million acre-feet of water were originally apportioned to the states; actually, the average annual supply is only 13.8 million. In addition, the Compact did not take into account Mexico's right to any Colorado River water at all, so the 1.5 million acre-feet later guaranteed to Mexico widen the gap between demand and supply. The Colorado is, in short, overbooked. —Adapted from David Sheridan, "The Colorado—An Engineering Wonder Without Enough Water' *Smithsonian* 13 (February 1983): pp. 46–47.

Topic Sentence: ____

____

3. As we approached our house so hurriedly abandoned the night before, we first saw the shrubs and flowers we had carefully planted last spring broken off at their bases and scattered in the pools of muddy water. Also in these dark pools, bits of windowpanes lay shattered. Looking at the house, I saw only gaping holes where windows had once been. Inside, the hurricane waters, which had by now receded, had washed everything a dirty brown. In the living room, chairs lay on their sides, the stereo system was propped up against the sofa, and my favorite lamp lay broken on the floor. Upon seeing all this, I sat down and wept.

Topic Sentence: ____

____

4. Anyone who saw him once never forgot his nose and his body. The first time anyone saw him, they were very surprised. The second time, they looked at his nose with admiration, as if it were a valuable treasure. His nose, which was longer than Barbra Streisand's, occupied most of his face. When he smiled, nothing but his nose was visible. He was recognized by it even in a crowd. The treasure made one think that in his previous life he had been a collie or an anteater. In addition, his nose was as thin as a razor. If he had flown like a jet, he could have divided the clouds. His body was also very skinny. He looked as if he had not eaten for ten days. He was a heavy eater, but one couldn't imagine where he kept food in his body. Finally, on a windy day, he was blown away and gone, like Mary Poppins. —*Nobutaka Matsuo*

Topic Sentence: ______________________________

____

5. We write because we want to understand our lives. This is why my closets are filled with boxes and boxes of musty old journals. It is why I found pages of poetry under my stepdaughter Kira's mattress when she went off to camp. It is why my father tells me he will soon begin his memoirs. As John Cheever explains, "When I began to write, I found this was the best way to make sense out of my life." —Lucy McCormick Calkins, *The Art of Teaching Writing* (Portsmouth, New Hampshire: Heinemann, 1986), p. 3.

Topic Sentence: ______________________________

____

6. Why do young jackals like Tejas stay on to help tend younger brothers and sisters? I have studied seventeen litters of pups, and twelve have had such helpers. Clearly, another family member capable of hunting and fighting is important to pup survival. Pairs that had no helpers raised on the average only one pup. With just a single helper, three pups survived. I observed one family with three helpers and six surviving pups. —Patricia D. Moehlman, "Jackals of the Serengeti," *National Geographic*, 158.6 (December 1980), pp. 846, 849.

Topic Sentence: ______________________________

____

____

Formulating the Topic Sentence

Thus far you have been given topics and controlling ideas to recognize and improve, but often you must find your own controlling idea. Once you have found a manageable topic for a paragraph, you need to examine that topic more closely to determine your own feelings or attitudes about it.

To decide on the controlling idea and what you want to say about a topic, begin by making a detailed list of things that come to mind about the topic. You can write the list using complete sentences, or you can just take brief notes. The form your notes take is not really important; what is important is writing down enough notes so that you can pick out an aspect of the topic that seems worthy of development. As you examine your notes, keep in mind that you should still try to narrow down the scope of your topic. For example, suppose you are asked to write about a place in your country and you narrow that broad topic down to a certain resort. The following is one example of how your notes could be done:

Topic: Lehai Resort
Notes:

- Pretty sandy beaches, palm trees along the shore, clear turquoise water, gorgeous mountains
- Tourists swarming every place, new hotels cropping up every month; one hotel blocks the view of the sea from the road, many tourist shops
- Resort provides many jobs, brings in $1 million in revenue from tourists, has attracted some new companies to the city

The list could, of course, be expanded. Once the list is completed, look through it for something striking. For example, you might realize that the resort has provided economic benefits to the local area. Or, in your notes, you might like to write about the beauty of the resort area. Several ideas could emerge from these notes. Here are a few:

Lehai Resort is set in one of the most scenic coastal areas in the world.
Lehai Resort has been ruined by the excessive influx of tourists.
Lehai Resort has brought direct and indirect economic benefits to our area.

EXERCISE 1-7

Study the topics that follow. On a separate sheet of paper, make a list of things that come to mind about each topic. After sorting through the list, write a topic sentence that has a controlling idea. If necessary, narrow the topic down. In the space provided, write your topic sentences, underline the topics, and circle the controlling ideas. Remember to focus your controlling ideas on an aspect of the topic.

1. Topic: Music Videos

   ____

2. Topic: Superstitions

   ____

3. Topic: Mathematics

   ____

4. Topic: Working Mothers

   ____

5. Topic: Pollution

   ____

____

Support

Once you have taken notes and formulated a controlling idea about your topic, the next step is to extract from your notes the material you can use to develop the paragraph. This material is used to support the opinion or attitude expressed in your topic sentence. It serves to back up, clarify, illustrate, explain, or prove the point you make in your topic sentence. Most often we use factual detail to support a point. Such detail may include facts from resource material, such as magazines, journals, and books, or details about things you or others have observed. Basically, support comes from the information you used to arrive at the view you have expressed in your topic sentence.

When you are examining your notes to find support for your topic sentence, you may find it necessary to add material to your notes. Let's take as an example the topic sentence "Lehai Resort has nearly solved our local employment problem." From the notes on this topic, we might extract "Lehai Resort provides many jobs" and "has attracted some new companies to the city." These two bits of information can serve as the basis for more notes and support. To generate more notes at this stage, you may find it useful to ask specific questions, such as "What are the companies that have opened up? How many jobs have they brought to our city? How else has the resort provided jobs? What are those jobs? What was the employment situation before the resort opened? What is the employment rate now?" The answers to these questions will serve as a foundation for the support for your paragraph. Your revised notes might be as follows:

Unemployment rate in 1970 = 35%; in 1980 = 8%

Hotel jobs—Statler Hotel, 100
Modern Inn, 50
New Wave Spa, 35

Five new shops on Beach Highway for tourists—15 new jobs

New companies (since 1972)—Jones Batiking
Mary's Dollworks
Julio's Tour Guide Service
J & M Corporation
Menk's Manufacturing Company

It is a good idea to write the support out as sentences and list them under your topic sentence in outline form, grouping related details together. For example, for the Lehai Resort example, your paragraph outline might look like this:

Topic Sentence:

Lehai Resort has nearly solved our local employment problem.

Support:

1. The unemployment rate has dropped from 35% in 1970 to 8% in 1980.
2. The tourist industry has created many jobs.
   a. Three new hotels have opened up.
      1) The Statler Hotel employs 100 local residents.
      2) The Modern Inn hired fifty.
      3) The New Wave Spa has thirty-five new workers.
   b. Five new shops have opened on Beach Hwy., for a total of fifteen jobs.
   c. Tourist-related industries have opened up: Jones Batiking, Mary's Dollworks, and Julio's Tour Guide Service.
3. The resort has attracted two nontourist companies: J & M Corp. and Menk's Mfg. Co.

Such an outline is useful in two ways: It provides a means for quickly checking your sentences to see if they deal with the topic, and it serves as a guide for checking whether the sentences are logically arranged. Here is an outline of the paragraph on page 3:

Topic Sentence:

Smoking cigarettes can be an expensive habit.

Support:

1. Cigarettes cost about one dollar.
2. The average smoker smokes two packs a day.
3. The annual expense for this smoker is $730.00.
4. The smoker must also pay for extra cleaning of carpeting, furniture, and clothes.

Obviously, not all the sentences in the original paragraph are listed or recorded verbatim. For example, the sentence "But the price of cigarettes is not the only expense cigarette smokers incur" is omitted here. This

sentence certainly relates to the topic and the controlling idea, but its main function is to provide a link in the sentences; it joins the section discussing the price of cigarettes with the section dealing with the hidden expense of cigarette smoking. This type of sentence is called a *transition*. (Transitions are discussed at length in the following chapters.) Also omitted from the outline is the last sentence: "Although it is difficult to estimate the cost of this additional expense, one can see that this hidden expense does contribute to making smoking an expensive habit." This type of sentence, which summarizes the main idea in the paragraph, is called the *concluding sentence.* Not all paragraphs need concluding sentences, but they are useful for ending the development of the support smoothly.

How you organize your sentences within a paragraph will depend on your topic and purpose. In the following chapters, you will learn how to support various kinds of topics and how to organize that support. At this stage, it is important to understand that the material you use to write the sentences in your paragraph should be directly supportive of the view you express in your topic sentence.

EXERCISE 1-8

Study the paragraph about cigarette smoking on page 8. In the space provided here, write the topic sentence, circle the controlling idea, and outline the support given in the paragraph. Write the concluding sentence if there is one.

Topic Sentence:

____

Support:

1. ______________________________
2. ______________________________
3. ______________________________
4. ______________________________

Conclusion:

____

EXERCISE 1-9

Choose one of the topics for which you developed a topic sentence in Exercise 1-7. In the space provided here, write the topic sentence, circle the controlling idea, and then list the support in sentence form.

Topic Sentence:

____

Support:

1. ____
2. ____
3. ____
4. ____
5. ____

____

Unity

Each sentence within a paragraph should relate to the topic and develop the controlling idea. If any sentence does not relate to or develop that area, it is irrelevant and should be omitted from the paragraph. Consider the topic sentence discussed earlier in this chapter:

Smoking cigarettes can be an expensive habit.

If a sentence in this paragraph had discussed how annoying it is to watch someone blow smoke rings, that sentence would have been out of place, since it does not discuss the expense of smoking.

A paragraph that has sentences that do not relate to or discuss the controlling idea lacks *unity*. Note the following example of a paragraph that lacks unity:

> Another problem facing a number of elderly people is living on a reduced income. Upon retiring, old people may receive a pension from their company or Social Security from the government. The amount of their monthly checks is often half the amount of the checks they received when they were employed. Suddenly, retirees find that they can no longer continue the life-style that they had become accustomed to, even if that life-style was a modest one. Many find, after paying their monthly bills, that there is no money left for a movie or a dinner out. Of course, sometimes they can't go out because of their health. Maybe they have arthritis or rheumatism and it is painful for them to move around. This can also change their life-style. Some older people, however, discover that the small amount of money they receive will not even cover their monthly bills. They realize with horror that electricity, a telephone, and nourishing food are luxuries they can no longer afford. They resort to shivering in the dark, eating cat food in order to make ends meet.

The topic of this paragraph is "another problem facing a number of elderly people," and the controlling idea is "living on a reduced income." Therefore, all of the sentences should deal with the idea of the problem of living on a reduced income. In the paragraph, though, there are three sentences that do not discuss this particular topic: "Of course, sometimes they can't go out because of their health. Maybe they have arthritis or rheumatism and it is painful for them to move around. This can also change their life-style." These sentences should be taken out of this paragraph and perhaps developed in another paragraph.

EXERCISE 1-10

Read the following paragraphs. Underline the topic sentence in each paragraph and cross out any sentences that do not belong in the paragraph. There may be one or more irrelevant sentences.

1. Since the mid-1960s, there has been a tremendous increase in the popularity and quality of Latin and South American novelists; in fact, some call this literary movement "El Boom." Mexico has produced, for example, Carlos Fuentes, who wrote *The Death of Artemio Cruz*. The 1967 Nobel Prize for Literature was awarded to the Guatemalan novelist, Miguel Ángel Asturias. Argentina has given us numerous impressive writers, such as Jorge Luis Borges, Julio Cortázar, Luisa Valenzuela, and Manuel Puig, whose *Kiss of the Spider Woman* was made into a film. William Hurt won the Oscar for Best Actor for his role in that movie. Another recent novelist who has impressed the world is Chile's Isabelle Allende (*The House of the Spirits*). The list could go on, but probably the biggest name associated with this movement is Gabriel García Márquez, a Colombian whose enormously popular *One Hundred Years of Solitude*, published in 1967, helped him earn the 1982 Nobel Prize for Literature.
2. Despite their reputation, some workers in American factories take pride in helping their companies. A good example of this is the 14,400 employees of the Lockheed-Georgia Company who submit ideas to management to help reduce production costs. In one year, these ideas, ranging from a new way to recharge a dead battery to a more efficient way to paint airplane wings, saved the company $57.5 million. Since 1979, employee suggestions have resulted in savings of over $190 million. While we might think that workers submit ideas in order to receive large rewards, this is not the case. According to Executive Vice President Alex Lorch, the financial benefit is minimum. The employee with the best idea each year receives only $100. The employees, Lorch says, submit ideas because they are motivated by a desire to do a good job. Japanese workers, on the other hand, are generally considered the best example of workers loyal to their company.*

*Information from *The Times-Picayune*, 27 May 1984, sec. 7, p. 7.

3. The common sponge, the skeleton of a sea creature of the Porifera phylum, has been put to many good uses. When mature, most sponges cannot move about in the ocean. In prehistoric times, groups living along seashores bartered with sponges for inland-grown items. The ancient Greeks used sponges for scrubbing their floors and furniture and for padding their armor. The Romans found them useful as mops and paintbrushes. As you may know, the Romans painted many of their famous statues with bright colors, so the harvesting of sponges became an especially thriving industry during Roman times. Today, sponges are used for washing cars, cleaning houses, applying shoe polish, and even dabbing on face cream. The humble sponge, sometimes called nature's wash-cloth, has proven to be extremely useful to humans throughout history.
4. At least two events in the life of Charles Darwin brought him to state his theory of natural selection. The first was his post on H.M.S. *Beagle* as naturalist. While on voyages of exploration to various parts of the world, Darwin noted differences in certain species of plants and animals, even when two species were living in close proximity. He began to wonder what caused these differences. From his observations, Darwin started to form his opinions about the necessity for change in the struggle for survival. The second event was Darwin's reading of *Essay on Population* by T. Malthus. According to Malthus, the rate of growth of the population of the world was outstripping the food supply. To bring population down to manageable levels, famine, pestilence, and war were inevitable. Darwin concluded from this book that in these ravages only the strong would survive. This reinforced his view that evolutionary changes can lead certain organisms to be stronger and survive. Another naturalist, Alfred Russel Wallace, after reading Malthus, came up with the theory of evolution at approximately the same time as Darwin.

Coherence

We have seen that a paragraph must have a topic and controlling idea, support, and unity. Another element that a paragraph needs is *coherence*. A coherent paragraph contains sentences that are logically arranged and that flow smoothly.

Logical arrangement refers to the order of your sentences and ideas. There are various ways to order your sentences, depending on your purpose. For example, if you want to describe what happens in a movie (that is, the plot), your sentences would follow the sequence of the action in the movie, from beginning to end—in that order. If, on the other hand, you want to describe the most exciting moments in the movie, you would select a few moments and decide on a logical order for discussion—

perhaps presenting the least exciting moments first and the most exciting last to create suspense. (In the following chapters, we study the various principles for ordering ideas and sentences.)

A paragraph can be incoherent even when the principle for ordering the ideas is logical. Sometimes, as students are writing, they remember something that they wanted to say earlier and include it as they write. Unfortunately, this sentence often ends up out of place. Study the following paragraph, in which one or more sentences are out of order:

> Although Grants Pass, Oregon, is a fairly small town, it offers much to amuse summer visitors. They can go rafting down the Rogue River. They can go swimming in the Applegate River. Lots of people go hunting for wild berries that grow along the roadsides. Campers will find lovely campgrounds that are clean. There are several nice hotels. Tourists can browse through a number of interesting shops in town, such as antique stores. One fun activity is shopping at the open market where local folks sell produce grown in their gardens. Grants Pass has a lot of places to eat, ranging from a low-calorie dessert place to lovely restaurants. Some of these restaurants offer good food and gorgeous views. One store to visit is the shop that sells items made from Oregon's beautiful myrtlewood. Fishing in the area is also a popular activity. Water sports are by far the main attraction. As you can see, Grants Pass offers a lot to do in the summer. If you want to give your family a nice, wholesome vacation, try visiting Grants Pass.

The paragraph seems to have a principle of organization: The first half is devoted to activities in the areas just outside of the city itself and the last half discusses activities within the city. However, toward the end of the paragraph the writer seems to throw in a few sentences as an afterthought. Three sentences—"One store to visit is the shop that sells items made from Oregon's beautiful myrtlewood," "Fishing in the area is also a popular activity," and "Water sports are by far the main attraction"—are out of place. This paragraph could be revised as follows:

> Although Grants Pass, Oregon, is a fairly small town, it offers much to amuse summer visitors. Water sports are by far the main attraction. Visitors can go rafting down the Rogue River. They can go swimming in the Applegate River. Fishing in the area is a popular activity. Lots of people go hunting for wild berries that grow along the roadsides. Campers will find lovely campgrounds that are clean. There are several nice hotels. Tourists can browse through a number of interesting shops in town, such as antique stores. One store to visit is the shop that sells items made from Oregon's beautiful myrtlewood. One fun activity is shopping at the open market where local folks sell produce grown in their gardens. Grants Pass has a lot of places to eat, ranging from a low-calorie dessert place to lovely restaurants. Some of these restaurants offer good food and gorgeous views. As you can see, Grants Pass offers a lot to do in the summer. If you want to give your family a nice, wholesome vacation, try visiting Grants Pass.

The order of the sentences in this revised version is improved, but it is still not completely coherent, for the sentences do not always flow smoothly.

Smooth flow refers to how well one idea or sentence leads into another. Smooth flow can be achieved through sentence combining and through the use of certain expressions, called transitions, that provide the links between ideas. Some transitional expressions include *for example, to begin with, in contrast, however, also*, among many others that we will cover throughout this text. Note how the addition of some expressions and the combining of some sentences improve the coherence of this paragraph:

> Although Grants Pass, Oregon, is a fairly small town, it offers much to amuse summer visitors. Water sports are by far the main attraction. Visitors can go rafting down the Rogue River or swimming in the Applegate River. Fishing in the area is *another* popular activity. Lots of people *also* go hunting for wild berries that grow along the roadsides. *In addition*, there are lovely, clean campgrounds where campers can park their vehicles. *For those who prefer to stay in town*, Grants Pass offers several nice hotels. In town, tourists can browse through a number of interesting shops, such as antique stores and the shop that sells items made from Oregon's beautiful myrtlewood. *Another* fun activity is shopping at the open market where local folks sell produce grown in their gardens. *And finally*, Grants Pass has a lot of places to eat, ranging from a low-calorie dessert place to lovely restaurants, some of which offer good food and gorgeous views. As you can see, Grants Pass offers a lot to do in the summer. If you want to give your family a nice, wholesome vacation, try visiting this charming town.

The expressions "another," "also," "in addition," "and finally" bridge the gaps in ideas. Some of the sentences have been combined as well. Combining sentences and adding transitions make the ideas and sentences easier to follow.

If the sentences are not logically arranged or if they do not connect with each other smoothly, the paragraph is *incoherent*. Coherence is an important quality of writing.

EXERCISE 1-11

Study each of the following paragraphs, in which one or more sentences are out of order. Revise these paragraphs for greater coherence by arranging the sentences in logical order.

1. In the hotel business, computers ease the load at the front desk. With a computer, a clerk can make a reservation easily and quickly, without the use of cards, racks, or registration books. So when guests come in to register, their reservations can be checked a they can be given available rooms without much fuss or h The hotel business is just one type of enterprise that h

by the invention of computers. And with a computer, the clerk can get an instant update of the room status. This tells the clerk which rooms are available to guests.

2. Political conventions in America attract all kinds of people besides delegates. You are sure to see an artist or two doing chalk portraits of the candidates on the sidewalks. Groups who wish to attract attention to their political and social causes demonstrate outside the convention halls. The pro-life people, the pro-abortionists, the supporters of nuclear energy, those against nuclear energy, and the pro-gays and anti-gays are probably the most common groups. Others just like to poke fun at the candidates. For instance, at most conventions you will find at least a couple people wearing masks of their favorite or least favorite candidates. Others dress in costumes and carry signs with outrageous comments about the candidates or the political process. Another social-political group is the one advocating more civil rights and better economic opportunities for minorities. No matter who they are or what their reasons are for going to the conventions, these people always add color to the sometimes boring conventions.
3. The story of Arachne, a mortal woman, showed the danger of claiming to be equal with a goddess. The goddess Minerva, a champion weaver, believed her fabrics were the most beautiful in the world. When Minerva head that a peasant girl, Arachne, had boasted that Arachne's were the most beautiful, Minerva became angry. Minerva tore Arachne's weaving into shreds. Arachne became angry at Minerva's destruction and hung herself. Minerva challenged Arachne to a weaving contest so Minerva had the opportunity to see how beautiful Arachne's weaving was. In the end, Minerva repented and changed the dead Arachne into the champion weaver of all time, the spider.

EXERCISE 1-12

Study the following paragraphs, which lack both unity and coherence. For each paragraph, rearrange the sentences for coherence and omit any sentences that do not belong.

1. First of all, teenagers work for their own current expenses. For example, my cousin Celia works at a clothing store and buys all her own clothes. Last week she bought herself a nice leather jacket. And one of my friends bought himself a used car just from the money he made after school. Young people want to make money for their future. Young people want to buy clothes and they want to save money to buy a car or a stereo or a television. An example of this is saving money for an education after high school. My cousin Robert is doing this for his future. He also told me that he is saving some money to set up a household after marriage.
2. The driving lesson I got from my fiancé was a very distressing one. I started off very well until my fiancé started getting bossy. I did one

wrong thing so he started shouting at me. The little incident occurred when he wanted me to make a U-turn in the middle of the street. As I was trying to do that, I turned the wheels too hard and the wheels hit the end of the curb. My fiancé started yelling at me as if he were crazy. So I calmly put the car in park and started to get out to let him drive since I obviously wasn't doing it the way he wanted. But he grabbed my arm and told me to finish getting the car out of the middle of the street. Oh, I forgot to tell you that when the tires hit the curb, the car stopped in the middle of the street. I guess that was why he was worried. My fiancé also tried to teach me to play tennis and he shouted at me then, too. He also wanted me to move the car because there were cars coming in both directions. I decided after this incident that my fiancé was not the right person to teach me to drive.

3. Your dollar seems to stretch a bit further at Frank's Grocery than at G & W. Whenever somebody I know goes to Frank's, they come out with more groceries in hand. Eggs on sale at Frank's are generally priced at eighty-nine cents a dozen, while eggs on sale at G & W cost ninety-nine cents. Meat on sale at Frank's is generally about ten cents less a pound than meat on sale at G & W. Frank's doesn't advertise its sales much, however. The workers post the newspaper listing the sales in front of Frank's, but G & W is better about advertising its sale items. They put them on the radio and in the newspaper. They also post sale signs right over the sale items in the store. Last week, for example, Frank's had sugar on sale for $1.59 for a five-pound bag. G & W also had it on sale, but it cost $1.89 for the same amount. All in all, Frank's Grocery is more economical than G & W.

EXERCISE 1-13

Writing Assignment

Write a paragraph using the topic sentence and support you developed in Exercise 1-9. After you write the paragraph, consult the checklist that follows.

Paragraph Checklist

1. Is your topic sufficiently narrowed down?
2. Does your paragraph have a topic sentence? If not, is the topic sentence implied?
3. Does your paragraph have a clear, focused controlling idea?
4. Is your paragraph unified; that is, do all of the sentences support the controlling idea?
5. Is your paragraph coherent; that is, are the sentences logically arranged and do they flow smoothly?

Chapter 2

The Narrative Paragraph

Readings: Personal Discovery

CERTAIN events in our lives help us to understand ourselves and the world around us. Perhaps you remember a specific incident from childhood or adolescence that taught you something about yourself. Through events like these we make important personal discoveries.

In the two readings that follow, the writers recount important events from childhood that lead to personal discoveries. As you read them, formulate answers to these questions:

1. What was the personal discovery that the writer made?
2. How did the writer make the discovery?

READING 1

THE STRUGGLE TO BE AN ALL-AMERICAN GIRL

ELIZABETH WONG

In this essay, which first appeared in the Los Angeles Times, *Elizabeth Wong tells of her painful experiences growing up in the bicultural atmosphere of Los Angeles' Chinatown. She describes the difficulty of being Chinese on the outside but American on the inside.*

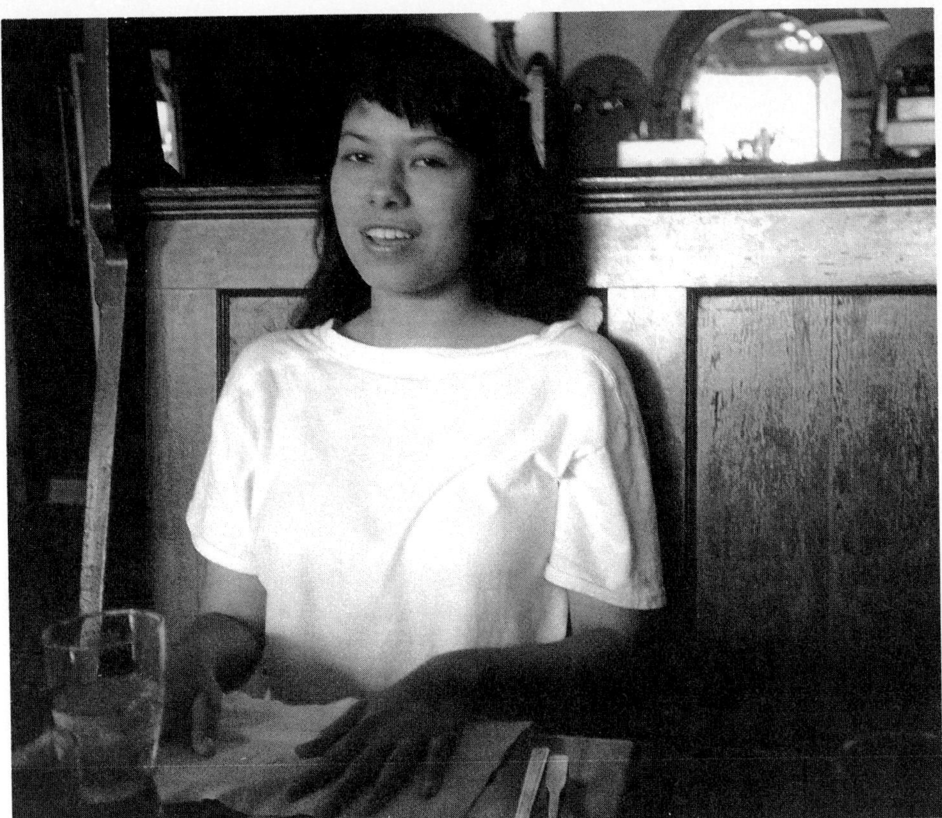

1 It's still there, the Chinese school on Yale Street where my brother and I used to go. Despite the new coat of paint and the high wire fence, the school I knew 10 years ago remains remarkably, stoically• the same. *without emotion*

2 Every day at 5 P.M., instead of playing with our fourth- and fifth-grade friends or sneaking out to the empty lot to hunt ghosts and animal bones, my brother and I had to go to Chinese school. No amount of kicking, screaming, or pleading could dissuade• my mother, who was solidly determined to have us learn the language of our heritage. *to talk out of*

3 Forcibly, she walked us the seven long, hilly blocks from our home to school, depositing our defiant tearful faces before the stern principal. My only memory of him is that he swayed on his heels like a palm tree, and he always clasped his impatient twitching hands behind his back. I recognized him as a repressed maniacal child killer, and knew that if we ever saw his hands we'd be in big trouble.

4 We all sat in little chairs in an empty auditorium. The room smelled like Chinese medicine, an imported faraway mustiness.• Like ancient mothballs or dirty closets. I hated that smell. I favored crisp new scents. Like the soft French perfume *staleness*

that my American teacher wore in public school.

5 There was a stage far to the right, flanked• by an American flag and the flag of the Nationalist Republic of China, which was also red, white and blue but not as pretty.

bordered

6 Although the emphasis at the school was mainly language—speaking, reading, writing—the lessons always began with an exercise in politeness. With the entrance of the teacher, the best student would tap a bell and everyone would get up, kowtow,• and chant, "Sing san ho," the phonetic for "How are you, teacher?"

bow

7 Being ten years old, I had better things to learn than ideographs• copied painstakingly in lines that ran right to left from the tip of a *moc but*, a real ink pen that had to be held in an awkward way if blotches were to be avoided. After all, I could do the multiplication tables, name the satellites of Mars, and write reports on "Little Women" and "Black Beauty." Nancy Drew, my favorite book heroine, never spoke Chinese.

Chinese picture symbols used to form words

8 The language was a source of embarrassment. More times than not, I had tried to disassociate• myself from the nagging loud voice that followed me wherever I wandered in the nearby American supermarket outside Chinatown. The voice belonged to my grandmother, a fragile woman in her seventies who could outshout the best of the street vendors.• Her humor was raunchy,• her Chinese rhythmless, patternless. It was quick, it was loud, it was unbeautiful. It was not like the quiet, lilting romance of French or the gentle refinement of the American South. Chinese sounded pedestrian.• Public.

to detach from association

sellers of goods

obscene

ordinary

9 In Chinatown, the comings and goings of hundreds of Chinese on their daily tasks sounded chaotic and frenzied. I did not want to be thought of as mad, as talking gibberish.• When I spoke English, people nodded at me, smiled sweetly, said encouraging words. Even the people in my culture would cluck• and say that I'd do well in life. "My, doesn't she move her lips fast," they would say, meaning that I'd be able to keep up with the world outside Chinatown.

confused, unintelligible speech

make an approving sound

10 My brother was even more fanatical than I about speaking English. He was especially hard on my mother, criticizing her, often cruelly, for her pidgin• speech—smatterings of Chinese scattered like chop suey in her conversation. "It's not 'What it is,' Mom," he'd say in exasperation. "It's 'What *is* it, what *is* it, what *is* it!" Sometimes Mom might leave out an occasional "the" or "a," or perhaps a verb of being. He would stop her in mid-sentence: "Say it again, Mom. Say it right." When he tripped over his own tongue,• he'd blame it on her: "See, Mom, it's all your fault. You set a bad example."

simplified speech, usually a mixture of two or more languages

tripped over . . . *stumbled in speaking*

11 What infuriated my mother most was when my brother cornered her on her consonants, especially "r." My father had

played a cruel joke on Mom by assigning her an American name that her tongue wouldn't allow her to say. No matter how hard she tried, "Ruth" always ended up "Luth" or "Roof."

12 After two years of writing with a *moc but* and reciting words with multiples of meanings, I finally was granted a cultural divorce. I was permitted to stop Chinese school.

13 I thought of myself as multicultural. I preferred tacos to egg rolls; I enjoyed Cinco de Mayo more than Chinese New Year.

14 At last, I was one of you; I wasn't one of them.

15 Sadly, I still am.

EXERCISE 2-1: COMPREHENSION/ DISCUSSION QUESTIONS

1. What did Elizabeth Wong and her brother do every day after school?
2. What was their attitude about this activity? How do you know?
3. Who wanted them to do this? Why?
4. According to Wong, what kind of man was the school principal?
5. Wong compares the smells of the Chinese school with those of the public school. What smells does she remember of each? How do these smells suggest her attitude toward each?
6. Wong compares what she learns at each school. What does she learn at Chinese school? At public school? In her opinion, which is more important? Why?
7. According to Wong, what was her grandmother like? What was Wong's attitude toward her? Why?
8. What was her brother's attitude about speaking English?
9. How did Wong's brother treat his mother when she spoke English? How do you account for this behavior?
10. Explain the problem Wong's mother had with her American name, "Ruth."
11. Wong sees herself as multicultural. What does she mean? What examples does she give to prove this? Are these examples surprising? Why?
12. Who are the "you" and "them" in paragraph 14?
13. Explain the significance of the last sentence. What is Wong's attitude toward Chinese school as an adult?

14. Wong and her brother resented being forced to attend Chinese school. Do you think their mother was right in making them go? Why, or why not?
15. Wong describes the clash of two cultures and the conflicts that can occur from it. Do you think it is possible for someone to maintain connections with his or her original culture and at the same time become an "all-American"? What does one gain or lose in becoming completely Americanized?

EXERCISE 2-2: VOCABULARY DEVELOPMENT

For each of the italic words that follows, choose the word or expression that most closely matches its meaning.

1. the *stern* principal (par. 3)
   a. military c. very old
   b. immoral d. strict
2. our *defiant* tearful faces (par. 3)
   a. fearful c. resistant
   b. relaxed d. funny
3. *repressed* maniacal child killer (par. 3)
   a. held back c. quiet
   b. ugly d. retired
4. repressed *maniacal* child killer (par. 3)
   a. embarrassed c. favorite
   b. crazy d. rich
5. a *fragile* woman (par. 8)
   a. elderly c. frail
   b. tall d. loud
6. thought of as *mad* (par. 9)
   a. childish c. angry
   b. foreign d. crazy
7. the quiet, *lilting* romance of French (par. 8)
   a. musical c. tilting
   b. soft d. complicated
8. what *infuriated* my mother most (par. 11)
   a. angered c. humiliated
   b. typified d. occurred to

READING 2

FROM *THE STORY OF MY LIFE*

HELEN KELLER

When Helen Keller was born, she could neither speak nor see. With the help of her teacher and longtime friend, Anne Sullivan, she learned to communicate with her hands. In

the following passage from her autobiography, Keller describes the most important discovery of her life.

1 The most important day I remember in all my life is the one on which my teacher, Anne Mansfield Sullivan, came to me. I am filled with wonder when I consider the immeasurable contrast between the two lives which it connects. It was the third of March, 1887, three months before I was seven years old.

2 On the afternoon of that eventful day, I stood on the porch, dumb, expectant. I guessed vaguely from my mother's signs and from the hurrying to and fro• in the house that something unusual was about to happen, so I went to the door and waited on the steps. The afternoon sun penetrated• the mass of honeysuckle that covered the porch, and fell on my upturned face. My fingers lingered almost unconsciously on the familiar leaves and blossoms which had just come forth to greet the sweet southern spring. I did not know what the future held of marvel or surprise for me. Anger and bitterness had preyed upon• me continually for weeks and a deep languor• had succeeded this passionate struggle.

back and forth

came through

bothered

lack of energy

3 Have you ever been at sea in a dense fog, when it seemed as if a tangible• white darkness shut you in, and the great ship, tense and anxious, groped her way toward the

able to be touched

shore with plummet and sounding-line,• and had no way of knowing how near the harbour was. "Light! give me light!" was the wordless cry of my soul, and the light of love shone on me in that very hour.

plummet . . . *nautical instruments for measuring the depth of water*

4 I felt approaching footsteps. I stretched out my hand as I supposed to my mother. Some one took it, and I was caught up and held close in the arms of her who had come to reveal all things to me, and, more than all things else, to love me.

5 The morning after my teacher came she led me into her room and gave me a doll. The little blind children at the Perkins Institution had sent it and Laura Bridgman had dressed it; but I did not know this until afterward. When I had played with it a little while, Miss Sullivan slowly spelled into my hand the word "d-o-l-l." I was at once interested in this finger play and tried to imitate it. When I finally succeeded in making the letters correctly I was flushed with childish pleasure and pride. Running downstairs to my mother I held up my hand and made the letters for doll. I did not know that I was spelling a word or even that words existed; I was simply making my fingers go in monkey-like imitation. In the days that followed I learned to spell in this uncomprehending way a great many words, among them *pin, hat, cup* and a few verbs like *sit, stand* and *walk*. But my teacher had been with me several weeks before I understood that everything has a name.

6 One day, while I was playing with my new doll, Miss Sullivan put my big rag doll into my lap also, spelled "d-o-l-l" and tried to make me understand that "d-o-l-l" applied to both. Earlier in the day we had had a tussle over the words "m-u-g" and "w-a-t-e-r." Miss Sullivan had tried to impress it upon me that "m-u-g" is *mug* and that "w-a-t-e-r" is *water*, but I persisted in confounding• the two. In despair she had dropped the subject for the time, only to renew it at the first opportunity. I became impatient at her repeated attempts and, seizing the new doll, I dashed it upon the floor. I was keenly delighted when I felt the fragments of the broken doll at my feet. Neither sorrow nor regret followed my passionate outburst. I had not loved the doll. In the still, dark world in which I lived there was no strong sentiment• or tenderness. I felt my teacher sweep the fragments to one side of the hearth,• and I had a sense of satisfaction that the cause of my discomfort was removed. She brought me my hat, and I knew I was going out into the warm sunshine. This thought, if a wordless sensation may be called a thought, made me hop and skip with pleasure.

confusing

emotion

front part of a fireplace

7 We walked down the path to the well-house, attracted by the fragrance of the honeysuckle with which it was covered. Some one was drawing water and my teacher placed my

hand under the spout. As the cool stream gushed over one hand she spelled into the other the word *water,* first slowly, then rapidly. I stood still, my whole attention fixed upon the motions of her fingers. Suddenly I felt a misty consciousness• as of something forgotten—a thrill of returning thought; and somehow the mystery of language was revealed to me. I knew then that "w-a-t-e-r" meant the wonderful cold something that was flowing over my hand. That living word awakened my soul, gave it light, hope, joy, set it free! There were barriers still, it is true, but barriers that could in time be swept away.

awareness

8 I left the well-house eager to learn. Everything had a name, and each name gave birth to a new thought. As we returned to the house every object which I touched seemed to quiver with life. That was because I saw everything with the strange, new sight that had come to me. On entering the door I remembered the doll I had broken. I felt my way to the hearth and picked up the pieces. I tried vainly• to put them together. Then my eyes filled with tears; for I realized what I had done, and for the first time I felt repentance and sorrow.

without hope

9 I learned a great many new words that day. I do not remember what they all were; but I know that *mother, father, sister, teacher* were among them—words that were to make the world blossom for me, "like Aaron's rod, with flowers."• It would have been difficult to find a happier child than I was as I lay in my crib at the close of that eventful day and lived over the joys it had brought me, and for the first time longed for a new day to come.

Aaron's rod . . . *a biblical reference to a dead stick suddenly blossoming*

EXERCISE 2-3: COMPREHENSION/ DISCUSSION QUESTIONS

1. How did Helen Keller feel before she met Anne Sullivan?
2. What was Helen learning when she learned to spell *d-o-l-l*?
3. Why did Helen break her doll?
4. What did Helen understand when the water flowed over her hand?
5. Why was Helen able to feel sorry about her broken doll?
6. Do you think Helen's personality changed after that day? Support your answers with evidence from the reading.
7. What was Helen's attitude toward the day she describes?
8. What was Helen's attitude toward her teacher, Anne Sullivan?
9. According to this account, what is language?
10. What is the relationship among language, thinking, and emotions?

EXERCISE 2-4

1. What is the *topic* of this passage? What is the *controlling idea*?
2. Summarize the main idea of the passage in one sentence. Do you find a sentence anywhere in the passage that states the main idea?
3. Does paragraph 2 have a topic sentence? If so, what is it? Does it have a controlling idea? If so, what is it?
4. Explain the comparison Helen gives in the third paragraph. How does this help support the main idea.
5. It is possible for a paragraph to have an *implied* topic sentence. Can you find any paragraphs in this passage that have implied topic sentences? If so, where? What is the implied topic sentence? Does the paragraph you chose lack unity because it does not have a stated topic sentence?
6. What is the topic sentence of paragraph 7? Where is it located in the paragraph?

EXERCISE 2-5: VOCABULARY DEVELOPMENT

Rewrite each of the following sentences by replacing the italicized word with the appropriate synonym from this list:

quivered (par. 8)	gushed (par. 7)	dashed (par. 6)
flushed (par. 5)	lingered (par. 2)	immeasurable (par. 1)
dumb (par. 2)	vaguely (par. 2)	groped (par. 3)
tussle (par. 6)		

1. The new mother looked with *great* pride at her new baby boy.

   ____

2. The little girl was *unable to talk*.

   ____

3. After he smoked the cigar, we could smell the smoke, which *stayed* in the air.

   ____

4. He *somewhat* understood the letter, but it was not very clear.

   ____

5. The blind woman *felt* her way through the room.

   ____

6. He was *red in the face* after jogging five miles.

   ____

7. In a fit of anger, he *threw* the delicate wine glass against the wall.

   ____

8. Rich black oil *flowed* from the well after the shaft was sunk.

   ____

9. The old car *vibrated* because it needed a tune-up.

 ____

10. The two other children *struggled* on the floor, each trying to keep the other down.

 ____

Writing

Present Narration

There are several ways to organize sentences in paragraphs. The arrangement of sentences and details depends on the writer's purpose. Suppose, for example, that you are asked to write about a typical morning at school. Obviously, you would not begin by telling what you do when you get home; instead, you would begin with what you do first and end with what you do at the end of the morning. In short, you would arrange your ideas according to the *time* in which they occurred. Likewise, to explain a process (how to do something), you would begin by explaining what to do first and finish by explaining what to do last. Ordering your sentences and ideas in order of time is referred to as *chronological* development.

There are principally two types of writing that require chronological development: narration and process description. (Process analysis is discussed in Chapter 9.) Although narration usually refers to the telling of a story, the term is used here to describe the relating of an experience. That experience may be in the past (past narration), or it may be a typical experience (what people usually do), or it may be going on now (present narration).

Ordering your sentences and ideas chronologically is not hard, as you know. However, deciding what to include and what to omit—in other words, making your paragraph unified—can be difficult. And what is perhaps more difficult is having a controlling idea for your paragraph. Imagine that you received a letter from your cousin back home who is very curious about the various American customs. If you lived in New Orleans, you might decide to write to your cousin about the famous Mardi Gras celebration. Your narration might begin like this:

> For many, Mardi Gras day begins on St. Charles Avenue with the Rex Parade. By nine o'clock, the avenue is lined with people dressed in all kinds of costumes. At around ten o'clock, the parade begins. First there is the sound of sirens. The police on motorcycles always lead the parade to clear the street. Then a band usually marches by. At this time the people start clapping and swaying to the music. Next come the masked men on horseback. Finally, the first float arrives carrying men in costumes and masks.

Immediately, everyone rushes toward the float. They wave their hands and yell, "Throw me something, Mister!" The men generally throw beads and coins at the crowd. Then the float passes, but soon another one comes and the people do the same thing over again. After about an hour, the parade passes by and the first part of Mardi Gras day ends.

The writer has narrowed down the topic to the Rex Parade on Mardi Gras day. The sentences are arranged logically; the topic suggests chronological development and the sentences are arranged in chronological order. The paragraph, then, is coherent. The paragraph is also unified; all of the sentences discuss what people do during this parade. But is the author's attitude about the event clear? Not really. The cousin back home would have a difficult time determining the author's attitude about this topic. Of course, the writer does not *have* to tell what he feels about this experience, but a controlling idea would help the reader get a clearer image of what that experience is like. The paragraph can be improved by revising it to have a strong controlling idea:

When people here talk of Mardi Gras, they use the expression "Mardi Gras Madness." This delightful madness begins for many on St. Charles Avenue with the Rex Parade. By nine o'clock, the avenue is lined with people of all ages in colorful costumes, from cavemen to Supermen. They stroll among the crowd and chat with friends and strangers alike. Some dance and some drink. At around ten o'clock, the excitement mounts as the parade begins. First there is the welcome sound of sirens. The police on motorcycles always lead the parade to make a path through the jubilant crowd. Then a band usually marches by, playing a popular tune such as the theme from *Star Wars*. At this time people start clapping and dancing to the music. Next come the masked men on horseback. They wave and the crowd waves back. Sometimes a girl goes up and kisses one of the riders! Finally, someone usually shouts, "There it is!" It is the first float carrying men in costumes and masks. Immediately, everyone rushes toward the float. They wave their hands and yell, "Throw me something, Mister!" The men throw beads and souvenir coins to the excited crowd. Usually, they catch the coins, but sometimes one hits the ground. Then several people rush to retrieve it, pushing and shoving if necessary. Then the float passes, but soon another one comes and the madness continues in the same way. After about an hour, the parade passes by and the first part of Mardi Gras day ends.

By adding a topic sentence with a strong controlling idea ("delightful madness"), the writer clearly establishes his attitude about the parade. In addition, the writer has changed some of the sentences and added some details to make sure that the support shows the delightful madness at the Rex Parade.

EXERCISE 2-6

Reread the preceding paragraph and underline the specific changes the writer has made. What effect do these changes have on the paragraph?

EXERCISE 2-7

To practice manipulating supporting sentences to convey an attitude, rewrite each of the following sentences in two ways. In the first version, assume that the controlling idea is "enjoyable." In the second version, assume that it is "awful." Study the following useful expressions. Select from this list or add other expressions and details.

Topic Sentence:

Fumiki enjoys his morning routine.

Useful Expressions:

jumps out of bed	happily
leaps out of bed	cheerfully
savors the flavor	carefully puts on
sips	selects with care
peaceful	sunlight

Topic Sentence:

Nobutaka considers his morning routine awful.

Useful Expressions:

drags himself out of bed	wearily
forces himself to get out	grumbles
gulps the tea down	depressing
throws on his clothes	glare of the sun
annoying	

1. He gets out of bed.

   Fumiki: ______________________________

   Nobutaka: ______________________________

2. He puts on his clothes.

   Fumiki: ______________________________

   Nobutaka: ______________________________

3. He opens the curtains.

   Fumiki: ______________________________

   Nobutaka: ______________________________

4. He drinks some tea.

   Fumiki: ______________________________

   Nobutaka: ______________________________

5. He says "Good morning" to his neighbor.

   Fumiki: ______________________________

   Nobutaka: ______________________________

EXERCISE 2-8: WRITING ASSIGNMENT

Select one of the following writing topics.

1. Using the information in Exercise 2-7, write a paragraph about either Fumiki or Nobutaka. You should add more information to support the controlling idea in your topic sentence.
2. Write a paragraph about what you do in the morning.
3. Reread the paragraph about the Rex Parade on page 34. The actions described in that paragraph are typical; that is, people do these things each year at the parade. People act differently at other kinds of parades. Think of a parade that is held in your country each year (such as an Independence Day parade). Make a list of the things people do before and during the parade. From that list, think of a controlling idea about your topic. Then write a paragraph about what people usually do at the parade. Be sure that the sentences all support the controlling idea. (If there is no annual parade in your country, describe what people generally do at any kind of parade or procession.)

COMPOSITION SKILLS

Coherence

Adverbials of Time and Sequence

The sentences in both of the paragraphs on the Mardi Gras celebration are arranged in chronological order. Each of the paragraphs is a short narration. A narration, as noted earlier, tells a story or describes a sequence of events. It is important in narrative writing to show the reader the time relationship between sentences and ideas; clarifying the time relationship helps to achieve coherence. After all, if any of the sentences could be switched around without any significant change in meaning, the paragraph is not coherent. In the revised paragraph about the Rex Parade, the following adverbial expressions of time and sequence tie the sentences together logically, thus clarifying the time sequence.

By nine o'clock. . . .

At around ten o'clock. . . .

First. . . .

Next . . .

Note that these adverbial expressions fall into two groups. The first group consists of time expressions of more than one word. They generally introduce a sentence and are followed by a comma. Here is a list of the most common ones:

by	+ time	*By nine o'clock,* the avenue is lined with people.
at	+ time	*At around ten o'clock,* the excitement mounts.

after + time	*After eleven o'clock,* the people go home.
before + time	Everyone gets there *before nine o'clock.*
after + noun	*After about an hour,* the parade passes by.
before + noun	*Before the parade,* everyone is excited.
during + noun	*During the morning,* the people have a good time.

The second group of adverbial expressions consists of one-word expressions of sequence. These generally introduce a sentence and are followed by a comma. Here is a list of the most common ones:

first	*First,* there is the welcome sound of sirens.
next	*Next,* the masked men arrive on horseback.
second	*Second,* they wave and the crowd waves back.
then	*Then,* a band usually marches by.
last	*Last,* the big floats come.
finally	*Finally,* the parade is over.

EXERCISE 2-9

Complete the following paragraphs with the appropriate adverbial expressions of time or sequence from the preceding lists.

1. My friend, Thuy, who has a private nursing business, has a demanding schedule. She does not work for a hospital or a doctor; instead, she nurses patients in their own homes. Every morning Thuy gets up ____________ 6:00 A.M. and fixes breakfast for her family. ____________, she takes her son to school and then goes to her office where she arrives ____________ 8:00 A.M. She stays there for about an hour. ____________ that time she checks to see if there are any phone messages on the answering machine. She also prepares some coffee or tea. While she drinks her beverage, Thuy reads the mail, studies the files of her patients, and prepares the work assignments for her other nurses. ____________ that, she is ready to visit her patients. ____________ she sees Mr. West and gives him an injection. Thuy goes to Mrs. Garcia's house to take her blood pressure. After seeing two more patients, she returns to the office where she eats her lunch. ____________ time she does clerical work, such as filling out forms for Medicare. She also studies recent medical reports and consults with the doctors, if necessary, of her patients. ____________ about two hours, Thuy is ready to visit four or five more patients ____________ the afternoon.

__________ she returns to the office and checks the reports of her other nurses. __________, after a long day, Thuy gets in her car and heads home.

2. Juan Prados, a diver on an oil barge off the coast of Mexico, enjoys his early morning dive to the ocean bottom to check on the oil and gas pipelines. Every morning his alarm rings at 5:30 A.M., but he is usually out of bed and dressed by that time. __________ 5:30, he generally heads to the warm, friendly galley for a leisurely cup of coffee. __________ 6:30, just as the sun is rising, he usually arrives on the main deck. __________, he stands there a few minutes, enjoying the sunrise and checking out the weather. He enjoys calm weather, for it means an easy dive with extra time for him to do some exploring on the ocean floor. __________, he goes to the back of the barge to the dive shack to prepare for his dive. __________, he carefully checks out his scuba bottles for adequate pressure. He jumps into his wet suit, his safety vest, mask, and fins. __________ that, he is ready for the exhilarating fifteen-foot jump to the surface of the water. Once in the water, Juan always relaxes in the weightless, quiet atmosphere and slowly swims down another seventy feet to the pipes lying on the ocean floor. __________, he carefully checks to see that the pipes are undisturbed and lying at the proper angle.

   __________ this part of the job, he begins to make his way back to the surface. On the way, he always watches for dolphins and frequently spots some. __________, he reaches the surface of the water, climbs the ladder of the barge to the deck, and removes his scuba gear. His early morning visit with nature is over.

Prepositions in Time Expressions

Since expressions indicating time sequence are important in achieving coherence and clarity, it is vital to use the correct prepositions in time expressions. Let us review the following prepositions in time expressions.

- *At* indicates a time of day:

  Adult students usually go to school *at night.*

  Most Americans eat lunch *at noon.*

  My first class begins *at eight o'clock.*

- ***In*** **indicates a part of the day, month, year, or season:**

  I like to get up early *in the morning.*

  I enjoy eating out *in the evening.*

  Final exams take place *in June.*

  My little sister was born *in 1968.*

  We get a week off from school *in the spring.*

- ***On*** **indicates a day:**

  In the United States, there is usually no school *on weekends.*

  My brother was born *on May 5, 1970.*

  On the morning of May 5, 1970, my brother was born.

- ***By*** **indicates up to but not later than a point in time:**

  I usually get up *by 6:30 A.M.,* sometimes earlier but never later.

  They always try to arrive home *by noon.*

- ***During*** **indicates an amount of time (followed by a noun phrase):**

  I have classes *during the day.*

  I sometimes fall asleep *during the biology lecture.*

- ***Until*** **indicates time up to a point, but not limited to that point in time:**

  I usually don't get home *until midnight,* rarely before and sometimes after.

  I like to sleep *until noon,* and sometimes I sleep later.

Special Time Expressions: *on time* and *in time*

The expression *on time* indicates the completion of an act at a designated time. It indicates the correct or exact time. If class begins at eight o'clock and you arrive at eight o'clock, you are *on time.* If you must turn in a paper on Friday and you get it on Friday, you have turned it in *on time.*

We arrived at the concert *on time.*

The expression *in time* indicates the completion of an act during a length of time that has a final limit. If class begins at eight o'clock, and you come any time before eight o'clock or you are there at eight o'clock, you are *in time. In time* is often followed by *for* and *to.* Note these examples:

We arrived *in time for* the first race.

We arrived *in time to* watch the first act.

EXERCISE 2-10

Fill in the blanks with appropriate prepositions.

1. I usually study ____________ the week, but not ____________ weekends.
2. We are leaving for Rome ____________ Friday, ____________ 3:30 ____________ the afternoon.
3. Unfortunately, we cannot leave now. We have to stay here ____________ the weekend when we can get some gasoline.
4. I arrived at the university ____________ September 2nd.
5. My mother generally does the laundry ____________ Saturday.
6. We went on vacation ____________ June.
7. Veronica did not get home ____________ eight o'clock. ____________ that time, it was too late to go to the movie.
8. I turned on the television ____________ time to catch the evening news.
9. My birthday is ____________ August. This year it is ____________ a Saturday.
10. I hate to stay up ____________ midnight.
11. We planned to get to a party at eight o'clock, and we got there ____________ time.
12. He is always late for class; he is never ____________ time.
13. He did not learn to play the piano ____________ last year.
14. I hope the package gets there ____________ time for Christmas.
15. He stays home ____________ the day.

EXERCISE 2-11

Fill in the blanks with the most appropriate prepositions.

1. Although we live in New York City now, every year ____________ August my wife and I go back to Hong Kong to visit my wife's family. We usually leave ____________ a Thursday or Friday and fly to San Francisco. ____________ the weekend, we visit our

favorite places in San Francisco—Golden Gate Park, Fisherman's Wharf, and Chinatown. Then we leave __________ Monday morning for Hong Kong. __________ the flight, I usually read a book or sleep, but my wife plans the details of our stay. We usually arrive in Hong Kong late Monday night, but sometimes we do not arrive __________ Tuesday. I like to arrive at the airport just __________ time to see the sunrise on Tuesday morning. If our flight is __________ time, my wife's uncle and family are generally at the airport to meet us. We greet each other warmly and then drive to my wife's parents' house. __________ the time we get there, we are chattering with anticipation. Whether it is __________ the morning, __________ noon, or __________ night, the old couple is always waiting quietly to welcome us.

2. Registration at this university occurs __________ the third week of August. It is usually __________ Wednesday, Thursday, and Friday. Depending on the first letter of their last name, students pick up registration materials __________ a certain time. Starting __________ 8:00 A.M., students can pick up their materials __________ their designated time. However, students do not have to pick them up __________ that time. They can pick them up any time after that time __________ the week of registration. But they should pick them up __________ the end of the week. It is not possible to pick them up __________ the weekend or __________ the first week of classes.

3. It seems that I always have trouble __________ the day I am supposed to register. The first time I registered was __________ August 17, 1989. I didn't realize that I had to wait __________ two o'clock, so I arrived __________ eight o'clock. I waited a long time! The next time, I was supposed to register __________ noon __________ Friday. I wanted to be __________ time so I left my house __________ ten o'clock. But there was a terrible traffic jam on the freeway so I barely arrived __________ time to pick up my materials. And __________ the time I went to get my class cards, all the classes I wanted were closed.

EXERCISE 2-12

Each of the following begins with a preposition. Using an appropriate time expression, complete each sentence.

1. On ____

____

2. During ____

____

3. In ____

____

4. After ____

____

5. By ____

____

GRAMMAR REVIEW

Single-Word Adverbs of Frequency

Adverbs of frequency tell how often something is done or how often someone does something. Single-word adverbs of frequency include the following:

always	usually	frequently	sometimes	rarely	ever
generally	often	occasionally	seldom	never	

Placement of single-word adverbs of frequency is as follows:

- ***In affirmative statements:*** Single-word adverbs of frequency usually go before the main verb of the sentence but after the verb ***to be***:

  He is *usually* out of bed and dressed by 5:30 A.M.

  She *generally* drinks coffee in the morning.

  A good nurse should *always* make sure that the patient is comfortable.

  My alarm clock is *seldom* set to go off at 5:00 A.M.

- ***In affirmative statements with auxiliaries:*** Adverbs of frequency are placed after the first auxiliary.

  I have *always* enjoyed movies.

  I will *never* forget the first time I saw Gloria Estefan and the Miami Sound Machine in concert.

  He should *never* have done that.

- ***In negative statements:*** **The adverb *always* must follow the negative auxiliary.**

  I do not *always* get up on time.

  I'm not *always* hungry at breakfast.

  The adverbs *frequently, sometimes,* and *occasionally* must come before the negative auxiliary.

  Nuri *frequently* does not catch the bus.

  We *sometimes* are not ready for class at eight o'clock.

  The adverbs *usually, generally,* and *often* can be placed either before or after the negative auxiliary.

- ***In questions:*** **Frequency adverbs follow the subject.**

  Are you *often* late to class?

  Does John *usually* watch television on Saturday night?

- ***For emphasis or variety:*** **Adverbs of frequency may be placed at the beginning or at the end of a sentence.**

  Sometimes I take a walk in the evening after dinner.

  I watch the news in the morning *occasionally.*

  However, the adverb *always* cannot be placed at the beginning or at the end of a sentence.

  Note: The adverbs of frequency *seldom, rarely,* and *never* convey a negative meaning. They are not used with *not.*

  I don't often stay home alone. = I *seldom* stay home alone.

  ***Seldom* and *rarely* can occur at the beginning of a sentence followed by an auxiliary or the verb *to be.* This construction is considered formal.**

  Seldom does he speak harshly.

  Seldom did she do anything wrong.

  Rarely is she at home.

  Rarely should a child be discouraged by his teacher.

  The adverb *ever* is used with a negative word and in questions.

  I don't *ever* eat chocolate because I am allergic to it.

  Do you *ever* eat chocolate?

EXERCISE 2-13

Think of a person you know who has a job that you are interested in, perhaps electrical engineering, nursing, or teaching. Write a sentence that tells the kind of job it is. Then answer the following questions using an adverb of frequency. Try to use a different adverb in each sentence. Change *she* to *he* if your friend is male.

Example:

My friend Li Ling is a photographer.

1. Does she like her job?

____

2. How does she get to work?

____

3. What time does she arrive at work?

____

4. What is one thing she does every day?

____

5. What is one thing she does not do very often?

____

6. What is one thing she sometimes does?

____

7. What is one thing she never does?

____

8. At what time does she eat during the day?

____

9. What does she do or not do after she eats?

____

10. At what time does she leave work?

____

EXERCISE 2-14: WRITING ASSIGNMENT

Using the information you generated in Exercise 2-13, make some notes about your friend's job. Add any information that comes to mind. From the data, find a controlling idea. Write a paragraph about what your friend generally does at work. You might want to review the model on page 37 before you begin.

EXERCISE 2-15: WRITING ASSIGNMENT

Review Exercise 2-9 on page 38. Using those examples as models, write a paragraph describing a typical morning in the life of a working person in your country, such as a doctor, farmer, businessperson, or computer programmer.

Verb Tense Review: The Simple Present vs. the Present Progressive

Thus far in our discussion of narrative paragraphs, we have restricted our narrations to the present tense. Review the two paragraphs (pages 33–34) that describe a typical morning at a Rex Parade. Which present tense is used? As you can see, the simple present tense predominates. Although the simple present tense is generally used in narrations that take place in the present time, occasionally you will need to use the present progressive (*be* + present participle) as well. Study the following passage and observe the use of the two present tenses:

> Much of David's life is centered around his future career. He wants to be a sports announcer, so he is attending the University of California and majoring in communications. This semester he is taking his first course in broadcasting. Next week he is giving his first demonstration broadcast, and he is planning to demonstrate his skills in sports announcing. He does not know how he will do; in fact, he worries about it all the time. He does not want to fail, so each night he practices in front of the television while a basketball game is going on. He always records his practice session on a tape recorder. A typical practice broadcast begins like this:
>
> "Good evening, Ladies and Gentlemen, this is David Swenson reporting live tonight from the press booth at the new sports arena in downtown Pleasantville. The arena is filled to capacity tonight, and the fans are anxiously waiting for the game to begin. As you know, the Pleasantville Bears are playing the Hick City Colts. There appears to be a good deal of excitement in the arena tonight! Here they come! The fans are cheering wildly! Yes, folks, this crowd loves its team. The game is about to begin as the players assume their positions on the court for the tip-off. The referee tosses the ball in the air, and Long Tall Jones, wearing jersey number twenty-two, tips it to his teammate Tommy Evans. Evans races down the court and slips the ball to Raoul Gomez. Gomez breaks through the defensive line, shoots, and he misses! Robinson is there. He catches the rebound and lays that ball in. The crowd is going wild! Pleasantville takes the lead. . . ."
>
> After he finishes the practice broadcast, David plays it back on his recorder and takes notes. Each time he improves his performance.

Although this passage is done in the present tense, the author uses both the simple present tense and the present progressive. Although both describe present time, the simple present and the present progressive convey different actions and times.

THE SIMPLE PRESENT TENSE

1. The simple present tense is usually used to describe repeated, habitual, or characteristic actions. The adverbs of frequency will help by signaling the need for the simple present, but sometimes those adverbs are not present, even though their meaning is there.

A band usually *marches* by, playing a popular tune.

Each night the lonely old lady *feeds* the ducks.

Each night he *practices* in front of the television.

Cigarette smoke *has* an offensive odor.

2. Some verbs, sometimes called ***stative verbs***, are almost always used in the simple present form when they are not describing the past. These verbs describe states of being, not actions. These verbs relate sensory perceptions, conditions, judgments, conclusions, emotional states, or states of being.

David *wants* to be a sports announcer.

There *appears* to be a good deal of excitement here.

The crowd *loves* its team.

His proposal *sounds* intriguing.

I *see* the roses in the garden.

You *seem* to be upset.

I *think* that we ought to consider changing our position.

This exercise *is* really easy.

My friend *has* a private nursing business.

3. A few verbs are used in the simple present tense even though they describe future actions. Fortunately, not many verbs are in this group. These verbs generally describe acts of arriving and departing, and beginning and ending.

The game *begins* in ten minutes.

The plane *leaves* for Bermuda in the morning.

The ship *departs* for Manila in two hours.

The train *arrives* tomorrow morning.

Note: These types of verbs can also be used in the present progressive to convey future actions.

4. The preceding three uses are the most common; however, there are some less common uses of the simple present to be aware of.

a. The simple present can be used to describe the steps in demonstrations, such as a scientific experiment.

We first *put* the solution in the flask, and then we *place* the flask in an area where it will get lots of light. When the solution is settled, we *add* two more ounces of soda.

b. The simple present is often used in commentaries on radio and television to describe what is taking place. In this case, the simple present often conveys a rapid sequence of events and provides a sense of drama.

The referee *tosses* up the ball. Jones *tips* it to his teammate, who *races* down the court.

c. **The simple present is often used in announcements and in newspaper headlines.**

Floods *destroy* ten homes in the canyon.

Earthquake *hits* Mexico City.

THE PRESENT PROGRESSIVE TENSE

1. The present progressive is used to describe a single action that is in progress at a specific moment, usually the moment of speaking or writing.

Samson *is studying* the lesson right now.

The people *are cheering* wildly!

2. The present progressive may also be used to describe an action in progress over a long period of time, even though the action may not be taking place at the moment of speaking or writing. This action, however, is perceived as temporary.

David *is attending* the University of California. (He may be on vacation at the moment of speaking, but he is still a registered student there.)

He *is taking* his first course in broadcasting this semester. (Again, he may not be in class right now, but he is enrolled in it.)

She *is writing* her first novel. (The pen may not be in her hand at this precise moment, but the activity is going on during the present time span and will end at some time in the future.)

3. The present progressive can be used to express a future action, especially when that action is in the near future. Usually, you need adverbials of time to clarify that the present progressive is indicating future time.

Next week he *is giving* his first demonstration.

Miss La Belle *is appearing* at the Orange Grove Theater tomorrow night.

The ship *is arriving* this afternoon at three o'clock.

We *are taking* the exam later this afternoon.

4. The present progressive can also express the beginning, progression, or end of an action in the present time.

It *is beginning* to get hot.

It *is starting* to rain again.

My writing *is getting* worse.

I *am becoming* a little irritated with you.

The movie *is* just *beginning.*

His temper tantrum *is ending* at last.

Note: The verb *to be* is rarely used in the progressive because it describes a general state of being. There are rare instances, however, when you do use the verb *to be* in the progressive:

My child *is being* obnoxious right now. Please excuse him.

In this instance, the progressive is used because the meaning is "My child is acting obnoxiously right now." The child is not generally obnoxious.

EXERCISE 2-16

Read the following passages carefully. Then fill in each blank with the correct present tense: the simple present or the present progressive.

1. At the end of each semester as final exams ____________ (approach), I ____________ (have) the same scary dream. I ____________ (dream) that I have forgotten to drop a class that I have not attended since the first week of school. I ____________ (rush) to the administration building where there ____________ (be) always a long line. After nervously waiting in line, I ____________ (get) up to the window and ____________ (inquire) about dropping the class. The clerk always ____________ (tell) me that I ____________ (can) not drop the course because it ____________ (is) too late. I then ____________ (realize) that I ____________ (have) to take the final exam. In the next scene, I ____________ (sit) in a room in a very old library, which ____________ (smell) like dusty books. There ____________ (be) several other students who ____________ (wait) at tables all around me. Everyone ____________ (look) very serious. All of the other students ____________ (wear) formal clothes. Suddenly, I ____________ (realize) that I ____________ (wear) my pajamas. Since I ____________ (feel) embarrassed and humiliated, I ____________ (try) to conceal my pajamas by sliding down in my chair. As I ____________ (sit) there at the table, I ____________ (look) around for a way to escape, but it ____________ (be) impossible. I cannot do anything because the instructor ____________ (start) to pass out the exams. When I ____________ (get) my exam and ____________ (read) the questions, my heart suddenly ____________ (sink), for I ____________ (find) that I ____________ (not know) any of the answers. In fact, I ____________ (not even recognize) any of the material on the

exam. Nevertheless, I try to take the exam. Just as I ____________ (start) to write, the bell ____________ (ring). While the bell ____________ (ring), I ____________ (cry) out, "No, no! Please, I need more time!" Then I ____________ (wake up) and ____________ (realize) that it is my alarm clock going off. Thank God it is always just a dream!

2. Our lecture in Professor Johnson's history class always begins the same way. We students ____________ (sit) in the big auditorium talking and laughing; sometimes somebody ____________ (eat) or even ____________ (smoke). Then the door on the left-hand side at the front of the auditorium ____________ (open). For a minute, it ____________ (seem) as if there ____________ (be) no one there. Then, old Professor Johnson ____________ (hobble) in. He ____________ (use) a cane, which he ____________ (have) in his right hand. In his left hand he ____________ (carry) nothing at all. He slowly ____________ (make) his way across the front of the room to the podium. All this time, the students ____________ (continue) to talk and laugh. When he ____________ (reach) the podium, he ____________ (hang) his cane on the right-hand side, but he ____________ (not say) anything. He just ____________ (wait). Gradually, the students ____________ (begin) to stop talking and ____________ (turn) around in their seats. In about five minutes, the room ____________ (be) absolutely quiet. Professor Johnson still just ____________ (wait). Then, after at least a full minute of silence, Professor Johnson ____________ (say) in a quiet but commanding voice, "Today, ladies and gentlemen, we shall concern ourselves with. . . ."

3. When I ____________ (want) to take a break from studying, I usually ____________ (go) to the computer lab. I ____________ (leave) my room or the library, wherever I ____________ (study) at the moment, and I ____________ (head) across campus to the computer building. When I ____________ (get) there, I ____________ (check) to see if anyone ____________ (use) the new Macintosh Plus. If not, I ____________ (settle) down in front of it for some fun. I ____________ (enter) my password and code and log on to the computer. Sometimes I ____________ (code)

in programs to do math problems or statistical analyses. Sometimes I ______ (prefer) to do word processing or play a game of kill the dragon. While students at other terminals ______ (moan) about botching up their programs, I just ______ (sit) and ______ (watch) the letters and numbers dance across the screen. Later, after I am relaxed, I ______ (return) to my books.

EXERCISE 2-17: WRITING ASSIGNMENT

Following are some topics for your writing assignment. Before you begin writing, make a list of ideas about the topic. Then decide on your controlling idea. Next, decide which of the ideas in your list you will use to support your controlling idea. Then, write your paragraph. Do not forget to use expressions of time and sequence and adverbs of frequency. Remember also to use simple present and present progressive tenses.

1. Review the model paragraphs in Exercise 2-16. Then relate a recurring dream or experience.
2. Review the model paragraph on page 45. Pretend that you are a news reporter at the scene of an accident or a fire. You are reporting live on camera. Your paragraph might begin like this: "This is ______ reporting for WKBY-TV News. . . ." Complete your report.
3. Review the model paragraph on page 34 about the Mardi Gras parade. Think of a holiday, ritual, or sports event in your country that occurs every year. Write down the sequence of events for one small part of the holiday. Then think of a controlling idea. Be sure to limit yourself to only one aspect of the holiday. Then choose your support and write a paragraph.

Past Narration

We have been concentrating on narrative paragraphs that describe a sequence of events in the present time. Just as common, if not more so, is narration that takes place in the past. Suppose, for example, that you were asked to describe a significant moment in your life. First, sum up the significance of this moment in one sentence. Then arrange your sentences logically and include only the sentences that relate to the topic. Study the following narration and see how the sentences are arranged, if it has a controlling idea, and if it has unity and coherence.

It was nearly dark when my two brothers and I arrived at the Ranger Station in the Shenandoah National Park. As the ranger was issuing us our camping permit, he warned us to be careful of bears. After we had put on our hiking boots and adjusted our backpacks, we set off down the nearest trail with only a flashlight to guide us. While we were tramping through the forest, we heard many strange noises. As soon as we arrived at a small clearing, we began to set up camp. I held the flashlight while my brothers were setting up the tent. I noticed that the light was getting dimmer and dimmer; apparently, the batteries were going dead. Soon, I could hear my brothers snoring and I could see the faint shadows of the forest as the moon began to rise. Just as I was about to fall asleep, I heard a strange scratching noise outside. I suddenly remembered the ranger's warning about bears. I woke my brothers up. My oldest brother grabbed the flashlight, but the batteries by then had gone dead. Suddenly, we heard a loud grunt. Upon hearing this awful sound, we all scrambled out of the tent and took off running as fast as we could, screaming for help. Exhausted, we finally reached our car near the station, jumped in, and took off. We never did return for our gear. In fact, after that scary experience, I have never gone camping again, and I do not think I ever will.

EXERCISE 2-18

On a separate sheet of paper, answer these questions about the preceding paragraph:

1. **Where in the paragraph is the topic sentence located? Why do you think the author placed the topic sentence there?**
2. **What is the controlling idea?**
3. **Is the paragraph coherent? Is it unified? Explain.**
4. **Make an outline of this paragraph.**

EXERCISE 2-19: WRITING ASSIGNMENT

1. **Think of a frightening or amusing experience you have had. Try to choose a relatively minor event so you can adequately describe it in one paragraph. Make an outline (review page 15) of the sequence of events in your experience. What is the point of your narration? Make the "point" your controlling idea, and use that in your topic sentence at the end.**
2. **Think of a time when you had to do something against your wishes. Make an outline of the sequence of events in your experience. You may wish to refer to Elizabeth Wong's essay, "The Struggle to Be an All-American Girl," on pages 24–27.**

COMPOSITION SKILLS

Coherence

Adverbial Clauses of Time

Time sequence is conveyed by terms like *after, first, then,* and *until,* followed by noun phrases or time expressions. Although these expressions help to achieve coherence in chronologically developed paragraphs, a more sophisticated technique for achieving coherence involves adverbial clauses of time.

Like adverbials, adverbial clauses tell when, where, how, how often, and why; they can also indicate contrast or concession. When you are writing chronologically developed paragraphs, you will probably use adverbial clauses of time more often than the other types of adverbial clauses.

Before discussing adverbial clauses, we should review some terms:

- *Clause*—A clause is a group of words consisting of at least a *subject* and *verb.*
- *Independent clause*—An independent clause can stand alone as a sentence.
- *Dependent clause*—Although a dependent clause has a subject and verb, it cannot stand alone because it does not express a complete thought. Dependent clauses begin with such words as *because, since, although, after, when, before, while, whereas, who,* and *why.* Dependent clauses must be attached to independent clauses.
- *Subordinator, subordinating conjunction*—These terms refer to adverbials that make a clause dependent, such as *when, because, although.*

Adverbial clauses are dependent clauses and must be attached to an independent clause. Adverbial clauses can come at the beginning or at the end of the independent clause. Look at these examples:

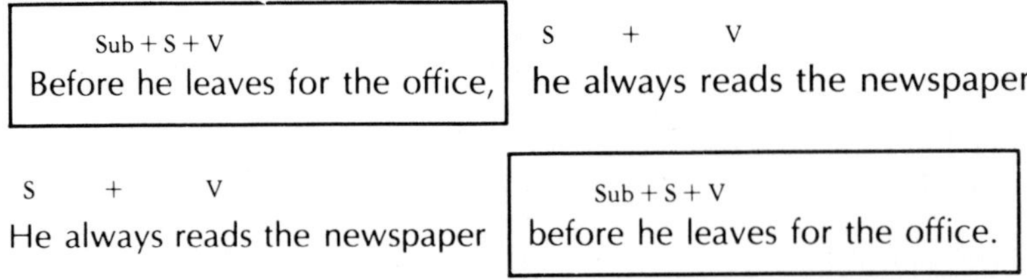

Note that when the adverbial clause comes at the beginning of the sentence, it is often followed by a comma. However, if it comes at the end, there is no comma separating it from the independent clause.

The adverbial clause is used to make the relationship between two clauses clearer and tighter. An adverbial clause of time clarifies and tightens the time relationship of two clauses. For example, look at the time relationship between these sentences:

First I go to the store. Then I go home.

To make this passage flow more smoothly and to tighten the relationship of the actions, these two clauses can be combined, making one an adverbial clause and leaving one an independent clause:

After I go to the store, I go home.

Note how the author uses adverbial clauses of time in the paragraph about the scary experience:

> It was nearly dark *when my two brothers and I arrived at the Ranger Station.*
>
> *As the ranger was issuing us our camping permit,* he warned us to be careful of bears.
>
> *After we had put on our hiking boots and adjusted our backpacks,* we set off down the nearest trail.

Adverbial clauses of time, however, do not express just time alone; they express time in relation to the independent clause in the sentence. The time in the adverbial clause of time can occur simultaneously with, before, or after the time in the independent clause. Let us review the time sequence in adverbial clauses of time.

1. ***While, as, during the time that, when, whenever.*** The adverbial clause subordinators listed here indicate that the action in the adverbial clause occurs during the same time period as the action in the independent clause.

- ***While, as***—These subordinators often indicate that an action is in progress; therefore, the progressive tenses are frequently used with them. When the progressive is used in this adverbial clause, the simple tenses (simple present, simple past) are often used in the independent clauses.

  > *As the ranger was issuing us our permit,* he warned us of the bears.
  >
  > *As I am sitting there at the table,* I look around for a way to escape.
  >
  > I *held* the flashlight *while my brothers were setting up the tent.*

- ***During the time that***—This expression is similar to ***while*** and ***when***. Both the progressive and simple tenses can be used with this expression, depending on the action conveyed.

  > *During the time that we remained in the tent,* I was very frightened.

- ***When***—This subordinator indicates a point in time or a repeated or habitual occurrence; therefore, the simple tenses are generally used with it. Sometimes, however, the progressive tenses are used with it when it is used to mean "while."

  > It was dark *when my two brothers and I arrived at the station.*

- ***Whenever***—Unlike the other subordinates in this group, ***whenever*** usually takes only the simple tenses because it indicates a repeated or habitual action. (It means "each time that, every time that.")

Whenever you call my name, I come running to you.

Sometimes ***whenever*** can indicate that the action in the independent clause is future but is expected to be repeated.

Whenever you call me up, I will come over immediately.

2. ***Before, after.*** These subordinators are used to indicate that the time in the adverbial clause occurs before or after the action in the independent clause.

After we had put on our hiking boots, we set off down the trail. (First we put on our boots. After that we set off down the trail.)

Before we set off down the trail, we put on our hiking boots.

Before the parade begins, the people stroll in the street.

In sentences like the first two, where there are two ***past*** actions and a sequence is established, the past perfect tense (***had*** + past participle) can be used to indicate the ***earlier*** of the two actions. However, it is common practice to use the simple past tense in the adverbial clause.

After we put on our hiking boots, we set off down the trail.

3. ***Until, till, up to the time that.*** These subordinators indicate that the time in the adverbial clause signals the end of the time in the independent clause.

I stayed in my tent *until it was light outside.* (Then she left the tent.)

"You cannot go outside *until you finish your spinach,*" the mother told her child.

4. ***Since, ever since, from the moment (time) that.*** These subordinators are used to indicate that the action in the independent clause began at the moment indicated in the adverbial clause and continues in the present. The simple past is usually used in the adverbial clause; the perfect tenses are used in the independent clause.

Ever since I was a child, I have had the tendency to get angry easily.

From the moment I first saw her, I have been in love with *her.*

5. ***As soon as, the moment that, when, once.*** These subordinators are used to indicate that the action in the independent clause will take place ***upon completion*** of the action in the adverbial clause. ***When*** is used less frequently in this way; if you want to make it clear that the action in the independent clause will take place right after the action in the adverbial clause, use ***as soon as*** or ***the moment that.***

As soon as we arrived at a small clearing, we began to set up camp.

I turn on the television set *the moment that I get home.*

Once I arrive in Hong Kong, I am going to visit my friend's parents.

Note: *Once* can also be used to mean "after."

Special Verb Tense Note

In adverbial clauses of time, the present tense is used even though the time indicated is future:

> Before you *begin* to write your paper, you need to think about it.
>
> I am going to stay here until he *arrives*.
>
> We are giving him a party after he *returns* from Japan.

EXERCISE 2-20

Combine each of the following sets of sentences into a single sentence. Use the appropriate subordinators to make sentences with adverbial clauses of time. The first one is done for you.

1. **I was driving down the road. During that time, I saw something or someone ahead by the side of the road.**
   While I was driving down the road, I saw something or someone ahead by the side of the road.
2. **I looked at it carefully. At that moment, it began to move.**

   ____
3. **It started to move and shake. Then, I slowed down.**

   ____
4. **I brought the car to a stop behind it. I was still trying to figure out what it was.**

   ____
5. **I got out of the car. Before that, I opened the glove compartment and took out something.**

   ____
6. **I walked over to it. It began to. . . . (Fill in the blank.)**

   ____

EXERCISE 2-21: WRITING ASSIGNMENT

Exercise 2-20 presents the beginning of a narrative. Complete the story.

EXERCISE 2-22: WRITING ASSIGNMENT

Read the following paragraphs about a Chinese folktale. Rewrite the paragraphs and combine the sentences using adverbial clauses of time. Be careful to use the appropriate subordinators. The first one is done for you. Your revised version should contain the following subordinators:

while	until	after
when	as soon as	whenever

(1) The night is clear and you can see shadows on the moon.
When the night is clear, you can see shadows on the moon.

(1) *The night is clear and you can see shadows on the moon.* According to an old Chinese folktale, they are the shadows of the cinnamon tree in the moon. This tree came to be because of the laziness of an immortal, Wu Kang.

Wu Kang was in charge of guarding the dragon. However, he was lazy. (2) *He drank wine and he often allowed the dragon to run away.* One day he went to Mount K'un Lun. (3) *He was there. During that time, he met some of his friends.* They began to drink wine, compose poems, and throw dice. He continued to drink, even after night came. (4) *He drank some more and finally, he became completely tipsy.* (5) *He saw some fellows playing chess, so he asked to join them.* They advised him to go home because they knew he was being negligent, but Wu Kang offered to wager the dragon pearl. (6) *They played a few moves of the game. Then Wu Kang lost the pearl.* (7) *He had wagered and lost the dragon pearl. Immediately, he wagered and lost the mighty dragon.* (8) *The Immortals learned of the loss. They were furious.* They immediately sowed a pearl in the ground and a tall cinnamon tree grew from it. (9) *The tree reached a great height. After that, they gave Wu Kang an axe and told him to cut off the branches.* (10) *He had cut off all the branches. Immediately after that, bigger ones sprouted and grew.* Wu Kang had to cut them off, too. Wu Kang is still there to this day cutting off branches. (11) *Now, you see shadows on the moon, and you will know that they are the branches of the cinnamon tree falling down.*

—Adapted from *A Harvest of World Folk Tales*, ed. Milton Rugoff (New York: Viking, 1968), pp. 193–95.

EXERCISE 2-23: WRITING ASSIGNMENT

Rewrite the paragraph you first wrote for Exercise 2-8 on page 36. In your version, use adverbial clauses of time for greater coherence.

EXERCISE 2-24: WRITING ASSIGNMENT

Using adverbial clauses of time, write one of the paragraphs you outlined for Exercise 2-19 on page 51.

GRAMMAR REVIEW

Verb Tense Review: The Simple Past, the Past Progressive, and the Past Perfect

To write a good narrative paragraph about something that happened in the past, it is imperative that you review the most common forms of the past tense used in this kind of writing: the simple past, the past progres-

sive, and the past perfect. Although these tenses are not the only ones used in paragraphs written about an event that takes place in the past, they are the most common ones. Study the following paragraph about a memorable and tragic day that the author remembers vividly. Note the author's use of the past tenses.

It started out as a nice enough day. The weather was unusually warm for the third week in November, so I was in a good mood when my mother dropped me off at school. Everything went as usual that morning; the classes were boring and nothing exciting was happening. At noon, I went to the cafeteria for lunch. While I was standing in line with my friends, I noticed that some of the other students were excited about something. Then a girl in line asked me if I had heard that someone had shot the president. I was surprised at this news; however, I figured that it was probably just a minor wound. Suddenly, a voice came over the loudspeaker announcing that the president was dead. There was a hush in the cafeteria. Students stopped eating. No one was moving; it was as if we were all frozen. That afternoon the teachers did not conduct the classes as usual; in fact, most of the teachers allowed the students to express their feelings about what had happened. Even my old stodgy English teacher did not conduct class as usual. She did not give us the exam that she had planned for that day. After school, I went home. Fortunately, no one was home, for I wanted to be alone. Finally, after three hours of containing my emotions, I began to cry. I was still crying when my mother arrived home. She came into my room, put her arms around me, and said, "This is a sad day for our country." Yes, November 22, 1963, was a sad day, a tragic day that was the beginning of a long, difficult period in American history.

EXERCISE 2-25

On a separate sheet of paper, answer the following questions about the preceding paragraph.

1. Where in the paragraph is the topic sentence located? What is the controlling idea?
2. Is the paragraph unified? Coherent? Why, or why not?
3. Make an outline of the paragraph.

THE SIMPLE PAST TENSE. The simple past tense indicates that an action occurred or a situation existed at a known moment in the past or during a period of time in the past.

It *was* nearly dark when my two brothers and I *arrived* at the ranger station.

Everything *went* as usual that morning.

THE PAST PROGRESSIVE TENSE. The past progressive tense indicates that an action began and continued over a period of time in the past. It is also used to describe an action that is going on at a particular time in the past.

> I *was* still *crying* when my mother arrived.
>
> No one *was moving* during that time.

The past progressive is often used in adverbial clauses of time with ***while*** and ***as*** to indicate an action that occurs at the same time as the action in the independent clause.

> *While* I *was standing* in line with my friends, I noticed that some of the students were excited about something.
>
> *As* the ranger *was issuing* us our camping permit, he warned us to be careful.

THE PAST PERFECT TENSE. The past perfect tense indicates that one past event occurred before another past event. The past perfect is used to describe the event that occurred first.

> She did not give us the exam that she *had planned* for that day.
>
> After we *had put* on our hiking boots, we set off down the trail.

In strict chronological sequence, or when adverbials make the time relationship clear, the past perfect is often unnecessary. In these cases, the simple past tense is used instead.

> First we *put* on our hiking boots, and then we set off down the trail.
>
> After we *put* on our hiking boots, we set off down the trail.

However, when the amount of time leading up to the first event is given, the past perfect is necessary.

> I *had known* her for three years when she left.
>
> It *had* just *begun* to rain when we got out of the theater.

The past perfect is often used with the expressions ***no sooner . . . than*** and ***hardly . . . when***.

> I *had no sooner begun* to work *than* the telephone rang.
>
> We *had hardly started* to fish *when* it began to rain.

EXERCISE 2-26

1. Following are some facts about Albert Einstein's life.* Keeping these facts in mind, fill in the correct verb tense for each verb in the paragraphs that follow. Use the simple past, past progressive, or past perfect tense.

*Information from G. J. Whitrow, ***Einstein—The Man and His Achievement*** (London: British Broadcasting Corp., 1967).

Albert Einstein

1879—born
1880—moved to a suburb of Munich
1889—sent to Leopold Gymnasium (high school)
1893—read a series of natural science books
1894—his parents moved to Milan, Italy
1895—left Munich for Milan
1896—admitted to Zurich Polytechnic Institute
1900—graduated from Zurich Polytechnic Institute
1901—began to publish
1902—obtained a job in the Swiss Patent Office in Berne

Albert Einstein was one of the greatest scientists of the twentieth century. His theories have affected all of modern science. However, as a child, this great man __________ (be) often considered dull and __________ (be) often misunderstood by his teachers.

Albert Einstein __________ (be) born in Ulm, Germany, on March 14, 1879. As a child, he __________ (be) taciturn and slow in learning to talk. Very often, while other children __________ (play), he __________ (daydream) and __________ (think).

Although he __________ (enjoy) learning, he __________ (have) problems in school. By the time Einstein __________ (be) twelve, his family __________ (move) to a suburb of Munich, and he __________ (attend) the Leopold Gymnasium there for two years. He did not enjoy learning Latin and Greek grammar or mathematics at school because the standard methods of solving problems __________ (not arouse) his imagination. However, he __________ (like) solving algebra problems in his own way at home. Also, by the time he __________ (be) fifteen, he __________ (read) a number of books on natural science and __________ (develop) an enthusiasm for it. Later in 1895, when Albert __________ (want) a discharge from the gymnasium to join his parents, who previously __________ (move) to Milan, his teacher __________ (help) him get one, telling Albert that he __________ (be) a disruptive influence in the class.

His problems with school __________ (follow) him to Milan. In 1895, he __________ (decide) that he __________ (want) to go to the famous Polytechnic Institute in Zurich, Switzerland. However, because he __________ (not receive) a gymnasium diploma from his school in Munich, the Institute __________ (refuse) to admit him. He __________ (go) to a gymnasium in Aarau to obtain his diploma. After Einstein __________ (receive) it, the Institute finally __________ (admit) him at the age of seventeen.

While Einstein __________ (study) at the Polytechnic Institute, he again __________ (clash) with the educational system. He often __________ (cut) classes to study more interesting subjects on his own. This __________ (anger) his professors. By the time he __________ (get) his diploma in 1900, he __________ (anger) his theoretical physics professor so much that this professor __________ (prevent) Albert from becoming an assistant at the Institute.

Finally, in 1910, Einstein __________ (begin) to publish his revolutionary ideas. Eventually, the whole world __________ (recognize) his genius.

2. Using the simple past, past progressive, or past perfect tense, fill in the correct verb tense in each blank.*

On July 20, 1969, people around the world __________ (watch) television in wonder as two men __________ (step) out of a spacecraft and onto the surface of the moon. __________ (aux.) humans really __________ (stand) on the moon? It __________ (seem) like science fiction had come to life. Since that time, astronauts have accomplished more difficult feats, but none have caught the imagination of the world as much as that mission by Apollo 11. From the time the astronauts, Neil Armstrong, Edwin Aldrin, Jr., and Michael Collins, __________ (blast) off at 9:30 A.M., Wednesday, July 16 until the time they __________ (return) eight days later, the world __________ (marvel) at this adventure in space.

The launching of the spacecraft __________ (be) a blaze of power. The astronauts __________ (ride) on top of a pillar of fire as the first-stage engines __________ (lift) the spacecraft off the launching pad. Once the first-stage rocket __________ (use) up all its fuel, the astronauts __________ (shut) off its engines and __________ (separate) it from the

*Information from *Collier's Encyclopedia* (New York: Macmillan, 1980).

rest of the Saturn-5 rocket. This drama __________ (occur) only nine minutes after the launch. The second-stage rocket __________ (take) over and __________ (boost) the vehicle to an altitude of 187 kilometers. As the second-stage rocket __________ (drop) into the Atlantic Ocean, the third stage __________ (power) the craft into an orbit around the earth. Only twelve minutes __________ (elapse) since blastoff. While the space vehicle __________ (make) one and a half revolutions around the earth, the ground controllers and the astronauts __________ (check) all the systems. They __________ (fire) the third rocket a second time. Once this __________ (be) done, they __________ (commit) the Apollo to a flight toward the moon. About three hours after liftoff, the third-stage rocket __________ (separate) from the craft and the astronauts __________ (settle) down for a seventy-three hour trip to the moon.

The world __________ (go) with the astronauts on the second and third days of the journey as the astronauts __________ (send) home television pictures of their view of the earth from many kilometers out in space. Everyone __________ (wait) for the fourth day of the mission, when the astronauts successfully __________ (maneuver) the spacecraft into orbit around the moon, which provided a spectacular backdrop to the event.

Then, the critical moment __________ (arrive). On the morning of July 20, the three men __________ (climb) into their spacesuits. Neil Armstrong and Edwin Aldrin __________ (transfer) to the landing module, separating it from the command module, and __________ (start) the descent to the surface of the moon. Approximately one hour later, Armstrong __________ (announce), "The Eagle has landed." The men __________ (set) the landing module down on a level, rocky plain near the southwestern shore of the Sea of Tranquility. At 10:56 P.M., the first human __________ (step) on the surface of the moon and Armstrong __________ (pronounce) those now historic words, "That's one small step for a man, one giant step for mankind." On earth, 600 million people __________ (watch) as Armstrong __________ (take) that step.

The drama __________ (continue) the next day as the landing module __________ (lift) off from the lunar surface and __________ (rejoin) the command module, still in orbit around the moon. The three astronauts __________ (settle) down for the three-day journey back to earth. Although dramatic, the reentry into the earth's atmosphere, the splashdown, and the hero's welcome were anticlimactic for the three men who __________ (have) this adventure in space and for the millions of people who __________ (watch) it.

3. Fill in the appropriate verb tense in each blank. Note that some should be in the past tense and some in the present tense.

I had known that some people __________ (freeze) in emergency situations; that is, they cannot move or speak. I, of course, __________ (think) that I __________ (be) immune to this reaction, but one day I __________ (experience) this terrible reaction.

When I was ten years old, our family __________ (live) on a farm in Texas. I __________ (use) to go swimming regularly in the large irrigation canal near our home. My younger brother, who __________ (can) not swim, usually just sat nearby and __________ (watch) me. One day, while I __________ (sit) on the bank drying off after a swim, my brother suddenly __________ (fall) into the water. I __________ (watch) his head go under and come up; it __________ (seem) to be happening in slow motion. I __________ (can) not move. No thoughts __________ (enter) my brain; I simply __________ (can) not react at all.

Fortunately, one of our neighbors was __________ (walk) along the bank on the other side of the canal when my brother __________ (fall) into the water. She __________ (hear) my brother __________ (yell) at the top of his lungs as he __________ (fall). The woman __________ (jump) into the water and __________ (swim) toward my brother. I __________ (watch) all this silently; I still __________ (can) not move. The woman __________ (pull) my brother out of the water and __________ (check) to see that he __________ (be) okay. Suddenly, I __________ (begin) to tremble. For several minutes, my knees __________ (shake) and my teeth

__________ (chatter). Then, the woman __________ (take) us back to our house and __________ (tell) our parents what __________ (happen). I __________ (be) deeply ashamed. I still __________ (carry) that shame with me today.

EXERCISE 2-27: WRITING ASSIGNMENT

Study the following list of information. As you will notice, all of the verbs are in the simple present tense. Use this information to write a narrative paragraph in the past time. The times given at the left will help you determine the chronological order; do not mention the times given in your paragraph. In the paragraph, use time-sequence markers and adverbial clauses of time. You must include at least one sentence for each of the following subordinators of time: *while, when, as soon as, after.* If you want to use others, you may. Be sure that the verb tenses accurately describe the time you want to indicate. In addition, the paragraph should have a topic sentence with a controlling idea about this incident. The controlling idea could deal with the lesson that Patrick learned. You can add information if you wish.

Thursday night: Patrick goes to a party instead of studying for his biology exam.

Friday

10:00—The bell rings.
10:00—The instructor distributes the biology exams.
10:02—The instructor reads the instructions for the multiple-choice exam.
10:03—The students begin answering the questions.
10:03— 10:50—The students take the exam.
10:03— 10:48—The instructor reads a book.
10:05—Patrick looks at the instructor. Patrick looks worried.
10:05—Patrick glances around the room.
10:30—Patrick sees the answers on Mario's answer sheet.
10:03 - 10:47—Mario writes out his answers.
10:30 - 10:47—Patrick hurriedly copies Mario's answers.
10:48—The instructor looks up.
10:50—The bell rings.
10:50—The instructor collects the exams.

Monday

10:00—The bell rings.
10:00—The instructor enters the classroom.
10:02—The instructor returns the exams to the students.
10:04—Patrick peeks at Mario's exam and sees an "A" on it.
10:05—Patrick gets his exam with an "F" on it.
10:06—Patrick compares his answers to Mario's answers.

10:06—Patrick sees that his answers are all incorrect. He had copied Mario's answers incorrectly.

Special Verb Usage: *would* + verb and *used to* + verb

Sometimes it is necessary to express actions that are repeated in the past; we can call them habitual actions, actions that occur again and again in the past. For such a habitual past action, you can use the expression *would* + a verb.

For example, suppose that every weekend your family went to the park. Your family did this regularly. You could say:

Every weekend my family *would go* to the park.

Although you could say "Every weekend my family went to the park," the use of *would* + a verb emphasizes the repetition of the act.

The expression *used to* + a verb is sometimes used in expressing the habitual past, but this expression is considered more informal.

I *used to* take the bus every day.

EXERCISE 2-28

Study the following passage from Carl Sagan's *Broca's Brain*. Underline the instances where he uses *would* + a verb to indicate habitual past actions.

In the early years of the twentieth century there was a horse in Germany who could read, do mathematics, and exhibit a deep knowledge of world political affairs. Or so it seemed. The horse was called Clever Hans. He was owned by Wilhelm von Osten, an elderly Berliner whose character was such, everyone said, that fraud was out of the question. Delegations of distinguished scientists viewed the equine marvel and pronounced it genuine. Hans would reply to mathematical problems put to him with coded taps of his foreleg, and would answer nonmathematical questions by nodding his head up and down or shaking it side to side in the conventional Western way. For example, someone would say, "Hans, how much is twice the square root of nine, less one?" After a moment's pause Hans would dutifully raise his right foreleg and tap five times. Was Moscow the capital of Russia? Head shake. How about St. Petersburg? Nod.

The Prussian Academy of Sciences sent a commission, headed by Oskar Pfungst, to take a closer look; Osten, who believed fervently in Hans's powers, welcomed the inquiry. Pfungst noticed a number of interesting regularities. Sometimes, the more difficult the question, the longer it took Hans to answer; or when Osten did not know the answer, Hans exhibited a comparable ignorance; or when Osten was out of the room, or when the horse was blindfolded, no correct answers were forthcoming. But other times Hans would get the right answer in a strange place, surrounded by skeptics, with Osten not only out of the room, but out of town. The solution eventually became clear. When a mathematical question was put to Hans, Osten would become slightly tense, for fear Hans would make too few taps. When Hans, however, reached the correct number of taps, Osten unconsciously and imperceptibly nodded or relaxed—imperceptibly to virtually all human observers, but not to Hans, who was rewarded with a sugar cube for correct answers. Even teams of skeptics would watch Hans's foot as soon as the question was put and make gestural or postural responses when the horse reached the right answer. Hans was totally ignorant of mathematics, but very sensitive to unconscious nonverbal cues. Similar signs were unknowingly transmitted to the horse when verbal questions were posed. Clever Hans was aptly named; he was a horse who had conditioned one human being and discovered that other human beings he had never before met would provide him the needed cues. But despite the unambiguous nature of Pfungst's evidence, similar stories of counting, reading, and politically sage horses, pigs, and geese have continued to plague the gullible of many nations.

Carl Sagan, *Broca's Brain: Reflections on the Romance of Science* (New York: Ballantine, 1979), pp. 59–60.

EXERCISE 2-29: WRITING ASSIGNMENT

Following are some topics for your writing assignment. Choose one that interests you. Before you begin writing, though, first establish the sequence of events. Then decide on your controlling idea. Also decide if your controlling idea should appear at the beginning or at the end of your paragraph. Remember to use adverbial clauses of time for coherence. Finally, since you are writing a past narrative, decide which of the past tenses to use. With these concerns in mind, write the paragraph.

1. Review the paragraph that you wrote for Exercise 2-27. Then write a paragraph that describes an incident in your life when you learned a lesson.
2. Review the paragraph on page 57 about President Kennedy's death. Then think of a significant historical event that took place in your lifetime, such as the explosion of the space shuttle Challenger, a devastating earthquake or other natural disaster, or an important political event. Write a paragraph about what you were doing on that day when you heard the news of the event.
3. Review the paragraph that you wrote for Exercise 2-22, the Chinese folktale. Then think of a short folktale you are familiar with and write a paragraph about it. Be sure to include a controlling idea.

4. Review the Helen Keller essay on pages 28–31. Then write a paragraph about a time in your life when you made an important discovery.

Narrative Paragraph Checklist

1. A narrative paragraph relates a story or incident. Does your paragraph tell a story?
2. A narrative paragraph presents the sequence of events in a story in chronological order. Are your ideas and sentences arranged in chronological order?
3. Does your paragraph have a clear topic sentence or an implied topic sentence?
4. Does your paragraph have a clear, focused controlling idea?
5. Is your paragraph unified; that is, do all of your sentences support the controlling idea?

Chapter 3

The Descriptive Paragraph

Readings: Important People, Important Places

OUR lives are filled with places, people, and events. We remember certain important places from our childhood and from our current lives—perhaps a particular room or outdoor scene. Often when we think of that place, we not only see it in detail but we also smell the smells and hear the sounds associated with it. We remember what important event happened there. So, too, with people. Certain people are important in our lives—our parents, family members, teachers, others. And, again, when we think of a particular person, we see the details and hear the sounds of that individual and remember, even with just a feeling, his or her impact on our lives.

In the following two readings, Jade Snow Wong and N. Scott Momaday both remember a particular person; Momaday also describes an important place. As you read the selections, try to answer these questions:

1. What important characteristics do the writers remember about the people they are describing?
2. In the second selection, what important characteristics of the place does Momaday describe?

READING 1

UNCLE KWOK

JADE SNOW WONG

In this reading selection from* Fifth Chinese Daughter, *the author's autobiography about growing up in San Francisco's Chinatown, Jade Snow Wong presents a memorable portrait of her Uncle Kwok. She describes his physical appearance and his actions from the time he enters the Wong factory (which also serves as the family's home) until he gets settled at his job. As you read the selection, try to discover Wong's attitude toward Uncle Kwok.

1 Among the workers in Daddy's factory, Uncle Kwok was one of the strangest—a large-framed, awkward, unshaven man whose worn clothes hung on him as if they did not belong to him. Each afternoon around three-thirty, as some of the workers were about to go home to prepare their early dinners, Uncle Kwok slowly and deliberately ambled• in through the Wong front door, dragging his feet heavily, and gripping in one hand the small black satchel• from which he was never separated.

ambled: walked in a leisurely way

satchel: a small bag for carrying clothes, books, or articles

2 Going to his own place at the sewing machine, he took off his battered• hat and ragged coat, hung both up carefully, and then sat down. At first Jade Snow was rather afraid of this extraordinary person, and unseen, watched his actions from a

battered: worn, beaten up

safe distance. After Uncle Kwok was settled in his chair, he took off his black, slipperlike shoes. Then, taking a piece of stout cardboard from a miscellaneous• pile which he kept in a box near his sewing machine, he traced the outline of his shoes on the cardboard. Having closely examined the blades of his scissors and tested their sharpness, he would cut out a pair of cardboard soles, squinting• critically through his inaccurate glasses. Next he removed from both shoes the cardboard soles he had made the day before and inserted the new pair. Satisfied with his inspection of his renewed footware, he got up, went to the waste can some seventy-five feet away, disposed of the old soles, and returned to his machine. He had not yet said a word to anyone.

having various kinds

looking with eyes partly closed

3 Daily this process was repeated without deviation.•

change

4 The next thing Uncle Kwok always did was to put on his own special apron, homemade from double thicknesses of heavy burlap• and fastened at the waist by strong denim ties. This long apron covered his thin, patched trousers and protected him from dirt and draft. After a half hour had been consumed by these chores, Uncle Kwok was ready to wash his hands. He sauntered• into the Wong kitchen, stationed himself at the one sink which served both family and factory, and with characteristic meticulousness,• now proceeded to clean his hands and fingernails.

coarse cloth made of hemp used for making sacks

walked carelessly or idly

extreme care about details

5 It was Mama's custom to begin cooking the evening meal at this hour so that the children could have their dinner before they went to the Chinese school, but every day she had to delay her preparations at the sink until slow-moving Uncle Kwok's last clean fingernail passed his fastidious• inspection. One day, however, the inconvenience tried her patience to its final limit.

not easy to please, excessively careful

6 Trying to sound pleasantly persuasive,• she said, "Uncle Kwok, please don't be so slow and awkward. Why don't you wash your hands at a different time, or else wash them faster?"

convincing

7 Uncle Kwok loudly protested the injustice of her comment. "Mama, I am not awkward. The only awkward thing about my life is that it has not yet prospered!" And he strode off, too hurt even to dry his hands finger by finger, as was his custom.

EXERCISE 3-1: COMPREHENSION/ DISCUSSION QUESTIONS

1. **What is the main point that Wong makes about Uncle Kwok? In which sentence is this point clearly established?**

2. What are some of the physical details that Wong gives to describe Uncle Kwok?
3. How does Uncle Kwok dress?
4. How does he move? Find five words that describe the way he moves.
5. Describe Uncle Kwok's daily routine. What does he do first? Next? Next?
6. What is Wong's mother's attitude toward Uncle Kwok?
7. What words would you use to describe Wong's attitude toward her Uncle?
8. What does Uncle Kwok's statement in paragraph 7 explain about his behavior? Does it help us to understand Uncle Kwok better? If so, how?
9. In the first paragraph, Wong describes Uncle Kwok as "strange." What makes him strange to her? What makes any person strange?

EXERCISE 3-2: VOCABULARY DEVELOPMENT

In describing Uncle Kwok, Wong uses adverbs of manner to tell about his actions. Adverbs of manner usually end in *-ly* and tell how something is done. Note these examples from the first paragraph of the essay:

Uncle Kwok *slowly* and *deliberately* ambled in through the Wong front door.

Slowly and *deliberately* tell how Uncle Kwok ambled or walked. In describing his walk, these words also help to indicate his character. Thus, they help us to understand Uncle Kwok better.

1. In the following phrases and sentences from the Wong reading, underline the adverbs of manner. Then tell what aspects of Uncle Kwok they help to convey.
   a. dragging his feet heavily (par. 1)
   b. he took off his battered hat and ragged coat, hung both up carefully (par. 2)
   c. Having closely examined the blades of his scissors and tested their sharpness (par. 2)
   d. he would cut out a pair of cardboard soles, squinting critically through his inaccurate glasses (par. 2)
2. The following adjectives all help to describe Uncle Kwok. Make them into adverbs of manner by adding *-ly*. Write the adverb in the blank provided. The first one is done for you.
   a. slow ______slowly______
   b. awkward ____________________
   c. meticulous ____________________
   d. fastidious ____________________

Now use each of the preceding adverbs in a sentence to describe a particular action of Uncle Kwok.

a. Uncle Kwok sauntered slowly to the sink to wash his hands.

b. ____________________

c. ____________________

d. ____________________

3. Wong relates some of Uncle Kwok's actions without a descriptive adverb. If she had used adverbs with the following actions, what words do you think she might have used? From your knowledge of Uncle Kwok's character, add an appropriate adverb to each of the following actions. Try to use a variety of adverbs.

a. tightly gripping in one hand the small black satchel (par. 1)

b. Going __________ to his own place at the sewing machine (par. 2)

c. he __________ traced the outline of his shoes on the cardboard (par. 2)

d. he __________ put on his own special apron (par. 4)

e. He sauntered __________ into the Wong kitchen (par. 4)

f. he proceeded __________ to clean his hands and fingernails (par. 4)

READING 2

FROM *THE WAY TO RAINY MOUNTAIN*

N. SCOTT MOMADAY

N. Scott Momaday, a Kiowa Indian, was born in Oklahoma in 1934 and was educated at the University of New Mexico and Stanford University. Momaday's works include House Made of Dawn *(1968), which won the Pulitzer Prize for fiction, and* The Way to Rainy Mountain *(1969), a collection of Kiowa Indian folktales.*

The following reading is taken from the autobiographical introduction to The Way to Rainy Mountain, *where Momaday describes the landscapes, the legends, and the people that were part of the Kiowa culture before it was disrupted by American settlers and the United States Army in the late 1800s. In the first two paragraphs reprinted here, Momaday describes the area of Oklahoma where the Kiowas, and*

specifically, his grandmother, lived. In the third paragraph, he describes his grandmother, who remembered many of the old tribal customs and stories, as he remembers her.

1 A single knoll• rises out of the plain in Oklahoma, north and west of the Wichita Range.• For my people, the Kiowas, it is an old landmark, and they gave it the name Rainy Mountain. The hardest weather in the world is there. Winter brings blizzards,• hot tornadic• winds arise in the spring, and in summer the prairie is an anvil's[1] edge. The grass turns brittle and brown, and it cracks beneath your feet. There are green belts along the rivers and creeks, linear groves• of hickory and pecan, willow and witch hazel.[2] At a distance in July or August the steaming foliage• seems almost to writhe• in fire. Great green and yellow grasshoppers• are everywhere in the tall grass, popping up like corn to sting the flesh, and tortoises• crawl about on the red earth, going nowhere in the plenty of time. Loneliness is an aspect• of the land. All things in the plain are isolate; there is no confusion of objects in the eye, but *one* hill or *one* tree or *one* man. To look upon that landscape in the early morning, with the sun at your back, is to

small hill
a group of mountains
severe snowstorms / a terrible windstorm
groups in lines
green leaves / twist and turn
insects, like locusts
turtles
a way of looking

[1]*an iron or steel block on which a blacksmith pounds metal*
[2]**hickory and pecan, willow and witch hazel** *types of trees*

lose the sense of proportion.• Your imagination comes to life, and this, you think, is where Creation[3] was begun.

comparative relation between things

2 I returned to Rainy Mountain in July. My grandmother had died in the spring, and I wanted to be at her grave. She had lived to be very old and at last infirm.• Her only living daughter was with her when she died, and I was told that in death her face was that of a child. . . .

feeble, weak

3 Now that I can have her only in memory, I see my grandmother in the several postures• that were peculiar to her: standing at the wood stove on a winter morning and turning meat in a great iron skillet;• sitting at the south window, bent above her beadwork, and afterwards, when her vision failed, looking down for a long time into the fold of her hands; going out upon a cane, very slowly as she did when the weight of age came upon her; praying. I remember her most often at prayer. She made long, rambling• prayers out of suffering and hope, having seen many things. I was never sure that I had the right to hear, so exclusive were they of all mere custom and company.[4] The last time I saw her she prayed standing by the side of her bed at night, naked to the waist, the light of a kerosene lamp moving upon her dark skin. Her long, black hair, always drawn and braided in the day, lay upon her shoulders and against her breasts like a shawl. I do not speak Kiowa, and I never understood her prayers, but there was something inherently• sad in the sound, some merest• hesitation upon the syllables of sorrow. She began in a high and descending pitch,• exhausting• her breath to silence; then again and again—and always the same intensity[5] of effort, of something that is, and is not, like urgency[6] in the human voice. Transported[7] so in the dancing light among the shadows of her room, she seemed beyond the reach of time. But that was illusion;• I think I knew then that I should not see her again.

ways of standing

frying pan

not sticking to the point

in the nature of it

slightest

sound / using up entirely

unreal or misleading idea

EXERCISE 3-3: COMPREHENSION/ DISCUSSION QUESTIONS

1. In Momaday's description of Rainy Mountain, he says: "The hardest weather in the world is there" (par. 1). How does he support this idea?

[3]*the beginning of the world*
[4]**exclusive were they of all mere custom and company** *private, unique*
[5]*strength, energy*
[6]*a need for something to be done immediately*
[7]*Taken out of her immediate surroundings*

2. How does Momaday support this statement: "Loneliness is an aspect of the land" (par. 1)?
3. Explain what the author means by, "To look upon that landscape in the early morning, with the sun at your back, is to lose the sense of proportion" (par. 1).
4. What does the writer mean when he says: "this, you think, is where Creation was begun" (par. 1)?
5. What is Momaday's controlling idea or main point about Rainy Mountain?
6. Why does he return to Rainy Mountain?
7. Momaday remembers his grandmother in "several postures" (par. 3). What are they?
8. How does he describe his grandmother at prayer?
9. Momaday does not understand the Kiowa language, but he describes the sound of his grandmother's prayers. To him, what did her prayers sound like? What emotions did she express in them?
10. Explain the meaning of the last two sentences in paragraph 3: "Transported so in the dancing light among the shadows of her room, she seemed beyond the reach of time. But that was illusion; I think I knew then that I should not see her again."
11. How do the last two sentences in paragraph 3 tie in with the description of the landscape in the first paragraph?
12. How does Momaday feel about Rainy Mountain? His grandmother?

EXERCISE 3-4: VOCABULARY DEVELOPMENT

The following words from the Momaday reading are used to give a physical description of a place. Be sure you understand each one.

knoll	plain	blizzard	groves	grasshoppers
range	prairie	tornadic	foliage	tortoises

The following words are not used in the reading but could be used to write a description of Rainy Mountain. For each word, write a clear definition. Then, using the word, write a sentence describing some aspect of Rainy Mountain.

1. slope ______________________________

____

2. torrent ______________________________

____

3. scorch ______________________________

____

4. clusters ______________________________

____

5. skyline ____

____

____

Writing

Narrative paragraphs describe a sequence of events or tell a story; in other words, narrative paragraphs describe an experience. The logical arrangement of ideas and sentences in a narrative paragraph is chronological—according to time order. But what if you were asked to describe how something looks—a place, a thing, or a person? How should you arrange your ideas and sentences in the paragraph? Obviously, time order would not be logical. When you are describing the way something looks—its physical appearance—it is not time but space that is important. Therefore, you should arrange your sentences and details according to where the objects being described are located. This type of organization is called *spatial organization.* In a descriptive paragraph, you must make the location of the objects being described very clear.

Description of a Place

In describing a room, what should you describe first? The walls? The floor? Unlike the chronologically developed paragraph, there is no set pattern for arranging sentences in a descriptive paragraph. It is not necessary to begin with one area and then proceed to another area. Nevertheless, the sentences should not be randomly arranged. The description must be organized so that the reader can vividly imagine the scene being described. Imagine that you are describing a scene for an artist to paint. Would you have the artist paint the ceiling white and the bed blue and then go back and put posters on the walls before painting the walls? Of course not! Those directions might irritate the artist. The same applies to describing for the reader, for you are the describer with words, and your reader is the painter who mentally re-creates what you are describing in the paragraph.

The arrangement of the details in a descriptive paragraph depends on the subject. The selection and the description of details depend on the describer's purpose. Suppose that your cousin wrote and asked you to describe your room. Remember that your cousin is very interested in what you think about your life in the United States. You might write your description like this:

> My dormitory room is on the second floor of Bienville Hall. It is a small rectangular room with a white ceiling and green walls. As you enter the room, straight ahead you will see two large windows with gold curtains. My bed, which is covered with a red and gold bedspread, is under the windows. On your left, against the wall, there is a large bookcase filled with

books. Close to the door, a desk and chair sit next to the bookcase, with a small woven wastepaper basket underneath the desk. There are several posters on this wall. The one that is over the bookcase shows an interesting scene from our country. The one that is over the desk is of my favorite singer. To your right, built into the wall opposite the bookcase and desk, is a closet with sliding doors. Behind you on your right and somewhat behind the door, is a dresser with a mirror over it.

Examine this description. Is the location of the objects in the room clear? Are the details arranged logically? The answer to both of these questions is yes. The objects are clearly arranged and the description is easy to follow. The paragraph is both unified and coherent. But is the controlling idea about the room clear? What impression is conveyed about the room? Would your cousin know if you liked the room or not? Probably not. To make the paragraph more interesting, you can add a controlling idea that states an attitude or impression about the place being described. After all, your cousin does want to know how you feel about your room. This paragraph could be revised to include a strong controlling idea. Read the following revised version and locate the topic sentence with the controlling idea:

My dormitory room, on the second floor of Bienville Hall, is small and crowded. The dark green walls and dirty white ceiling make the room seem dark, and thus even smaller than it is. As you walk into the room, you are stopped short by my bed, which fills half of the room The two large windows over the bed are hidden by heavy dark gold drapes. Against the wall on your left, pushed into a corner behind the head of the bed, is a large bookcase that is crammed with papers, books, and knickknacks. Wedged in between the bookcase and the wall opposite the bed is a small gray metal desk. It has a brown wooden chair that seems to fill the left end of the room. Stuffed under the desk is a woven wastepaper basket overflowing with paper and debris. The wall above the bookcase and desk is completely taken up with two small posters. On the right hand side of the room is a narrow closet with clothes, shoes, hats, tennis racquets, and boxes bulging out of its sliding doors. Every time I walk out of the door, I think, "Now I know what it is like to live in a closet."

This revised version is quite different from the original one, even though both versions describe the same room. The addition of a topic sentence with a strong controlling idea has dictated not only what is included, but also how the objects in the room are described. A strong controlling idea gives the paragraph focus. Reread the preceding paragraph and underline the changes from the earlier version. These changes reinforce the controlling idea and give a clear idea of what you think about your little room.

EXERCISE 3-5: WRITING ASSIGNMENT

Rewrite the preceding paragraph using "comfortable" as the controlling idea in the topic sentence. Change the description to show that the room is comfortable. Feel free to add or delete details as necessary.

EXERCISE 3-6: WRITING ASSIGNMENT

Think of a room in your dormitory, apartment, or house. Write down the objects in the room. Then think about how you could describe them. What will you use for a controlling idea? Outline a paragraph, and then write a complete paragraph.

The arrangement of the details in your description depends on your subject and purpose. When painting a picture with words, you can begin from left to right, from right to left, from top to bottom, or from bottom to top. Note how Alfred Kazin does this in the following description of his family's kitchen.

The kitchen held our lives together. My mother worked in it all day long, we ate in it almost all meals except the Passover *seder*, I did my homework and first writing at the kitchen table, and in winter I often had a bed made up for me on three kitchen chairs near the stove. On the wall just over the table hung a long horizontal mirror that sloped to a ship's prow at each end and was lined in cherry wood. It took the whole wall, and drew every object in the kitchen to itself. The walls were a fiercely stippled whitewash, so often rewhitened by my father in slack seasons that the paint looked as if it had been squeezed and cracked into the walls. A large electric bulb hung down the center of the kitchen at the end of a chain that had been hooked into the ceiling; the old gas ring and key still jutted out of the wall like antlers. In the corner next to the toilet was the sink at which we washed, and the square tub in which my mother did our clothes. Above it, tacked to the shelf on which were pleasantly ranged square, blue-bordered white sugar and spice jars, hung calendars from the Public National Bank on Pitkin Avenue and the Minsker Progressive Branch of the Workman's Circle; receipts for the payment of insurance premiums, and household bills on a spindle. . . . —Alfred Kazin, "The Kitchen," anthologized in Judith Fishman, *Responding to Prose* (Indianapolis: Bobbs-Merrill Ed. Pub., 1983), p. 233. From *A Walker in the City.* Copyright 1951, 1979 by Alfred Kazin. Reprinted by permission of Harcourt Brace Jovanovich, Inc.

Sometimes, though, the description can focus on some object that dominates the scene or on something that is unusual in the scene. In this case, it may be desirable to focus on that object and describe it first, since it is the first thing noticed. In the paragraph describing a room, for

example, the first thing the writer describes is the first thing the viewer sees: the walls, ceiling, and the bed straight ahead.

Read the following description of a backyard and note the organization of the details. What is the controlling idea in the description?

> Our backyard is dominated by a huge old live oak tree. The base of the trunk measures approximately ten feet around. The thick muscular trunk rises solidly for about eight feet and then separates into four main branches. From these, the lower branches spread out horizontally over the ground, reaching into the neighbors' yards. The main branches continue to rise, up and up, where they compete with each other for air and sunlight. From these heights, the neighborhood cardinals and blue jays sing to each other, keeping a sharp eye out for cats. As the birds sway in the wind, they look as if they are riding a ship across a gently swelling ocean. From these heights, too, it is easy to see the variety of shrubs and sweet-smelling flowers lining the two long sides of our rectangular yard, the small walkway along the back of the house, and the back fence that runs along the alley.

Here the author describes not only what he or she sees but also the sounds and smells in the backyard. Describing what can be perceived with the senses—sights, sounds, smells, touch, taste—makes the scene even more vivid and interesting.

EXERCISE 3-7: WRITING ASSIGNMENT

1. Study the picture that follows. Assume that you are a real estate agent who is trying to sell this house. You want to persuade your reader to buy the house. Think of a controlling idea and write a paragraph describing the house. If you want some ideas of short descriptions, read the real estate section in the classified ads of your Sunday newspaper. Following are some useful vocabulary words.

single story	front porch	shrubbery
corner lot	shutters	lawn
three bedrooms	aluminum gutters	pine tree
two baths	new roof	landscaping
central air/heat	freshly painted	garage

2. Find a picture of a room or a house. Decide on a controlling idea and write a paragraph describing it. Submit the picture with your paragraph.

COMPOSITION SKILLS

Coherence

Adverbs of Place

Details in descriptive paragraphs are organized spatially to give the reader a clear picture of the scene being described. Clarifying the spatial relationship helps to achieve coherence. These spatial expressions are called *adverbs of place*; most of them are prepositional phrases (preposition + noun phrase). Some of the expressions used to clarify space relationships include:

on the second floor	on the right-hand side	along the back of the house
straight ahead	against the wall	underneath the desk
under the windows	above the bookcase	opposite the bed
on your left	next to the toilet	from these heights
over the table	in the corner	

Here are some other expressions that clarify space relationships:

Behind the chair is a guitar.

On top of the refrigerator is a plant.

The desk is *adjacent to the bookcase*.

Special Sentence Construction

Adverb of place + verb phrase + subject
Under the desk *is* *a basket.*

The normal word order for this sentence is

Subject + verb phrase + adverb of place
A basket *is* *under the desk.*

However, in descriptive writing it is common to place the adverb of place in the subject position at the beginning of the sentence. This special sentence construction is useful for achieving coherence, especially if the noun in the adverb of place has been mentioned in the previous sentence:

There is a *ball* under the bench. Next to the *ball* is a bat.

Note: You can, of course, include the "dummy subject" (expletive) *there* in the subject position before the verb:

Next to the ball *there* is a bat.

In this sentence, if the adverb of place is moved to the end of the sentence, *there* is necessary to fill the subject position.

There is a bat next to the ball.

Since *there* is a dummy subject, the verb agrees with the real subject even though it follows the verb.

There is a *bookcase* in the corner.
There are several *towels* on the rack.

Note the use of this special sentence construction in the previous paragraphs and attempt to use it in your writing assignments.

EXERCISE 3-8

Study the following picture of a room. In the paragraph that follows, fill in the blanks with prepositions from this list to describe the room in the picture:

against	close to	in	at
on	in front of	to	next to
behind	near	in the middle of	of
to the right of	on the other side of	adjacent to	opposite
			on the left side of

The Cooper's spacious living room is neatly arranged. The floors are of polished wood. ____________ the room, there is a large wool rug with a glass coffee table sitting ____________ it. A newspaper is neatly folded ____________ the coffee table, which is ____________ a sofa. ____________ the sofa and sitting ____________ a right angle ____________ it is a chair. A coat rack stands ____________ the chair ____________ the corner ____________ the door. ____________ the door is a large plant. ____________ the curtains ____________ the corner sits a wooden stand with a stereo speaker ____________ it. ____________ the wooden stand is a leather rocking chair. A small wicker chest sits ____________ the rocking chair. A large lamp is ____________ the chest.

Modification

The details in a descriptive paragraph should not only be logically arranged but vivid as well. As a painter with words, you want to give the reader as precise a picture as possible; otherwise, the reader will have only a vague sense of what you are describing. To make the details more vivid, you need to modify them. (*Modify* means to restrict or narrow down the meaning.)

Nouns can be modified in three ways: by adding adjectives, by adding adjective and prepositional phrases, and by adding clauses. Each time a modifier is added to a noun, the class to which it belongs is restricted. For example, consider the word *book*. The word *book* describes a rather large class. A book can be large, small, green, old, or new; it can be a textbook or a novel. The word *book*, therefore, does not conjure up a precise image in the reader's mind. If the adjective *red* is added, then the class of books is restricted to those that are no other color but red; if *paperback* is added, the class of books is further restricted to those that are red paperback books. The class can be restricted even more by adding an adjective clause and a prepositional phrase: a red paperback book *that has a torn page in the middle.* Now the reader has a clear image of the book.

Always strive to make details specific. Instructors become impatient with vague descriptions, for vague descriptions suggest that the student's thoughts are vague and imprecise. Moreover, specific detail makes writing more interesting.

Adjectives

Adjectives modify nouns. Single-word adjectives are generally placed before the nouns they modify. Adjectives in English *do not change form* to agree with the number of the noun (an *old* car, some *old* cars). Since it is not unusual when striving to be more specific to use more than one adjective to modify a noun, it is important to review the order of the adjectives before the noun they modify. Study the following chart:

PRE-DETER-MINER NUMBER PRONOUN	ARTICLE	GENERAL ADJECTIVE	SIZE	SHAPE	AGE	COLOR	ORIGIN	NOUNS AS ADJECTIVES: MATERIAL	NOUNS AS ADJECTIVES: NON-MATERIAL	NOUN
Most of	the	pretty	little					rubber		toys
	A	beautiful			antique		Mayan		flower	vase
Some				round		white				discs

Most of the pretty little rubber toys.
A beautiful antique Mayan flower vase.
Some round white discs.

This chart is a guide, so some exceptions can be expected. For example, it is appropriate to say, "a tall, dark, handsome man" even though the general adjective (*handsome*) would normally occur before the adjective that indicates size. Note these descriptive phrases from the preceding paragraphs in this chapter:

the dark green walls and dirty white ceiling

the two large windows

a small metal desk

a huge old live oak tree

the thick muscular trunk

Generally speaking, it is wise to limit the number of adjectives before the noun to two or three; including more than that may confuse the reader. Here are some other descriptive phrases:

a dirty old man	a beautiful Italian painting
a shining new car	a gorgeous antique Greek vase

Note: When two or three adjectives are used, each of which belongs to a different class (size, age, etc.), it usually is not necessary to separate the adjectives with commas. But when there are two adjectives of the same class, they should generally be separated with commas:

a big red European automobile

vs.

a deep, peaceful sleep

EXERCISE 3-9

Study the following paragraphs. Insert the adjectives in parentheses in their proper order before the nouns they modify.

1. Some people like elegant restaurants, but I prefer small "hole-in-the-wall" places like Pete's Grill. Pete's Grill is a (*little/cute/hamburger*) __________ __________ __________ place on Downey Road. The (*yellow, triangular*) __________ __________ building sits on the corner across from a camera shop. As you enter, you see a (*narrow/crowded*) __________ __________ room with tables on the right and the counter on the left. The tables are always filled with (*college/hungry*) __________ __________ students, (*old/friendly/newspa-*

per) ____________ ____________ ____________ men, (*talkative/little*) ____________ ____________ kids, and just about any other type of person. As you wait to order, you can smell the (*French/delicious*) ____________ ____________ fries, and you can watch the cooks prepare the (*huge/tantalizing/beef*) ____________ ____________ ____________ patties for the burgers. When you get your order, if you're lucky to find a seat, you can eat to your heart's content. Everyone in Pete's Grill shares the same experience.

2. When I am feeling depressed, my favorite place to go is the lake, where I like to sit under a (*old/tall/oak*) ____________ ____________ ____________ tree overlooking the shoreline. On a (*summer/clear*) ____________ ____________ day, the (*crystal/blue*) ____________ ____________ water looks peaceful and calm. The (*foamy/white*) ____________ ____________ waves gently caress the (*white/shore/sandy*) ____________ ____________ ____________ leaving (*wavy/thin*) ____________ ____________ lines on the sand among the (*little/multicolored*) ____________ ____________ shells. While listening to the reassuring whispers of the waves, I also watch the (*white/graceful*) ____________ ____________ seagulls hovering above the water as they look for (*tasty/small*) ____________ ____________ fish for their meals. I usually remain under that tree for several hours. When the (*apricot/oval*) ____________ ____________ sun begins its slow, languorous descent into the horizon, I know that it is time to go home, and I reluctantly leave. But before I go, I take one more look at the (*serene/beautiful*) ____________ ____________ scene and I feel that this (*short/difficult*) ____________ ____________ life is worth living after all.

EXERCISE 3-10: WRITING ASSIGNMENT

Choose one of the following writing assignments.

1. Write a paragraph describing your favorite place, either indoors

or outdoors. Since you are writing just one paragraph, be sure to narrow down the area you are going to write about. For example, if this place is a park, choose just one small area of the park.

2. Using the first paragraph of Momaday's ***The Way to Rainy Mountain*** (page 72) as an example, describe a place where you lived as a child or a place that you remember well. Again, be sure to narrow down the area that you describe and to begin with a controlling idea.

Participles as Adjectives

Adjectives like ***beautiful, tall,*** and ***soft*** are necessary in good writing because they give specific, vivid detail. Two other kinds of adjectives that are useful but also very troublesome are the present participle (***-ing***) and past participle (***-ed***) forms. Although they are actually verb forms, they can be used as adjectives. Note these examples:

When I am *depressed,* my favorite place to go is the lake.

My dormitory room is small and *crowded.*

The one that is over the bookcase shows an *interesting* scene from our country.

Maria is *fascinating.*

Sometimes it is difficult to tell whether you should use the present or past participle as an adjective. The problem lies in the verb that the adjective comes from. A number of verbs describe psychological states or reactions. They tell how a person feels about something or someone. The meaning of these psychological verbs implies two things: a person who experiences the feeling (this person is called the ***experiencer***) and the thing or person who stimulates the feeling (this thing or person is called the ***stimulus***). Note the experiencer and stimulus in these examples:

EXPERIENCER	VERB	STIMULUS
I	love	old movies.
John	enjoyed	the candy.

In the first example, I am experiencing or feeling the emotional or psychological state of love. The thing that is stimulating me to feel that is old movies. In the second example, John is experiencing the psychological state of enjoyment and the candy is stimulating this state.

Note that the experiencer must be capable of feeling the psychological state the verb denotes. This means that the experiencer must be human or animal. It cannot be a thing because things cannot experience; they cannot feel as humans do. The stimulus is often a thing, but it may be a person also. Note these examples:

EXPERIENCER	VERB	STIMULUS
Maria (*human*)	hates	that book. (*thing*)
Maria (*human*)	hates	Bill. (*human*)
His dog (*animal*)	enjoys	old bones. (*thing*)

Many psychological verbs require the same word order as ordinary verbs. In this case, the experiencer is the subject of the sentence and the stimulus is the object. Note the word order of the following sentences:

SUBJECT	ORDINARY VERB	OBJECT
John	read	the book.

SUBJECT (EXPERIENCER)	PSYCHOLOGICAL VERB	OBJECT (STIMULUS)
James	can't stand	spinach.

In this last example, the experiencer, James, is the subject of the sentence, and the stimulus, spinach, is the object of the sentence.

Following is a list of ***straightforward psychological verbs***, requiring the word order experiencer – verb – stimulus:

love	admire	hate	regret
like	respect	fear	mistrust
enjoy	prefer	dread	trust
remember	not mind	dislike	understand
miss	forget	resent	not be able to stand

Because these psychological verbs have the same word order as ordinary verbs, they generally do not cause trouble for writers.

However, there is another group of psychological verbs that do cause trouble for writers, and this is because the word order is reversed. With the verbs in this group, the stimulus is in the subject position and the experiencer is in the object position. Here are some examples:

STIMULUS	VERB	EXPERIENCER
The movie	interested	me.
The book	depressed	the professor.
Maria	fascinates	Bill.

In the first example, the movie is the stimulus. It is causing me to feel the psychological state called ***interest***. In the second example, the book is the stimulus, and in the third example, Maria is the stimulus. In these cases, they are causing the professor and Bill to experience something. The verbs in these examples are part of a group called ***reverse psychological verbs***.

Note the contrast in word order among an ordinary verb, a straightforward psychological verb, and a reverse psychological verb:

Ordinary Verb:

Bill ate the spinach.

Straightforward Psychological Verb:

Bill (*experiencer*) hated the spinach. (*stimulus*)

Reverse Psychological Verb:

The spinach (*stimulus*) disgusted Bill. (*experiencer*)

Following is a list of some ***reverse psychological verbs*** requiring the word order stimulus–verb–experiencer:

delight	surprise	bother	disgust
thrill	interest	worry	shock
charm	fascinate	disappoint	scare
amuse	satisfy	depress	frighten
excite	relieve	annoy	horrify
elate	reassure	bore	appall
impress	overwhelm	confuse	insult
please	flatter	mislead	offend

These verbs tend to cause trouble for writers because of the reverse word order they require. It is necessary to distinguish these verbs and learn the reverse word order for them.

EXERCISE 3-11

The sentences that follow contain both straightforward and reverse psychological verbs. First determine which word is the experiencer and which word is the stimulus. Then answer these questions about each sentence:

Who is experiencing a psychological state or feeling?
What is the psychological state?
Who or what is causing or stimulating this psychological state?
Is the verb a straightforward or reverse psychological verb?

1. The student missed his family.
   a. Experiencer—the student
   b. Psychological state—missing
   c. Stimulus—family
   d. Straightforward psychological verb
2. The answer pleased the teacher.
   a. Experiencer—the teacher
   b. Psychological state—pleasing
   c. Stimulus—the answer
   d. Reverse psychological verb
3. Bob dreaded the test.
4. Mari's boyfriend flatters her.
5. The children dislike sitting still.
6. The thunder frightened the dog.
7. John insulted the principal.
8. The monkeys thrilled the children.
9. The children alarmed the monkeys.

10. The citizens mistrusted the government.
11. The teacher bored the students.
12. Steve excited his fans.

Almost all reverse psychological verbs can be made into adjectives by adding *ing* (the present participle) or *ed* (the past participle). The problem generally occurs in knowing whether to use the present or past participle. The rule is that the present participle modifies the stimulus and the past participle modifies the experiencer. Look at these examples:

The movie interested me.

STIMULUS		EXPERIENCER
The movie	was interesting	to me.

EXPERIENCER		STIMULUS
I	was interested	in the movie.

In these examples, you can see that the movie is the stimulus. It has the quality of being interesting. It is causing my interest. I am the experiencer because I am feeling the psychological state of interest. Thus, I am interested.

The book depressed the professor.

EXPERIENCER		STIMULUS
The depressed professor	stopped reading	the depressing book.

In this case, the book is the stimulus. It has the quality of being depressing. It is causing depression. The professor is experiencing depression. Thus, he is depressed.

In order to determine which adjective form to use, you must first decide if the noun is a stimulus or an experiencer. Look at the following example:

The television program was (bore) ______________.

Is the television program a stimulus? Can it cause boredom? If so, choose the present participle. Is the television program experiencing boredom? Can a television program experience boredom? If so, choose the past participle. It is easy to see that the television program is a stimulus. It has the quality of boredom. It can cause boredom in me, but it cannot feel boredom. Thus, the correct answer is ***boring.***

Here is another example:

When Mr. Chong looked at his daughter's report card and saw several Fs, he was (disappoint) ______________.

In order to determine the correct adjective, rewrite the sentence so that the stimulus and experiencer are clear:

Mr. Chong was ______________ by his daughter's report card.

Is Mr. Chong the stimulus or the experiencer? He is experiencing the feeling of disappointment. Therefore, the correct answer is the past participle:

When Mr. Chong looked at his daughter's report card and saw several Fs, he was *disappointed.*

Note: The following psychological verbs do not have *-ing* (present participle) adjective forms. Note the adjective forms for them:*

bother	bothersome
delight	delightful
impress	impressive
scare	scary

EXERCISE 3-12

For the following sentences, first identify the stimulus, the verb, and the experiencer and write them in the blanks. Then, write a sentence using the present participle to modify the stimulus. Next, write a sentence using the past participle to modify the experiencer. The first one is done for you.

1. The sound of the bear terrified my brothers and me.

	STIMULUS	VERB	EXPERIENCER
a.	sound	terrified	my brothers and me

b. The sound was terrifying.

c. My brothers and I were terrified.

2. The lecture bored the entire class.

	STIMULUS	VERB	EXPERIENCER
a.	lecture	______	______

b. ______________________________

c. ______________________________

3. The price of the car surprised my father.

	STIMULUS	VERB	EXPERIENCER
a.	______	______	______

*Information from Marina K. Burt and Carol Kiparsky, *The Gooficon: A Repair Manual for English* (Rowley, Mass.: Newbury House, 1972).

b. ______________________________

c. ______________________________

4. The painting interested the art dealer.

	STIMULUS	VERB	EXPERIENCER
a.	________	________	________

b. ______________________________

c. ______________________________

5. The ball game excited the fans.

	STIMULUS	VERB	EXPERIENCER
a.	________	________	________

b. ______________________________

c. ______________________________

6. The directions misled the driver.

	STIMULUS	VERB	EXPERIENCER
a.	________	________	________

b. ______________________________

c. ______________________________

7. Her emotions overwhelmed her.

	STIMULUS	VERB	EXPERIENCER
a.	________	________	________

b. ______________________________

c. ______________________________

8. The good news relieved the family.

	STIMULUS	VERB	EXPERIENCER
a.	________	________	________

b. ______________________________

c. ______________________________

EXERCISE 3-13

Read the situations that follow and fill in either the present or past participle in the blanks.

1. John is sitting nervously at the racetrack watching his horse. He wants to see the beginning of the race. He is ____________ (excite). He

thinks the race will be __________ (excite).

2. Steve just learned that he got a D on his chemistry test. He is __________ (depress). He thinks he got a D because he is not __________ (interest) in chemistry.
3. Today is Monday. Janet just got home from work. Mondays at work are always __________ (tire) so Janet is __________ (exhaust).
4. The movie on television last night showed new discoveries about cancer. The show was __________ (interest).
5. My history teacher always talks in a monotone and never looks at the students. He is the most __________ (bore) teacher I have. All of the students are __________ (bore).
6. Veronica has just gotten a job with an architect's firm. She is doing an excellent job. Her employer is __________ (impress).
7. Mary's mother has always wanted Mary to finish college. She was __________ (disappoint) when Mary told her that she had quit school. Mary's mother sobbed when she heard the __________ (disappoint) news.
8. John went to the doctor because he had a pain in his chest. The doctor's comments were __________ (reassure) to John. Before the doctor told him that the pain was just heartburn, John had been __________ (frighten).
9. Last night Julio cooked a huge Mexican dinner for all of us. It was very __________ (satisfy). Julio was __________ (delight) that we liked it.
10. I didn't understand the __________ (confuse) income-tax forms that I got from the government. I was so __________ (worry) about them that I asked my neighbor to help me. However, he gave me a lot of __________ (mislead) information. Finally, I went to a tax consultant who had a __________ (depress) office. He helped me fill out the forms correctly.
11. When I went to New York, I was __________ (disgust) at the condition of the subway stations. The litter was __________ (appall) and I was __________ (shock) at the graffiti on the walls.
12. The computer lab is a __________ (fascinate) place. I go there when I am __________ (bore) and want something __________ (interest) to do.

13. The new Stephen King movie is ____________ (frighten). I was ____________ (scare) by the monster who ____________ (amuse) the little children and then ate them.

GRAMMAR REVIEW

The Passive Voice vs. the Active Voice

Most writing involves the use of the *active voice*, whether verbs are in the present or past tense. The active voice is used when the subject performs the action directly:

I *bought* a book.

Sometimes, however, when the doer of the action is unknown, or perhaps the doer of the action is unimportant, the *passive voice* is appropriate.

Our house *was built* in 1953.

Who built the house? Perhaps the builder is unknown, or perhaps the writer of the sentence thinks that it is not important to identify the builder. In addition, the passive voice is used when the subject is the main topic of discussion.

The Coopers' spacious living room *is* neatly *arranged.*

Although the passive voice is used in all kinds of writing, it is particularly useful for descriptive writing, especially descriptions of places.

Study the following passage and observe the use of the passive voice:

One of the most enduring symbols of New York City is the Empire State Building. This famous structure is located on Fifth Avenue in Manhattan. Construction was begun in 1930 and was completed in 1931. This enormous building rises 1,250 feet into the air. It has 102 stories, most of which are used for offices. The Empire State Building was once the tallest building in the world, and became especially famous as the building from which the original King Kong fell. Many tourists who have ridden the elevators to the observation deck have enjoyed a fascinating and unforgettable view of New York City.

Underline the passive verbs in the preceding paragraph. Why is the passive voice used in this paragraph?

THE PASSIVE VOICE: FIVE POINTS TO REVIEW

1. The passive voice always adds a form of the verb *to be* and the past participle to the sentence.

This famous structure *is located* on Fifth Avenue in Manhattan.

2. Only transitive verbs (verbs with object and indirect objects) can be made passive. With a direct object, the passive voice is formed as follows:

	Subject	Verb	Direct Object	
Active:	An architect	designed	our house	in 1952.
Passive:	Our house	was designed	by an architect	in 1952.

In the following example, the indirect object of the active sentence becomes the subject of the passive sentence:

	Subject	Verb	Direct Object		Indirect Object
Active:	The architect	sold	the plans	to	my mother.
Passive:	My mother	was sold	the plans	by	the architect.

Intransitive verbs (verbs that do not take a direct object) *cannot* be made passive. If you are uncertain whether a verb is transitive or intransitive, consult the dictionary. In most dictionaries, directly next to the verb is an abbreviation, either *vt* ("transitive verb") or *vi* ("intransitive verb"). Read the definition of the verb carefully; some verbs can be used as transitive and intransitive verbs, though their meanings change with each use.

With some intransitive verbs, the object of a preposition following the verb may become the subject of the passive sentence.

	Subject	Intransitive Verb	Preposition	Object of Preposition	
Active:	They	spoke	to	him	about it.
Passive:	He	was spoken	to		about it.

3. The tense of the active sentence is used in the corresponding passive sentence.

A huge oak tree *dominates* our backyard.
Our backyard *is dominated* by a huge oak tree.

Edith Head *designed* the costumes for *My Fair Lady*.
The costumes for *My Fair Lady were designed* by Edith Head.

They *are building* a subway in my hometown.
A subway *is being built* in my hometown.

You *should* not *order* the sentences randomly.
The sentences *should* not *be ordered* randomly.

They *were discussing* the plans when I came in.
The plans *were being discussed* when I came in.

They *have* already *completed* the apartment building next door.
The apartment building next door *has* already *been completed.*

They *will form* a new committee to discuss this issue.
A new committee *will be formed* to discuss this issue.

Someone *is going to consider* John for promotion.
John *is going to be considered* for promotion.

The people *had built* the church before the revolution.
The church *had been built* before the revolution.

4. The *by* phrase is often omitted, especially if the information it contains is not specific or important.

The university *was founded* in 1920. (by John Smith)

5. Although every sentence in English has an active form, the passive is especially useful in two situations:

a. When the doer of the action is unimportant or unknown.
b. When the subject of the passive sentence is the main topic of discussion.

EXERCISE 3-14

Study the following pairs of sentences. For each pair, indicate which sentence is in the appropriate voice. Be prepared to explain the reason for your choice!

1. The new students were lectured to by the counselor about academic honor.
   The counselor lectured the new students about academic honor.
2. A sailboat was sailed around the world by me.
   I sailed a sailboat around the world.
3. The four-minute-mile record has been broken several times.
   Someone has broken the four-minute-mile record several times.
4. The dinner will be enjoyed by everyone.
   Everyone will enjoy the dinner.
5. It has been advised by my teacher that we study every night.
   My teacher has advised that we study every night.

Special Note: The Verb *locate*

The verb *locate* poses a problem for many students, for it can be used in both the active voice and the passive voice.

1. When *locate* is used in the *active voice*, it means "to find the location of":

   John *located* his sister's house.

2. When *locate* is used in the *passive voice*, it indicates location and is often followed by an adverbial phrase of place (preposition + noun).

   His sister's house *is located* in Minneapolis.

   The Empire State Building *is located* in Manhattan.

   The store *is located* on the corner of Main and Broad Streets.

EXERCISE 3-15

Read through the following paragraphs and decide which active verbs need to be converted to passive ones. Write the correct verb phrase in the blank. Be sure to keep the tense the same as it is now. For some of the passive verbs, it may be necessary to add *by*.

1. This smooth, rectangular metal box ________ (sits) in almost every living room in the United States. "Rabbit ears" ________ (grow) out of the top, and one side of the box ________ (covers) a piece of gray glass. Some small knobs or buttons ________ (have placed) next to the glass. If one of the knobs ________ (pushes) in, a moving picture ________ (appears) in the glass. If another knob ________ (pushes), the volume of the sound that ________ (accompanies) the picture can ________ (control). Although most people ________ (not look) inside the box, the contents of the box ________ (look) like a bowl of spaghetti and meatballs. Hundreds of wires and other components ________ (connected and arranged) to transmit the moving picture. Since it ________ (invented) in the 1920s and ________ (introduced) at the World's Fair in 1939, this nondescript yet

magic box ____________ (has captured) the imagination of people all over the world. What is it?

2. The Qualicare Building was originally Turner's Hall, built in 1849 for a New Orleans society of German immigrants. The building ____________ (contained) a large gymnasium and a two-and-a-half story ballroom. The building ____________ (served) Tulane University as the first home of its architecture school and ____________ (renovated) for Qualicare, a hospital management corporation. The building ____________ (has changed) hands again and now ____________ (will use) as an entrepreneurial center.

   The exterior facades of the building ____________ (have restored and painted) decoratively to emphasize their architectural elements. On the upriver side of the building is a blank brick wall facing a parking lot. That wall ____________ (has decorated) with a painting of the building's principal facade. The treatment of the exterior of the building is a somewhat fanciful and imaginative restoration. It's a very dramatic statement and one that calls a lot of attention to a handsome building in an area where a touch of beauty ____________ (needs) badly. On the Lafayette Street side of the building, the old galleries ____________ (have restored) lovingly.

   On the inside, the building ____________ (has thoroughly redesigned and adapted) to its new uses. A sense of the volume of the old ballroom ____________ (retains) by adding a fourth story, which does not extend all the way to the building's wall. Clerical offices ____________ (place) around the perimeter of the old ballroom and the large ballroom windows ____________ (expose). The new fourth-floor offices ____________ (have) interior windows, which pick up light from the original ballroom windows. The new fourth floor ____________ (constructed) from salvaged materials.*

*Adapted from Gary Esolen, "A Modest Renaissance," *Gambit*, 26 May, 1984.

EXERCISE 3-16: WRITING ASSIGNMENT

Describe a building or an object without revealing its identity. The first paragraph in Exercise 3-15 may serve as a model.

EXERCISE 3-17: WRITING ASSIGNMENT

Find a picture of a building, a disaster area, an outdoor area, or a room. Plan a paragraph about the picture. Decide on a controlling idea. Be sure to use spatial organization when you write the paragraph.

Description of a Person

In college writing, occasionally it will be necessary to describe an animate subject, such as a person, animal, or insect. For example, in biology class, it might be necessary to describe the Cro-Magnon human or perhaps even a certain species of butterfly. In a sociology class, it might be necessary to describe a typical middle-class person. How would you describe a person? Depending on the subject or assignment, you could describe the person's physical appearance, behavior, or both. At this point, the discussion will be restricted to physical appearance, since the principle of organization is spatial, for the most part.

You can describe a person's appearance in many ways. You can tell about the person's style of clothing, manner of walking, color and style of hair, facial appearance, body shape, and expression. You can also describe the person's way of talking. Just what you select to describe depends on your topic and purpose. For example, how would you begin to describe your girlfriend to your cousin? Her hair? Her eyes? Her voice? Remember, you are the painter with words, so you want your description to be vivid, coherent—logically arranged so that your cousin can envision the face of your girlfriend. Look at the following description and see if you can get a good image of what Marie looks like:

> Marie has long black hair that falls down to her shoulders and surrounds her diamond-shaped face, which is usually suntanned. She has dark brown eyebrows over her blue eyes, which are rather large. Her nose is straight, and on the left side of the bottom of her nose, by her nostril, is a small mole. She has a small mouth, with lips that are usually covered with light pink lipstick. Her teeth are straight and white.

Is this paragraph coherent? Do you get a good picture of Marie in your mind's eye? Yes, the paragraph is coherent and the picture is clear—as far as it goes. But is the young lady attractive or plain? Does she have a regal appearance, or does she look rather ordinary? It is difficult to tell what the author's attitude is about the girlfriend's appearance; there is no real controlling idea here. In addition, the picture the author has painted with words is rather vague. Is Marie's hair curly or straight? Is her complexion smooth or blemished? Is her nose long? Are her lips thin or full? Are her teeth large or are they in proportion? Does she have an overbite? Are her eyebrows arched, or are they thick and straight? There are a lot of descriptive details the author has not included; as a result, his picture is not very vivid. Let us see how this description can be improved:

> Marie is as beautiful as any Hollywood star. Her thick, wavy, long black hair gracefully falls down to her shoulders and surrounds her exquisite, diamond-shaped face. A golden suntan usually highlights her smooth, clear complexion. Her slightly arched chestnut brown eyebrows draw attention to her deep blue eyes, which remind me of a lake on a stormy day. Her eyes are large, but not too large, with thick eyelashes. Her nose is straight and neither too long nor too short. A small black mole on the left side of her mouth adds to her beauty. And her mouth! It is a small mouth that looks delicate and feminine. Her lips are rather thin, but not too thin; her light pink lipstick adds another touch of beauty. When she smiles, which is often, her well-formed and even, white teeth brighten up her whole face. There is nothing but extraordinary beauty in the face of Marie.

Now can you tell what the attitude is about the girlfriend's appearance? Yes, indeed! In this version, we get a vivid image of Marie through the eyes of her friend. The paragraph has a strong controlling idea—beautiful—and has much more specific descriptive detail than the first version.

EXERCISE 3-18: WRITING ASSIGNMENT

In the preceding paragraph, underline the changes the author has made. Do these changes support the controlling idea? Then outline the paragraph on a separate sheet of paper.

EXERCISE 3-19: WRITING ASSIGNMENT

Using the same descriptive detail as the original paragraph, about Marie, write a paragraph that describes Marie as plain. Make any changes that you feel necessary.

When describing a person, you are not obliged to describe every single detail about the person's appearance. Sometimes it is better to focus on one or two outstanding features that convey something about the person's character. Read the following description of a young boy. What is the general impression you get about him from this description?

WALLACE

The two most impressive things about him were his mouth and the pockets of his jacket. By looking at his mouth, one could tell whether he was plotting evil or had recently accomplished it. If he was bent upon malevolence, his lips were all puckered up, like those of a billiard player about to make a difficult shot. After the deed was done, the pucker was replaced by a delicate, unearthly smile. How a teacher who knew anything about boys could miss the fact that both expressions were masks of Satan I'm sure I don't know. Wallace's pockets were less interesting than his mouth, perhaps, but more spectacular in a way. The side pockets of his jacket bulged out over his pudgy haunches like burro hampers. They were filled with tools—screwdrivers, pliers, files, wrenches, wire cutters, nail sets, and I don't know what else. In addition to all this, one pocket always contained a rolled-up copy of *Popular Mechanics*, while from the top of the other protruded *Scientific American* or some other such magazine. His breast pocket contained, besides a large collection of fountain pens and mechanical pencils, a picket fence of drill bits, gimlets, kitchen knives, and other pointed instruments. When he walked, he clinked and jangled and pealed.

—Richard Rovere, "Wallace," *The New Yorker*, 4 Feb. 1950.

EXERCISE 3-20

On a separate sheet of paper, answer the following questions about the preceding paragraph.

1. What is the general impression you get about Wallace?
2. What is the topic sentence? Is the controlling idea stated or implied?
3. Look up the following words in the dictionary and answer these questions:
   a. *pucker*—When do people pucker their lips?
   b. *unearthly*—What does Wallace's "unearthly" smile suggest that he has done?
   c. *bulge*—Where do you often find bulges?
   d. *pudgy*—Does this word suggest an ugly image or a cute image?
   e. *haunches*—Where are haunches located?
   f. *picket fence*—Draw a picket fence.
   g. *clink, jangle, peal*—Name at least one other thing for each of these words that makes the same sound.

In addition to using colorful verbs, nouns, and adjectives, the author of "Wallace" makes his description even more vivid by making comparisons between unlike things to convey what Wallace looks like:

". . . his lips were all puckered up, like those of a billiard player . . ."

". . . The side pockets of his jacket bulged out over his pudgy haunches like burro hampers."

The expression *like* + *noun phrase* is a valuable tool for descriptive writing. This expression makes a comparison between things that do not otherwise seem similar. This type of comparison is called a *simile* and is often used in poetry; however, you can use similes in your writing, especially when you do not know a vocabulary word or when you just want to add an extra touch. For example, imagine describing someone's eyes that were green with specks of brown in them—a deep hazel. If that person had just been crying, the description could be, "Her eyes look like the forest after a rainstorm—dark green and brown and moist." Obviously, original comparisons can be overdone, but it is a good idea to try to use fresh, interesting comparisons once in a while.

Note how N. Scott Momaday uses similes in his passage from *The Way to Rainy Mountain*:

"Great green and yellow grasshoppers are everywhere in the tall grass, popping up *like corn* to sting the flesh. . . ."

"Her long, black hair . . . lay upon her shoulders and against her breasts *like a shawl.*"

Alfred Kazin also makes use of the simile:

". . . the old gas ring and key jutted out of the wall *like antlers.*"

EXERCISE 3-21

Complete each of the following sentences with a noun phrase. Try to use a noun phrase that is creative.

1. Bill's outfit is quite colorful. In it he looks like ______________________________.
2. Julio Iglesias sings like ______________________________.
3. What beautiful hair you have! Your hair looks like ______________________________.
4. It's raining very hard. It sounds like ______________________________.
5. Just look at these "dishpan" hands. They look like ______________________________.

6. What an ugly car! It looks like ______________________________

____.

EXERCISE 3-22: WRITING ASSIGNMENT

Listen to the radio, television, recordings, or other people for interesting similes. Write down at least five.

EXERCISE 3-23: WRITING ASSIGNMENT

Choose one of the following topics and write a paragraph of description. Plan the paragraph carefully. Be sure you have a controlling idea that is supported with vivid, descriptive language. Try to use a comparison with *like.*

1. **Review the model paragraph that describes Marie on page 98. Write a description of the most beautiful or the most unattractive person you know.**
2. **Review the model paragraph about Wallace on page 99. Write a description of a person that focuses on only one or two features. Here are some useful vocabulary words and expressions for this exercise.**

FACIAL EXPRESSIONS	FACIAL SHAPES	EYES
scowl	round	beady
frown	broad	smiling
smirk	narrow	snapping
worried	heart-shaped	flashing
pained	moon-shaped	empty
blank	angular	staring
vivacious	oval	hard
delicate	flat	sad
lively		bulging
peaceful		
placid		

VOICE	MOUTH	EYEBROWS
booming	full-lipped	thick
rasping	thin-lipped	arched
squeaky	set	neatly plucked
harsh	sensuous	uneven
growling		
deep		
melodious		

OTHER EXPRESSIONS

crow's feet	protruding forehead
knitted brow	bony face

3. N. Scott Momaday describes his grandmother at prayer in "The Way to Rainy Mountain" (pages 72–73). Describe someone you know—a friend, a family member, a teacher—doing something, such as your little sister watching television, your father reading, or your brother standing in front of a mirror.

What you decide to describe depends on your purpose. Let us say, for example, that you were asked to describe, not a person, but an animal, for one of your classes. What would you begin with? Depending on the assignment, you could begin with a physical description using much the same principle used to describe human beings. If the purpose is to explain what the creature looks like, you probably will not need a "strong" controlling idea expressing an attitude; your description will probably be more objective. Look at the following two paragraphs describing a gorilla and find their controlling ideas and the writer's purpose.

> The gorilla is the bulkiest of the primates. Gorillas are not as tall as most people imagine, being on the average only about five and a half feet. Weights up to 670 pounds have been recorded. As in the other apes, the forelimbs are longer than the hind limbs. Undoubtedly the gorilla is the strongest of all primates. Gorillas have bare chests, not hairy ones as is commonly believed. Otherwise, they are covered with black hair except on the face. Some of the hairs on the top of the head may be variously colored. While the orang can grow a beard and mustache, the chimpanzee and gorilla cannot.
>
> The average male cranial capacity is 550 cc, while that of the female is about 460 cc. Males sometimes attain a cranial capacity of as much as 750 cc. The face is most interesting because the nasal bones show a slight elevation, so that the nose, while still quite flattish, is more like that of man than the nose of any of the other apes. The lips, as in all apes, are thin with hardly any of the reddish-looking mucous membrane furled outward as in ourselves.
>
> —Ashley Montagu, *Man: His First Two Million Years* (New York: Columbia University Press, 1969), pp. 33–35.

EXERCISE 3-24

On a separate sheet of paper, answer these questions about the preceding passage:

1. What is the topic of the first paragraph? The controlling idea?
2. What is the topic of the second paragraph? The controlling idea?
3. Is each paragraph unified? Coherent?
4. Outline each paragraph.
5. Do these paragraphs describe a particular gorilla or a typical gorilla?

6. What do you think Montagu's purpose is in writing this?
7. Who do you think this text is addressed to; in other words, who is the audience?

Now contrast Montagu's paragraphs with this passage from *West with the Night* by Beryl Markham, in which she describes a zebra. Explain Markham's purpose in the paragraph.

> But to men the zebra is a complete ambiguity. He resembles a donkey, but will not be trained and cannot stand work; he runs wild like Thompson's gazelle and eland and eats the same food, but his meat lacks even the doubtful succulence of horse. His hide, while striking in appearance, is only fairly durable and has made its greatest decorative triumph as panelling for the walls of a New York night club. Ostrich and civet cat have contributed more to the requirements of civilized society, but I think it not unjust to say that the zebra clan, in spite of it all, is unaffected by its failure to join in the march of time. I based this conclusion on a very warm friendship that developed, not too long ago to remember, between myself and a young zebra.
>
> —Beryl Markham, *West with the Night* (San Francisco: North Point Press, 1983), p. 39.

EXERCISE 3-25: WRITING ASSIGNMENT

1. Assume that you are a scientist interested in unusual creatures. You travel to the mountains to find the legendary "Bigfoot," and you are successful. You actually saw the beast, but unfortunately you did not have a camera with you. Write a physical description of the creature. Remember to be objective!
2. Describe an animal with an interesting or peculiar appearance.

COMPOSITION SKILLS

Coherence

Adjective Clauses

Chapter 2 emphasizes two ways of improving coherence in chronologically developed paragraphs: using time sequence markers, such as *first*, and *after that*, and using adverbial clauses of time. In this chapter, the emphasis has been on achieving coherence in spatially organized descriptive paragraphs by using adverbial phrases of place. Another technique for improving coherence is the use of the adjective clause.

An *adjective clause* (sometimes called a *relative clause*) modifies a noun and, like an adverbial clause, is a dependent clause that cannot stand alone as a sentence; it must be connected to an independent clause. But unlike adverbial clauses, which can be placed either at the beginning or at the end of a sentence, an adjective clause can be placed *only after the noun it modifies*; it can never be placed at the beginning of a sentence.

The subordinators that introduce adjective clauses include *who*, *whom*, *whose*, *that*, and *which*. Less common adjective clause subordinators are *when*, *where*, and *why*. Observe the use of adjective clauses in some of the passages you have read thus far:

> It's a small mouth *that looks delicate and feminine.*
>
> From these heights, too, it is easy to see the variety of shrubs and sweet-smelling flowers *that line the two long sides of our rectangular yard.*
>
> Many tourists *who have ridden the elevators to the observation deck* have enjoyed an unforgettable view of New York City.

You have learned that a coherent paragraph is one that has logically arranged sentences and ideas; in addition, in order for a paragraph to be coherent, the sentences should flow smoothly. *Smoothly* is the key word here. If the sentences in a paragraph are mostly short and if the sentences contain a lot of repeated words, the paragraph is choppy. To illustrate, look at this description of a famous character in fiction:

> One of the ugliest creatures in literature is the monster in the novel *Frankenstein, The Modern Prometheus.* The novel was written by Mary Shelley in the nineteenth century. The monster was created by Victor Frankenstein when he was a student at a university. The monster has flowing black hair. The hair is lustrous. The monster has pearly white teeth. These fine features form a horrid contrast with his other features. He has yellow skin. The skin barely covers his facial muscles. His complexion is shrivelled. The monster has hideous, watery, almost colorless eyes. The eyes seem to be almost the same color as the sockets. They are set in the sockets. Even uglier, perhaps, are his lips. His lips are straight and black.

Does the paragraph have a controlling idea? Yes, the controlling idea is that the monster is one of the *ugliest* creatures in literature. Is the paragraph unified? Yes, it describes the monster as ugly. Are the sentences and ideas logically arranged? Yes, the paragraph provides an organized description of the monster's face. But do the sentences flow smoothly? No. The paragraph has too many short sentences and too many repeated words and phrases. Adjective clauses can improve this paragraph:

> One of the ugliest creatures in literature is the monster in the novel *Frankenstein, The Modern Prometheus,* which was written by Mary Shelley in the nineteenth century. The monster, which was created by Victor Frankenstein when he was a student at a university, has flowing lustrous black hair. The monster has pearly white teeth. These fine features form a horrid contrast with his other features. He has yellow skin that barely covers his facial muscles. His complexion is shrivelled. He has hideous, watery, almost colorless eyes which seem to be almost the same color as the sockets that they are set in. Even uglier, perhaps, are his lips, which are straight and black.

By combining a few sentences using adjective clauses, some of the repeated words have been eliminated and the sentences flow more smoothly. More revisions of the paragraph can be done to make it flow even more smoothly, of course, but it is evident here that the use of adjective clauses helps achieve coherence.

EXERCISE 3-26

Underline all the changes in the preceding revised version. Do the changes improve the coherence of the passage?

EXERCISE 3-27: WRITING ASSIGNMENT

Think of a horrible-looking creature from a movie or photograph. Write a paragraph describing its face or another part of it—such as its hands. Narrow down your topic and write a detailed descriptive paragraph.

A REVIEW OF ADJECTIVE CLAUSES. The subordinators ***who, whom, that, whose,*** and ***which*** can function either as the subject or as the object of an adjective clause. Compare:

S V
The Empire State Building, *which is the second tallest building in New York City,* rises 1,250 feet in the air.

O S V
The Empire State Building, *which many tourists visit each year,* is the second tallest building in New York.

If the subordinator functions as the subject of an adjective clause, its verb agrees in number with the noun that the subordinator refers to:

S V
Mr. Jones, *who is a marvelous cook,* invited us to dinner.

S V
Bill and Eva Failla, *who are members of the Audubon Social Club,* are avid birdwatchers.

If the subordinator functions as an object in the adjective clause, the verb in the adjective clause agrees in number with its subject:

O S V
The house *that you are thinking about buying* has already been sold.

O S V
David Marchand, *whom I find unbearable,* has been assigned to my team.

ADJECTIVE CLAUSE SUBORDINATORS

1. ***Who*** is used when referring to a person. ***Who*** is used as the subject of the adjective clause:

   The little girl is playing the violin. The girl is my cousin.
   = The little girl *who is playing the violin* is my cousin.

2. ***Whom*** **is also used when referring to a person, but** ***whom*** **is used as an object in the adjective clause:**

   My Uncle Boris is a writer. You met him earlier today.

   = My Uncle Boris, *whom you met earlier today,* is a writer.

3. ***Whose*** **is used to show possession and functions as a possessive pronoun in the adjective clause:**

   The artist is coming to our area soon. You adore his paintings.

   = The artist, *whose paintings you adore,* is coming to our area soon.

4. ***Which*** **is used when referring to something other than a person.** ***Which*** **can function as the subject or object of an adjective clause:**

   He has hideous eyes. These eyes are also colorless.

   = He has hideous eyes *which are also colorless.*

   You see the books here. These books are special.

   = These books *which you see here* are special.

5. ***That*** **can be used when referring to a person, an animal, or a thing.** ***That*** **can function as the subject or the object of an adjective clause.**

   I have really enjoyed the book. You gave me the book for my birthday.

   = I have really enjoyed the book *that you gave me for my birthday.*

   The trees are going to be cut down soon. The trees line Main Street.

   = *The trees that line Main Street* are going to be cut down soon.

   (Also: The trees *that are going to be cut down soon* line Main Street.)

6. ***When*** **means approximately "*in which time*" or "*at which time.*" Note the word order in this clause:** ***when*** **+ subject + verb.**

   My friends are still talking about the day. On that day I fell in the river.

   = My friends are still talking about the day *when I fell in the river.*

7. ***Where*** **can be used to mean approximately "*at which place*" and introduces the adjective clause: The word order is** ***where*** **+ subject + verb.**

   Tourists in New Orleans visit the Old Mint. At that place United States currency used to be made.

   = Tourists in New Orleans visit the Old Mint *where United States currency used to be made.*

8. ***Why*** **means "for which" when used to introduce an adjective clause: Again, the word order is** ***why*** **+ subject + verb.**

   You have not given me any reason *why I should go out with you.*

EXERCISE 3-28

Study the following sets of sentences carefully. Combine each set into one sentence using an adjective clause. Be careful to select the appropriate adjective clause subordinator. Note that there may be more than one way to combine the sentences.

1. The human eye is a remarkable optical instrument.
   The eye consists of very specialized structures.

   ____

2. On the outside of the eye is the conjunctiva.
   The conjunctiva is a membrane.
   The membrane lines the inner surface of the eyelid and the outer surface of the front of the eyeball.

   ____

3. Behind the conjunctiva is the cornea.
   The cornea forms the image of an object.

   ____

4. The cornea is provided nutriment by the aqueous humour.
   The aqueous humour is located behind the cornea.

   ____

5. The colorful part of the eye is the iris.
   The iris helps control the amount of incoming light.

   ____

6. In the middle of the iris is the pupil.
   The pupil is really a hole.
   Light passes through this hole to the lens.

   ____

7. The crystalline lens is elliptical in shape.
   The lens helps the cornea bend the image.

   ____

8. On the sides of the lens are the ciliary muscle and zonula.
   These structures make the lens change shape, so the image changes in size.

   ____

9. Behind the lens is a big cavity.
   The cavity contains the vitreous humour.
   The vitreous humour is a clear, colorless jelly.

   ____

10. At the back of the cavity is the retina.
    The retina is a thin layer of interconnected nerve cells.
    These cells convert light to electrical pulses.

    ____

PREPOSITIONS IN ADJECTIVE CLAUSES. Occasionally, verb phrases in English are followed by prepositional phrases, such as "*John walked into the room.*" Sentences like these can, of course, be combined with other sentences using adjective clauses, but the preposition must be retained. Study these two sentences. How can they be combined, changing one to an adjective clause?

> John found himself in a room.
> The room was very large and dark.

The sentences can be combined in this way:

> John found himself in a room *that was very large and dark.*

This sentence is correct and may serve the purpose. However, what if the emphasis should be placed on the room instead of on John? Remember, the emphasis is always on the independent, or main, clause. To place the emphasis on the room, subordinate "*John found himself in a room*" into an adjective clause:

> The room *that John found himself in* was very large and dark.

In this sentence, ***that*** refers to ***room***; therefore, ***in*** is associated with ***that*** (replacing "in a room" of the original sentence), and ***that*** becomes the object of the preposition ***in***.

An old grammar rule in English states that a clause should never end in a preposition; however, in formal writing, ending a clause in a preposition has become generally acceptable. In writing a formal report or term paper, it is wise to follow the old rule. Move the preposition to its more formal position before the subordinator, and when you do so, change ***that*** to ***which***:

> The room *in which John found himself* was very large and dark.

This construction is considered formal.

Note the two uses of prepositions in adjective clauses in passages in this chapter.

1. He has hideous, watery, almost colorless eyes that seem to be almost the same color as the sockets ***that they are set in***.
2. The Empire State Building was once the tallest building in the world and became especially famous as the building ***from which the original King Kong fell.***

Note: *That* cannot take the preposition before it. To change sentence 1 to its formal form, use ***which***:

> He has hideous, watery, almost colorless eyes that seem to be almost the same color as the sockets *in which they are set.*

EXERCISE 3-29

Part A

Mrs. Liv Borg's son is missing. In Part A, she reports her son missing to a police officer in a conversation. In the blanks provided, combine the sentences with adjective clauses, leaving the prepositions at the end of the sentences. Note that not all sentences contain prepositions. The first one is done for you.

OFFICER: I understand that you want to report a missing person.
MRS. BORG: Yes, sir. It's my son, Johann. He has been gone for two days. I've called all the people. He usually spends time with them.

1. I've called all the people that he usually spends time with. But no one seems to know where he is. I'm really worried.

OFFICER: Would you give us a description? We can publicize the description in order to find him.

2. ______________________________

MRS. BORG: Yes, sir. He is only twelve years old, about five feet, two inches tall, and weights about 100 pounds.
He has a dark face. His face is full and round.

3. ______________________________

He has short, black hair. He is very careful about his hair.

4. ______________________________

He has a scar above his left eye. He is ashamed of the scar.

5. ______________________________

He often tries to cover it with his hand or something. He is carrying something.

6. ______________________________

He has big brown eyes. His eyes are always smiling.

7. ______________________________

OFFICER: Do you remember the clothes. He was dressed in the clothes when he disappeared?

8. ______________________________

MRS. BORG: Yes. He had on a pair of new blue jeans. He was very proud of them.

9. ______________________________

He also was wearing a faded blue jacket. He used to play baseball in that jacket.

10. ______________________________

He was wearing an old pair of tennis shoes. He did not care much about the tennis shoes.

11. ______________________________

I think he had on a red baseball cap. He used to pin his scout medals on this cap.

12. ______________________________

He probably had with him a new baseball and baseball glove. He used to practice with them.

13. ______________________________

OFFICER: Thank you for the description. We will send it out and start checking our files. I will let you know as soon as we hear anything.

Part B

The police officer has asked Mrs. Borg to write a letter describing her missing son. The beginning of her letter follows. On another piece of paper, write the entire letter. Because a letter is more formal, place the prepositions in the adjective clauses in front of the relative pronouns.

Dear Sir:

You have asked me to write a description of my son, Johann Borg, who has been missing for two days.

First, let me give you a physical description. He is twelve years old, five feet, two inches tall, and weighs 100 pounds. He has . . .

Here is a description of the clothes my son was wearing when I last saw him. He had on . . .

Sincerely,
Mrs. Liv Borg

PUNCTUATION OF RESTRICTIVE AND NONRESTRICTIVE ADJECTIVE CLAUSES. Sometimes adjective clauses are set off by commas and sometimes they are not:

The trees *that line Main Street* are going to be cut down soon.

David Marchand, *whom I find unbearable*, has been assigned to my team.

The primary function of the clause determines the punctuation: to restrict the class of the noun it modifies, or simply to add information about the clause. There are two types of adjective clauses: ***restrictive*** and ***nonrestrictive***.

• *Restrictive adjective clauses: no commas.* Although all adjective clauses modify nouns, some adjective clauses serve mainly to ***identify or define*** the noun—in other words, to distinguish that noun from all other nouns in its class. If the clause serves this purpose, it is called ***restrictive*** and requires ***no commas***. Look at the sentence cited earlier:

The trees *that line Main Street* are going to be cut down soon.

If the adjective clause ***that line Main Street*** were omitted, would the reader be able to tell which trees are being referred to? Unless the trees have been referred to earlier in the context, the reader would have no idea what trees were being discussed. Therefore, because the adjective clause is ***necessary for identifying*** the noun ***trees***, it is a restrictive clause and no commas are used. Study these other examples of restrictive clauses:

Many tourists *who have ridden the elevators to the observation deck* have enjoyed an unforgettable view of famous Manhattan.

The room *that John found himself in* was very large and dark.

• *Nonrestrictive adjective clauses: commas.* When the adjective clause is used primarily to provide additional information about the noun, the adjective clause is considered unessential for identifying the noun. This type of adjective clause is called ***nonrestrictive*** because it does not serve to restrict the class to which the noun belongs. Nonrestrictive adjective clauses require commas.

David Marchand, *whom I find unbearable*, has been assigned to my team.

In this sentence, ***"whom I find unbearable"*** does not serve to identify the subject. The name David Marchand clearly identifies this person and distinguishes him from anyone else. Generally speaking, when the noun modified is a proper noun, the adjective clause modifying it is nonrestrictive and must be set off with commas. If the noun is not a proper noun—that is, if it is a common noun (such as ***tree***) that has been identified earlier in the context—then its adjective clause will most likely be nonrestrictive, functioning merely to add information about the noun.

John Lennon was a member of the rock group the Beatles until it disbanded in the early 1970s. This talented musician, *who was loved by millions*, was murdered in New York City on December 8, 1980.

In this passage, the adjective clause ***who was loved by millions*** modifies ***this talented musician***—a common noun phrase—but that common noun phrase was identified in the previous sentence. The adjective clause does not help to identify ***this talented musician*** and therefore needs commas.

Observe these other examples of nonrestrictive clauses:

The Empire State Building, *which is the second tallest building in New York City,* rises 1,250 feet in the air.

Mr. Jones, *who is a marvelous cook,* invited us to dinner.

The rest of his costume, *which is also black,* hides his entire body, even his hands.

> **Special Note: *that* to Introduce Adjective Clauses**
>
> ***That*** is always used in restrictive clauses; therefore, ***that*** adjective clauses are not set off by commas.

EXERCISE 3-30

In the following sentences, insert commas where appropriate.

1. My mother whom I love very much has decided to go to college.
2. One of the reporters who was assigned to South America was not able to go.
3. The cars that were parked along one block of Wilshire Boulevard were ticketed for illegal parking.
4. The man who played the Frankenstein monster in several movies was Boris Karloff.
5. Olaus Römer who was Danish was responsible for the first measurement of the velocity of light in 1676.
6. In 1859 Charles Darwin's *Origin of Species* which set forth the idea of the natural selection of living things was published.
7. The Ivory Coast which is located on the western coast of Africa is considered the richest former French West African colony.
8. Trygve Halvdan Lie who was born in Oslo, Norway, was the first secretary-general of the United Nations.
9. The Space Needle which was built for the 1962 World's Fair is one of Seattle's most popular attractions.
10. Anne Boleyn who was the second wife of Henry VIII of England was beheaded in 1536.
11. Ivan who was a civilian now was waiting for me at the Charlotte airport, and at first I didn't recognize him. The crew cut which was symbolic of the man, the career, and the era, was gone. His hair was longer now, a point of debate within his family whose members had insisted that a crew cut was passe. He had grudg-

ingly consented, but it was also clear that he had to resist an almost primal instinct to have it cut flat once again.

The civilian in front of me, Mr. Ivan Slavich, was a prosperous middle-management executive with McGuire Properties which was a very successful Charlotte commercial real estate firm. This man who stood in front of me was no longer Col. Ivan Slavich of the United States Army. Instead he was Colonel, U.S. Army Retired, which was a title he did not use, for he disliked those colleagues of his who had left the Army but held on to their rank and who remained, years after their last day in uniform, still colonels.*

EXERCISE 3-31: WRITING ASSIGNMENT

Look again at the description of the creature that you wrote in Exercise 3-27. Can it be improved with the use of adjective clauses? Rewrite your paragraph, revising it to include adjective clauses.

REDUCTION OF ADJECTIVE CLAUSES TO PREPOSITIONAL PHRASES. Adjective clauses often include prepositional phrases that tell where something or someone is. Note this example:

The store *that is on the corner* sells newspapers and maps.

It is possible to omit the relative pronoun and the verb ***to be***, leaving just the prepositional phrase:

The store *on the corner* sells newspapers and maps.

Reducing adjective clauses to prepositional phrases is useful when describing people and what they are wearing. The preposition ***in*** is used to describe a main piece of clothing. Note the reduction:

The woman *who is wearing the blue dress* is from Egypt.

The woman *in the blue dress* is from Egypt.

The preposition ***with*** is used to indicate a physical attribute, or possession. Note the examples:

The boy *who has curly hair* is from Venezuela.

The man *who is wearing a diamond ring* must be rich.

The woman *who is holding the book* is obviously the teacher.

These sentences reduce like this:

The boy *with curly hair* is from Venezuela.

The man *with the diamond ring* must be rich.

The woman *with the book* is obviously the teacher.

*Adapted from David Halberstam, "The Bravest Man I Know," *Parade*, 10 June 1984, p. 14.

EXERCISE 3-32

Reduce the following adjective clauses to prepositional phrases. In some sentences, adding the prepositions *in* or *with* will be necessary.

1. The apartment that is next to mine is empty right now.

   ____

2. The landlord brought a woman who was wearing blue jeans and a sweater to see it.

   ____

3. He also brought a man wearing a long gray overcoat.

   ____

4. Next, he brought an attractive young woman who had flashing black eyes.

   ____

5. None of them liked it because the building that is next door has very noisy tenants.

   ____

6. Then he showed it to a small man who was wearing glasses and who had a big nose.

   ____

7. Next, he brought a family. The little boy who was carrying a toy truck was crying.

   ____

8. They did not want it because the park that is across the street is dirty.

   ____

9. Finally, a tall man who was wearing cowboy boots and a white hat rented the apartment.

   ____

10. I guess he did not mind the noisy building that is next door or the dirty park that is across the street.

    ____

Participles as Adjectives

Earlier, we studied present and past participial adjectives that derive from psychological verbs. It is possible to use the present and past participles of other verbs as adjectives as well. Note these examples:

She enjoys the sound of *running* water.

I only eat *cooked* vegetables.

The *stuffed* moose hung on the wall.

Sometimes it is difficult to tell whether to use the present or past participle as adjective with these ordinary verbs. In this case, it helps to make the adjective into an adjective clause. Doing this will show that the past participle derives from a passive verb while the present participle derives from an active verb:

She enjoys the sound of water that is *running*.

I only eat vegetables that have been *cooked* (by someone).

The moose that was *stuffed* (by someone) hung on the wall.

You can see in each of these examples that the choice of present or past participle depends on the verb of the underlying adjective clause—is it passive or active? When you want to make a choice between the present and past participle, look at the noun and ask if it is acting or being acted upon, if it is doing or being done to. Look at this example:

The *torn* book lay on the table.

Is the book tearing or has someone torn the book? In other words, is it active or passive? Make the adjective into a clause in order to check:

The book that has been *torn* (by someone) lay on the table.

You can see that the adjective clause comes from a passive verb, and thus the past participle is the appropriate adjective.

EXERCISE 3-33

In the following sentences, write either the present or past participle in the blanks. Remember that some past participles are irregular.

1. Last Friday, my friend, Jack, and I spent a ______________ (pack) day at the natural history museum.
2. First, we toured the ______________ (mount) displays of prehistoric animals.
3. In that section, we saw a huge, ______________ (stuff) replica of a brontosaurus.
4. In the next room, we came across some ______________ (preserve) fossils of the earliest- ______________ (know) plants.
5. As we went on, we encountered the displays of ______________ (develop) *Homo sapiens*.

6. The Neanderthal man was short and had a ____________ (shrink) head.
7. The Cro-Magnon man was taller and more ____________ (advance) physically than the Neanderthal man.
8. We agreed that ours was an ____________ (endure) species.
9. Finally, we watched a planetarium show in which countless ____________ (wander) stars and planets filled the sky.
10. After we emerged from the ____________ (darken) planetarium, we went to the ____________ (crowd) restaurant to talk over the day's events.

EXERCISE 3-34: WRITING ASSIGNMENT

Assume you have a pen pal in another country. Write a paragraph to your pen pal describing your physical appearance. You might want to describe your face, or you may prefer to describe one or two of your outstanding features. Plan your paragraph carefully. Remember to have a controlling idea that is supported with vivid detail. Try to use adjective clauses in the description.

Descriptive Paragraph Checklist

1. Descriptive writing uses sensory details to paint a picture of a place, a person, or an object. Does your paragraph use sufficient vivid detail?
2. The controlling idea of a descriptive paragraph is often an attitude or an impression about the subject. Does your paragraph have a clear, focused controlling idea?
3. Is the controlling idea in your paragraph contained in a clear topic sentence? An implied topic sentence?
4. The details and support of the controlling idea in a descriptive paragraph often follow spatial organization or some other logical format. Are the topic sentence and details logically arranged in your paragraph?
5. Is your paragraph unified; that is, do all the sentences support the controlling idea?
6. Is your paragraph coherent; that is, do the sentences flow smoothly?

Chapter 4

The Expository Paragraph

Readings: Learning and Education

WHEN cultural anthropologists speak of learning, they mean the adaptations human beings learn to make in order to function in a particular culture. As children we learn the language that is spoken around us, we learn to eat our food in the manner common in our culture, we learn to be polite to the appropriate people, and so forth. From a cultural point of view, then, a great deal of learning is necessary for us to become independent, mature members of society. Yet when educators speak of learning, they usually mean the specific type of learning that occurs in an educational context. What is a student supposed to learn in a beginning calculus class? In a four-year engineering program? In the context of school, then, learning often means a body of knowledge that is passed along in a formal educational setting. While not all people in the world have the opportunity for this type of formal education, all people in all cultures learn constantly as they go about their daily lives. For those of us who have attended school, it is interesting to try to separate what we have learned in a general way from what we have learned through our formal education.

Following are two readings that might help us to do that. As you read the selections about human learning, try to answer these questions:

1. What have you learned through general experience? Through formal education?
2. Which kind of learning is easier for you? Why?
3. What are the advantages of each kind of learning? The disadvantages?

READING 1

WHAT IS INTELLIGENCE, ANYWAY?

ISAAC ASIMOV

Born in the Soviet Union in 1920, Isaac Asimov came to the United States in 1923. Author of more than three hundred books, he is internationally recognized as a great popularizer of science. Asimov's works also include science fiction and books on history, Shakespeare, and the Bible. As you read the essay that follows, try to identify Asimov's definition of intelligence.

1 What is intelligence, anyway? When I was in the army I received a kind of aptitude• test that all soldiers took and, *ability*

against a normal of 100, scored 160. No one at the base had ever seen a figure like that, and for two hours they made a big fuss over me. (It didn't mean anything. The next day I was still a buck private with KP• as my highest duty.)

kitchen patrol

2 All my life I've been registering scores like that, so that I have the complacent• feeling that I'm highly intelligent, and I expect other people to think so, too. Actually, though, don't such scores simply mean that I am very good at answering the type of academic questions that are considered worthy of answers by the people who make up the intelligence tests—people with intellectual bents• similar to mine?

self-satisfied

tendencies

3 For instance, I had an auto-repair man once, who, on these intelligence tests, could not possibly have scored more than 80, by my estimate. I always took it for granted that I was far more intelligent than he was. Yet, when anything went wrong with my car I hastened to him with it, watched him anxiously as he explored its vitals,• and listened to his pronouncements as though they were divine oracles•—and he always fixed my car.

insides

prophecies, foretelling the future

4 Well, then, suppose my auto-repair man devised questions for an intelligence test. Or suppose a carpenter did, or a farmer, or, indeed, almost anyone but an academician. By every one of those tests, I'd prove myself a moron.• And I'd *be* a moron, too. In a world where I could not use my academic training and my verbal talents but had to do something intricate• or hard, working with my hands, I would do poorly. My intelligence, then, is not absolute but is a function of the society I live in and of the fact that a small subsection of that society has managed to foist• itself on the rest as an arbiter• of such matters.

a person of below-average intelligence

elaborate, complicated

to impose by fraud / a settler of disputes

5 Consider my auto-repair man, again. He had a habit of telling me jokes whenever he saw me. One time he raised his head from under the automobile hood to say: "Doc, a deaf-and-dumb guy went into a hardware store to ask for some nails. He put two fingers together on the counter and made hammering motions with the other hand. The clerk brought him a hammer. He shook his head and pointed to the two fingers he was hammering. The clerk brought him nails. He picked out the sizes he wanted, and left. Well, Doc, the next guy who came in was a blind man. He wanted scissors. How do you suppose he asked for them?"

6 Indulgently,• I lifted my right hand and made scissoring motions with my first two fingers. Whereupon my auto-repair man laughed raucously• and said, "Why, you dumb jerk, he used his *voice* and asked for them." Then he said, smugly,• "I've been trying that on all my customers today." "Did you catch many?" I asked. "Quite a few," he said, "but I knew for sure I'd catch *you*." "Why is that?" I asked. "Because you're

giving in

loudly

in a self-satisfied way

so goddamned educated, Doc, I *knew* you couldn't be very smart."

7 And I have an uneasy feeling he had something there.

EXERCISE 4-1: COMPREHENSION/ DISCUSSION QUESTIONS

1. What was the effect of Asimov's high IQ score on army officials? On his army-related duties?
2. According to Asimov, why does he rank high on IQ tests?
3. Does Asimov consider his auto repairman intelligent? Why, or why not?
4. What does the author mean by, "My intelligence, then, is not absolute but is a function of the society I live in. . . ." (par. 4)? Explain.
5. What distinction does Asimov make between being educated and being smart?
6. What is Asimov's definition of intelligence?
7. How do you define intelligence? Be prepared to support your answer.

EXERCISE 4-2: VOCABULARY DEVELOPMENT

The following words are all adverbs used in the reading. Each of these words also has an adjective form. For each one, give the adjective form and then use it in an original sentence. For example:

Example:

actually—actual

The *actual* result of his high IQ score in the army was negligible.

---

1. indulgently (par. 6)

   ____

2. raucously (par. 6)

   ____

3. smugly (par. 6)

   ____

The following are adjectives used in the reading. Write the adverb form and an original sentence for each one.

1. complacent (par. 2)

   ____

2. intelligent (par. 2)

___

3. divine (par. 3)

___

4. intricate (par. 4)

___

READING 2

FORGETTING

CAMILLE B. WORTMAN AND ELIZABETH F. LOFTUS

Psychologists have long been interested in the mechanisms of human learning. They have engaged in a great deal of research on the learning process, especially on the role of human memory in learning. Although less research has been done on memory loss, psychologists are intrigued with this part of the learning process that causes us to forget events, people, or ideas.

The following reading, taken from a psychology textbook, presents some of the theories that researchers believe may explain human forgetting. Before you begin reading, try to answer these questions:

1. What kinds of things—events, names, people, ideas—are you most likely to forget?
2. Why do you think you forget these things?

While the reading discusses only one aspect of human learning—forgetting—it also serves as an example of the type of information considered important in formal education. That is, this information would likely be part of the body of knowledge that a student would learn in a psychology class. Earlier we noted the difference between general cultural learning and school learning. As you read the following selection, try to answer these questions:

1. What aspects of the reading make it typical of textbook information?
2. How is this type of information different from the type acquired through general cultural learning?

1 Until now we have concentrated primarily on the successful side of human memory. We have seen that people can instate, store, and retrieve• information from long-term mem- *recover*

ory with a reasonable degree of speed and accuracy, even if some distortions• of memory occur. But what about the all-too-familiar process called forgetting? It, too, is of interest to psychologists.

misrepresentations

2 Psychologist Marigold Linton (1978), frustrated by the undependability of her own memory, set out in the early 1970s to investigate the phenomenon• of forgetting personal experiences. Following the lead of the nineteenth-century memory researcher Hermann Ebbinghaus (1885), Linton chose herself as the most willing and reliable• subject available. For six years she recorded on file cards two or more distinct events that happened to her each day. The entries varied from such mundane• occurrences as eating dinner at a Chinese restaurant to rather unusual happenings, such as an important job interview. Every month she tested her recall of the dates of some 150 events selected at random• from the card file as well as some other information related to the events. The results were not encouraging. By the end of 1978, Linton had slowly but steadily forgotten almost a third of the events she had considered memorable six years earlier.

occurrence
trustworthy
everyday
without order or purpose

Theories of Forgetting

3 What are the reasons for this persistent• forgetting? Psychologists have suggested three major causes: decay, interference, and motivation to forget. Although these explanations conflict with one another in several important ways, they are not entirely incompatible.• A full account of forgetting should probably include all three.

continuing
do not go together

4 **Decay of Memory Traces.** Perhaps the oldest theory of forgetting is that memories simply fade away, or decay, with the passage of time if they are not renewed through periodic use. This notion has a certain romantic appeal and tends to fit well with some of our personal experiences. The memory of a movie seen last week, for example, is usually stronger and more detailed than that of a movie seen last year. Nevertheless, some of the things we know about human memory appear to contradict• decay theory. For one thing, not all long-term memories seem to dissipate• with time. Motor skills, for instance, are particularly resistant to decay. An adult who has not ridden a bicycle in twenty years usually has no trouble demonstrating the skill to a child. Second, if long-term memories do in fact fade over the years, then the structural or chemical changes in the brain that originally encoded those memories must also break down in some way. As yet, however, we do not know why such a breakdown would regularly and spontaneously occur. The concept of decay, then, may

not go together with / go away

be useful in explaining loss from fragile• short-term memory, but its application to long-term memory is open to question.

delicate

5 **Interference.** The phenomenon of interference is another cause of forgetting. According to this view, memory of a year-old movie fades because of the unavoidable confusion that results when you subsequently encounter very similar experiences (other movies or television shows with similar characters and plots). Marigold Linton was surprised at how much of her forgetting was attributable• to this kind of confusion. As a string of similar events in her life became longer (the sixth time she dined at a certain restaurant, or the twelfth time she attended a certain professional meeting), she found it increasingly difficult to distinguish one episode from another. The details of the separate episodes blended together, until none could be clearly recalled (Linton, 1982).

the reason for

6 Interference may hinder• recall of verbal information, too. You may have had this experience yourself when you studied for exams. If you have just memorized the names of various bones of the body for a test in human anatomy, for instance, reading about the related muscles could begin to confuse you. When information learned later interferes with information learned earlier, psychologists say that retroactive interference has taken place. (*Retro* means "backward in time.") Conversely, when material learned earlier interferes with recall of material learned later, proactive interference has occurred. (*Pro* means "forward in time.") You may have had this experience when you introduced someone by her maiden name, even though she has been using a married name for months.

slow down

7 Sleep seems to be one of the best temporary safeguards against interference. Research has shown that people forget substantially• less if they sleep for several hours after learning than if they continue their waking activities. In one experiment, subjects who stayed awake for eight hours recalled only about 10 percent of material they had previously learned, whereas subjects who slept for eight hours remembered about 60 percent of the same material (Jenkins and Dallenbach, 1924). Presumably those who went to sleep were not subject to interference. These findings can be applied to your own study habits. Getting a good night's sleep after studying for an exam will probably increase your powers of recall in the morning.

a significant amount

8 **Motivated Forgetting.** It is not hard to believe that we sometimes forget because we *want* to. Such motivated forgetting is, in fact, the foundation of Freud's psychoanalytic theory. According to Freud, people often push unacceptable, anxiety•-provoking thoughts and impulses into their unconscious so as to avoid confronting• them directly. This psycho-

worry

facing

logical defense mechanism is called repression. Sirhan Sirhan's inability to remember shooting Robert Kennedy• is probably an instance of repression. In fact, repression seems to be quite common among people who have committed violent crimes of great passion; it occurs in an estimated one out of three such cases (Bower, 1981).

candidate for the American presidency, killed by Sirhan Sirhan in 1967

9 Not all motivated forgetting is a defense mechanism against severe anxiety, however. Research shows that people generally tend to forget unpleasant experiences more readily than pleasant ones, even when the unpleasant events are not especially threatening. In one early experiment, students returning to college after Christmas vacation tended to remember more pleasant than unpleasant things about the holiday. And when the same students were unexpectedly interviewed again six weeks later, they remembered even fewer unpleasant holiday experiences in proportion to pleasant ones (Meltzer, 1930). Negative memories, it appears, are banished more readily than positive ones.

10 Part of this tendency to remember the past as better than it actually was may be motivated by a desire to enhance• our own self-esteem.• Research shows that people often remember themselves as having held more responsible, better-paying jobs than they actually had. They also recall donating• more to charity, voting more frequently, and raising more intelligent children than objective records indicate (Cannell and Kahn, 1968). We tend, in other words, to edit our personal memories in order to cast• ourselves in a more favorable light (Myers and Ridl, 1979). From this point of view, forgetting is partly self-serving. . . .

increase

good feelings about oneself

giving

put

EXERCISE 4-3: COMPREHENSION/ DISCUSSION QUESTIONS

1. Describe the experiment that researcher Marigold Linton undertook (par. 2). Why did she do it? What did she do? What were the results?
2. Explain the decay theory of memory loss (par. 4).
3. What are the objections to the decay theory?
4. How does interference cause forgetting?
5. Explain the difference between retroactive and proactive interference (par. 6).
6. According to the authors, what are the two causes of motivated forgetting?
7. Why do we sometimes remember the past as better than it actually was?

8. Can you think of a personal example of any of these types of forgetting? Be prepared to explain it to the class.

EXERCISE 4-4: VOCABULARY DEVELOPMENT

The reading contains a number of terms related to the study of psychology in general and to memory in particular, some of which are listed here. For each of the following terms, write an original sentence.

1. long-term memory (par. 1)

   ____

2. short-term memory (par. 4)

   ____

3. phenomenon (par. 2)

   ____

4. subject (par. 2)

   ____

5. motor skills (par. 4)

   ____

6. recall (par. 2)

   ____

7. experiment (par. 7)

   ____

8. defense mechanism (par. 8)

   ____

9. anxiety (par. 8)

   ____

10. self-esteem (par. 10)

    ____

Writing

The organization and content of a paragraph are determined by the topic and the controlling idea of that paragraph. A topic sentence must be supported with details organized chronologically in a narrative paragraph and spatially in a descriptive paragraph. Not all topics are best developed into narrative or descriptive paragraphs, however. Let us suppose, for instance, that you are asked to develop the topic sentence, "Going to college can be expensive." The controlling idea is, of course, *expensive*. What kind of support would you use for this topic sentence? Obviously, the topic sentence does not suggest that you tell a story or describe a scene or a person; rather, it suggests that you support the controlling idea with information, explanation, facts, or illustrations. A paragraph that explains or analyzes a topic is an ***expository paragraph.*** (***Expository*** comes from the term *expose*, meaning "to reveal.") Although explaining a topic can be done in several ways, the most common approach to developing an expository paragraph requires using specific details and examples. (In subsequent chapters, other methods of developing expository paragraphs and essays are discussed.)

No matter what type of paragraph you are writing, you will need specific detail and examples to support the controlling idea in your topic sentence. The controlling idea is the word or phrase in the topic sentence that states an *idea* or an *attitude* about the topic; this idea or attitude is frequently referred to as a *generalization*. A generalization is a statement that applies in most cases to a group of things, ideas, or people. A generalization can be a value judgment or an opinion ("Mr. Mantia is a *nice* person") or a factual statement ("The English language has borrowed many terms from the French").

EXERCISE 4-5

Study the following sets of sentences carefully. In the space provided, write a topic sentence that contains a pertinent generalization.

1. *Topic Sentence:* ______________________________

   Support:
   a. Antarctica appears frozen in time, an icy world surrounded by frigid seas where winds of 100 mph are not uncommon.
   b. Temperatures regularly plunge to −100°F or below.
   c. Giant crevasses can open in the ice, swallowing people and machines.
   d. Sudden storms often blend ground and sky into one snowy blur that hopelessly disorients the most skilled aviators.*

2. *Topic Sentence:* ______________________________

   Support:
   a. Many products on grocery store shelves are conspicuously labeled "cholesterol free."
   b. Two books, Robert E. Kowalski's *The 8-Week Cholesterol Cure* and Dr. Kenneth H. Cooper's *Controlling Cholesterol*, have been major best-sellers this year.

*Adapted from "Scramble on the Polar Ice" by Wolf Von Eckardt and reported by Walter Galling, *Time*, 22 Feb. 1982, p. 64.

c. Oat bran, which moderately lowers cholesterol levels, is selling so fast that some manufacturers are working around the clock to meet the demand.
d. During the recent presidential campaign, doctors released medical reports with the leading candidates' cholesterol levels.

3. *Topic Sentence:* ______________________________
Support: a. Approximately $161 million were lost when lightning struck an Atlas-Centaur rocket carrying a navy satellite as the rocket rose from the launch pad at Cape Canaveral on March 26, 1987.
b. A one-day delay in the launch of the Space Shuttle because of the threat of lightning costs $3 million.
c. If an overnight delivery service has to clear its loading docks because of the threat of lightning, it does so at a cost of $1,000 per minute.
d. Millions of dollars were lost in New York City in 1977 when lightning caused a major blackout that resulted in large-scale vandalism and looting.

4. *Topic Sentence:* ______________________________
Support: a. People used to think that Neanderthal man was quite stupid because of the shape of his head. However, scientific investigation has shown that head shape does not have anything to do with intelligence.
b. Neanderthal man made beautiful tools.
c. He also made flint balls, perforators, discs, scrapers, and stone knives.
d. Neanderthal man developed the use of mineral pigments such as red ocher.
e. He also introduced ceremonial burial of the dead, suggesting that he had a highly developed religious system.*

5. *Topic Sentence:* ______________________________
Support: a. Thirty-three percent of all high-school athletes are female, a sixfold increase since the early 1970s. In colleges, the figure is 30 percent, an increase in ten years of 250 percent.

*Adapted from Ashley Montagu, *Man: His First Two Million Years* (New York: Columbia University Press, 1969), p. 67.

b. Since 1970, the number of female tennis players in the country has jumped from about 3 million to 11 million, the number of golfers from less than a half million to more than 5 million.
c. According to one survey, of the nation's 17.1 million joggers, over one third are women; in 1970, there were too few to count.
d. In 1980, financial rewards for female athletes topped more than $16 million, up from less than $1 million ten years ago.*

Support of the Generalization

Specific Details

The topic sentence "Going to college can be expensive" should yield a paragraph that provides some information or explanation about the controlling idea—expensive. The topic sentence might be developed as follows:

> Going to college can be expensive. Everyone knows that tuition and room and board aren't cheap, but there are other expenses that make going to college even more expensive. For instance, the cost of books and supplies is high. In addition, there are all kinds of special fees tacked onto the bill at registration time. Students usually have to pay for parking and even for adding and dropping courses after registration. The fees never seem to end.

Does this paragraph effectively demonstrate that going to college can be expensive? Although the writer mentions a few of the expenses that students must incur, the writer has not provided the reader with enough hard evidence to support the controlling idea—*expensive*. Specific details would help support this statement more strongly. Just as specific descriptive details help to support the controlling idea in a description and make the description more vivid and interesting, specific details help "prove" or support the generalization in an expository paragraph. This paragraph can be improved by using specific detail:

> Going to college can be expensive. Everyone knows that tuition and room and board can cost anywhere from $3,000 to $10,000 per semester, but there are other expenses that make going to college even more expensive. For instance, books typically cost between $150 and $400 each term.

*Adapted from "Female Athletes: They've Come a Long Way, Baby," *Reader's Digest*, Oct., 1980, p. 126.

Supplies, too, are not cheap, for as any student knows, paper, notebooks, writing utensils, and the many other supplies needed usually cost more at the college bookstore than at a local discount department store. For instance, a package of notepaper costing $1 at a discount store might cost $2 at a college bookstore. In addition, there are all kinds of special fees tacked onto the bill at registration time. A student might have to pay a $30 insurance fee, a $15 activity fee, a $10 fee to the student government association, and anywhere from $20 to $100 for parking. If a student decides to add or drop a course after registration, there is yet another fee. The fees never seem to end.

Instead of just referring to the expenses of attending college, in this revised version the writer uses specific details—in this case, factual details—to illustrate or prove the generalization.

In expository writing, then, the writer is like a lawyer who is trying to prove a point; a lawyer cannot make generalizations without giving proof to support his or her statements. Good proof is factual detail.

EXERCISE 4-6

To illustrate the difference in the support given in the two paragraphs about the expense of college, make an outline of each paragraph. On the left side of your paper write the outline for the first version of the paragraph; on the right side write the outline for the revised version. Then compare the support. For example:

INEFFECTIVE SUPPORT	EFFECTIVE SUPPORT
Tuition and room and board aren't cheap.	Tuition and room and board can cost anywhere from $3,000 to $10,000 per semester.

EXERCISE 4-7

Study the following bits of information about the mythical town of Decasia, Illinois.

January 3:	Rose's Giant Boutique moves to the Town Mall shopping center.
January 23:	Heartland Department Store moves to the Town Mall.
February 1:	Thirty-six potholes are counted on Main Street.
February 15:	Fire destroys Boolie's Restaurant.
March 3:	During the night someone paints "The Killers" on four buildings.
March 16:	An "adult" (pornographic) bookstore moves into the building formerly occupied by Rose's Giant Boutique.
April 5:	The elegant Chandler Theater closes down.
May 3:	The famous Chez Pierre restaurant closes down for lack of business.
June 15:	Forty potholes are counted on Main Street.
July 3:	Bus service is discontinued.
August 1:	The remains of Boolie's Restaurant are condemned.
August 15:	Shank's Men's Clothing Store moves to the Town Mall in the suburbs.
September 2:	An "adult" movie theater opens at the old Chandler theater.
October 12:	Three more buildings have "The Killers" painted on them.
November 3:	All of the windows of the old Heartland Department Store are shattered by stones.
December 1:	A pawnshop opens where Chez Pierre used to be.

Using the information from this list, rewrite the weak support given below and provide strong support for the topic sentence given. You do not have to use all the information provided. Write out the topic sentence and the strong support on a separate sheet of paper.

Topic Sentence:

The downtown area of Decasia is rapidly decaying.

Support:

1. Many of the stores are moving out.
2. Some of the buildings are unsightly.
3. The street is in bad shape.
4. Several sleazy places have opened up.

But support should not only be specific; it should be relevant as well. All of the supporting sentences in a paragraph should relate to the controlling idea in order for the paragraph to be unified.

EXERCISE 4-8

Study the following groups of topic sentences and details. For each topic sentence, circle the letter of the detail that does not support the generalization (controlling idea).

1. Smoking cigarettes is unhealthy.
   a. Studies have indicated that cigarette smoking increases the risk of cancer.
   b. Smokers have a higher rate of respiratory diseases, such as emphysema and bronchitis.
   c. Studies have also shown that cigarette smokers have a higher rate of heart attacks.
   d. Moreover, cigarette smoke stains the teeth.
2. In the 1960s, nuclear power was expected to provide most of the additional electrical energy needed for the United States for the rest of the century. The West Coast seemed ideal for locating future nuclear power plants.
   a. Much of the coast is sparsely populated, so if a radiation leak occurred, it would affect only a few people.
   b. The urban centers requiring most of the electric power are close enough to the coast so that the costs of building power lines and transmitting electricity could be kept to a minimum.
   c. The West Coast is one of the most active earthquake areas in the United States, with the San Andreas fault running the length of the state of California.
   d. The ocean water from the Pacific Ocean would provide an efficient means of cooling a nuclear reactor—a major consideration since two-thirds of the heat generated by a nuclear power plant is wasted heat that must be dispersed.
   e. Because of the mountainous coastline, power plants could be constructed out of reach of potential floods.*
3. The very words for *left* and *right*, in most languages, testify to a universal right-handed bias.
   a. Our word *right* suggests that it is "right" to use the right hand.
   b. Many authorities today estimate that about 25 percent of people are born left-handed.
   c. It may be that our word *left* has its origin in the fact that the left hand is so little used that it is "left out" of most tasks.

*Adapted from Charles C. Plummer and David McGeary, *Physical Geology*, 2nd ed. (Dubuque, Iowa: Wm. C. Brown, 1982), p. 292.

   d. Our word *sinister*, suggesting something disastrous or evil, is from the Latin word for left; *dexterous* or *dextrous*, meaning adroit and skillful, is from the Latin word for right.
   e. The French word for left is *gauche*, which also means crooked or awkward; the French word for right is *droit*, which also means just, honest, and straight.
   f. Spaniards speak of the left hand as *zurdo*, and the Spanish phrase "a zurdas" means the wrong way.*

4. There are examples of behavior suggesting that animals can process information and make judgments.
   a. James Gould of Princeton University points out that honey bees, fed sugar water that is gradually moved away from the hive, anticipate where the food will be placed.
   b. Seagulls break open shellfish by dropping them on hard surfaces, flying low when their target is small.
   c. At the Yerkes Regional Primate Research Center in Atlanta, chimpanzees have been conditioned to communicate through symbols and are able to distinguish between signs that mean food and those that refer to nonedible items.
   d. The chimps also have demonstrated self-awareness. One chimp, while watching itself on a television monitor, directed a flashlight beam into its mouth, apparently curious about what its throat looked like.
   e. One of the most widely held misconceptions is that dolphins have an authentic language.**

Examples

Since factual details are not always available and since not all generalizations can be "proven," other kinds of support are necessary for the expository paragraph. The most common kind of support is *examples*. What exactly is an example? By definition, an example is an item that represents a group of things, people, or ideas. In other words, an example is a specific representative of a general category. An example of a horror movie is *The House of Wax;* an example of a tennis player is Bjorn Borg. In short, examples make the controlling idea — the generalization — clearer and more convincing, and therefore are an effective means of support.

EXERCISE 4-9

Complete the following sentences, drawing on personal experiences and observations. The first one is done for you.

*From Martin Gardner, *The Ambidextrous Universe* (New York: Scribner's, 1974), p. 70.
**Adapted from "Birds May Do It, Bees May Do It," *Time*, 2 May, 1983, p. 55.

1. An example of a famous rock-and-roll singer is Bruce Springsteen.
2. An example of a dangerous drug is ______________________.
3. An example of a difficult course is ______________________.
4. Albert Einstein is an example of a ______________________.
5. Driving while under the influence of alcohol is an example of ______________________.

It is not usually sufficient just to name an example; often it is necessary to explain the example to show how it relates to and supports the generalization. For instance, notice the simple generalization in this topic sentence: "Tornadoes can be devastating." The topic is *tornadoes* and the controlling idea (generalization) is that they can be *devastating*. It would be insufficient to support that generalization by simply stating, "Take, for example, the tornado that hit Wichita Falls, Texas, in 1979." That does not really show that the tornado was devastating; in reality, the tornado might have caused very little damage. It is necessary to add an explanation of that example: "This tornado destroyed an entire block of homes and damaged many other houses and places of business. In addition, the tornado caused the death of several people." Now the reader is convinced that the example is relevant. The paragraph might conclude by discussing one or two more examples:

> Tornadoes can be devastating. Take, for example, the tornado that hit Wichita Falls, Texas, in 1979. This tornado destroyed an entire block of homes and damaged many other houses and places of business. In addition, the tornado caused the death of over twenty people. More recently, in 1982, at least twenty-five tornadoes hit Arkansas, Texas, Mississippi, and Florida, killing 26 people, injuring over 300, and causing more than $50 million in property damage. In 1984, the town of Barneveld, Wisconsin, was leveled by a tornado that killed 7 and injured about 200. Even though not all tornadoes cause such massive devastation, if they touch down in populated areas, you can expect considerable damage.*

The explanation of an example does not have to be lengthy; sometimes all you need to do is add a few words. Consider another example:

Generalization:

The cost of living has been rising lately.

Support:

The average one-bedroom apartment goes for $350 a month.

*Information from "The Winter That Refused To Die," *Time*, 19 April, 1982, p. 24.

Does this example really show that the cost of living has been rising lately? After all, there may have been no change in the average monthly rent for several years. The writer could add a clause to explain the example:

> The average one-bedroom apartment goes for $350 a month, *whereas only two years ago it went for $275.*

Using this same generalization, the writer might discuss four or five additional examples to show that the cost of living has been rising, but among those examples should be at least one that provides information about a specific case. In other words, it is useful to provide specific detail for support.

Here is how the support might look for this generalization:

The cost of living has been rising lately.

1. The average one-bedroom apartment goes for $350 a month, whereas only two years ago it went for $275.
2. The cost of regular gasoline has increased from 92 cents a gallon to $1.10 a gallon in only six months.
3. When I first came to this town three years ago, it cost 10 cents to use the public telephone, but now it costs 25 cents.
4. In addition, my water bill has increased $2 in three months, even though my water consumption has not gone up.
5. Finally, my cable television bill has just jumped up another $1.35 per month for basic service.

EXERCISE 4-10

In the preceding sentences underline the part that clarifies its support of the generalization.

EXERCISE 4-11

For each of the following topic sentences, circle the controlling idea (generalization) and then write out two examples that support that idea. Be sure that the examples are adequately explained. For the second example, use a specific incident. The first one is done for you.

1. Mr. Morales displays kindness wherever he goes.

   a. When he is on the bus, he talks to people who look sad. He tells them funny stories that invariably make them smile.

   b. Last week when he heard that his neighbor was sick, he made some soup and delivered it to her, along with a bouquet of flowers.

2. There are several things you can do to reduce pollution.

   a. ______________________________

   b. ______________________________

3. Some things definitely need to be changed at this school.

   a. ______________________________

   b. ______________________________

4. I have learned a lot about __________ in the last year.

   a. ______________________________

   b. ______________________________

5. You can find some unusual items at the bookstore.

   a. ______________________________

   b. ______________________________

EXERCISE 4-12: WRITING ASSIGNMENT

Select one of the following writing assignments.

1. Choose one of the generalizations in Exercise 4-11. Develop a paragraph with examples drawn from personal experience.
2. The devastation from such natural disasters as floods, tornadoes, hurricanes, hail storms, or droughts is awesome. Write a paragraph giving examples of the devastation caused by a natural disaster.

Illustrations and Anecdotes

It is not always necessary to give several examples to support the controlling idea; sometimes one example that is explained in greater detail will suffice to support the controlling idea. This kind of extended example is useful, not so much for "proving" the statement in the generalization but for illustrating it; therefore, this kind of example is called an *illustration*. Study the following paragraph:

> Wherever there are great forests, modern methods of insect control threaten the fishes inhabiting the streams in the shelter of the trees. One of the best-known examples of fish destruction in the United States took place in 1955, as a result of spraying in and near Yellowstone National Park. By the fall of that year, so many dead fish had been found in the Yellowstone River that sportsmen and Montana fish-and-game administrators became alarmed. About 90 miles of the river were affected. In one 300-yard length of shoreline, 600 dead fish were counted, including brown trout, whitefish, and suckers. Stream insects, the natural food of trout, had disappeared.
>
> —Rachel Carson, *Silent Spring* (Boston: Houghton Mifflin, 1962).

What is the controlling idea in this paragraph?

Another type of illustration is an *anecdote*. An anecdote is a brief story that dramatizes the point made in the generalization. In other words, it is a brief narrative. (To review the narrative paragraph, return to Chapter 2.) Study the following paragraph and note its organization:

> There is a story, possibly apocryphal, about a psychologist who shut a chimpanzee in a soundproof room filled with dozens of mechanical toys. Eager to see what playthings the ape would choose when he was all alone in this treasure house, the scientist bent down on his knees and put his eye to the keyhole. What he saw was one bright eye peering through from the other side of the aperture. If this anecdote isn't true, it certainly ought to be, for it illustrates the impossibility of anticipating exactly what an animal will do in a test situation. —Frank A. Beach, "Can Animals Reason?" *Natural History*, March 1948.

What is the topic sentence of this paragraph? How are the sentences arranged?

COMPOSITION SKILLS

Coherence

Organization of Details and Examples

When a paragraph contains several details and examples, it is necessary to consider the order of their presentation. Unlike narratives, whose sentences logically are ordered chronologically, and descriptions, whose sentences are logically organized on a spatial principle, the sentences in the expository paragraph follow no prescribed or set pattern of organization. The ordering depends on the subject and often on the author's logic. There are, however, some common patterns that might be considered guidelines.

ORDER OF IMPORTANCE: SAVING THE BEST FOR LAST. Often, when you are developing a topic sentence with details and examples, one of the examples is more impressive than the others. Since readers generally remember what they read last, and since it is a good idea to leave a good impression on the reader, it is wise to place the most impressive example at the end of the paragraph. Study the following paragraph and note that the last example is the most startling one:

> A search through etymologies will reveal other examples of words which have narrowed in meaning since their early days. *Barbarian* was originally a vague designation for a foreigner of any kind; *garage*, when it was borrowed from France, meant "a place for storage." In the United States *lumber* has specialized to mean "timber or sawed logs especially prepared for use," but in Britain the word still retains its more general meaning of "unused

articles," which are stored, incidentally, in a *lumber room*. *Disease* originally meant what its separate parts imply, *dis ease*, and referred to any kind of discomfort. The expression "to give up the ghost" and the biblical reference to the Holy Ghost may be the only remnants of an earlier, more general meaning for *ghost*, which once meant "spirit" or "breath." Now *ghost* has specialized to mean "a specter or apparition" of some kind. Perhaps the most startling specialization has taken place with the word *girl*; even as late as Chaucer's time it was used to mean "a young person of either sex."

—Richard R. Lodwig and Eugene F. Barrett, *The Dictionary and the Language* (New York: Hayden, 1967), p. 159.

ORDER OF FAMILIARITY: FROM THE MORE FAMILIAR TO THE LESS FAMILIAR. When the details in the expository paragraph are mostly factual, it is common to begin with the most obvious or familiar detail and move toward the less obvious or less familiar detail. This is the pattern of the following paragraph about the expenses of smoking cigarettes. The writer begins with details that most people would consider when thinking about expense: the price. Then the writer discusses the less obvious or familiar expense of smoking cigarettes: the cleaning expenses. Read the paragraph and note how the writer connects the more obvious expense to the less obvious expense:

Smoking cigarettes can be an expensive habit. Considering that the average price per pack of cigarettes is about one dollar, people who smoke two packs of cigarettes a day spend $2 per day on their habit. At the end of one year these smokers have spent at least $730. But the cost of cigarettes is not the only expense cigarette smokers incur. Since cigarette smoke has an offensive odor that permeates clothing, stuffed furniture and carpet, smokers often find that they must have these items cleaned more frequently than nonsmokers do. Although it is difficult to estimate the cost of this additional expense, one can see that this hidden expense does contribute to making cigarette smoking an expensive habit.

ORDER OF TIME: FROM THE PAST TO THE PRESENT. When the details and examples in a paragraph are taken from history or are events that have taken place in the past, it is often a good idea to order the examples according to chronology.

The seventeenth century was a period of great advances in science. For example, early in this century Galileo perfected the telescope and in 1609 published "The Sidereal Messenger," in which he reported the results of his observations of the Milky Way, the moon, and the planet Jupiter. Only a few years later, the Dutch scientist, Anton van Leeuwenhoek performed pioneering research with the microscope, discovering among other things that weevils, fleas, and other minute creatures come from eggs rather than being spontaneously generated. Not long after this, William Harvey, an English physician, discovered the method by which blood circulates in humans and other animals and in 1628 published his findings in the historic treatise "On the Motion of the Heart and Blood in Animals." Finally, in the 1660s, Isaac Newton discovered the law of gravitation and the laws governing the physics of light, and he also invented differential calculus.

EXERCISE 4-13

Study the following topic sentences and their supporting details. Rearrange the support so that each detail is in its most logical position. Remember, there is no set order, but you must be able to justify your choices.

1. China has suffered from some of the worst disasters in history.
   a. The worst disaster of all time occurred in 1931, when the Huang He River flooded, killing 3.7 million people.
   b. On January 24, 1556, 830,000 people died in an earthquake.
   c. In 1642, 300,000 Chinese perished as a result of flood waters.
   d. In 1887, the Huang He River flooded, causing the death of 900,000 Chinese.
   e. The year 1927 saw another devastating earthquake, killing 200,000 people.
   f. As recently as 1976, there was an earthquake in Tangshan that killed 242,000 people.
   g. In 1982 and 1983, over 1,700 people died from floods.
2. American women have been fighting for equal rights for over one hundred years.
   a. In 1920, the Nineteenth Amendment to the Constitution was adopted. This amendment gave women the right to vote.
   b. In 1976, the U.S. military academies admitted women for the first time.
   c. Women began to fight for better working conditions in New York in 1868.
   d. In 1978, Congress passed the Pregnancy Disability Bill, which makes pregnancy an insurable disability.
   e. Women were still fighting to get the Equal Rights Amendment passed in 1980.
   f. Congress passed an act forbidding discrimination on the basis of sex by employers of fifteen or more employees in 1964.
3. Any household repair, no matter how complicated, is made easier if you use the right tool for the job.
   a. To make holes in wood and for marking the place where a screw or nail goes in, you can use the scratch awl. It is about 6 inches long and has a wooden handle shaped like a 25-watt lightbulb.

b. A claw-hammer is useful because its curved prongs pull out tacks and nails.
c. Side-cutting, square-nosed pliers are used for cutting and stripping wires.
d. A smaller tack hammer is designed to hammer in tacks or headless nails on surfaces that are easily bruised by a larger striking force.
e. Needle-nosed pliers have long and narrow noses that allow you to apply strong pressure for bending or straightening metal objects even in hard-to-reach areas.
f. A gimlet, which looks like a long corkscrew, is used for drilling the start of a hole before inserting the screw.
g. Of course, you always need a good set of screwdrivers of varying sizes, along with a Phillips head screwdriver.*

4. Some people think that enjoying work is more important than the amount of money earned.
   a. Mary Bright, an Atlanta cab driver, has an annual income of $7,800. She is fifty-three and has been driving a taxi since 1961. She says "I love it."
   b. Bob Jones, a fifty-five-year-old patrol officer in Boston, has been on the job twenty-five years. He likes it a lot and thinks his salary of $23,000 is just fine. "Everything about it is great except for the politicians," he says.
   c. Susan Smith helps build homes in Concord, New Hampshire, for $5,000 a year. It's enough for her to get by on while she pursues a second profession in art.
   d. Al Johnson of Wyoming could be making more doing maintenance on the government's Minuteman missile system. Instead, he makes $10,000 a year as a photographic technician for the Wyoming Fish and Game Dept.
   e. Sixty-year-old Roberta Howell is a senior food service aide at Tampa General Hospital in Florida. Although she could make more in New York, she is satisfied with the $15,000 she earns per year and loves her home in Tampa.

EXERCISE 4-14: WRITING ASSIGNMENT

Every culture has proverbs. Some popular ones in the United States are "The early bird catches the worm" and "A stitch in time saves nine." Think of a popular proverb in your country and translate it into good English. Using the proverb as your topic sentence, write a paragraph with an anecdote from your life that shows the truth of this statement.

---

*Adapted from J. Flanagan, "Tools for the Task," *The Consumers' Almanac, 1989* (1988), p. 100.

Transitional Words and Phrases

Not only should sentences and ideas in a paragraph be logically arranged, but they should flow smoothly as well. Expressions such as *next, then, after that,* and the like signal time sequence; expressions such as *above, farther on, next to,* and so forth signal location. These types of words and phrases help to achieve coherence by establishing the relationship between sentences in a paragraph. Because they provide transitions —links or connectors—between ideas and sentences by signaling what is going to follow, they are called *transitional words and phrases.* Here the focus is on some transitions to be used to achieve coherence in the expository paragraph developed by example.

- *An example of, the most significant example.* These expressions are used to identify the example in the sentence; this approach is probably more commonly used for illustrations.

> *An example of* a brilliant scientist is Albert Einstein.

It is also a good way to clarify the significance of the example, especially when your paragraph goes from least important to most important:

> *The most startling example* of a word that has specialized in meaning is *girl.*
>
> *One of the best-known examples* of fish destruction in the United States took place in 1955. . . .

- *Another example, an additional example.* These expressions are used to introduce the second or third example for the same generalization when the examples are equally significant.

> *Another example of* a brilliant scientist is Georg Ohm.

- *To illustrate.* This infinitive phrase is used to introduce an illustration and is generally placed at the beginning of the sentence:

> *To illustrate,* let us look at a topic sentence to identify the topic and controlling idea.

- *For example, for instance.* These expressions are the most frequently used transitional words for introducing examples and illustrations. They occur most often at the beginning of a sentence, but they can be placed in the middle of the sentence (after the introductory phrase, after the verb phrase, or after the subject) and at the end.

> Take, *for example,* the tornado that hit Wichita Falls. (after the verb)
>
> In the paragraph describing a room, *for example,* the author begins with the first thing the viewer sees. . . . (after the introductory phrase)

For instance, let us say that you made the simple generalization in this topic sentence: Tornadoes can be devastating. (beginning)

Let us say, *for instance,* that you made the simple generalization. . . . (after the verb)
Let us say that you wrote a long letter, *for example.* (end)

- ***First, second, next, then, last, finally.*** **These transitional expressions, also used to indicate chronological order, can be used to signal examples, especially when the examples are given in time order. They can also be used when it is established that a limited number of things are to be discussed; these terms signal the progression of the discussion.**

There are several things that I do not like about registration. *First,* it takes too long. The entire process takes the average student three hours. *Second,* it is too impersonal. No one knows your name, not even the counselors who stamp their names on your registration card. *Next,* I do not like the atmosphere where registration is held. The constant sound of voices is irritating and so are the fluorescent lights, which make everyone look a little sick. And *finally,* I do not like the way it is organized. First-year students always get in last; consequently, they end up with classes at inconvenient times.

- ***To begin with.*** **This expression can often be used instead of *first.***
- ***Also, furthermore, moreover, in addition, besides that.*** **These expressions are used to number or to include more information about an idea already stated.**

This tornado destroyed an entire block of homes and damaged many other houses and places of business. *In addition,* the tornado caused the death of over twenty people.

This tornado destroyed an entire block of homes and damaged many other houses and places of business. *Moreover,* the tornado caused the death of over twenty people.

Also, the tornado caused the death of over twenty people.

Besides that, the tornado caused the death of over twenty people.

Furthermore, the tornado caused the death of over twenty people.

These expressions can be placed at the beginning of a sentence or at the beginning of an independent clause joined to another independent clause. In the latter case, you need to punctuate as follows:

This tornado destroyed an entire block of homes; *in addition,* it caused the death of over twenty people.

The expressions *moreover* and *also* can occur after the subject:

The tornado, *moreover,* caused the death of over twenty people. (use commas)

The tornado *also* caused the death of over twenty people. (no commas)

> **Special Note: *besides***
>
> ***Besides*** means approximately the same as ***in addition;*** that is, it indicates a supplement to a point just started. However, ***besides*** is usually considered less formal. It is generally a good idea to use ***in addition*** in formal essays.

- *Finally, in conclusion.* These expressions signal the last example or the conclusion of a paragraph:

In conclusion, although I do not like the registration process, I know that at this point I have no choice but to go through with it.

Remember, there are many ways to achieve coherence; do not rely entirely on one way. Try to use a variety of coherence devices—a mixture of clauses, phrases, and transitional expressions. Do not overdo the use of transitions; it could be repetitious. Generally, two or three transitional expressions in a paragraph are sufficient.

EXERCISE 4-15

Which of the transitions in the preceding lesson would be appropriate in the following blanks? Make a list of those that fit in each blank.

Although the United States has become an advanced technological country, many old-fashioned superstitions still remain. ____________, when walking down a street in New York City past ingeniously built skyscrapers, you might see a sophisticated New Yorker walk around instead of under a ladder. Of course, he or she knows that walking under a ladder brings bad luck. Or, should a black cat wander from a back alley to that same bustling street, some people would undoubtedly cross to the other side of the street to avoid letting a black cat cross their paths. ____________, it is true that most buildings in the United States do not have a thirteenth floor and many theaters do not have a thirteenth row. Again, we all know that thirteen is an unlucky number. ____________, if you take a drive through Pennsylvania Dutch country, you will see large colorful symbols called hex signs attached to houses and barns. Of course, the people who live there say they are just for decoration, but sometimes I wonder.

EXERCISE 4-16

Using transitions studied in the preceding lesson, add transitions to the following paragraphs wherever appropriate.

1. In the past several years, we have become much more aware of hazardous conditions in the environment. Scientists recently reported that ozone, the natural shield protecting us from the sun's ultraviolet rays, has declined significantly. They noted that a hole in the ozone layer over Antarctica has developed and blamed the widespread use of certain chemicals for the ozone decrease. Scientists have warned us about the greenhouse effect, the gradual warming of the earth because the heat from the sun's rays is prevented from radiating back into space by a blanket of artificial gases. The chief gas in the greenhouse effect is carbon dioxide, a byproduct of burning fossil fuels in cars and factories. Waste disposal has become a significant problem. We not only have tons and tons of household garbage to get rid of, but we also have hazardous waste from nuclear facilities and plants. While all of these are significant problems that must be solved in the near future, at least we are now more aware of them.

2. When surnames began appearing in Europe eight hundred years ago, a person's identity and occupation were often intertwined. A surname was a direct link between who a person was and what the person did. Taylor is the Old English spelling of tailor, and Clark is derived from clerk, an occupation of considerable status during the Middle Ages because it required literacy. The names Walker, Wright, Carter, Stewart, and Turner indicate occupations. A walker was someone who cleaned cloth; a wright was a carpenter or metalworker; a carter was someone who drove a cart; a steward was a person in charge of a farm or estate; and a turner worked a lathe. One of the few occupational surnames reflecting the work of women is Webster, which refers to a female weaver.*

EXERCISE 4-17: WRITING ASSIGNMENT

Choose one of the following writing assignments.

1. **Develop a topic sentence about superstitions in your country. Then write a paragraph of support using examples.**
2. **Develop a topic sentence about polluting the environment. Support it with specific examples in a paragraph.**

---

*Information from *The Times Picayune*, 17 June, 1984, sec. 3, p. 5.

GRAMMAR REVIEW

Verb Tense Review: The Present Perfect vs. the Simple Past

An important verb tense that is useful not only for expository writing but for all kinds of writing is the *present perfect tense*. Since the time period referred to in the present perfect tense is often the same as in the simple past tense, these two tenses are often confused. Study the following paragraph and note the use of the present perfect and simple past tenses:

Before I came to the United States to study, I was afraid. I heard from my friends about widespread crime in the United States and about the unfriendliness of Americans. Since my arrival here six months ago, I can say I have been pleasantly surprised. I have not found crime everywhere, and, while not all Americans have been friendly, many of them have. In fact, I have found this country to be as safe and almost as friendly as the one I left. Let me give you an example. One night two weeks ago, I had to walk back to the dorm from a friend's house. It was quite late and the streets were lonely and deserted. As I was walking along, I saw a man walking toward me. I said to myself, "Oh no, this is it." But when the stranger finally got close to me, he just said "hey man" and kept walking. I realized then that America is not as dangerous as I thought.

EXERCISE 4-18

On a separate sheet of paper, answer the following questions about the preceding paragraph.

1. What is the controlling idea in this paragraph? Where is it stated?
2. How many examples does the writer use?

THE PRESENT PERFECT TENSE. The present perfect tense (*has/have* + past participle) indicates a state or action that started in the past and continues to the present moment. It indicates that that state or action is relevant to the present time. The duration of the state or action is often indicated or implied.

Since my arrival here six months ago, I can say I *have been* pleasantly *surprised.* (The duration of time here is from the arrival until the present.)

My hometown *has changed* from a friendly small town into a busy modern suburb. (Although the duration of time is not stated, it is implied — from the time I lived there until the present.)

The present perfect tense is also used to indicate an action that has been completed at some *indefinite* time in the past, usually in the recent past.

The president *has signed* the bill into law. (No specific time of the signing is given, but it was probably recently.)

The present perfect tense is used as well to indicate that an action that occurred in the past has the capability of happening again.

I *have had* three headaches today. (This person will probably have another one.)

There *have been* six hijackings this week. (It is possible that there will be another hijacking).

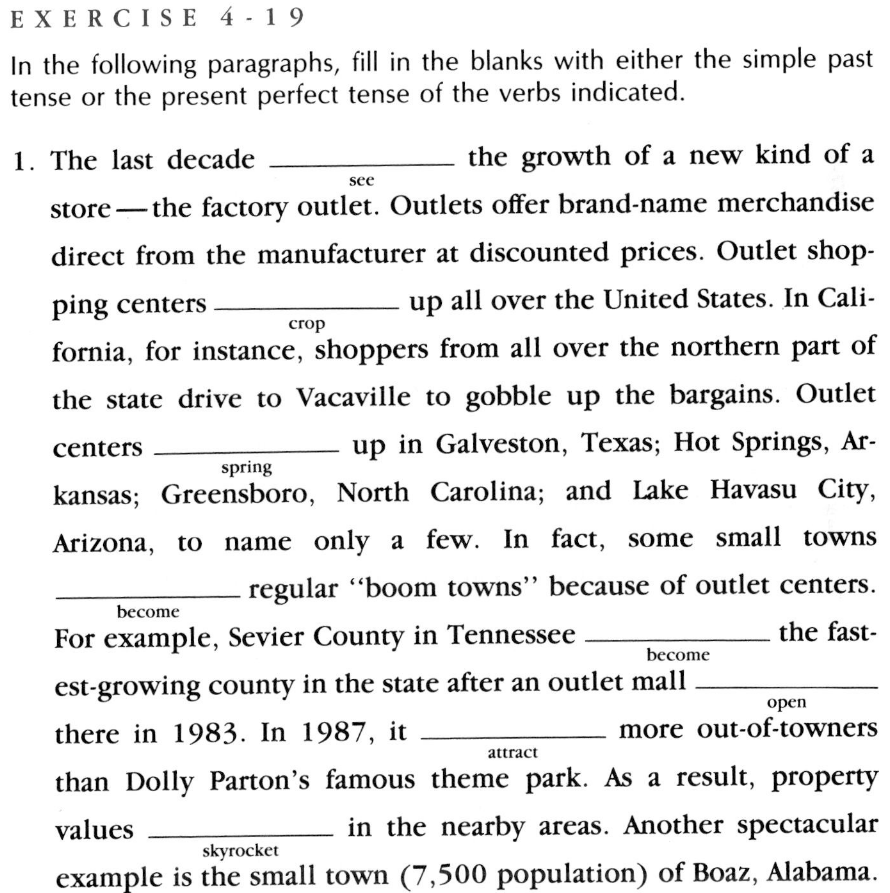

EXERCISE 4-19

In the following paragraphs, fill in the blanks with either the simple past tense or the present perfect tense of the verbs indicated.

1. The last decade ____________ (see) the growth of a new kind of a store—the factory outlet. Outlets offer brand-name merchandise direct from the manufacturer at discounted prices. Outlet shopping centers ____________ (crop) up all over the United States. In California, for instance, shoppers from all over the northern part of the state drive to Vacaville to gobble up the bargains. Outlet centers ____________ (spring) up in Galveston, Texas; Hot Springs, Arkansas; Greensboro, North Carolina; and Lake Havasu City, Arizona, to name only a few. In fact, some small towns ____________ (become) regular "boom towns" because of outlet centers. For example, Sevier County in Tennessee ____________ (become) the fastest-growing county in the state after an outlet mall ____________ (open) there in 1983. In 1987, it ____________ (attract) more out-of-towners than Dolly Parton's famous theme park. As a result, property values ____________ (skyrocket) in the nearby areas. Another spectacular example is the small town (7,500 population) of Boaz, Alabama. It ____________ (experience) an even more amazing rebirth. Since 1982, five outlet shopping centers ____________ (attract) there. These centers attract as many as 75,000 shoppers on a good weekend. Sales-tax revenues ____________ (increase) from $665,000 to $4 million since

1982. On one Saturday in 1988, ninety-eight buses ______ (pull) into the town filled with eager shoppers. Although some of the more traditional store chains may not be as enthusiastic as the shoppers, you can bet that people will continue to flock to outlet malls.*

2. Although computer programmers ______ (make) some progress in designing programs enabling humans to talk to computers, they still have a long way to go. The company that ______ (make) the most progress in this area so far is the Artificial Intelligence Corporation. This company recently ______ (produce) a program that can respond to limited conversational English, if it has a specific data base. Since 1981, the company ______ (install) more than two hundred copies of the program in companies such as Federal Express, Citibank, and Atlantic Richfield. The success of this program ______ (encourage) other companies to turn from pure research to the field of business. Two other companies already ______ (enter) this infant marketplace. Last August, Texas Instruments ______ (release) Natural Link, which constructs questions from a list of acceptable phrases. Another firm, Cognitive Systems, Inc., ______ (pursue) a more ambitious course, designing programs for specific companies.

Despite the limited success of these programs, conversations with computers are still limited and dull. In fact, researchers ______ (be) more optimistic about conversing with computers thirty years ago than they are today. At the dawn of the computer age, computer programmers ______ (write) many programs to translate from Russian or English into other languages. Their approach ______ (be) quite straightforward. A Russian to English program, for example, simply ______ (look) up each Russian word in a bilingual dictionary and ______ (rearrange) the English

*Information from A. Miller, with E. Williams and J. Howard, "Bargain Basements Move Upscale," *Newsweek* 19 Dec. 1988, pp. 40–41.

equivalents into a sensible sentence. Unfortunately, these literal translations often ____________ (leave) much to be desired. When programmers ____________ (translate) the biblical text "the spirit is willing but the flesh is weak" from Russian it ____________ (become) "the wine is agreeable but the meat is spoiled." Another program ____________ (translate) the advertising slogan "Coke adds life" into the Chinese equivalent "Coke brings our ancestors back from the grave."

Even with the new advances that some companies ____________ (make), it will still be some time before we will be having interesting conversations with computers.*

ADVERBIALS USED WITH THE PRESENT PERFECT AND SIMPLE PAST TENSES. Note the position of the following adverbs. They usually occur at the end of a sentence. However, for emphasis or variety, these adverbs and adverbial phrases can also be placed at the beginning of a sentence.

	PRESENT PERFECT		SIMPLE PAST
Today	I haven't seen him today.	*Today*	I saw him at school today.
		Yesterday	I broke my arm yesterday.
This week	It has rained three times this week (year, month)	*Last week (This week)*	It rained three times last week (month, etc.).
In my life	I have done some silly things in my life.		
Up to now	He has been successful up to now.		
So far	We have won every race so far.		
Recently	Three shows have been cancelled recently.	*Recently*	Three shows were cancelled recently.
Lately	Have you seen any good movies lately?		
Since	I have lived in New York since May. (This means that I am still living in New York.)		

*Information from "Hacking in Plain English," *Psychology Today*, June 1984, p. 42.

	PRESENT PERFECT		SIMPLE PAST
For	I have lived in New York for three years. (This means the last three years, I am still living in New York.)	*For*	I lived in New York for three years. (This means that I no longer live in New York. I once lived there.)

The following adverbial phrase can be placed only at the end of the sentence.

			SIMPLE PAST
		Ago	I lived in New York two years ago. (This means I no longer live in New York.)

Note: A time expression that follows *since* represents a point in time:

I have been here *since three o'clock.*

We have been in the city *since Friday.*

A time expression that follows *for* represents an amount of time:

I have been in Canada *for three years.*

We have studied at the university *for two months.*

The following adverbs have definite restrictions on their placement:

- *Just.* *Just* can occur only in the middle of the sentence after the first auxiliary verb. *Just* indicates that the action was completed a few months ago; it is in the very recent past.

  We have *just* eaten dinner.

- *Already.* *Already* can occur in two places: after the first auxiliary verb or at the end of the sentence. *Already* is used in affirmative statements to emphasize that the action has occurred. It implies that the action occurred earlier than expected.

  He has *already* finished his homework.

  He has finished his homework *already.*

- *Yet.* *Yet* can also occur in two places: after the first auxiliary verb or at the end of the sentence. *Yet* is used in negative statements to emphasize that the action has not occurred.

  They have not *yet* gone to school.

  They have not gone to school *yet.*

Note that none of these adverbs—*just, already, yet*—can occur at the beginning of the sentence.

EXERCISE 4-20

Write the information and relevant dates for each of the following situations. Then write three sentences for each one, using *ago*, *since*, and *for* and either the present perfect tense or simple past tense as appropriate. The first one is done for you.

1. The first school you attended and the dates you attended it: Lakewood Elementary School—1968–1974
   a. I first went to Lakewood Elementary School twenty-two years ago.
   b. I haven't been there since 1974.
   c. I attended that school for seven years.

2. The next school you attended and the dates you attended it: ______
   ______
   a. ______
   b. ______
   c. ______

3. Your current school and when you started there: ______
   ______
   a. ______
   b. ______
   c. ______

4. Something you learned to do and when you learned it: ______
   ______
   a. ______
   b. ______
   c. ______

EXERCISE 4-21

Using the following information,* write three sentences for each item. Use *ago, since,* and *for* and either the present perfect tense or simple past tense as appropriate. The first one is done for you.

*Information from L. Sprague De Camp, *The Heroic Age of American Invention* (Garden City, N.Y.: Doubleday, 1961).

1. *1791*—Eli Whitney, a native of Connecticut working in Georgia, took out a patent on the cotton gin.
   The cotton gin separates seeds from cotton.
   Today's machines are built on the same principle as Whitney's.
   a. Eli Whitney invented the cotton gin over 190 years ago.
   b. Machines have been used to separate seeds from cotton for 191 years.
   c. The principle used in Whitney's cotton gin has been in use since 1791.
2. *1815*—Robert Fulton, from Pennsylvania, built the first steam warship. Steam warships were used until the early twentieth century.
   a. ______________________________
   b. ______________________________
   c. ______________________________
3. *1831*—Cyrus McCormick, from Pennsylvania, demonstrated his first grain harvester. It cut as much grain as six people with scythes or twenty-four with sickles. Improved McCormick harvesters are still in use.
   a. ______________________________
   b. ______________________________
   c. ______________________________
4. *1869*—George Westinghouse, born in New York, got the first patent on air brakes for trains.

   Air brakes use compressed air in a cylinder to stop a train.
   a. ______________________________
   b. ______________________________
   c. ______________________________
5. *1903*—Orville and Wilbur Wright, from Ohio, flew the first small-engine aircraft. Improved engine aircraft are still used.
   a. ______________________________
   b. ______________________________
   c. ______________________________

EXERCISE 4-22: WRITING ASSIGNMENT

Using the information in Exercise 4-21, write a paragraph developed by examples. First, look at the information to decide on a topic sentence with a controlling idea. What generalization can you make? Can you make a better, more concise generalization if you omit some of the information? If so, omit what you like. Then write your paragraph, using examples to support the topic sentence. Be sure to use transitions as well.

EXERCISE 4-23

In the following verb tense review exercise, use the tense that you think is most appropriate. You may use any of the verb tenses studied so far.

By the time I reached the middle of my law career, I __________ (become) a workaholic. That __________ (be) two years ago. Then Tim, an old high school friend, __________ (persuade) me to take a break. Together we __________ (plan) a 250-mile walk down the New Jersey and Delaware coasts.

On Day Four of the expedition, I __________ (call) my office and __________ (announce) that I __________ (extend) my vacation a few more days. "You sound like a different person," my secretary __________ (say). By Day Seven of the walk a remarkable strength and vigor __________ (come) over me.

Tim, meanwhile, __________ (undergo) a dramatic transformation of his own. Before the marathon, he __________ (be) a chain smoker and normally __________ (go) through two or three packs a day. As we __________ (increase) our daily walking distance from eighteen to twenty-five miles, however, he __________ (smoke) fewer cigarettes, and before long he __________ (replace) the smoking habit with the walking habit.

What __________ (happen) to the two of us __________ (be) an example of what I __________ (call) the natural powers of walking. By merely increasing the amount of daily walking—without regard to technique or exercise regimen—you __________ (benefit) greatly. Research done since 1960 __________ (show) that walking __________ (be) the most efficient exercise for improving overall fitness. It __________ (use) more muscles in a continuous uniform action than most other forms of exercise, and it __________ (remain) accessible to you throughout your life. Since that research, doctors often __________ (use) it as an integral part of medical programs to prevent heart-related diseases and to rehabilitate those already stricken with heart trouble.

If your walking muscles __________ (decline), then your whole body __________ (decline). So you might as well give walking your fullest attention; it __________ (be) the best life insurance policy around.*

Definite and Indefinite Articles

Since the articles in English (*a, an, the, some*) are troublesome for many students, it is useful to review the use of these articles now.

THE INDEFINITE ARTICLE. The most common use of the indefinite article *a* (*an* before a vowel sound) is to signal an unspecified item. Note the examples:

He wants *a* bicycle.

A man is at the door.

A picnic is always fun.

Note that there is not an attempt to make the noun specific. The noun is indefinite. This indefiniteness is indicated in the plural of countable nouns with *some* or with no article at all. When no article is used, the noun itself is emphasized. With *some*, the indefiniteness is emphasized.

He wants *some* bicycles.

Some men are at the door.

Picnics are always fun.

A singular countable noun always requires an article, even if an adjective precedes it:

I need *a* new car.

The only time an article is not necessary before a single countable noun is when another determiner is used instead:

I need this new car.

We need another new car.

However, a noncountable noun cannot be preceded by the indefinite article *a*.

I requested new information.

But *some* can be used with noncountable nouns:

I bought *some* gasoline this morning.

*Adapted from Gary D. Yanker, "Walk Your Way to Health and Fitness," *Reader's Digest*, June 1984, pp. 141–142.

EXERCISE 4-24

Put the article *a/an* in the blank if it is needed. If the indefinite article is not necessary, put "O."

1. I used to play __________ soccer for my high school team.
2. He gave me __________ good advice.
3. This is __________ difficult situation.
4. Superman is __________ example of a fictional hero.
5. I like __________ Indian food because it's spicy.
6. We had __________ bad weather last week.
7. __________ anecdote is __________ type of illustration.
8. We wrote __________ book about our travels in Guatemala.
9. John is going to build __________ garage next week.
10. __________ exercise is important for good __________ health.

THE DEFINITE ARTICLE. The definite article *the* signals a specific or particular person, place, or thing. Nouns can be made specific in several ways.

1. The noun has been identified in a previous sentence. When the noun is first mentioned, it is unspecified, so the article *a* may be used. The first mention of the noun serves to identify it. When it is mentioned a second time, the article *the* is used:

   We bought *a* new car last year. After we got *the* car home, one of its tires went flat.

   I ordered *some* soup from the delicatessen. When *the* soup arrived, it was cold.

2. The noun has a modifying phrase or clause in the sentence that identifies it as a specific item.

   The information *that I got from this book* was helpful.

   The information *in this book* was helpful.

   Notice in the following sentence *information* is unspecified; it means information in a general sense. Therefore, no article is used:

   Information comes to us in a variety of ways.

   In certain situations with a modifying phrase or clause, *the* is omitted. ***The*** is used with modifying phrases or clauses when the sentence is not a generalization but is about one event:

The cars in the driveway just had their tires stolen.

The luggage in the cars was also stolen.

In a generalization when the modifying phrase or clause limits the noun to one item in a class, ***the*** is also used:

The car in the driveway is a good one.

However, ***the*** is often omitted in generalizations (and sometimes must be) when the modifying phrase or clause is not referring to one item in a class but merely serves to narrow down the class. Compare with the previous sentences:

Cars from Germany are quite expensive.

Luggage that is made of leather is also expensive.

3. The situation identifies the noun. When both the writer and reader are familiar with the item that is being referred to, ***the*** is used. Often there is only one such item.

   Let's go to *the* post office.

   John just returned from *the* doctor.

   Where is *the* baby?

4. The noun is specific because it is unique.

   When I look at *the* sky, I am filled with wonder.

   Hurricanes usually come from *the* south.

5. The use of superlatives, ranking adjectives, and ordinal numbers makes a noun specific.

   He was definitely *the* most exciting singer.

   The main speaker is next.

   The first person in line got the prize.

EXERCISE 4-25

Put *a*, *an*, or *the* in the blanks. If no article is needed, put "O."

1. ____________ life brings many strange events.
2. ____________ food is necessary for survival.
3. ____________ food we had at that restaurant was excellent.
4. ____________ most useful magazines are those that tell you how to do something.

5. We all have ____________ need for ____________ love.
6. ____________ fascinating place to visit is Samoa.
7. It is difficult to estimate ____________ cost of his hidden expenses.
8. One example of ____________ useful invention is ____________ cotton gin.
9. ____________ extended example is often called ____________ illustration.
10. He always puts his coat in ____________ closet when he gets home.
11. All of ____________ dogs in ____________ neighborhood started to bark when ____________ lights went out.
12. ____________ people who do not eat meat are generally healthy.
13. Let's go to ____________ grocery store. I need ____________ loaf of bread.
14. ____________ books about ____________ economy are quite popular right now.
15. Please shut ____________ window.
16. Rosa bought ____________ new white dress and hat for graduation. Unfortunately, ____________ dress was too big.
17. We saw ____________ woman with ____________ baby on ____________ Main Street bus. ____________ woman was frantic because ____________ baby was sick and crying. ____________ passengers could not believe it when ____________ bus driver stopped ____________ bus and asked ____________ woman and baby to get off.
18. Yesterday, while we were standing at ____________ corner of Fifth and Main Streets, we saw ____________ accident. ____________ old blue Ford ran ____________ red light and crashed into ____________ white van that was going through ____________ intersection. ____________ old man who owns ____________ little grocery store on ____________ corner called ____________ police.

EXERCISE 4-26

Study the following paragraphs and insert *a*, *an*, *the*, or "*O*" (for no article) in the blanks.

1. Word processors are great for people who can type, but what about ____________ people who can't type? Ralph Sklarew has solved ____________ problem. He has invented ____________ computer that doesn't have ____________ keyboard. Instead, it has a screen that you write on with ____________ special pencil. ____________ computer translates ____________ handwritten letters into its own code. ____________ inventor sees many ____________ uses for ____________ lap-top computer. For example, it is good for filling out forms. Homeowner's insurance agents and adjusters, for example, fill out ____________ considerable number of ____________ forms when they measure rooms and list their contents. This computer can take down all this information, then calculate ____________ square footage and add up value automatically. In ____________ suburb of Chicago, ____________ nurses are experimenting with using ____________ machine to keep track of ____________ emergency-room supplies. Sklarew also foresees lawyers and executives using ____________ machine to keep notes and write ____________ memos. He says, "Eventually, it could be used for taking ____________ notes over ____________ phone, in ____________ schools, or in ____________ workplace. That's all on ____________ way."*

2. ____________ usual answer to ____________ obstreperous stream, one that erodes or floods out its banks, is to build ____________ dam. But ____________ dams cost up to $100,000 apiece, even for ____________ very small streams. Now, ____________ Bureau of Land Management (BLM) is cutting

*Adapted from T. Waters, "Back to Basics," *Discover The World of Science*, 9 (Dec. 1988): pp. 26–27.

costs by using local labor: beavers. For three years, __________ three beavers have been at work on Wyoming's Current Creek, whose spring runoff had yearly gouged out its banks and flooded neighboring farms. There were no trees left for __________ beavers to use, so __________ BLM helped by dragging __________ apsens from __________ distant forest. It also wired __________ truck tires together and laid them across __________ stream, making __________ sturdy foundations for __________ beavers' dams. It worked. __________ beavers restored __________ creek's ecological balance and saved its banks from erosion. __________ dams slowed __________ stream, and nutrient-rich silt has settled behind them. __________ rye grass and __________ willows are coming back along __________ banks, and spring flooding has been regulated; __________ creek now widens by about 50 feet. __________ cost to __________ federal government? Less than $3,000.*

ARTICLES WITH QUANTIFIERS. The following quantifiers indicate a number or amount:

USED WITH PLURAL-COUNT NOUNS	USED WITH NONCOUNT NOUNS	USED WITH SINGULAR-COUNT NOUNS
few (students)	little (money)	one (student)
a few	a little	each
several	some	every
some	much	neither, either
many	any	no
any	all	
most	no	
all		
no		
both		
two, three, and so on.		

*Adapted from "Toxic Wastes—Another Solution?" *Science Digest*, July 1984, p. 36.

Examples:

Some students spoke out about the restrictions.

John has a little money.

Neither student was late.

In these examples, the quantifiers indicate how many or how much of something there is.

Special Note: *a few/a little; few/little*

These words refer to a small quantity or amount of something. *Few* and *little* have a negative meaning. They indicate dissatisfaction.

I have *few* friends. (I am unhappy about it.)

I have *little* time. (I cannot help you.)

A few and *a little* have a positive meaning. They indicate satisfaction.

I have *a few* friends. (And I am happy about it.)

I have *a little* time. (It is enough. I can help you.)

We can add *of the* after all of the quantifiers listed earlier.

Some *of the* students spoke out about the restrictions.

John has a little *of the* money.

Neither *of the* students was late.

Notice that when we add *of the* to the quantifiers with singular-count nouns, the noun becomes plural but the verb remains singular, agreeing with the singular subject (*neither, each,* and so on).

One of the students *is* late.

Each of the students *has* agreed to help.

In the lists given previously, there are two exceptions. *Every* must become *every one* and *no* must become *not one* or *none*.

Every one of the apples *is* rotten. (This means "every single one.")

None of the teachers *is* coming.

In informal usage, the following is also acceptable:

None of the teachers *are* coming.

When *of the* is added to the quantifiers listed previously, the meaning changes. Because the definite article was added, there is a definite meaning: part of an already known group or item. In the sentence, *"Some of the students did the homework,"* the writer has either mentioned the group of students earlier or assumes the reader is familiar with the group. Perhaps he means: *"Some of the students in our class did the homework."* In the sentence, *"John has a little of the* money," perhaps he said earlier: *"John and I got some money for mowing the lawn."*

EXERCISE 4-27

Put *of the* in the blanks, if it is needed.

1. Many ____________ Americans have started to buy small cars.

   Most ____________ drivers owned large cars and station wagons before.
2. Most ____________ Americans on the trip were from California.
3. On our trip, we visited ten cities. Several ____________ cities were using solar power.
4. All ____________ people are created equal.
5. Some ____________ professional athletes receive critical injuries while playing.

EXERCISE 4-28

Rewrite the following sentences, using the quantifiers given in italics. Make any necessary changes. The first one is done for you.

1. Most of the trees are dead because of the drought.

   One One of the trees is dead because of the drought.
2. All of the books on the second floor of the library have been stolen.

   None ____________
3. Twelve of the members of Congress contact the president every day.

   Each ____________
4. Several of the basketball players are sick.

   Each ____________
5. Both of the singers also play the piano.

   Neither ____________

EXERCISE 4-29

Use *a, an, the,* or *of the* wherever you think necessary in the following paragraphs.

1. In last few years, people have become more interested in learning another language. Not only do they want to learn second language for educational purposes, but also to know more about culture. Most important for today's careers, knowing another language offers lot of opportunities.
2. I think that high schools and universities should require their students to study foreign language, for educational purposes. In my case, for example, I started to study and learn English at age 13. Even though my mother spoke only English at home and I understood most of it, it was not until I changed to bilingual school that I started to learn more and speak it more fluently.
3. At same time it was kind of fun because I was reading stories and articles that interested me. At movies I no longer had to read the translation in Spanish and at home we played all kinds of board games like Clue and Monopoly.
4. Learning another language offers lot of opportunities, too. Many jobs now require that person know another language. Jobs related to travel, hotels, and airlines are few examples. There are others, like working with government and in business. One example of this is friend of mine who recently changed jobs. She used to be working in travel agency; she said her knowledge of English made lot of things easier for her. Just few weeks ago I received letter from her saying that she is now working with U.S. Embassy in Honduras. She said that without English language she wouldn't be working there.
5. As we can see, students should learn second language. There are many advantages, especially when finishing school and job opportunities are great. For me it's great experience. Without knowing English, I wouldn't be working and studying in this university.

—*Carlos Palacio*

EXERCISE 4-30: WRITING ASSIGNMENT

Choose one of the following topics for this writing assignment. In planning your paragraph, be sure to arrange your details carefully and to use specific details.

1. Discuss the techniques you use to remember important things. You can choose what you have learned through general experience or through formal education.
2. Write a paragraph about the things you don't want to forget and explain why.
3. Make a generalization about a person you know and then write a paragraph supporting that generalization with examples or an anecdote. For instance, you might begin with, "My little brother has done some amusing things." You could support this generalization with an illustration, an anecdote, or perhaps you could give several examples of amusing things he had done.

Expository Paragraph Checklist

1. An expository paragraph supports the controlling idea with explanation, facts, and illustrations. Does your paragraph use sufficient details and examples?
2. The controlling idea, or generalization, of an expository paragraph conveys the writer's attitude about the topic. Does your paragraph have a clear, focused generalization?
3. The organization of details and support of the generalization in an expository paragraph depends on the subject and the writer's logic. Are the generalization and support logically arranged in your paragraph?
4. Is your paragraph unified; that is, do all the sentences support the controlling idea?
5. Is your paragraph coherent; that is, do the sentences flow smoothly?

Unit Two

THE ESSAY

Chapter 5

Introduction to the Essay

Emphasis thus far has been on writing paragraphs with good, detailed support. Since a paragraph develops only one idea, the topics being developed are necessarily quite limited. Often, however, topics are too complex or too broad to be developed in a single paragraph. In this case, it is necessary to write an *essay*. An essay is a group of paragraphs that develops one central idea. How are the paragraphs organized in an essay? How many paragraphs are there in an essay? How does an essay begin and end? These are questions this unit will answer.

Unlike the paragraph, the essay is a more formal composition. Each paragraph in an essay has a designated function:

1. *Introduction.* The introduction is usually one paragraph (sometimes two or more) that introduces the topic to be discussed and the central idea (the thesis statement) of the essay.

2. *Developmental paragraphs.* These paragraphs develop various aspects of the topic and the central idea. They may discuss causes, effects, reasons, examples, processes, classifications, or points of comparison and contrast. They may also describe or narrate.

3. *Conclusion.* This paragraph concludes the thought developed in the essay. It is the closing word.

How many paragraphs an essay contains depends entirely on the complexity of the topic; some essays have only two or three paragraphs, whereas others may have twenty or thirty. However, for most purposes, the essays written in class for most first-year college English courses contain from four to six paragraphs, with the most common number being five: one introductory paragraph, three developmental paragraphs, and one concluding paragraph.

✓

The Thesis Statement

The essay, like the paragraph, is controlled by one central idea. In the essay, the sentence containing the central idea is called the *thesis statement.* The thesis statement is similar to the topic sentence in that it contains an expression of an attitude, opinion, or idea about a topic; unlike the topic sentence, however, the thesis statement is broader and expresses the controlling idea for the entire essay. In fact, each of the developmental paragraphs should have a controlling idea that echoes or relates to the controlling idea—the central idea—in the thesis statement.

Here are a few points to remember about the thesis statement.

1. *The thesis statement should be expressed in a complete sentence.* Since the thesis statement is the main statement for the entire essay, it should express a complete thought; therefore, it should be expressed in a complete sentence. And since it makes a statement, it should not be written as a question.

Not a thesis statement:

My fear of the dark.

Thesis statement:

My fear of the dark has made my life miserable.

2. *A thesis statement expresses an opinion, attitude, or idea; it does not simply announce the topic the essay will develop.*

Not a thesis statement:

I am going to discuss the effects of radiation.

Thesis statement:

The effects of radiation are often unpredictable.

3. *A thesis statement should express an opinion; it should not express a fact.* Since the thesis statement expresses an attitude, opinion, or idea about a topic, the thesis statement is really a statement that someone could disagree with. The thesis statement, therefore, is a statement that needs to be explained or proved.

Not a thesis statement:

Cows produce milk.

Thesis statement:

The milk cows produce is not always fit for human consumption.

Not a thesis statement:

There are many advantages and disadvantages to going to college. (Not an arguable point.)

Thesis statement:

The advantages to going to college far outweigh the disadvantages.

4. ***A thesis statement should express only one idea toward one topic; if a thesis statement contains two or more ideas, the essay runs the risk of lacking unity and coherence.***

Not a thesis statement:

Going to college in the Midwest can be fun, and I have found that living in a suburb of a large city is the best way to live while at college.

Thesis statement:

Going to college in the Midwest can be fun.

EXERCISE 5-1

Study the following statements carefully. If the statement is a thesis statement, write *yes* in the blank; if it is not a thesis statement, write *no*.

1. ____ The advantages of majoring in engineering.
2. ____ I would like to discuss my views on the Olympic Games.
3. ____ Students should be allowed to manage the bookstore.
4. ____ When I first came to the United States, I wasn't used to eating in fast-food places, and I was amazed at the shopping centers.
5. ____ Why do I want to be a lawyer?
6. ____ The differences between Mandarin and Hunan cuisine.
7. ____ Knowing a foreign language can be beneficial to anyone.
8. ____ Being honest is important.
9. ____ I am going to describe my home.
10. ____ There are many similarities and differences between New York and Hong Kong.

EXERCISE 5-2

Study the following statements, which are not thesis statements. Rewrite each of the sentences to make it a thesis statement. The first one is done for you.

1. I am going to explain why I decided to go to college.

   Choosing to go to college was a difficult decision.
2. The hazards of storing chemical wastes.

   ____
3. There are many similarities and differences between life in the country and life in the city.

   ____
4. New York City is the largest city in the United States.

   ____
5. Universities in the U.S. should require more humanities courses; they should also have more social activities.

   ____

The Introduction

The thesis statement is the main statement for the entire essay. But where should the thesis statement be placed? Although there is no law that requires the thesis to be placed in any particular place in the essay, the thesis statement is usually in the introductory paragraph. After all, the thesis is the statement that the developmental paragraphs are going to explore. But where in the introduction should the thesis statement be placed? Before we answer this question, let us look at the characteristics of an introductory paragraph.

1. *An introductory paragraph should introduce the topic.* Do not forget that the introductory paragraph is the first thing that a reader sees. Obviously, this paragraph should inform the reader of the topic being discussed.

2. *An introductory paragraph should indicate generally how the topic is going to be developed.* A good introductory paragraph should indicate whether the essay is going to discuss causes, effects, reasons, or examples; whether the essay is going to classify, describe, narrate, or explain a process.

3. *Generally speaking, an introductory paragraph should contain the thesis statement.* This is a general rule, of course. In more sophisticated writing, the thesis statement sometimes appears later in the essay, sometimes even at the end. In some cases, too, the thesis is just implied. For college essays, however, it is a good idea to state the thesis clearly in the introduction.

4. *Ideally, an introductory paragraph should be inviting; that is, it should be interesting enough to make the reader want to continue reading.* Since the introductory paragraph functions to introduce the topic and since the introductory paragraph should be inviting, it makes good sense not to put the thesis statement right at the beginning of the introductory paragraph. Not only should you introduce the topic before you state an opinion about it (the thesis statement), but you should try to entice the reader to continue after reading the first sentence. Stating an opinion about something in the first sentence is not usually very inviting; in fact, if readers disagree with the opinion, it may very well discourage them from reading your essay. Therefore, *it is generally a good idea to place the thesis statement at or near the end of the introductory paragraph.*

Since the introduction is the first paragraph the reader reads, it is often the first paragraph the student plans and can be, therefore, the most difficult. There are many ways to begin an essay. In this text we discuss four basic types of introductions: (1) the "Turnabout," in which the author opens with a statement contrary to his or her actual thesis (Chapter 8); (2) the "Dramatic Entrance," in which the author opens with a narrative, description, or dramatic example pertinent to the topic (Chapters 9 and 10); (3) the "Relevant Quotation," in which the writer opens with a quotation pertinent to the topic (Chapter 10); and (4) the "Funnel."

The Funnel approach is perhaps the most common type of introductory paragraph. It is so-called because the ideas progress from the general to the specific just as a funnel is wide at the top and narrow at the bottom. The approach is to open with a general statement about the topic and then to work toward the more specific thesis statement at or near the end of the introduction. Not only should the opening statement be general, it should be congenial as well: do not alienate the reader. See how this technique is applied in this introductory paragraph.

> Traveling to a foreign country is always interesting, especially if it is a country that is completely different from your own. You can delight in tasting new foods, seeing new sights, and learning about different customs, some of which may seem very curious. If you were to visit my country, for instance, you would probably think that my people have some very strange customs, as these three examples will illustrate.

In this introductory paragraph, the writer introduces the general topic of "traveling to a foreign country" in the first sentence and narrows down that topic to a more specific aspect—the customs in the writer's country. The thesis statement comes at the end with the central idea being "strange." Illustrations should appear in the developmental paragraphs.

Just how general should the introductory paragraph be? One way to avoid beginning too generally or too far back is to have one key word in the first sentence reappear in the thesis statement, or if not the word itself, a synonym of the word or an idea. In the preceding paragraph, *visit* echoes *traveling*, and the word *country* appears in the first and last sentences.

Here is another example of this type of introduction, taken from a popular science magazine.

America is a throwaway society. From both industrial and municipal sources, the U.S. generates about 10 billion metric tons of solid waste per year. Every five years the average American discards, directly and indirectly, an amount of waste equal in weight to the Statue of Liberty. Municipal solid waste alone accounts for 140 million metric tons per year. The municipal solid waste produced in this country in just one day fills roughly 63,000 garbage trucks, which lined up end to end would stretch 600 kilometers, the distance from San Francisco to Los Angeles. The repercussions of our waste habits, however, stretch to every city. Let us demonstrate by example.

—P. O'Leary, P. Walsh, and R. Ham, "Managing Solid Waste," *Scientific American* 6 (Dec. 1988): p. 36.

EXERCISE 5-3

Study the following introductory paragraphs. Underline the word or words that appear in the first sentence and are restated in the thesis statement.

1. Computers are advanced machines that can store and recall information at very high speed. Computers are easy and interesting to use; however, some people are afraid of computers. I used to be afraid of computers, too, because of the fear of failure and because I knew nothing about programming. But actually I have learned that the procedures of working on computers are very easy.
   —*Nader Alyousha*
2. When we were very young, we believed that parents could do no wrong. Indeed, they seemed to us to be perfect human beings who knew all the answers to our problems and who could solve any problems that we had. However, as we grow older, we find that parents can make mistakes, too.
3. We live in an era where television is the national pastime. Since the invention of the television set, people have been spending more of their free time watching television than doing anything else. Many of the television addicts feel that this particular pastime is not a bad one; indeed, they argue that people can learn a great deal watching television. I am sure that if you look long and hard enough, you can probably find some programs that are educationally motivating. But, for the most part, I say that watching television is a waste of time.
   —*Pamela Moran*
4. Today's children are our future men and women. They will become the dominant force one day. If they receive proper guidance and have a nice childhood, they will contribute immeasurably to

our society after they have grown up. In other words, today's children are going to have a significant impact on our society in the future; therefore, parents should not neglect the proper conditions that children need during their childhood. —*Chun Lee*

5. When we see a blind person nearing a street corner or a door, many times we try to help by opening the door or taking the person's arm and guiding him or her across the street, and while we do that, some of us talk to the blind person in a loud voice, as if the blind person is not only helpless but also deaf. Rushing to help a blind person without asking if that person needs help and speaking loudly are just two of the inappropriate ways people react to blind people. If you want to help a blind person whom you perceive as in need of help, you should bear in mind the following tips.

EXERCISE 5-4

On pages 168–69 are the characteristics of a good introductory paragraph. Using those characteristics, evaluate the following introductory paragraphs. Does the paragraph introduce the topic? Does it indicate how the topic is going to be developed? Does it contain a thesis statement? Is it inviting? If one or more of these are missing, write the missing element in the space provided. Some of the paragraphs may be good introductory paragraphs.

1. We are all familiar with the image of the fat, jolly person, right? Unfortunately, this is an inaccurate stereotype. Fat people are not always so happy.

   ____

2. "We are moving to the city!" These are the words of many villagers today. When they are asked to give reasons for their movement, they simply reply that life in the city is more developed than that in the village. In the city, there are communication, transportation, education and medical services. Also there are more chances for jobs. I positively agree with these people, but have these people thought about their lives and health? Have they thought about the danger that might happen to their children? It might not be during the first six months of living, but in the future when the city becomes more inhabited by different people of different nationalities and when the streets get crowded with cars. Although the village is lacking some of the services mentioned above, it is still the best type of environment for me to live in.

   —*Habeeb Al-Saeed*

   ____

3. I would like to tell you about my hometown, Hlatikulu, Swaziland. It is a small town of only 8,000 people. The main industries there are farming and working for the government, since it is the capital of the southern region.

   ____

4. Last year, my cousin, Julio, went to a bank to apply for a job. As you know, when you apply for a job, you must be ready to answer a lot of ambiguous questions. Some of the questions that an interviewer may ask you include: educational background, previous jobs, and salaries you earned. The problem with Julio was that he wasn't prepared for the questions. The interviewer asked Julio a lot of things that he couldn't answer. Because Julio wasn't prepared for the interview, he didn't get the job. If you do not want to be in that situation, you may want to follow these steps.

—*Mauricio Rodriguez*

EXERCISE 5-5: WRITING ASSIGNMENT

Six thesis statements follow. On a separate sheet of paper, write an introductory paragraph for each one.

1. My country has some of the most beautiful sights you will ever see.
2. Speaking in a foreign language can create some embarrassing misunderstandings.
3. The wheel is one of the greatest inventions in history.
4. Watching television is not a waste of time.
5. I can suggest several improvements needed at this school.
6. The New Year is one of the happiest occasions. (You may choose a favorite holiday in your country.)

The Developmental Paragraphs

Developmental paragraphs, which range in number in the typical student essay from about two to four, are the heart of the essay, for their function is to explain, illustrate, discuss, or prove the thesis statement. Keep in mind these points about the developmental paragraphs:

1. *Each developmental paragraph discusses one aspect of the main topic*. If, for example, you were asked to write a paper about the effects of smoking cigarettes on a person's health, then each paragraph would have as its topic an effect.

2. *The controlling idea in the developmental paragraph should echo the central idea in the thesis statement*. If your thesis statement about the effects of smoking cigarettes is "Cigarette smoking is a destructive habit," then the controlling idea in each paragraph should have something to do with the destructiveness of the effects.

3. *The developmental paragraphs should have coherence and unity*. The order of your paragraphs should not be random. As you

have seen in the last three chapters, there are various ways to order the sentences in a paragraph; similarly, there are various ways to order your paragraphs. The same principles apply as you learned in Chapter 4, and additional strategies will be presented in this chapter. Just as your sentences need to flow smoothly, the train of thought at the end of one paragraph should be picked up at the beginning of the next paragraph; this can be achieved through the use of transitions. Again, much attention will be devoted to transition use in this text.

In Chapter 1, you learned how to formulate a restricted topic sentence from your notes. The same technique can be used to arrive at a thesis statement; you need simply to remember that the thesis statement is more general than a topic sentence. After all, each developmental paragraph does discuss an aspect of the main topic expressed in the thesis statement. Once you have decided on your thesis, you need to break the thesis down logically into topics for your paragraphs. These topics are, in essence, supporting points for your thesis. Let us say, for example, that you wanted to write about the beautiful sights in your country—perhaps to persuade people to visit them or simply to inform your reader about your country. After you have taken considerable notes on the topic, you might come up with this thesis statement: "My country has some beautiful sights." The main topic of the essay is "sights in my country" and the central idea is "beautiful." The main topic then needs to be broken down into topics for paragraphs—perhaps two to four. Logically, the topics would be "sights," with one sight perhaps discussed per paragraph, and the controlling idea for each of these topics should be something akin to "beautiful," such as "charming," "lovely," "enchanting," "glorious," and so on. We could illustrate this breakdown as follows for an essay about beautiful sights in Mexico:

MEXICO HAS SOME BEAUTIFUL SIGHTS.

= beach at Progreso + Aztec Ruin + Monument

Just how you break down your thesis into topics depends on your thesis statement. There are several principles for logically breaking down your thesis. You can break it into topics according to causes, effects (benefits, advantages, disadvantages, results), steps in a process, types (kinds, categories, classes), examples, points of comparison and contrast, and reasons; these are the basic principles, and those that we will cover in depth in this text. One way to break your thesis down logically into topics is to turn your thesis statement into a question, keeping in mind what your topic and central idea are. The answers to this question might help you come up with possible topics for your developmental paragraphs; they can also help you determine a strategy for organizing your essay. (These strategies, or patterns of organization, are discussed in great detail in subsequent chapters.) Here are some thesis statements and possible breakdowns into topics for the developmental paragraphs:

1. THESIS STATEMENT:

The village is the best environment for me to live in.

Question:

What makes it a good environment?

Answers:

The cooperation among people.

Its lack of pollution.

Its security.

The central idea in the thesis statement is *best environment*, so this is a logical basis for the breakdown. Each paragraph would discuss a different element of the environment that is attractive to the writer.

2. THESIS STATEMENT:

In order to make a good impression at a job interview, you should prepare well for the interview.

Question:

What should you do to prepare for the interview?

Answers:

Plan your answers to the possible questions.

Plan and prepare what you are going to wear.

Make sure you arrive on time.

The central idea in the thesis is *prepare well*. Here the writer chose to break down the thesis into the steps of a process.

3. THESIS STATEMENT:

Watching television is not a waste of time.

Question:

Why isn't it a waste of time?

Answers:

Because it is a valuable educational tool.

Because it cheers us up.

Because it provides something for our family to discuss.

With the central idea of *not a waste of time*, the writer's approach here is to discuss the reasons television is not a waste of time, in other words, to discuss the advantages of having television.

4. THESIS STATEMENT:

New York and Hong Kong are more alike than people think.

Question:

In what ways are they alike?

Answers:

They are both enormous.
They both have lots of different ethnic groups.
They are both port cities.

In this breakdown, the writer selected points of similarity to develop the thesis.

5. THESIS STATEMENT:

Students should be allowed to manage the bookstore.

Question:

Why should they be allowed to manage it?

Answers:

Because it would benefit the students.
Because the bookstore would benefit.
Because the school would benefit.

In this essay, the student discusses the reasons for allowing students to manage the bookstore, and in this case the reasons are the benefits.

EXERCISE 5-6

Following are thesis statements, each with two supporting topic sentences. Study the thesis statements and their supporting topics sentences to determine the logic or the principle behind the breakdown. Then fill in a topic sentence for each.

1. THESIS STATEMENT:

The city is the place for me to live.

1. I like its excitement.
2. I like the availability of resources.
3. ______________________________

2. **THESIS STATEMENT:**

Smoking cigarettes is harmful to your health.

Topic Sentences:

1. Heavy cigarette smoking can cause throat diseases.
2. Smoking can damage the lungs.
3. ______________________________

3. **THESIS STATEMENT:**

Jogging isn't the only way to improve your circulation.

Topic Sentences:

1. Many have found cycling an excellent aerobic exercise.
2. Another way to improve your circulation is to swim.
3. ______________________________

4. **THESIS STATEMENT:**

A foreign student enrolled at an American university often finds that his or her life isn't such a happy one.

Topic Sentences:

1. The complex registration procedure is frustrating.
2. It is difficult to make friends.
3. ______________________________

5. **THESIS STATEMENT:**

Taking a foreign language should be required in high school.

Topic Sentences:

1. Students can learn about other cultures.
2. It can help in business in the future.
3. ______________________________

EXERCISE 5-7

Study the following thesis statements. On a separate sheet of paper, write out at least three possible topic sentences for two of the thesis statements.

1. Learning English isn't so easy.
2. My country has some of the most beautiful sights you will ever see.
3. Speaking in a foreign language can create some embarrassing misunderstandings.
4. You can see some unusual people on the bus.
5. Fixing a flat tire is not a difficult task.
6. Students whose native language is not English may face many problems that English speakers do not encounter.
7. People go to shopping centers for many reasons.
8. Athletic teams bring universities a number of advantages.

Read the following student essay about sights to see in Quebec, Canada. Try to find the central idea for the essay; then try to find the controlling idea for each of the developmental paragraphs.

MY FAVORITE SIGHTS

In each country in the world, there are always some beautiful sights to see. They might be a monument, a garden, or a cathedral. Every country is proud of them, and everyone is interested in talking about them. In my country, three important points of interest attract a great number of

tourists all year. No portrait of these sights is complete without mentioning their historical and seasonal aspects. Because of these aspects, Quebec is a place where you can find some of the most interesting sights you will ever see.

Old Quebec City is the living witness of our history. The first example is the church Notre-Dame des Victoires. Located at the bottom of Cap Diamant, this church was the first one built in North America. It commemorates the establishment of Quebec in 1608. It is a modest and charming church, constructed of stones and dominated by a single belfry from where you can still hear authentic chimes ringing. Another example is the Ramparts. Originally, they were long fortifications all around the city with three main doors to enter in. Now, the three doors are renovated and part of the fortifications is preserved, offering a harmonious blend of history and innovation. Finally, the focal point of Old Quebec City is the Plaines d'Abraham. It is a very large hill from which we can have a scenic view of the Saint Lawrence River and the city. It was on this site that our founders won many battles, but unfortunately, lost the most important one. Nevertheless, the spot is now a wonderful park where is still present, with its many cannons, a past which is not so far away. Regardless of the season, those three points are colorful: red in autumn, white in winter, light green in spring, and dark green in summer.

From the Plaines d'Abraham, it is easy to discover the majestic Saint Lawrence River. This beautiful broad river was the open door for our founders. Traveling in canoes, they established the first three cities in the lands drained by the Saint Lawrence: Quebec, Montreal, and Trois-Rivieres. They must have been impressed with the clear, sweet water, the tree-studded islands, and the banks lined with pine and hemlock. Today, the river is an exceptional waterway extending 1,500 miles into the interior. Like the Mississippi River, it is, in every season, the location for great activities. Although the most important one is commercial, pleasure and sport are considerable; for example, boating, water-skiing, and fishing. These are particularly popular in summer. Furthermore, even though there are three to five feet of ice on the river in the winter, the Saint Lawrence is still navigable.

On the north shore of the Saint Lawrence River, five miles from Quebec, the famous Montmorency Falls are located. These beautiful falls were discovered by a French explorer in the sixteenth century. About 350 feet high, and with frothing, foaming sheets of water, they are the highest falls in North America. During the summer, it is popular to go to one of the huge park areas near the falls to admire their cascades. At night, it is possible to hear and see a lovely sound and light show. During the winter, the main activity is at the bottom. The small drops of vapor in the air form a huge, round block of ice at the bottom of the falls which becomes bigger and bigger. This strange sight draws a lot of children and adults who spend time climbing up and down.

Is it possible to find a country where the beauty, the history, and the variety in the scenery are combined in such perfect harmony? Of course, our four seasons mean four different aspects of the same sight. I don't know if it is because I am far from my country, but I am convinced that Quebec has some of the most beautiful sights that I have ever seen.

—*Louisette Caron*

EXERCISE 5-8

On a separate sheet of paper, answer the following questions about the preceding essay.

1. What is the main topic of the essay? What is the central idea?
2. What are the subtopics? What are the controlling ideas for the subtopics?
3. Are the paragraphs descriptive, narrative, or expository, or are they a combination?

In general, *interesting* is considered rather vague and general for a controlling idea; however, in "My Favorite Sights," Louisette clarifies what she means by *interesting:* interesting for its history and beauty during the seasons. In choosing *interesting* as a controlling idea, restrict its meaning by clarifying what you mean by this word.

Sometimes the writer chooses to present part of the thesis statement in the introduction and the rest of it later in the essay, often in the conclusion. This approach is useful when the writer wants to build up to a point rather than stating it prematurely. The following essay is an example of this approach. The writer gives a generalized thesis statement at the end of the introductory paragraph and specifies what the generalized thesis statement means in the conclusion. As you read the essay, underline the two parts of the thesis statement.

WHY PEOPLE SAVE BOOKS

Many people who like to read also save the books they have read. If you walk into any home you are likely to see anywhere from a single bookshelf to a whole library full of all kinds of books. I know a family whose library has shelves reaching up to their ceiling; they keep a ladder for climbing up to the high books. Obviously, they have collected books for many years and though they rarely actually open the books again, they keep them on the shelves, dusted and lined up neatly. Why do people save their books? There may be several reasons, but three stand out.

One reason people save their books is to use them as reference materials. People whose job training included studying a lot of textbook material may save some of those books for future reference. A doctor, for instance, may keep his *Gray's Anatomy* and his pharmacology books; an English teacher will hold on to *The Norton Anthology of British Literature* and other anthologies and novels for reference; a lawyer usually keeps her case books. But it isn't only the professionals who save their books. People who like to cook keep recipe books. Those interested in electronic equipment hold on to their books about stereos, computers, videotape machines, and the like. Many families keep encyclopedias and almanacs handy for their children to use for school. Having your own reference book available is so much more convenient than running to the library every time you want to check a fact.

Another reason some people save books is to make a good impression. Some think that a library full of the literary classics, dictionaries, and books about art, science, and history make them look well read and therefore sophisticated. Of course, this impression may be inaccurate. Some have never bothered to read the majority of those books at all! In fact, a few people even have libraries with fake books. Also, some people like to reveal to visitors their wide range of tastes and interests. They can subtly reveal their interests in Peruvian art, Indian music, philosophy, or animals without saying a word.

While some people may keep books for practical reference and for conveying an impression, I suspect that there is a deeper reason. People who enjoy reading have discovered the magic of books. Each book, whether it's *The Treasury of Houseplants* or *Murder on the Orient Express*, has transported the reader to another place. Therefore, each book really represents an experience from which the reader may have grown or learned something. When I sit in my study, I am surrounded by my whole adult life. *The Standard First Aid and Personal Safety* manual, in addition to providing information, reminds me of the first-aid course I took and how more assured I felt as a result. *Bulfinch's Mythology* brings the oral history of Western civilization to my fingertips, reminding me of my link with other times and people. Of course, all of the novels have become part of the mosaic of my life. In short, saving books makes me feel secure as I hold on to what they have given me.

In fact, if you think about it, security is at the bottom of all these reasons. It's a secure feeling to know you have information at hand when you need it. There is a kind of security, even though it may be false, in knowing you make a good impression. Finally, books that you've read and kept envelop you with a warm and cozy cloak of your life.

EXERCISE 5-9

On a separate sheet of paper, answer the following questions about the preceding essay.

1. What is the main topic of the essay?
2. The generalized thesis can be stated as "People save books for three reasons." What is the central idea about those reasons?
3. What are the subtopics (reasons)? What are the controlling ideas for the subtopics?
4. What kind of paragraph is each developmental paragraph?
5. Identify specific details in each of the developmental paragraphs.

The Conclusion

Just as the introductory paragraph functions to open the essay discussion by introducing the topic and the central idea (thesis), so the concluding paragraph wraps up the discussion, bringing the development to a logical end. If the developmental paragraphs have done their job—that is, developed the thesis—then the conclusion should follow logically.

But what does one *say* in the conclusion? What is said depends entirely on what was developed in the essay. However, there is a standard approach to writing concluding paragraphs. Here are some points about conclusions.

1. *A conclusion can restate the main points (subtopics) discussed.* This restatement should be brief; after all, you have already discussed them at length.

2. *A conclusion can restate the thesis.* Generally, to avoid sounding repetitious, it is a good idea to restate the thesis in different words. The restatement of the thesis is really a reassertion of its importance or validity.

3. *A conclusion should* not, *however, bring up a new topic.*

For example, an essay about the most interesting places to visit in Mexico could conclude as follows:

> There are, of course, many more things to visit while you are in Mexico, but the beach at Progreso, the Aztec ruin, and the famous monument represent some of the more significant and beautiful sights to see. When you go to Mexico, visit these sights and you will be guaranteed a fond memory after you go home.

A concluding paragraph about allowing students to manage the bookstore might look like this:

> Providing jobs for students, jobs that would help cut the cost of managing the bookstore and providing on-the-job experience—which can only enhance the university's reputation for graduating knowledgeable students—are excellent reasons for allowing students to manage the bookstore. In fact, it is amazing that such a system is not in practice now.

EXERCISE 5-10

Reread the essay "My Favorite Sights" by Louisette Caron on pages 177–79. Then answer the following questions on a separate sheet of paper.

1. Are the main points in Louisette's essay mentioned in the conclusion?

2. If not, does the conclusion seem appropriate anyway? Why?
3. If yes, what are the main points she restates?

EXERCISE 5-11

Thesis statements, their supporting topic sentences, and conclusions follow. Study each conclusion to determine if it logically concludes. If the conclusion is not appropriate, write *not good* in the blank and write the reason it is not good in the space provided. If the conclusion is appropriate, simply write *logical* in the blank.

1. ______________________________

____

Thesis Statement:

Watching television is not a waste of time.

a. It is a valuable educational tool.
b. It provides entertainment to cheer us up.
c. It provides something our family can have in common to discuss.

Critics of television will continue to put down the "boob tube." But, because of its educational value, its entertainment value, and its provision of things we can discuss together, our family is going to continue watching television for a long time, and so should others. Indeed, watching television is a good way to spend one's time.

2. ______________________________

____

Thesis Statement:

Communicating in a foreign language can create some embarrassing misunderstandings.

a. Mispronouncing words can lead to real embarrassment.
b. Misunderstanding what someone says to you can create amusing problems.
c. Misusing vocabulary words can really make you blush.

Everyone who speaks a foreign language is bound to have misunderstandings from time to time. What you need to do is go to the laboratory as often as you can to improve your language skills. The people there are very nice and they will help you with your grammar and pronunciation.

3. ______________________________

____

Thesis Statement:

Television commercials are entertaining.

a. The Coca-Cola commercial is a good example of an entertaining commercial.
b. The Chevrolet commercial is as good as any situation comedy.
c. The Fritos commercial is particularly amusing.

If you do not have a television, you are certainly missing out on the fun of commercials. There are also a lot of entertaining programs to see. In addition, the news programs can keep you informed about the world. Indeed, everyone should have a television set.

4. ____

____

Thesis Statement:

My reasons for coming to State University center around the services it provides.

a. State University offers a superior program in my major.
b. In addition, the university has high-quality academic resources.
c. State also offers quality student services.
d. The recreational activities make State even better.

The challenge of a diversified and excellent program, the academic resources, the student services, the recreational activities, and the low tuition are the reasons I decided to come to State University. I really think I made a wise decision. If you are looking for a quality education at a reasonable price, then consider State as the place to enroll.

5. ____

____

Thesis Statement:

In order to make a good impression at a job interview, you should prepare well for the interview.

a. The first thing you should do is plan your answers to the possible questions the interviewer might ask.
b. Then you should carefully plan and prepare what you are going to wear.
c. Finally you should make sure that you arrive on time.

As you can see, it is necessary to be well prepared for the job interview. Having the answers ready, being properly dressed, and being on time can all help to make a good impression on the interviewer. If you follow these steps, you will find yourself sitting behind the desk at that coveted job in no time at all.

The Outline

To determine if an essay is well organized and if the paragraphs discuss the thesis statement, it is important to outline the essay. In Unit One, the paragraph outlines were essentially topic sentences with the supporting sentences written out on separate lines. In outlining an essay, however, you do not need to write out all the sentences in the paragraphs. An outline is the skeleton of the essay; it is the structure around which the details and explanations are organized.

There are many ways to write outlines for essays. It is not necessary to follow any strict outline form. For example, technically, in an outline if there is a 1 there must be a 2 and if there is an "A" there must be a "B." When you are asked to write formal outlines for formal papers, you should follow this rule; but for most other purposes, an outline can be informal. Here is a suggestion for an outline form for planning your essay:

Thesis Statement:

Write out the thesis statement in a complete sentence.

I. Write out the first developmental paragraph topic sentence.
- *A.* Identify the support. This can be a detail or an idea that the paragraph will discuss.
  - 1. Mention any additional detail about "A."
  - 2. If appropriate, mention another detail about "A."
- *B.* If you have another detail or example you are going to discuss in this paragraph, mention it here.

II. Write out the next topic sentence.
- *A.* Support.
- *B.* Support.

III. Write out the next topic sentence.
- *A.* Support.
  - 1. Detail if necessary.
- *B.* Support.

A quick glance at such an outline should reveal if the paragraphs are unified and coherent. Study the following outline of Louisette Caron's essay:

Thesis Statement:

Because of these aspects, Quebec is a place where you can find some of the most interesting sights you will ever see.

I. Old Quebec City is the living witness of our history.
- *A.* Historical aspects.

1. Notre-Dame des Victoires.
2. Ramparts.
3. Plaines d'Abraham.

B. Seasonal aspects — beautiful in all seasons.

II. From the Plaines d'Abraham, it is easy to discover the majestic Saint Lawrence River.

A. Historical aspects.

1. Open door for our founders who established cities.
2. Today, the river is an exceptional waterway.

B. Seasonal aspects.

The location for great activities in every season, particularly boating, water-skiing, and fishing in summer.

2. The river is navigable in winter.

III. On the north shore of the Saint Lawrence River, five miles from Quebec, the famous Montmorency Falls are located.

A. Historical aspects.

1. Discovered by a French explorer in the sixteenth century.
2. Highest falls in North America.

B. Seasonal aspects.

1. During the summer
   a. Go to park to admire falls.
   b. Sound and light show.
2. During the winter — play on the block of ice.

Supporting details can be expressed in words or phrases in an outline.

EXERCISE 5-12

Reread "Why People Save Books" on pages 179–80 and write an outline using the form given on pages 184–85.

The following essay is about an important invention. As you read it, try to locate the thesis statement and the supporting points. Also determine if the thesis is sufficiently supported.

THE HEAT ENGINE

The heat engine is certainly one of the most important devices that man ever invented. In its simplest meaning, the heat engine is a device that transforms heat energy into other forms of energy, such as mechanical and electrical energy. A great majority of the engines used today lie under this definition, and this gives us a quick glimpse of the importance of the heat engine. An observation of the contributions that the heat engine made in the fields of industry, transportation, and the production of electricity gives us a deeper and more detailed look at the importance of heat engines.

The heat engine had a great role in the Industrial Revolution of the nineteenth century. Scientists developed machines, based on heat engines, that could increase the amount of goods produced, and, at the same time, decrease the amount of time and money consumed. The manufactured goods became affordable to almost everyone, and they were not a luxury anymore. After the introduction of the heat engine in the industrial field, the concept of mass production was first realized, and industry flourished as never before.

Through history man has always tried to invent efficient means of transportation. However, it was not until the invention of the heat engine that this became possible. A new era replaced the old era of animal-powered transportation, an era whose characteristics were speed and comfort. The train was the first means of transportation that used the heat engine, and it introduced new horizons of long-distance traveling. However, it was another machine that replaced the horse as a personal means of transportation. It was called the car, and it also used the heat engine. The achievements of the car in a few decades erased centuries of horse transportation.

Scientists realized the importance of electricity since the day it was discovered. Unfortunately, electricity was not available in nature for direct use. Scientists had to come up with ways of producing it. Here again, the heat engine was used to produce mechanical energy, which in turn can produce electricity. Today, many power-producing stations all over the world still use heat engines. They use coal or fuel oil to evaporate water; then the steam is used to turn a turbine which can produce electricity.

In conclusion, heat engines proved to be one of the most important inventions. It is enough to observe the importance of industry, transportation, and electricity in our lives to know the importance of heat engines. Although the engines used today are quite different from the early ones, the same concept of changing heat into other kinds of energy is still used.

—*Tammam Dandashi*

EXERCISE 5-13

On a separate sheet of paper, answer the following questions about the heat engine essay.

1. **Does the introductory paragraph seem appropriate? Is it inviting?**
2. **Is the essay unified? Coherent?**
3. **Do you think there are enough examples provided? Are they discussed adequately?**
4. **Are the main points briefly mentioned in the conclusion? If so, in what sentence (or sentences)? Does the conclusion follow from the discussion?**
5. **Is the thesis restated in the essay? Where?**

EXERCISE 5-14: WRITING ASSIGNMENT

Topics for 300- to 400-word essay. Plan your essay carefully, first making a list of ideas, then finding a central idea on which to base a thesis statement. Make an outline and then write the essay.

1. Think of some noteworthy or interesting sights in your country or hometown. Formulate a central idea—thesis—about those sights. Try to avoid using "interesting" unless you modify it. Are these sights beautiful? Are they of historical significance? Are they unusual? Now break down your topic into three or four subtopics and write your essay.
2. What are some of the areas where computers are being used? Write about some of the uses of computers. If you wish, you may discuss another important invention, such as satellites.
3. Write an essay explaining why you think people save books or some other objects. For example, many people save stamps, coins, dolls, even toys!

Essay Checklist

1. Is your introduction inviting? Does it introduce the topic?
2. Does your essay have a clear thesis?
3. Do your topic sentences support the thesis?
4. Does the support in your paragraphs support the topic sentences?
5. Does your conclusion end the discussion logically?
6. Is your essay coherent? Unified?

Chapter 6

The Example Essay

Readings: The Power of Culture and Language

Both the culture we live in and the first language we learn to speak are powerful forces in shaping our behavior and worldview. From them we determine how to act in the world and how to make sense of it. Usually, we are unaware of the power of language and culture until we experience firsthand a different culture or learn to speak a different language. These activities help us to gain a perspective on our own culture and to see some of its unspoken but powerful "rules." But our first language not only shapes the way we see the world; it also acts in important ways to control our lives and to give us guidance.

The two selections that follow use examples to show the power of culture and language in our lives. As you read the essays, try to answer these questions:

1. How has your culture shaped your behavior?
2. What are some examples of unacceptable behavior in your culture? In American culture?
3. What sentences or ideas in your language have had a powerful effect on your life?

READING 1

HOW UNWRITTEN RULES CIRCUMSCRIBE OUR LIVES

BOB GREENE

Bob Greene's newspaper columns and articles are collected in* Johnny Deadline Reporter: The Best of Bob Greene *(1976) and* American Beat *(1983). In the article reprinted here, Greene writes about the power of unwritten cultural rules in our lives. As you read the essay, consider these questions:

1. **Are Greene's examples confirmed by your own experiences in American culture?**
2. **Would these same examples be true in your culture?**
3. **Can you think of additional examples of unwritten cultural rules?**

1 The restaurant was almost full. A steady hum of conversation hung over the room; people spoke with each other and worked on their meals.

2 Suddenly, from a table near the center of the room, came a screaming voice:

3 "Damn it, Sylvia. . . ."

4 The man was shouting at the top of his voice.• His face was reddened, and he yelled at the woman sitting opposite him for about fifteen seconds. In the crowded restaurant, it

at . . . *very loudly*

seemed like an hour. All other conversation in the room stopped, and everyone looked at the man. He must have realized this, because as abruptly• as he had started, he stopped; he lowered his voice and finished whatever it was he had to say in a tone the rest of us could not hear.

suddenly

5 It was startling• precisely because it almost never happens; there are no laws against such an outburst, and with the pressures of our modern world you would almost expect to run into such a thing on a regular basis. But you don't; as a matter of fact, when I thought about it I realized that it was the first time in my life I had witnessed• such a demonstration. In all the meals I have had in all the restaurants, I had never seen a person start screaming at the top of his lungs.•

surprising

seen

at . . . *very loudly*

6 When you are eating among other people, you do not raise your voice;• it is just an example of the unwritten rules we live by. When you consider it, you recognize that those rules probably govern our lives on a more absolute basis than the ones you could find if you looked in the lawbooks. The customs that govern us are what make a civilization; there would be chaos• without them, and yet for some reason—even in the distintegrating• society of 1982—we obey them.

speak loudly

without organization /

falling apart

7 How many times have you been stopped at a red light late at night? You can see in all directions; there is no one else around—no headlights, no police cruiser• idling behind you. You are tired and you are in a hurry. But you wait for the light to change. There is no one to catch you if you don't, but you do it anyway. Is it for safety's sake? No; you can see that there would be no accident if you drove on. Is it to avoid getting arrested? No; you are alone. But you sit and wait.

police car

8 At major athletic events, it is not uncommon to find 80,000 or 90,000 or 100,000 people sitting in the stands.• On the playing field are two dozen athletes; maybe fewer. There are nowhere near enough security guards on hand to keep the people from getting out of their seats and walking onto the field en masse.• But it never happens. Regardless of the emotion of the contest, the spectators stay in their places, and the athletes are safe in their part of the arena. The invisible barrier always holds.

grandstands, seating area at an athletic stadium

all together

9 In restaurants and coffee shops, people pay their checks. A simple enough concept. Yet it would be remarkably easy to wander away from a meal without paying at the end. Especially in these difficult economic times, you might expect that to become a common form of cheating. It doesn't happen very often. For whatever the unwritten rules of human conduct are, people automatically make good• for their meals. They would no sooner walk out on a check than start screaming.

pay, do the right thing

10 Rest rooms are marked "Men" and "Women." Often there are long lines at one or another of them, but males wait to enter their own washrooms, and women to enter theirs. In an era of sexual egalitarianism,• you would expect impatient people to violate• this rule on occasion; after all, there are private stalls inside, and it would be less inconvenient to use them than to wait. . . . It just isn't done. People obey the signs.

equality
go against

11 Even criminals obey the signs. I once covered a murder which centered around that rule being broken. A man wanted to harm a woman—which woman apparently• didn't matter. So he did the simplest thing possible. He went to a public park and walked into a rest room marked "Women"—the surest place to find what he wanted. He found it. He attacked with a knife the first woman to come in there. Her husband and young child waited outside, and the man killed her. Such a crime is not commonplace,• even in a world grown accustomed to nastiness.• Even the most evil elements of our society generally obey the unspoken rule: If you are not a woman, you do not go past a door marked "Women."

evidently
usual, normal
badness, evil

12 I know a man who, when he pulls his car up to a parking meter, will put change in the meter even if there is time left on it. He regards it as the right thing to do; he says he is not doing it just to extend the time remaining—even if there is sufficient time on the meter to cover whatever task he has to perform at the location, he will pay his own way. He believes that you are supposed to purchase your own time; the fellow before you purchased only his.

13 I knew another man who stole tips• at bars. It was easy enough; when the person sitting next to this man would depart for the evening and leave some silver or a couple dollars for the bartender, this guy would wait until he thought no one was looking and then sweep the money over in front of him. The thing that made it unusual is that I never knew anyone else who even tried this; the rules of civility• stated that you left someone else's tip on the bar until it got to the bartender, and this man stood out because he refused to comply.•

money left for waiter or bartender, gratuity
good manners
conform, go along with

14 There are so many rules like these—rules we all obey—that we think about them only when that rare person violates them. In the restaurant, after the man had yelled "Damn it, Sylvia" and had then completed his short tirade,• there was a tentative aura• among the other diners for half an hour after it happened. They weren't sure what disturbed them about what they had witnessed; they knew, though, that it violated something very basic about the way we were supposed to behave. And it bothered them—which in itself is a hopeful sign that things, more often than not, are well.

outburst, long angry speech / *feeling of uncertainty*

EXERCISE 6-1: COMPREHENSION/ DISCUSSION QUESTIONS

1. What is Greene's thesis in "How Unwritten Rules Circumscribe Our Lives"?
2. What are some of the examples he gives to support it?
3. Are all of his examples equally strong? Do any of them strike you as unconvincing?
4. Why is it important that the laws discussed by the writer are *unwritten*? Do you agree that these laws govern our lives more strongly than written ones?
5. Which of the laws given by the writer are true in your culture? Give examples to support your answer.
6. Can you give additional examples of unwritten cultural laws in any culture?
7. In your view, which unwritten laws mentioned in the essay seem basic to life in any civilized society and which seem relatively minor matters of form or taste? Explain your answers.
8. Where does Greene first state his thesis? Does he state it again? If so, where? Do you think his organization is effective?
9. Are the author's examples selected from a broad enough range of experience to support his thesis effectively?
10. Why are so many of Greene's examples exceptions—that is, examples of people who do not follow the unwritten laws?

EXERCISE 6-2: VOCABULARY DEVELOPMENT

The following idiomatic expressions are used in Greene's essay. Study the sections of the reading in which the expressions occur. From the context clues or surrounding information, determine the meaning of each idiomatic expression. Then use each one in an original sentence.

1. at the top of his voice (par. 4)

   The man was shouting at the top of his voice. His face was reddened, and he yelled at the woman sitting opposite him for about fifteen seconds.

   ____

2. at the top of his lungs (par. 5)

   . . . There are no laws against such an outburst. . . . In all the meals I have had in all the restaurants, I had never seen a person start screaming at the top of his lungs.

   ____

3. run into (par. 5)

   . . . and with the pressures of our modern world you would almost expect to run into such a thing on a regular basis. But you don't; as a matter of fact, when I thought about it I realized that it was the first time in my life I had witnessed such a demonstration.

____

4. **raise your voice (par. 6)**

In all the meals I have had in all the restaurants, I had never seen a person start screaming at the top of his lungs. When you are eating among other people, you do not raise your voice; it is just an example of the unwritten rules we live by.

____

5. **nowhere near enough (par. 8)**

At major athletic events, it is not uncommon to find 80,000 or 90,000 or 100,000 people sitting in the stands. On the playing field are two dozen athletes; maybe fewer. There are nowhere near enough security guards on hand to keep the people from getting out of their seats and walking onto the field en masse. But it never happens.

____

6. **make good (par. 9)**

In restaurants and coffee shops, people pay their checks. . . . It would be remarkably easy to wander away from a meal without paying at the end. . . . It doesn't happen very often. For whatever the unwritten rules of human conduct are, people automatically make good on their meals.

____

READING 2

FROM "WORDS THAT COUNT"

LETTY COTTIN POGREBIN

In this essay, which first appeared in* Ms. *magazine, Pogrebin points up the power of language in our lives. She notes that while past generations may have used religious or philosophical statements to guide their lives, today we often have a personalized statement that is important to us. To support this point, the author gives examples of axioms and aphorisms that different people use as their guiding light. As you read the essay, ask yourself the following question: "What statement or maxim is most important to you?"

1 The power of a single sentence to alter• behavior is quirky[1] and unpredictable. Maybe past generations reacted personally to the maxims[2] of religion, classical philosophy, and literature, but regardless of their sagacity,• the Golden Rule and lines like "To thine own self be true" have suffered from overexposure.• What resonates• for us today are "custom made"[3] axioms and aphorisms;[4] advice fashioned just for us by our family, friends—and friends' therapists. . . . Whereas common wisdom says, "Don't just stand there, *do* something," to counteract• my compulsiveness,• I tell myself "Don't do something, just stand there. You don't have to do anything now."

change
wisdom
overuse / is meaningful
balance against / acting quickly without thinking

2 "Can you think of one sentence that has had a profound• effect on you?" I asked everyone I met this week.

deep, important

3 The results were astonishing. People had their answers on the tip of their tongues, like kids waiting to be quizzed, or yogis confessing their mantras.[5]

4 *"Move toward anxiety,"* the television producer says with her eyes closed. "Years ago, I found that line taped to the bathroom mirror at a friend's and I try to live by it. When I feel anxious about something, I know that's the direction where growth lies. I face the fear. I go to the place, make the phone call, give the speech. Those three words have made me bold."

5 An actress in her mid-twenties got her sentence from a high school teacher: *Don't mistake vulnerability• for weakness.* "That advice is very important for my acting and my happiness. I have to work hard to let go, open up, and trust my emotions to others."

openness

6 A futurist once told a businessman, *The future is stupid—unless you change it,* and though that doesn't exactly make sense to me, to the businessman it has been a catalytic• message.

causing change

7 Apologizing for being guided by a cliché,• a lawyer admits his inspiration is *You only come this way once.* "Most people behave as though they're going to have a second go-around," he says. "I'm aware I have only one chance to be young, to enjoy my kids before they grow up, to take advantage of my health before it goes."

overused expression

8 *What will you remember?* That's the litmus test[6] for a busy journalist. "It's the way I set my priorities.• If I suspect

most important things

[1] *behaving in strange ways*
[2] *wise sayings, proverbs*
[3] *made differently for each individual*
[4] *wise sayings*
[5] **yogis confessing their mantras** *Indian religious men chanting and praying*
[6] *statement by which he judges what to do*

that some activity will later blur in memory, I don't do it. I choose the activity that most promises to be remembered."

9 These are humble platitudes,• not eloquent slogans or lines of epic verse. What makes them stick in the mind and reverberate• in the psyche•? Of all the written and spoken counsel directed at us, why do we hear one sentence louder than the rest? The answer may lie in your one sentence and what it reveals about your particular needs and fears. Or the "custom made" axiom may carry mystical weight because it is so precisely tailored to your experience.

proverbs, predictable sayings

echo, sound again and again / the mind

EXERCISE 6-3: COMPREHENSION/ DISCUSSION QUESTIONS

1. In paragraph 1, Pogrebin gives two examples to show that past generations used maxims of religion or philosophy to guide their lives. What are these maxims and what do they mean?
2. What is the writer's thesis (paragraph 1)?
3. What personal maxim does Pogrebin use to live by?
4. When the writer asked different people for their important personal statements, what most astonished her?
5. Explain the meanings of the television producer's maxim and the actress' maxim.
6. Pogrebin wonders why a particular maxim is important to each of us. She gives several possible reasons. What are they? Do you agree?
7. In the essay, the writer gives six maxims—her own and five others. Of these six, which one would you most likely choose for your own guiding principle? Why?
8. Do you have a maxim or important saying that you use to guide your life? What is it? Why is it important to you?
9. Do you think most people use a maxim to live by? Ask several of your friends to describe their maxims. Explain your results to the class.

EXERCISE 6-4: VOCABULARY DEVELOPMENT

In "Words That Count," Pogrebin uses a number of words that have the same meaning as the word *maxim*. However, most of these words are not true synonyms; that is, each has a slightly different meaning. Using your dictionary, try to distinguish the slight differences in meaning among the following words. Then use each one in an original sentence that makes its particular meaning clear.

1. maxim (par. 1)

2. line (par. 1)

3. axiom (par. 1)

4. aphorism (par. 1)

5. advice (par. 1)

6. cliché (par. 7)

7. inspiration (par. 7)

8. litmus test (par. 8)

9. platitude (par. 9)

10. slogan (par. 9)

11. counsel (par. 9)

Writing

The way you develop your topic depends on what the topic is and on what you want to say. Let us suppose, for example, that you are asked to write about the difficulties of being a foreign student. How could you develop this topic? You would probably want to develop it with examples that illustrate the difficulties. Could you adequately cover this topic in a single paragraph? Probably not. The topic is simply too broad. You will need to write a longer essay to cover this topic adequately. How to organize and develop the examples for such a topic in the multiparagraph essay is the focus of this chapter.

Number of Examples

Just how many examples you use in an example essay depends on the topic. Some topics require numerous examples, whereas others can be

effectively developed with three or four extended examples (illustrations). For instance, the thesis statement "San Francisco has some of the most unusual sights in California" does not commit the writer to giving numerous examples; after all, the claim is only that this city has "some" unusual sights. Therefore, three or four extended examples should suffice. As you read the following essay about a student's first year in the United States, determine if the writer provides enough examples.

AMERICANS ARE FRIENDLY TO STRANGERS

I came to the United States one year ago and I had no idea about life in the United States and American traditions, except that life was complicated and people are strange. At the time I arrived at J. F. Kennedy airport, I felt very happy because I am fond of traveling around the world. Coming to America had been one of my dreams, so I could go to Jamaica or any island in the Caribbean. A few minutes later, however, I felt afraid. I asked myself why I had come to this strange world and what I was doing here. The reason for that was what I remembered my friends in Saudi Arabia saying about Americans and how they treat strangers. After I attended college, however, I discovered the opposite of what I had expected.

Even though American social relations are complex, hard to form, and hard to maintain, I managed to bridge the gap and I was able to have close friendships with some Americans. For example, the first semester I attended college, I became friends with one of the American students who used to attend math class with me. We used to study together, go to parties together, and he used to help me a lot with my English. Even though he transferred to another university, we always keep in touch with each other.

From my experience, I have come to understand that Americans are generally verbal and long, silent periods are uncomfortable to them. So, when I sit with Americans, I start a conversation with them by talking about the weather, sports, or about teachers' skills in the classroom. I think conversations make a friendly atmosphere among people.

The second example that proved to me that I had the wrong idea about Americans was when my wife and I drove across the country from New Orleans to San Diego. When I told my friends that my wife and I were going to drive across the United States and if they wanted to they could join us, they said, "It is dangerous to drive across America. You might get killed by one of the truck drivers or get robbed." However, we didn't pay attention to them because we wanted to find out what America is really like and how people treat strangers.

On the way from San Antonio to El Paso, our car stopped because it ran out of fuel. We got out of the car and waited for anyone to give us a ride. Ten minutes later, a truck driver pulled off the road. I approached him carefully and I asked him, "Could you please give us a ride to the nearest gas station?" He asked me why. I said, "Our car ran out of gas and we have to get some." He said, "The nearest station is thirty-five miles away and you might not find anyone who can drive you back to your car." Then he came up with a solution to our problem. He towed our car to the nearest station. When we reached it, I took a fifty-dollar-bill from my pocket and handed it to him, but he wouldn't accept it. He told me that he helped me because we needed help.

In general, Americans are friendly to strangers. From my experience, a person who treats people well will put them in a position where they have to respect him in return, but if he treats them badly they will treat him in the same way. Human beings are born with a good nature and they will not behave badly unless they are forced to. I think a person should judge people by dealing with them, not by listening to his friends.

—*Nader Alyousha*

EXERCISE 6-5

On a separate sheet of paper, answer the following questions about the preceding essay.

1. **What is the thesis statement? What is the central idea?**
2. **How many examples does the writer give? Are the examples explained adequately?**
3. **Are there enough examples?**
4. **Are the examples relevant?**
5. **Are the paragraphs coherent and unified?**
6. **How are the paragraphs organized?**

An outline of Nader Alyousha's essay might look like this:

Thesis Statement: Americans are friendly to strangers.

I. I was able to have close friendships with some Americans.
  A. One example is a student in my math class during my first semester.
    1. We studied together.
    2. We went to parties together.
    3. He helped me with my English.
    4. We still keep in touch.
  B. I begin friendships by starting a conversation about . . .
    1. The weather.
    2. Sports.
    3. Teachers' skills in the classroom.

II. I had the wrong idea about Americans.
  A. An example is our trip across the country.
    1. My friends said it was dangerous.
    2. When we ran out of gas, a stranger helped us.
      a. He towed our car.
      b. He wouldn't accept any money.

Conclusion: People will treat you well if you treat them well.

Some topics require numerous examples for adequate development. For instance, suppose the thesis statement is "Our city streets are in terrible condition." Would three extended examples of streets in bad condition be sufficient to develop this thesis statement? Probably not. Asserting that all—or even most—of the city streets are in terrible condition based on only three or four examples would be rather unwise; after all, a city has many streets and, in this case, most of them may in fact be in good condition. A generalization such as "Our city streets are in terrible condition" based on an insufficient number of examples is called a ***hasty generalization***; in other words, it is a generalization made too hastily before examining enough evidence. Making such a generalization without giving sufficient examples for support sacrifices credibility with the reader. In short, thesis statements that state or imply "most" or "all" may need numerous examples for adequate support; thesis statements that are more moderate, stating or implying "some" or "a few," can often be supported with fewer, but more developed, examples.

Choices of Examples

Since an example is a "representative member" of a class or category, the examples you use to develop the thesis statement should be representative examples, examples that fairly support the thesis. Let's say, for instance, that you were writing an essay about the items found in mail-order catalogues, and in planning the essay you noticed that there were many items that were ridiculous. So, you might have arrived at the thesis statement, "Many items offered in mail-order catalogues are just superfluous, absurd trifles." If you used for your examples only items of one type, such as toys, clearly the examples would be unfairly chosen — not representative of most of the items offered in these catalogues. To be fair and effective, the examples should be from a range of areas. Study the following essay to determine if the examples are sufficient in number and if they are fairly chosen.

USELESS TRIFLES

For many years, people living in remote areas relied on the Sears or Montgomery Wards catalogues to purchase the necessities of life. These "wishbooks," as they were often called, helped people to improve the quality of their lives. Nowadays, nearly every household in the country receives a barrage of various catalogues selling everything from electric golf carts to padded coat hangers. The descriptions of these items suggest that they, too, will help improve the quality of our lives by providing convenience, comfort, and/or shortcuts to improve our appearance. But so often these items are just superfluous, absurd trifles.

Whoever does the cooking has a great deal of work to do and anything to ease that workload is certainly appreciated by any homemaker. Unfortunately, some of these clever items that claim to save time might actually end up making us waste time. Take, for example, devices to save time cutting. A specially designed cutter will slice six pieces of pie at the same time, each piece the same size. Another device cuts an apple in thin slices and removes the core all in one shot. Still another removes the corn from the cob, easily and quickly. Although these devices may save time in the actual cutting, just think of how much time the person lost trying to find the device in the first place and then cleaning it up afterward! The same problem applies to a hand-sized electric drink mixer. It might save the host or hostess some muscle, but not aggravation when he or she finds the batteries are dead and there are none in the house.

Certainly anyone would also appreciate items that make our lives more comfortable, but some of the items for the bathroom border on the absurd. For about $8 you can buy an inflatable pillow to rest against in the bathtub. (It's held secure by suction cups.) An inch-thick foam rubber pad will cushion you from the hard bottom of the tub as you bathe. Of course, if it gets mildew on it, it might be better located in the trash can. Finally, you can sit in comfort on the toilet on a plush toilet seat cover and listen to music from a radio built into a toilet paper container.

Comfort and convenience are carried to extremes in the area of personal care. Without any real effort at all, or so the ads in these catalogues claim, you can go to bed and wake up feeling and looking better. After taking special pills to melt away excess pounds, you can crawl into your bed and let it massage you all night long. (A curious electric device makes the bed vibrate.) In addition, you can rest your head on a wedge-shaped pillow that is supposed to help you sleep better. To protect your hairstyle while you sleep, you can don a special cap. To keep your chin from sagging, you can wrap a band around your face, under your chin, and up over the front part of your head. Finally, to prevent your eyes from getting puffy, all you need to do is slip on a water-filled face mask. Of course, if you wake up to find your mate gone, do not be surprised!

All of these items, whether they are designed to help us in the kitchen, comfort us in the bathroom, or improve the way we look and feel, are for the most part unnecessary. Rather than improve the quality of our lives, such items detract from it by wasting our time and money and cluttering up our cupboards and closets. And cluttering up our coffee tables and end tables are those stacks of catalogues offering more such useless trifles.

EXERCISE 6-6

On a separate sheet of paper, answer the following questions about the preceding essay.

1. What is the thesis statement? The central idea?
2. What are the topic sentences? The controlling ideas?
3. Does each of the paragraphs develop an aspect of the thesis statement?
4. Are there enough examples in the essay? Are the examples representative?
5. What is the principle of organization of the paragraphs? Why, for example, does the writer discuss items for personal care last?
6. Is the conclusion logical?
7. Make an outline of this essay.

EXERCISE 6-7

Following is information on the dumping of hazardous chemical wastes in the United States.* Read the thesis sentence and the examples in the list. Then answer the questions that follow.

Thesis:

Dangerous chemical substances are polluting our water supplies.

1. Pine Barrens, New Jersey—135-acre Jackson Township Dump. One hundred wells poisoned by chemicals from dump, causing kidney problems: One man had one kidney removed. His daughter died of kidney cancer when nine months old.
2. Elizabeth, New Jersey—50,000 barrels of hazardous chemicals exploded in abandoned dump and spread toxic fumes.
3. Love Canal, New York—landfill area. Chemicals were dumped in landfill. Contamination seeped into water supply. Twelve

*Information from Ed Magnuson, "The Poisoning of America," *Time*, 22 Sept. 1980, pp. 58–69.

hundred houses and a school nearby. High incidence of cancer, birth defects, and respiratory and neurological problems.

4. The United States generates about 77 billion pounds of hazardous waste per year—much of it is dumped indiscriminately.
5. Massachusetts—twenty-two towns have contaminated water supplies.
6. Michigan—300 places where wastes have polluted ground water.
7. Carlstadt, New Jersey—Fire in paint factory spread smoke and fumes over city. Citizens temporarily evacuated.
8. Pennsylvania—Wastes poured in abandoned mine shafts and tunnels in hills above Susquehanna River. Seeped into river, which is the water supply for a number of towns.
9. Kentucky—Outside Daniel Boone National Forest—200 containers loaded with dangerous solvents were dumped without permission.
10. Now substances that are very dangerous are beginning to show up in our water supply.
11. Charles City, Iowa—Deep wells 30–40 miles downstream from chemical dump are contaminated.

Questions

1. Which of the examples would be useful in supporting the thesis?
2. Which could not be used?
3. How many examples would be necessary to support the thesis?
4. Write an essay using the thesis given. Support it with the preceding information as necessary.

EXERCISE 6-8: WRITING ASSIGNMENT

Choose one of the following writing topics. Decide on a controlling idea and a thesis statement. Then decide on the examples needed to support the thesis. Write a brief outline of the essay. Then write the essay.

1. Review the essay "Americans Are Friendly to Strangers" on pages 197–98. Write an essay about the Americans you encountered when you first came to the United States. Were they friendly or not? Give examples to support your thesis.
2. On page 199 is a suggested thesis, "Our city streets are in terrible condition." Using this as your thesis, write an essay about the streets in the city where you live. If you think something else needs improvement, write an essay giving examples to illustrate your thesis. You could choose the food in the cafeteria, the buildings on campus, or even something in your neighborhood or your country.
3. Do you or your family get mail-order catalogues? Write an essay about the items in these catalogues that you find particularly interesting. Review the essay on pages 200–201.

COMPOSITION SKILLS

Coherence

Organization of Examples

The examples and details in an expository paragraph can be organized according to time, familiarity, and importance. In an example essay, the principle of organization is essentially the same. For example, the author of the essay about friendly Americans chose to organize his examples according to both time and importance, whereas the writer of "Useless Trifles" chose to begin with the least interesting examples and end with the most interesting ones—those that are personal.

Transitions Between Paragraphs

Developmental paragraphs in the example essay must be connected so that they flow smoothly. Just because a paragraph introduces an additional aspect of the topic does not mean that the shift from one topic to the next should be abrupt; indeed, the shift should be smooth so that the reader understands clearly the progression of thought. Remember, just as a paragraph is coherent if the sentences can be switched around without significant change in meaning, an essay is incoherent if the paragraphs can be switched around without significant change.

There are two ways to connect the paragraphs in an essay: (1) with transitional expressions and (2) with the repetition of key words and phrases.

TRANSITIONS TO INTRODUCE EXAMPLES. In the first developmental paragraph of an example essay, there are several phrases that can be used to introduce the first example or group of examples:

Take, for example, this topic.

One example of a person who is kind is my neighbor.

One area of town where there are examples of improvement is uptown.

One thing that bothers me is air pollution.

First, consider the case of Mr. Martinez.

To begin (To begin with), consider my roommate.

In the second developmental paragraph, the examples can be introduced in a variety of ways:

Another example of a good teacher is Mrs. Hahn.

An additional example is Mr. Ming.

Another thing is the safety issue.

Second, consider Mr. Jones.

Next, consider Ms. Evans.

In the last developmental paragraph, you can use the same type of transitions as above, but in an example paragraph that introduces the most important or most significant example, you should indicate its importance in the beginning of the paragraph:

Still another example of a good teacher is Ms. Lin.

A final example is the street near my house.

Third, consider Main Street.

Finally, there is the problem of air pollution.

The most important example of a helpful person is my advisor.

The most significant (interesting) example of air pollution is provided by Los Angeles.

To see how these types of transitions can be used to connect paragraphs, study the following essay.

WORDS THAT CAMOUFLAGE

People use words, of course, to express their thoughts and feelings. And as everyone knows who has tried to write, choosing just the right word to express an idea can be difficult. Nevertheless, it is important to choose words carefully, for words can suggest meanings not intended at all; words can also be used to deceive. In order to express ourselves accurately and to understand what other people express, we must be aware that words can camouflage real attitudes; English is full of examples.

Take, for instance, the language of advertising. Advertisers obviously want to emphasize the virtues of their products and detract from their faults. To do this, they use carefully chosen words designed to mislead the unwary customer. Carl P. Wrighter in his book *I Can Sell You Anything* has dubbed these expressions "weasel words," which the dictionary defines as words "used in order to evade or retreat from a direct or forthright statement or position."* Let's say, for example, that the advertiser wants you to think that using his product will require no work or trouble. He cannot state that the product will be trouble free because there is usually no such guarantee; instead, he suggests it by using the expression "virtually," as in this product is "virtually trouble free." The careless listener will ignore the qualifier "virtually" and imagine that the product is no trouble at all. Another misleading expression is "up to." During a sale a car dealer may advertise reductions of "up to 25 percent." Our inclination again is to ignore "up to" and think that most of the reductions are 25 percent, but too often we find that only a few products are reduced this much. The other day I saw a sign on a shoe store advertising "up to 40 percent off" for athletic shoes. Needing some walking shoes and wanting a good bargain, I went in, only to find that there were only a few shoes marked down by 40 percent; most of the shoes weren't even on sale.

A second example of words that camouflage meaning is euphemisms. A euphemism is defined as "the substitution of an agreeable or inoffensive

* *Webster's New Collegiate Dictionary* (Springfield: G&C Merriam Company, 1973), p. 1327.

expression for one that may offend or suggest something unpleasant."* We often use euphemisms when our intentions are good. For instance, it is difficult to accept that someone we love has died, so people use all kinds of euphemisms for death, such as "She passed away," "He's gone to meet his maker," or "She is no longer with us." To defend against the pain of such a reality some use the humorous euphemism, "He's kicked the bucket." To make certain jobs sound less unappealing, people use euphemisms. A janitor is now a "custodial worker" or "maintenance person." A trash man may be called a "sanitation engineer." Such euphemisms are not harmful, but sometimes euphemisms can be used to camouflage potentially controversial or objectionable actions. For example, instead of saying we need to raise taxes, a politician might say we need "revenue enhancement measures." When psychologists kill an animal they have experimented with, they prefer to use the term "sacrifice" the animal. Doctors prefer "terminate a pregnancy" to "abort the fetus."

A final example of language that conveys unintended impressions is sexist language. Sexist language refers to expressions that demean females in some way. For instance, when someone refers to a grown woman as a "girl," the implication is that she is still a child. Therefore, instead of an employer saying, "I'll have my girl type that," what should be said is "I'll have my assistant (or secretary) type that." Other offensive expressions include "young thing," as in "She's a cute young thing." The proper term, "girl," should be used in this case, since the "thing" is a young female. Further, the names of many jobs suggest women should not fill these positions. Thus, we use "chair" or "chairperson" instead of the sexist "chairman." Likewise, a "foreman" should be called a "supervisor."

We must always be careful to choose the words that convey what we really mean. If we do not want to give offense, then we should always be on guard against sexist (as well as racist) language. If we do not want to be misled by advertisements, we must keep our ears open for weasel words. Finally, when we use a euphemism, we should be aware that we are trying to make an idea more acceptable. At times this may be preferable, but let's not forget that euphemisms camouflage reality. After all, "coloring the truth" is still lying.

EXERCISE 6-9

On a separate sheet of paper, answer the following questions about the preceding essay.

1. **What is the thesis of this essay?**
2. **What is the principle of organization of the paragraphs?**
3. **How many examples does the writer discuss? Are there enough examples?**
4. **Outline this essay.**

* *Webster's New Collegiate Dictionary* (Springfield: G&C Merriam Company, 1973), p. 394.

Repetition of Key Words and Phrases. The standard transitional expressions are useful for making paragraphs connect logically; however, these phrases used all of the time can become mechanical and repetitious. For variety and for even more smoothness, pick up a key idea, word, or phrase from one paragraph and use it in the sentence introducing the next paragraph. Compare the first version of "Words That Camouflage" with the following revised version.

WORDS THAT CAMOUFLAGE

People use words, of course, to express their thoughts and feelings. And as everyone knows who has tried to write, choosing just the right word to express an idea can be difficult. Nevertheless, it is important to choose words carefully, for words can suggest meanings not intended at all; words can also be used to deceive. In order to express ourselves accurately and to understand what other people express, we must be aware that words can camouflage real attitudes; English is full of examples.

Experts at camouflage are those in advertising. Advertisers obviously want to emphasize the virtues of their products and detract from their faults. To do this, they use carefully chosen words designed to mislead the unwary customer. Carl P. Wrighter in his book *I Can Sell You Anything* has dubbed these expressions "weasel words," which the dictionary defines as words "used in order to evade or retreat from a direct or forthright statement or position."* Let's say, for example, that the advertiser wants you to think that using his product will require no work or trouble. He cannot state that the product will be trouble free because there is usually no such guarantee; instead, he suggests it by using the expression "virtually," as in this product is "virtually trouble free." The careless listener will ignore the qualifier "virtually" and imagine that the product is no trouble at all. Another misleading expression is "up to." During a sale a car dealer may advertise reductions of "up to 25 percent." Our inclination again is to ignore "up to" and think that most of the reductions are 25 percent, but too often we find that only a few products are reduced this much. The other day I saw a sign on a shoe store advertising "up to 40 percent off" for athletic shoes. Needing some walking shoes and wanting a good bargain, I went in, only to find that there were only a few shoes marked down by 40 percent; most of the shoes weren't even on sale.

Just as "weasel words" are used to engender favorable impressions, so are euphemisms. A euphemism is defined as "the substitution of an agreeable or inoffensive expression for one that may offend or suggest something unpleasant."* We often use euphemisms when our intentions are good. For instance, it is difficult to accept that someone we love has died, so people use all kinds of euphemisms for death, such as "She passed away," "He's gone to meet his maker," or "She is no longer with us." To defend against the pain of such a reality some use the humorous euphemism, "He's kicked the bucket." To make certain jobs sound less unappealing, people use

* *Webster's New Collegiate Dictionary*, pp. 1327, 394.

euphemisms. A janitor is now a "custodial worker" or "maintenance person." A trash man may be called a "sanitation engineer." Such euphemisms are not harmful, but sometimes euphemisms can be used to camouflage potentially controversial or objectionable actions. For example, instead of saying we need to raise taxes, a politician might say we need "revenue enhancement measures." When psychologists kill an animal they have experimented with, they prefer to use the term "sacrifice" the animal. Doctors prefer "terminate a pregnancy" to "abort the fetus."

What many find objectionable today is sexist language. Sexist language refers to expressions that demean females in some way. For instance, when someone refers to a grown woman as a "girl," the implication is that she is still a child. Therefore, instead of an employer saying, "I'll have my girl type that," what should be said is "I'll have my assistant (or secretary) type that." Other offensive expressions include "young thing," as in "She's a cute young thing." The proper term, "girl," should be used in this case, since the "thing" is a young female. Further, the names of many jobs suggest women should not fill these positions. Thus, we use "chair" or "chairperson" instead of the sexist "chairman." Likewise, a "foreman" should be called a "supervisor."

We must always be careful to choose the words that convey what we really mean. If we do not want to give offense, then we should always be on guard against sexist (as well as racist) language. If we do not want to be misled by advertisements, we must keep our ears open for weasel words. Finally, when we use a euphemism, we should be aware that we are trying to make an idea more acceptable. At times this may be preferable, but let's not forget that euphemisms camouflage reality. After all, "coloring the truth" is still lying.

Although both versions of "Words That Camouflage" are coherent, the second version flows more smoothly because the transitions are more subtle. A variety of transitions reduces monotony.

EXERCISE 6-10

Underline the changes made by the author in the second version of "Words That Camouflage."

Observe how the writers of the essays in Chapters 5 and 6 use transitions between paragraphs:

FROM "WHY PEOPLE SAVE BOOKS"

Another reason some people save books is to make a good **impression.** Some think that a library full of the literary classics, dictionaries, and books about art, science, and history make them look well read and therefore sophisticated. Of course, this impression may be inaccurate. Some have never bothered to read the majority of those books at all! In fact, a few people even have libraries with fake books. Also, some people like to reveal to visitors their wide range of tastes and interests. They can subtly reveal their interests in Peruvian art, Indian music, philosophy, or animals, without saying a word.

While some people may keep books for practical reference and for conveying an **impression**, I suspect that there is a deeper reason.

FROM "MY FAVORITE SIGHTS"

From the Plaines d'Abraham, it is easy to discover the majestic **Saint Lawrence River**. This beautiful broad river was the open door for our founders. Traveling in canoes, they established the first three cities in the lands drained by the **Saint Lawrence**: Quebec, Montreal, and Trois-Rivieres. They must have been impressed with the clear, sweet water, the tree-studded islands, and the banks lined with pine and hemlock. Today, the river is an exceptional waterway extending 1,500 miles into the interior. Like the Mississippi River, it is, in every season, the location for great activities. Although the most important one is commercial, pleasure and sport are considerable; for example, boating, water-skiing, and fishing. These are particularly popular in summer. Furthermore, even though there are three to five feet of ice on the river in winter, the **Saint Lawrence** is still navigable.

On the north shore of the **Saint Lawrence River**, five miles from Quebec, the famous Montmorency Falls are located.

FROM "USELESS TRIFLES"

Certainly anyone would also appreciate items that make our lives more **comfortable**, but some of the items for the bathroom border on the absurd. For about $8 you can buy an inflatable pillow to rest against in the bathtub. (It's held secure by suction cups.) An inch-thick foam rubber pad will cushion you from the hard bottom of the tub as you bathe. Of course if it gets mildew on it, it might be better located in the trash can. Finally, you can sit in comfort on the toilet on a plush toilet seat cover and listen to music from a radio built into a toilet paper container.

Comfort and convenience are carried to extremes in the area of personal care.

EXERCISE 6-11

Study the following sets of paragraphs. Assume that each set also contains the next two paragraphs after an introduction. Change the beginning of the second paragraph in each set so that it contains a key word linking it to the previous paragraph.

1. One of the things I do to improve my English is to watch television. This is no doubt one of the most popular techniques that all foreign students use. I find that the situation comedies and detective shows help me improve my listening skills the most because the actors speak very rapidly. Documentaries and news programs help me build my vocabulary because they contain material that interests me. All of the shows help me improve my speaking skills because I consciously try to imitate the way the actors speak, especially the newscasters because they enunciate each word so well.

   I work the crossword puzzles in the daily newspaper. Sometimes I can figure out a word if several of the letters are in it, and sometimes I have to ask somebody. If I cannot finish the puzzle, I keep it until the solution appears in the next edition of the newspaper. Then I look up the words I did not know and write them down. I have learned dozens of new vocabulary words this way, and by doing the puzzles every day, I have found that many of the words reappear, thus reinforcing my knowledge of the new words.
2. Many people who want to stay young looking ask their doctors for Retin-A. This is an ointment that was originally made to help people with acne, but researchers found that it also reduces the number of fine wrinkles and makes the skin look smoother and healthier. Unfortunately, the effects from the ointment do not come immediately.

   The results of dermabrasion can be seen quickly, usually within a week or so. This is a minor surgical technique that some anti-agers have had done. It involves peeling off a layer or so of skin. The result is skin that looks younger and smoother, subtracting fifteen or more years from someone's appearance.
3. One popular mythical character that youngsters in America love is the tooth fairy. When a child loses a tooth, she puts it under her pillow and during the night the tooth fairy will come and take the tooth, leaving in its place some money. Some children leave their extracted teeth in special boxes to make them easier for the tooth fairy to find. There is no typical description of what the tooth fairy looks like; most kids are content to imagine it as a mysterious benevolent spirit.

   The Easter Bunny is a favorite mythical character. During Easter week, children go on Easter egg hunts to find colored and candy eggs hidden in yards and parks. A white bunny, sometimes called Peter Cottontail, has supposedly hidden these treats. In addition, on Easter morning children wake up to find that the Easter bunny has left them a basket full of chocolate eggs, jelly beans, candy eggs—all in a bed of green stuff that looks like grass.
4. Vending machines dispense almost any kind of food imaginable. Of course, it is common to get snacks, such as candy bars, peanuts, potato chips, cookies, crackers and cheese, doughnuts, and cupcakes, from these familiar machines. In addition, a person can

obtain nearly any kind of beverage — cola, root beer, lemon-lime sodas, coffee, and even beer. A person can also get a lunch of cold sandwiches and apple pie. But I will never forget the roomful of big green machines I saw at an airport. They were all spitting out complete plate dinners of chicken and rice, hot dogs and sauerkraut, and roast turkey.

Vending machines contain products for personal grooming. In almost any airport you can get anything you need to take care of your hair — hair pins, combs, brushes, hair nets, even hair spray. Also available from vending machines are toothbrushes, toothpaste, dental floss, and mouthwash. If you want to smell nice, hit the right button and you have aftershave lotion or expensive French perfume. And if by chance you have lost a button, a machine will give you a needle with a variety of colored thread. To make your personal grooming complete, simply put in your quarters and out will come a new belt, a pair of socks, and a matching necktie.

EXERCISE 6-12: WRITING ASSIGNMENT

Select one of the following topics for your writing assignment.

1. Reread the paragraphs in item 3, Exercise 6-11. What are some mythical characters that children in your country believe in? Write an essay using at least three examples of mythical characters. Try to arrive at a thesis statement that expresses your opinion about them.
2. Many groups of people have been victims of prejudice. Develop a thesis statement, outline your examples, and write an essay about people you are familiar with who have been victims of prejudice.
3. Clothes often tell a lot about a person. What are some things that you can tell about someone judging from the clothes he or she wears? Using this idea, develop a thesis, outline the examples, and write an essay.

GRAMMAR REVIEW

Gerunds and Infinitives

Gerunds and Infinitives as Subjects

We all are familiar with nouns — persons, places, or things — that act as subjects. In the following sentences, notice that the subjects are nouns:

Bill is learning to play tennis.

This *university* has a good track team.

Hard *work* is essential for an athlete.

However, there are some verb forms in English that can also function as nouns. They are the *ing* form—or gerund—and the *to* + verb form—or infinitive. In the following sentences, the gerund and infinitive function as nouns in the subject position:

Jogging is good for your circulation.

To find a jogging partner can be difficult.

When the infinitive is the subject, as in the second sentence, it is very common to move it (and its modifiers) to the end of the sentence and place *it* in the subject position:

It can be difficult *to find* a jogging partner.

Special Note: Degrees of Formality

While it is possible to use gerunds and infinitives as subjects for sentences, the resulting sentences differ in degree of formality and common usage. Generally, a sentence with *it* and the infinitive is the most common. The next most common is a sentence with the gerund as subject. The least common and most formal sentence is one that uses the infinitive as subject. A sentence with *it* and a gerund is quite informal and is not appropriate for essay writing.

If the infinitive has a specific subject in front of it, *for* is placed in front of that subject:

For Mark to run a mile is extremely rare.

Of course, this could be changed:

It is extremely rare *for* Mark to run a mile.

If the gerund has a specific subject in front of it, the possessive form is used:

Bill's running down the hall in the dorm disturbs us.

His running down the hall in the dorm disturbs us.

Finally, when the subject of a sentence is a gerund or infinitive, the subject of the sentence is singular and must agree with a singular verb:

The boy's *stealing* the basketballs *is* a serious offense.

EXERCISE 6-13

Combine the following sentences, using first a gerund, then an infinitive, and finally *it* in the subject position. Then determine which is the most common usage. The first one is done for you.

1. She takes a math course every semester. This is difficult.
   Taking a math course every semester is difficult.
   To take a math course every semester is difficult.
   It is difficult to take a math course every semester.
2. She decides which course to take at registration. This is easy.

3. During the semester, she goes to class every day. This is a good idea.

4. She listens carefully to the professor's lecture. This helps her understand.

5. She takes notes as the professor does the sample problems on the board. This is useful.

6. She does the homework problems regularly. This takes time.

7. She turns the homework in every day. This gives her a sense of satisfaction.

8. She gets good grades. This is the best reward.

Gerunds and Infinitives as Objects

As noted earlier, regular nouns are often used as subjects. It is also common to use regular nouns as direct objects (DO):

DO
The coach arranged the *meeting*.

Further, gerunds and infinitives can function as subjects of sentences. Like regular nouns, after certain verbs, gerunds and infinitives can also function as objects. Observe the following examples:

He agreed *to run* four miles a day.

He enjoys *playing* tennis.

The number of verbs that can use gerunds and infinitives as objects is limited. For a complete list of these verbs, see Appendix VII. There are several other restrictions on these verbs to keep in mind.

1. The following verbs cannot have a second subject before the gerund or infinitive.

   a. These are some of the most common verbs followed by gerunds: ***avoid, enjoy, finish, keep on, practice, resume, quit***

      He enjoys *playing* tennis.

   b. These are some of the most common verbs followed by infinitives: ***agree, decide, hope, learn, pretend, try, want.***

      He is learning *to play* tennis.

   c. These verbs can be followed by either gerunds or infinitives: ***begin, continue, intend, like, start.***

      Bill starts *jogging* at 7:00 A.M.

      Bill starts *to jog* at 7:00 A.M.

Note: After the verbs *remember* and *stop*, the gerund and infinitive have different meanings:

I remember *buying* stamps yesterday. (I bought stamps yesterday and now I remember that action.)

I remembered *to buy* stamps yesterday. (I bought stamps yesterday because I remembered that I was supposed to.)

Anna stopped *visiting* me. (She doesn't visit me anymore.)

Anna stopped *to visit* me. (Anna visited me.)

2. The following verbs must have a second subject before the infinitive. Most of the verbs in this class involve one person telling or advising another person.

   a. Here are some common verbs: ***advise, permit, remind, tell, warn.***

He advised *me* to practice for the interview.

b. After the following verbs, the *to* of the infinitive is deleted:
   (1) Causatives: *have, let, make.*
   (2) Verbs of observation: *feel, hear, notice, see, watch.*

   Bill *had* the janitor *open* the door.

   We *saw* Kim *leave* the office.

3. The following verbs can occur with or without a second subject: *ask, choose, expect, help, like, want.*

   I expected *to go* to the track meet.

   I expected Mario *to go* to the track meet.

   Notice that there is a difference in meaning between the two sentences. In the first sentence, the subject of the verb *expect*, *I*, will perform the action of *to go*. In the second sentence, *I* is the subject of *expect*, but Mario is the subject of *to go*.

EXERCISE 6-14

Write either the gerund or infinitive form of the verbs in the blanks. If both are possible, write both. If an infinitive is preceded by a second subject, draw a line under the second subject. Remember to check Appendix VII, pages 456–63, for a list of verbs followed by infinitives and gerunds.

1. Pedro Reyes is a good example of a young philanthropist. Born in Mexico, Pedro came to the United States with his mother and sister in 1980 when he was six years old. They were hoping ____________ (have) a good future. But that was difficult ____________ (achieve) because they were poor and lived in a part of Los Angeles where there were gangs. In high school, Pedro joined the Youth Community Service Club; this experience changed his life. He decided ____________ (improve) himself and ____________ (contribute) to the community. He became interested in helping other people. He has volunteered his services numerous times. In 1987, he encouraged some of his classmates ____________ (join) him in helping newly arrived students from Cambodia and South America ____________ (adjust) to their new life. He has also helped ____________ (lead) outdoor games for the blind at the Braille Institute. This is impressive since he only

learned __________ (speak) English fairly recently. In addition, he has kept students from dropping out of school and has encouraged at least one __________ (stay) away from street gangs. He has also enjoyed __________ (do) other volunteer community work. For example, he once helped __________ (organize) a "Wipe Out Weekend," during which students from all over the Los Angeles area agreed __________ (paint) over the ugly graffiti that can be seen all over the area. He has also spent some of his weekends __________ (clean up) inner-city neighborhoods for the Los Angeles Beautiful group and has even helped __________ (plant) trees around L.A. He has also volunteered __________ (help) at the Children's Museum __________ (handle) the weekend crowds. Pedro plans __________ (go) to college next year, but he expects __________ (continue) __________ (do) volunteer work. He is truly a "teenager who learned philanthropy as a second language."

—Adapted from D. Devoss, "Angels Among Us," *Los Angeles Times Magazine*, December 18, 25, 1988.

2. The service at our university's bookstore continues __________ (be) poor. To begin with, the manager has not learned __________ (hire) the right number of clerks. During registration and the first week of classes, a lot of students try __________ (buy) their books, but the manager only hires three or four clerks to check out customers. Unless you enjoy __________ (stand) in a long line for hours, you should avoid __________ (go) to the bookstore at this time. Then, when the initial rush is over, the manager starts __________ (hire) more clerks. Of course, they spend a lot of their time just standing around. However, if you ask the clerks __________ (help) you, you can expect them __________ (be) rude. One time I noticed a new student __________ (ask) a clerk where to find a particular book. The clerk didn't even look at him. I watched him __________ (turn) around and __________ (walk) away! The poor student just kept on

______ (search) for the book by himself. Perhaps the worst experience I have had there was one day when I asked the assistant manager ______ (cash) a check for me. He enjoyed ______ (tell) me that the bookstore didn't intend ______ (start) ______ (cash) checks for students. He made me ______ (feel) so angry and embarrassed that I have just quit ______ (go) to the bookstore entirely.

Gerunds as Objects of Prepositions

There are a number of common expressions and verbs in English that are predictably followed by a certain preposition. These expressions and verb + preposition combinations can be followed by gerunds. Some of the most common are the following:

look forward to	plan on	be nervous about	be afraid of
get used to	count on	be excited about	be tired of
be used to	insist on	be concerned about	be capable of
be accustomed to	be interested in	be good at	be accused of

Observe the following examples:

I am looking forward to *seeing* you on Tuesday.

I did not plan on *spending* so much money on my vacation.

The advisor is interested in *helping* him.

The new students were nervous about *living* in the dormitory.

The president is capable of *handling* the situation.

EXERCISE 6-15

Write either the gerund or infinitive form of the verb in each blank. If both are possible, write both. Where (P) is indicated, fill in the correct preposition.

Most college students go to college in order to be trained for a particular profession. Many look forward ______ (P) ______ (work) as competent engineers, teachers, or chemists. Before they can begin ______ (work), however, they must find a job. Usually, they are interested ______ (P) ______ (find) a job that offers a good salary and a chance for promotion. The first hurdle for them __________ (jump) is the job interview. Even though they may be well qualified, getting the right job can be difficult if you are not prepared __________ (handle) the job interview. Kim's experience is a good example.

While in school, Kim worked hard to learn his chosen profession, computer science. When a program did not work properly, Kim kept __________ (P) __________ (try) until it did. He never hesitated __________ (ask) his professors about aspects of computer science that he did not understand. He even managed __________ (work) in the computer room on campus to get experience. All of his professors agreed that Kim was a well-qualified graduate.

A month before Kim graduated with a B.S. degree, his advisor encouraged him __________ (sign) up for an interview with a large company. The company needed someone __________ (be) a programming supervisor. Kim thought he would be good __________ (P) __________ (do) that job because he had always enjoyed __________ (work) with people.

A week before the interview, Kim became nervous __________ (P) __________ (make) a bad impression. So, he asked his advisor __________ (give) him some help. His advisor told him __________ (make) a list of possible questions and __________ (practice) __________ (answer) them. He also urged him __________ (not be) afraid __________ (P) __________ (say) anything too controversial. Finally, his advisor assured him that he was capable __________ (P) __________ (handle) the job. Kim thanked his advisor for his encouragement and agreed __________ (practice) __________ (answer) some possible questions.

As Kim waited in the outer office to meet the interviewer, however, all of this good advice seemed __________ (fly) out the window. For a brief moment Kim considered __________ (escape) out the side door. The next thing he knew he was sitting across the desk from the interviewer trying __________ (remember) all the answers he had planned

__________ (P) __________ (give). Although he had practiced and was used __________ (P) __________ (give) the right answers, at the moment he could only stutter and stammer. To this day, he can only remember that the interview was very short!

You can see that a person can be well qualified for a job but fail __________ (get) it because he or she is not accustomed __________ (P) __________ (perform) in a job interview. Perhaps for students like Kim, how to manage a job interview should be a required course in college.

EXERCISE 6-16: WRITING ASSIGNMENT

Write a paragraph about a person who you know or who you have heard about who is a philanthropist. Develop the paragraph with an anecdote or some examples of the person's philanthropy. You may wish to review the first paragraph in Exercise 6-14 about Pedro Reyes.

EXERCISE 6-17: WRITING ASSIGNMENT

Write an essay about something learned from past experience. It might be about getting a job or entering a new school. Use an extended example to develop your topic.

Noun Clauses

In the preceding section, we learned that gerunds and infinitives as well as simple nouns can function in a sentence as a noun. There is another structure that functions as a noun: the noun clause.

In the following sentence, note that the direct object is a simple noun:

I know his *name* (DO).

In this sentence, a noun clause functions as the direct object:

He said *that he was confused and overwhelmed his first day at State University* (DO).

A noun clause is a sentence ("He was confused and overwhelmed his first day at State") to which a subordinate conjunction (*that*) has been added. The introductory conjunction for the noun clause depends on whether the clause was originally a statement or a question.

Noun Clauses Derived from Statements

AS DIRECT OBJECTS. The most common use of noun clauses derived from statements is as direct objects. Note the following example.

I think *(that) he is a liar.*

Notice that the conjunction connecting the two sentences is ***that***. ***That*** can be deleted if the meaning of the sentence remains clear. Next, notice the verb ***think***. There are only certain verbs, like ***think***, that are commonly followed by noun clauses. (For a complete list, see Appendix VII, pages 456–63.) Some of the most common are: ***agree, answer, believe, claim, decide, explain, forget, hear, know, learn, mean, realize, say, think***.

A common use of noun clauses is in indirect or reported speech. Normally, quotation marks are used to indicate the *actual* words spoken by someone.

"The strike isn't over yet."

When these words are "reported" or told to a third person, they are often changed into indirect speech:

He said *that the strike wasn't over yet.*

The tense of the main verb affects the tense of the verb in the noun clause. If the tense of the main verb is *past*, the tense in the indirect statement changes as follows:

1. Present forms change to past:

   "We *are* on strike."

   He replied that they *were* on strike.

2. Simple past tense changes to past perfect tense:

   "We *went* on strike last week."

   He answered that they *had gone* on strike the week before.

   Note: Pronouns and time expressions often must change to conform to the new time relationship.

3. The modals ***will*** and ***can*** change to ***would*** and ***could***. When ***must*** means ***have to***, it changes to ***had to***.

   "The university *will* not offer more money."

   He asserted that the university *would* not offer more money.

   Note: The modals ***may, might***, and ***should*** remain the same.

4. If the noun clause expresses a generalization or historical fact, the tense in the reported statement may remain in the present.

   He said that John *hates* to jog. (a generalization)

   He said that Helena *is* the capital of Montana. (a historical fact)

EXERCISE 6-18

You are a reporter for the school newspaper. Your assignment is to cover the strike by student workers in the cafeteria. Here is your interview with Ben Foster, the student who organized the strike.

REPORTER'S QUESTIONS	MR. FOSTER'S RESPONSES
"Mr. Foster, just who is on strike here?"	"All of the student workers are."
"How long have you been on strike?"	"Four days."
"Are any of the civil service employees on strike?"	"No, they are not on strike because they already have a satisfactory contract."
"Exactly why are the student workers on strike?"	"It's simple. We need higher wages."
"How much money do you make now? How much are you asking for?"	"Now we only get $3 an hour. That is below minimum wage. We must get at least $5 an hour."
"How has the strike affected the people who eat in the cafeteria?"	"The service is slower because there are no student workers to carry the trays or wash the dishes. Now the cooks have to do our jobs."
"How long do you expect to continue the strike?"	"We will not go back to work until the administration is willing to negotiate."

On a separate sheet of paper, change all of *Mr. Foster's statements* into indirect speech. Try to use a variety of verbs to begin the sentences. (Check the list on page 219 for possible verbs.)

Example:

Mr. Foster said that all the student workers were on strike.

(answered)

(replied)

AS SUBJECTS. Just as noun clauses can function as direct objects, they can also function as subjects. Note the noun clause as subject in this sentence:

That they have not settled the strike surprises me.

This sentence pattern is considered quite formal and sometimes awkward because the subject is so long and "heavy." It is common to add a simple noun subject to this kind of sentence, thereby turning the noun clause into an adjective clause. The sentence, however, still tends to be quite formal.

The fact that they have not settled the strike surprises me.

Only certain nouns can be used in this sentence pattern: ***the fact, the idea, the belief, the evidence.*** Only certain verbs and ***be*** + adjective combinations can follow the noun clause in this pattern. Some common ones are ***surprise, annoy, please, amaze, irritate, be clear, be unfortunate, be unlikely, be obvious, be possible, be apparent, be true.***

The fact that they have not settled the strike is irritating.

The idea that he will cheat on the exam is ridiculous.

The evidence that he stole the money is clear.

Perhaps the most common and less formal use of the noun clause as subject, however, is after the verb phrase. In this case, ***it*** is added to fill the subject position:

It is surprising that they have not settled the strike.

It surprises me that they have not settled the strike.

It is clear that he stole the money.

Note that ***the fact*** cannot be used before the noun clause here. Also remember that the same verbs and ***be*** + adjective combinations are used here. Clauses beginning with ***the fact that*** can also function as objects of prepositions.

The students talked about *the fact that they have not settled the strike.*

EXERCISE 6-19

You are a reporter for your school newspaper. Your assignment is to cover the strike by student workers in the cafeteria. You have just interviewed the president of the university. Below are your notes. Write two complete sentences for each note. First write a sentence with *the fact, the belief,* and so forth, in the subject position. Next write a sentence with *it* in the subject position. Then decide which sentence sounds more formal. Pay attention to tense. It may be necessary to add articles and quantifiers. The first one is done for you.

1. Students' demands—unreasonable—clear.
   The fact that students' demands are unreasonable is clear.
   It is clear that the students' demands are unreasonable.
2. Strike—continue—too long—obvious.
   ____
   ____

3. None — civil service employees — cooperate — please me.

4. Student workers — not need higher wages — apparent.

5. Strike — slow down service — annoying.

6. Students — lazy bums — disappointing.

7. Students — not want to work for a living — disgusting.

8. Administration — not negotiate — clear.

9. Administration — hire new workers — necessary.

EXERCISE 6-20: WRITING ASSIGNMENT

Write an essay with the thesis, "In many situations, compromise is necessary." Include a standard introduction in which the thesis sentence appears at the end.

Develop the essay with examples. Use the situation of the student worker strike given in Exercises 6-18 and 6-19 as the first example. Develop this example in one paragraph. Pretend the strike happened at a local university. Add as many details as you wish to make the writing specific.

Develop two more examples in separate paragraphs. Try to use indirect speech in the examples. You might give as an example a conflict between a youngster and parents.

Complete the essay with an appropriate conclusion.

Noun Clauses Derived from Questions

AS DIRECT OBJECTS. Statements are often used as noun clauses to function as direct objects. Noun clauses derived from questions, often called indirect questions, can also function as direct objects. Look at both "yes/no" questions and "WH" questions (that is, questions asking *who*, *what*, *where*, and so on).

1. *Yes/no questions*. Note the following direct questions:

   "Does Mark like to jog?"

   "Is the president going to cooperate?"

   These yes/no questions are made into indirect questions by adding the conjunction *whether* (or *if*):

   I don't know *whether* (or not) Mark likes to jog.

   He didn't say *whether* the president was going to cooperate.

   Note that when the indirect yes/no question is added to the main clause the auxiliary *do/does/did* is omitted and the subject and verb revert to statement word order.
2. *WH-questions*. Note the following direct questions:

   "Who is he?"

   "Who is living there?"

   "What does he want?"

   All of these questions can be added to a main clause by omitting the *do/does/did* auxiliary and changing the question to statement word order:

	WH-WORD	SUBJECT	VERB	
I don't know	who	he	is.	
I don't know	what	he	wants.	
I don't know		who	is living	there.

   Note the subject–verb agreement when the *do/does* auxiliary is deleted:

   "What does he want?" I don't know what he wants.

The verbs commonly used in the main clause before statements are also used in the main clause before indirect questions. See page 219. Noun clauses derived from questions are common in indirect or reported speech. The rules for tense change in indirect speech given for statements also apply to questions.

EXERCISE 6-21

Turn all the reporter's questions in Exercise 6-18 into indirect speech. Try to use a variety of verbs to begin the sentences.

Examples:

The reporter asked Mr. Foster who was on strike.

I asked him who was on strike.

AS SUBJECTS. Just as noun clauses derived from statements can function as subjects, so can noun clauses derived from questions. Let us look at both yes/no questions and WH-questions.

1. *Yes/no questions.* Look at these examples:

 "Does Mark like to jog?"

 "Is the president going to cooperate?"

 Note that the conjunction ***whether*** (***if*** is not possible) is added and the ***do/does/did*** auxiliary is deleted. The question then can act as the subject of the sentence. These noun clauses are quite formal.

 Whether (or not) Mark likes to jog is not important.

 Whether (or) the president is going to cooperate does not concern me.

 The use of the yes/no question as the subject is quite restricted. Note the following verbs and expressions that can follow it:

Whether Mark likes to jog (or not)	*is* not *important.*
	does not *concern* me.
	tells me something about him.
	depends on past experience.
	remains a mystery.
	indicates something about him.
	influences my decision.

2. *WH-questions.* Note the following examples:

Who he is	*is* not *important.*
Who is living there	*is irrelevant.*
What he wants	*is confidential.*
	is something to consider.
	affects my decision.

 Many restrictions also exist for the use of WH-questions as subjects. The preceding verbs and expressions given for yes/no questions can also follow WH-questions as subjects.

AS OBJECTS OF PREPOSITIONS. Indirect questions can also occur as objects of prepositions. Note the examples:

We are concerned about *whether (or not) he is telling the truth.*

She is interested in *how many people are striking.*

His question about *when to do the report was ignored.*

EXERCISE 6-22

You are a supervisor in a company about to interview a computer programmer for a job. Following are some questions you are supposed to ask the prospective employee. What is your attitude about these questions? Turn each question into the subject of a sentence and finish the sentence with one of these expressions:

Be (not)	important	(not)	affect . . .
	irrelevant		concern . . .
	confidential		tell . . .
	something to consider		depend on . . .
			remain . . .
			indicate . . .
			influence . . .

1. What is his name?
   What his name is is not important.
   What his name is does not affect my decision.
2. Where did he go to school?
   ______
   ______
3. What was his major?
   ______
   ______
4. What was his grade point average?
   ______
   ______
5. Does he have good references?
   ______
   ______
6. Does he have any experience?
   ______
   ______
7. What are his hobbies?
   ______
   ______
8. Who are his parents?
   ______
   ______

9. Will he fit in with the other employees?

____

____

10. Is he available to begin work immediately?

____

____

11. What is his attitude about politics?

____

____

EXERCISE 6-23: WRITING ASSIGNMENT

Choose one of the following writing topics. First decide on a controlling idea and thesis statement. Then decide on the examples to use to support the thesis. Write a brief outline of the essay. Then write the essay.

1. Do you have a maxim or important statement that helps you guide your life? If so, can you give examples of times when you have used it. Write an essay stating your maxim and showing its importance to you by using examples. You may want to refer back to Pogrebin's essay, "Words That Count," for typical maxims (pages 193–95).
2. What are some of the unwritten rules that you think cultures use to regulate behavior? Can you think of relevant examples of these rules either in American culture or in some other culture? Write an essay using these examples to support a thesis. You may want to refer back to Greene's essay, "How Unwritten Rules Circumscribe Our Lives" (pages 189–91).
3. When you first came to the United States, you were undoubtedly surprised by something. Can you think of examples? Did you find anything particularly difficult to adjust to? Can you think of examples? Choose one of these topics, develop your thesis, and support it with examples.

Example Essay Checklist

1. An example essay supports its thesis with an appropriate number of examples. Does your essay have sufficient examples to support its point?
2. The examples you use to support your thesis should be representative or fair examples. Are your examples fairly chosen?
3. The organization of details and examples in an example essay depends on the subject and the writer's logic. Typical organizing principles are time, familiarity, and importance. Are the thesis and supporting examples logically organized in your essay?
4. Transitions between paragraphs and repetition of key words and phrases help to make an essay coherent. Have you used a variety of techniques to make your essay flow smoothly?

Chapter 7

The Comparison and Contrast Essay

Readings: People and Nature

The relationship of human beings to nature is complex. On the one hand, we are part of nature—participants in a biological life cycle in which we depend on the natural world for our food and indeed our very existence. On the other hand, we are often uncomfortable with our dependence on nature, preferring instead an independent relationship in which we can control nature and exploit it for our own purposes. We like to think that our technology has freed us from the demands of living in a natural world. The complexity of our relationship with nature is often shown in the way we treat nature, particularly in how we attempt to minimize our dependence on nature and concentrate on our mastery of it. Our attempts to master and control nature have had serious consequences for the natural environment, including in recent years an increase in pollution, threats to the ozone layer, and the possibility of the greenhouse effect. Yet at the same time we cannot deny our human nature, part of which is to explore the unknown, to push nature to its limits.

The two essays that follow explore in different ways the relationship of human beings to nature. In the first, "A Fable for Tomorrow," Rachel Carson shows us the dangers facing our natural environment if we continue to treat nature irresponsibly. In the second, "Columbus and the Moon," Tom Wolfe affirms that part of human nature is the need to explore the environment, to discover the unknown. As you read both selections, consider the following questions:

1. What are the major problems facing the world's environment?
2. What can or should be done about these problems?
3. Is space exploration a valuable enterprise? Why, or why not?

4. In your opinion, what is the ideal relationship between humans and nature?

READING 1

A FABLE FOR TOMORROW

RACHEL CARSON

In the 1950s and 1960s, Rachel Carson wrote a number of books alerting Americans to the dangers facing our natural environment. One of her most popular works is* Silent Spring *(1962), from which the following excerpt is taken. In it Carson tells a fable—a short story with a moral—about an imaginary American town that undergoes a serious change. As you read the selection, try to answer these questions:

1. What happened to the town?
2. What was the town like before the change? After the change?

1 There was once a town in the heart of America where all life seemed to live in harmony• with its surroundings. The town lay in the midst of a checkerboard of prosperous farms, with fields of grain and hillsides of orchards where, in spring, white clouds of bloom drifted above the green fields. In au-

orderly, peaceful, friendly

tumn, oak and maple and birch set up a blaze of color that flamed and flickered across a backdrop of pines. Then foxes barked in the hills and deer silently crossed the fields, half hidden in the mists of the fall mornings.

2 Along the roads, laurel, viburnum and alder, great ferns and wildflowers delighted the traveler's eye through much of the year. Even in winter the roadsides were places of beauty, where countless birds came to feed on the berries and on the seed heads of the dried weeds rising above the snow. The countryside was, in fact, famous for the abundance and variety of its bird life, and when the flood of migrants• was pouring through in spring and fall people traveled from great distances to observe them. Others came to fish the streams, which flowed clear and cold out of the hills and contained shady pools where trout lay. So it had been from the days many years ago when the first settlers raised their houses, sank their wells, and built their barns.

birds that move from one place to another

3 Then a strange blight[1] crept over the area and everything began to change. Some evil spell[2] had settled on the community: mysterious maladies• swept the flocks of chickens; the cattle and sheep sickened and died. Everywhere was a shadow of death. The farmers spoke of much illness among their families. In the town the doctors had become more and more puzzled by new kinds of sickness appearing among their patients. There had been several sudden and unexplained deaths not only among adults but even among children, who would be stricken• suddenly while at play and die within a few hours.

sicknesses

afflicted

4 There was a strange stillness. The birds, for example—where had they gone? Many people spoke of them, puzzled and disturbed. The feeding stations in the backyards were deserted. The few birds seen anywhere were moribund;• they trembled violently and could not fly. It was a spring without voices. On the mornings that had once throbbed with the dawn chorus of robins, catbirds, doves, jays, wrens, and scores of other bird voices there was now no sound; only silence lay over the fields and woods and marsh.

dying

5 On the farms the hens brooded,• but no chicks hatched. The farmers complained that they were unable to raise any pigs—the litters were small and the young survived only a few days. The apple trees were coming into bloom but no bees droned among the blossoms, so there was no pollination and there would be no fruit.

sat on their eggs

6 The roadsides, once so attractive were now lined with browned and withered• vegetation as though swept by fire.

dried up

[1]*disease or condition that kills or diminishes growth*
[2]*harmful condition brought about by magic or charms*

These, too, were silent, deserted by all living things. Even the streams were now lifeless. Anglers• no longer visited them, for all the fish had died. *fishermen*

7 In the gutters under the eaves[3] and between the shingles of the roofs, a white granular• powder still showed a few patches; some weeks before it had fallen like snow upon the roofs and the lawns, the fields and streams. *grainy*

8 No witchcraft, no enemy action had silenced the rebirth of new life in this stricken world. The people had done it themselves.

9 This town does not actually exist, but it might easily have a thousand counterparts• in America or elsewhere in the world. I know of no community that has experienced all the misfortunes I describe. Yet every one of these disasters has actually happened somewhere, and many real communities have already suffered a substantial number of them. A grim specter[4] has crept upon us almost unnoticed, and this imagined tragedy may easily become a stark[5] reality we all shall know. *others just like it*

EXERCISE 7-1: COMPREHENSION/ DISCUSSION QUESTIONS

1. How does Carson describe the town in the first two paragraphs?
2. What are some of the natural objects that Carson describes in the first two paragraphs? Why does she not focus on just one aspect of nature, such as trees?
3. What happened to the town? How does Carson describe the "evil spell" that settled over the town and countryside?
4. Is it significant that the evil spell descends in the spring? Why, or why not?
5. What is the "white granular powder" that falls from the sky (paragraph 7)? Why does Carson not explain what it is or where it came from?
6. Where in the essay is the author's main point stated? What is the main point?
7. List some of the uses of chemicals today, especially in our food and water. In your opinion, would Carson see these uses as progress? Do you? Are these chemicals safe? Are there adequate safeguards for human health in regulating their use?
8. What should be the relationship of factories to the environment?

[3]**gutters under the eaves** *metal troughs around the roof of the house for catching rainwater*
[4]*a ghost or object of fear*
[5]*bleak, barren, standing out sharply*

Should factories be required to protect and restore the environment they use? Can you think of examples?

9. In your view, is it possible for humans to live in harmony with the environment? Support your answer.

EXERCISE 7-2: VOCABULARY DEVELOPMENT

For each of the following sentences, fill in the blank with the word from the list that best completes the meaning of the sentence. Then write five original sentences each containing a word from the list.

harmony (par. 1)	blight (par. 3)	maladies (par. 3)
migrants (par. 2)	stricken (par. 3)	granular (par. 7)
counterparts (par. 9)	grim (par. 9)	specter (par. 9)
stark (par. 9)		

1. He was ___________ with a strange illness and died suddenly.
2. The ideal situation is for humans to live in ___________ with nature.
3. All the farmers' crops had a strange ___________ and were unfit to harvest.
4. For towns close to nuclear power plants, the power plants become a fearful ___________.
5. Both animals and crops can be stricken with countless ___________ if the environment is polluted.

READING 2

COLUMBUS AND THE MOON

TOM WOLFE

Tom Wolfe is a journalist who has popularized a particular style of writing known as "new journalism"—a style of news reporting that is dramatic, frequently subjective, and uses many of the techniques of the novel. Wolfe has also authored a number of books, including The Right Stuff *(1979), from which this reading is taken. In it the author shows his interest in space exploration. As you read the selection, consider the following questions:*

1. What similarities exist between Christopher Columbus's voyages of discovery to the New World in

the fifteenth century and America's trips to the moon and beyond in the twentieth century?

2. Were Columbus's voyages of discovery important events? Why, or why not?
3. Is space exploration a valuable enterprise? Why, or why not?

1 The National Aeronautics and Space Administration's moon landing 10 years ago today was a Government project, but then so was Columbus's voyage to America in 1492. The Government, in Columbus's case, was the Spanish Court of Ferdinand and Isabella. Spain was engaged in a sea race with Portugal in much the same way that the United States would be caught up in a space race with the Soviet Union four and a half centuries later.

2 The race in 1492 was to create the first shipping lane to Asia. The Portuguese expeditions• had always sailed east, around the southern tip of Africa. Columbus decided to head due west, across open ocean, a scheme• that was feasible• only thanks to a recent invention—the magnetic ship's compass. Until then ships had stayed close to the great land masses even for the longest voyages. Likewise, it was only thanks to an invention of the 1940's and early 1950's, the high-speed electronic computer, that NASA would even consider propelling• astronauts out of the Earth's orbit and toward the moon.

voyages
plan / practical, possible
sending

3 Both NASA and Columbus made not one but a series of voyages. NASA landed men on six different parts of the moon. Columbus had to keep coming back to the Government with their hands out, pleading for refinancing.• In each case the reply of the Government became, after a few years: "This is all very impressive, but what earthly good is it to anyone back home?"

more money

4 Columbus was reduced to making the most desperate• claims. When he first reached land in 1492 at San Salvador, off Cuba, he expected to find gold, or at least spices. The Arawak Indians were awed• by the strangers and their ships, which they believed had descended from the sky, and they presented them with their most prized possessions, live parrots and balls of cotton. Columbus soon set them digging for gold, which didn't exist. So he brought back reports of fabulous riches in the form of manpower; which is to say, slaves. He was not speaking of the Arawaks, however. With the exception of criminals and prisoners of war, he was supposed to civilize all natives and convert them to Christianity. He was talking about the Carib Indians, who were cannibals• and therefore qualified as criminals. The Caribs would fight down to the last unbroken bone rather than endure captivity, and few ever survived the voyages back to Spain. By the end of Columbus's second voyage, in 1496, the Government was becoming testy.• A great deal of wealth was going into voyages to Asia, and very little was coming back. Columbus made his men swear• to return to Spain saying that they had not only reached the Asian mainland, they had heard Japanese spoken.

extreme, wild
filled with respect and fear
people who eat human flesh
impatient
promise

5 Likewise by the early 1970's, it was clear that the moon was in economic terms pretty much what it looked like from Earth, a gray rock. NASA, in the quest• for appropriations,[1] was reduced to publicizing the "spinoffs"• of the space program. These included Teflon-coated frying pans, a ballpoint pen that would write in a weightless environment, and a

search
secondary benefits

[1]*government money*

computerized biosensor system that would enable doctors to treat heart patients without making house calls. On the whole, not a giant step for mankind.*

6 In 1493, after his first voyage, Columbus had ridden through Barcelona at the side of King Ferdinand in the position once occupied by Ferdinand's late son, Juan. By 1500, the bad-mouthing• of Columbus had reached the point where he was put in chains at the conclusion of his third voyage and returned to Spain in disgrace. NASA suffered no such ignominy,• of course, but by July 20, 1974, the fifth anniversary of the landing of Apollo 11, things were grim enough. The public had become gloriously bored by space exploration. The fifth anniversary celebration consisted mainly of about 200 souls, mostly NASA people, sitting on folding chairs underneath a camp meeting canopy• on the marble prairie outside the old Smithsonian Air Museum in Washington listening to speeches by Neil Armstrong, Michael Collins, and Buzz Aldrin and watching the caloric waves ripple.**

criticizing

shame, dishonor

open tent

7 Extraordinary rumors had begun to circulate about the astronauts. The most lurid• said that trips to the moon, and even into earth orbit, had so traumatized[2] the men, they had fallen victim to religious and spiritualist manias• or plain madness. (Of the total 73 astronauts chosen, one, Aldrin, is known to have suffered from depression, rooted, as his own memoir makes clear, in matters that had nothing to do with space flight. Two teamed up in an evangelical organization, and one

sensational, startling

obsessions, mental disorders

[2]*psychologically upset*

---

*On July 20, 1969, the first astronauts walked on the moon. As astronaut Neil Armstrong took the first step on the moon, he said, "That's one small step for a man, one giant step for mankind." Here Wolfe is referring to that statement. He is saying, however, that the items that NASA is publicizing, like frying pans and ballpoint pens, are not at all important but that the step on the moon was. To Wolfe, it is ironic that people would be more interested in these spinoff items than in a truly great and historic event.

**Wolfe's description of the fifth anniversary celebration has a number of allusions to the American traditions of the camp meeting and the song "America the Beautiful," reminding us of American patriotism. In the late 1800s and early 1900s, religious preachers commonly held camp meetings. They traveled from one rural area to another, setting up a large tent in an empty field and inviting all the local people to attend a one- or two-week series of nightly meetings. These meetings were popular both for the opportunity they provided settlers living in remote areas to gather together and for the religious fervor and excitement they generated. In describing the fifth anniversary celebration of the landing of Apollo 11, Wolfe compares the gathering of people on the marble area outside the Smithsonian Air Museum to such a camp meeting. He describes the people as sitting on folding chairs underneath an outdoor tent. Because it is July, it is hot and uncomfortable. Wolfe refers to the July heat when he says they watched "the caloric waves ripple"—that is, they watched the heat waves coming up off the marble. In this same line, the author alludes to the first line of "America the Beautiful," which says that America is beautiful because of its "amber waves of grain," or its fields of golden grain. However, Wolfe's point here is that people are patriotic out of duty; they are more concerned about the heat than the space program.

set up a foundation for the scientific study of psychic• phenomena — interests the three of them had developed long before they flew in space.) The NASA budget, meanwhile, had been reduced to the lightbill level.•

sensitive to supernatural forces

very low

8 Columbus died in 1509, nearly broke and stripped of most of his honors as Spain's Admiral of the Ocean, a title he preferred. It was only later that history began to look upon him not as an adventurer who had tried and failed to bring home gold — but as a man with a supernatural sense of destiny,[3] whose true glory was his willingness to plunge[4] into the unknown, including the remotest• parts of the universe he could hope to reach.

farthest

9 NASA still lives, albeit• in reduced circumstances, and whether or not history will treat NASA like the admiral is hard to say.

although

10 The idea that the exploration of the rest of the universe is its own reward is not very popular, and NASA is forced to keep talking about things such as bigger communications satellites that will enable live television transmission of European soccer games at a fraction of the current cost. Such notions as "building a bridge to the stars for mankind" do not light up the sky today — but may yet.

EXERCISE 7-3: COMPREHENSION/ DISCUSSION QUESTIONS

1. Because this reading is an excerpt from a book, it does not contain a true introduction. Instead, it begins by describing the similarities between Columbus's voyages of discovery and NASA's trips into space. What similarity does Wolfe give in the first paragraph? In the second paragraph?
2. In the third paragraph, Wolfe gives two similarities. What are they?
3. What is the main idea of paragraph 4? What previously stated idea does it support? What are some of Columbus's "desperate claims"?
4. What is the main idea of paragraph 5? What previously stated idea does it support?
5. In paragraph 6, Wolfe describes the attitudes of people toward Columbus and toward the NASA space program. How are the attitudes similar?
6. In paragraph 7, Wolfe continues the idea begun in paragraph 6. How are the astronauts being compared to Columbus?

[3]**supernatural sense of destiny** *unusual idea of his purpose in life*
[4]*dive or rush forward*

7. Wolfe gives his opinion of Columbus in paragraph 8. What is his opinion? What kind of man was Columbus?
8. From paragraph 10, what is Wolfe's opinion about space exploration? Is he in favor of it? How do you know?
9. According to Wolfe, what is the basic similarity between Columbus's voyages and NASA's space program? Do you agree?
10. In your view, is space exploration important? Why, or why not? Would the money spent on space exploration be better spent here on earth?
11. What relationship between humans and nature does space exploration exemplify?
12. What characteristics of human nature does space exploration point up?

EXERCISE 7-4: VOCABULARY DEVELOPMENT

In the following sentences taken from the reading, a word or phrase is italicized. Using your dictionary if necessary, rewrite the sentence with a different word or phrase that is similar in meaning to the italicized word.

1. Spain was *engaged* in a sea race with Portugal in much the same way that the United States would be caught up in a space race with the Soviet Union four and a half centuries later. (par. 1) ________

   ____

2. As a result both NASA and Columbus had to keep coming back to the Government *with their hands out*, pleading for refinancing. (par. 3) ____________________________

   ____

3. Columbus *was reduced* to making the most desperate claims. (par. 4) ____________________________

   ____

4. NASA, in the quest for appropriations, was reduced *to publicizing* the "spinoffs" of the space program. (par. 5) ____________

   ____

5. . . . by July 20, 1974, the fifth anniversary of the landing of Apollo 11, things were *grim* enough. (par. 6) ____________

   ____

6. . . . one set up a *foundation* for the scientific study of psychic phenomena. . . . (par. 7) ________________________

   ____

7. Such *notions* as "building a bridge to the stars for mankind" do not light up the sky today—but may yet. (par. 10) __________

   ____

Writing

Although details and examples can be used in all kinds of expository writing, not all essay topics are best developed in an example essay pattern. Very often, for example, you are asked to compare and contrast two things, items, or people. In your history class you might be asked to compare and contrast the Greek and Roman empires; in your biology class you might be required to compare and contrast DNA and RNA. Comparing and contrasting is a process we all do every day. We compare and contrast to determine the superiority of one thing over another. When we buy a car, for instance, we usually shop around and compare deals. We explain something that is unknown by comparing it to something that is known. We might explain what a barometer is by saying it looks like a thermometer but measures atmospheric pressure instead of temperature. We also compare and contrast when we want to show that two apparently similar things are in fact quite different in important ways, or to show that two apparently dissimilar things are really quite similar in significant ways. It might, for instance, be quite enlightening to discover that two very different cultures have some important things in common. We also compare and contrast to show how something or someone has changed, such as Armenia before and after the earthquake in 1988.

We have many reasons for comparing and contrasting, and since the process of comparison and contrast is such a common method of thinking and of developing topics, it is important to write a well-organized comparison and contrast paper. There is one thing to keep in mind, however. With comparison and contrast, the purpose is not just to point out similarities and differences or advantages and disadvantages; the purpose is to persuade, explain, or inform. Think of comparison and contrast as a *method of development*—not as a purpose for writing.

When you are planning a comparison and contrast essay, there are several points to consider.

Points of Comparison

Let us suppose that you are asked to compare and contrast two people —perhaps two generals, two politicians, or two religious leaders. What would you compare and contrast about them? You could compare their looks, backgrounds, philosophies, the way they treat people, their attitudes toward life, their intelligence, their life-styles, and so on. The list could continue, but this is just the problem: you would have a list. When comparing and contrasting two things, people, countries, and so forth, especially for a standard 300- to 500-word essay, it is best to restrict the points of comparison to two to four. Therefore, be selective and choose the most significant points for comparison that will support the central idea in your essay. For instance, if you wanted to compare two politicians in order to show that one is better as a public servant, you would not bother comparing and contrasting their tastes in food because this point would be irrelevant.

EXERCISE 7-5: WRITING ASSIGNMENT

Choose one of the following writing assignments.

1. Think of two educational systems that you are familiar with, such as the university system in your country and the system in the United States. Write a list of the things they have in common—their similarities—and another list of the ways they differ—their differences. From these lists, find three or four general points of comparison.
2. Choose two products—such as two different automobiles, cameras, hair dryers, or stereos—and make a list of their similarities and differences. From that list, find three or four general points of comparison.

Emphasis on Comparison or Contrast

In a comparison and contrast essay, the emphasis is usually on one or the other; that is, you spend more time either comparing or contrasting, depending on your purpose. If you are comparing two rather similar things, you should acknowledge the obvious similarities but focus on the differences. If you are comparing two obviously dissimilar things, you should acknowledge the obvious contrasts but emphasize the less obvious similarities.

Patterns of Organization

There are two basic patterns of organization for developing the comparison and contrast essay. Although they are called by various names, we refer to them here as Pattern A and Pattern B. To show how these patterns work, let's consider the topic of two automobiles: the Road Runner XL and the Speed Demon 280. Your points of comparison might be the cost of maintenance, performance, and comfort. Using Pattern A, you could organize the essay in this way:

Pattern A (Point-by-Point) or "Slice" method

Thesis Statement: The Speed Demon 280 is a better car than the Road Runner XL.

I. Cost of Maintenance
  A. The Road Runner XL
  B. The Speed Demon 280
II. Performance
  A. The Road Runner XL
  B. The Speed Demon 280

III. Comfort
   A. The Road Runner XL
   B. The Speed Demon 280

Pattern A—Point-by-Point—is useful for organizing more complex topics. It is also an easy pattern to follow because the comparison-contrast is made clear throughout the essay.

A developmental paragraph in a comparison and contrast essay following Pattern A appears to be more complex than a developmental paragraph in an example essay. In the developmental paragraph in the comparison and contrast essay, the writer introduces a topic (the point of comparison), but the topic is broken down into two parts to make the comparison. For example, let us say you were asked to compare the two automobiles, the Road Runner XL and the Speed Demon 280. For one of your points of comparison, you have chosen the cost of maintenance. You have found that the Road Runner XL is expensive to maintain and the Speed Demon is economical. What you have, then, are really two controlling ideas: one for each car. Here is how that paragraph might be developed:

> The Road Runner XL and the Speed Demon 280 differ in cost of maintenance. The Road Runner is rather expensive to maintain. This car gets rather poor mileage, with 23 miles per gallon on the highway and 18 miles per gallon in the city. Moreover, it requires the more expensive premium gasoline. In addition, the Road Runner has to have a tune-up every four months and an oil change every ninety days. The average driver who owns a Road Runner must pay approximately $1,400 a year to keep this car running. The Speed Demon, on the other hand, is quite economical. It gets an impressive 40 miles per gallon on the highway and 35 in the city, and unlike the Road Runner, the Speed Demon takes the less costly regular gasoline. In addition, whereas the Road Runner requires tune-ups and oil changes, the Speed Demon requires little maintenance. It needs to be tuned-up only every twelve months; the oil needs to be changed only every four months. In summary, instead of paying $1,400 per year to keep the car running, the owner of a Speed Demon only has to pay $600, which is significantly less.

This paragraph can be outlined as follows:

I. The Road Runner XL and the Speed Demon 280 differ in cost of maintenance.
   A. The Road Runner is rather expensive to maintain.
      1. Mileage.
      2. Tune-ups.
      3. Oil changes.
      4. Average cost of maintenance.
   B. The Speed Demon is economical to maintain.
      1. Mileage.
      2. Tune-ups.
      3. Oil changes.
      4. Average cost of maintenance.

In this outline, the Roman numeral *I* introduces the point of comparison (the topic); the next point of comparison would be outlined as Roman numeral *II*. Since the paragraph is rather long, it is possible to break it into two paragraphs, with the second one beginning "The Speed Demon, on the other hand, is quite economical."

EXERCISE 7-6: WRITING ASSIGNMENT

Study the following information about the comfort of the Road Runner XL and the Speed Demon 280 and find a controlling idea about the difference in comfort. Then write a paragraph comparing and contrasting the comfort of the Road Runner and the comfort of the Speed Demon.

THE ROAD RUNNER XL	THE SPEED DEMON 280
Spacious interior	Not as spacious interior
Ample head and leg room in both front and back.	Ample head and leg room in front, but cramped in the back (less used).
Two people can sit comfortably in the front and three in the back.	Two can sit comfortably in front but only two can sit comfortably in back.
Uncomfortable seats	Comfortable seats
Although the seats are large, they are vinyl and get very hot in spring and summer.	Suede seats are cool in the summer and pleasant all year round.
Cooling and heating not ideal	Excellent air conditioning and heating system
The air conditioner does not cool the back seat area; the heater is effective.	The air conditioner cools the entire car rapidly; the heater is equally effective.

This same topic can be developed in another way: Pattern B, called "All of one/All of the other."

Pattern B (All of One/All of the Other) "Chunk" method

Thesis Statement: The Speed Demon 280 is a better car than the Road Runner XL.

I. The Road Runner XL
- *A.* Cost of Maintenance
- *B.* Performance
- *C.* Comfort

II. The Speed Demon 280
- *A.* Cost of Maintenance
- *B.* Performance
- *C.* Comfort

Note that the points of comparison are the same and that they are discussed in the same order under each section in both patterns of organization. One of the problems with Pattern B, however, is that it is sometimes difficult to remind the reader in the second section of how the points compare or contrast with the points mentioned in the first section. Therefore, generally speaking, Pattern B is more useful for more limited topics.

As you read the following essay, determine whether it focuses more on comparison or contrast. Also, which pattern of development does the essay use?

TWO UNIVERSITY SYSTEMS

It was not until I joined an American university that I realized the fact that the American and Lebanese systems of college education differ in many ways. Perhaps the circumstances under which each system was established lay behind these differences; but whatever the causes were, the differences exist and they are major. As a result, studying in America seems to be much easier than doing so in Lebanon.

The first step toward earning a college degree is being admitted to the university, whether in America or in Lebanon. The conditions for admission, however, are very different. In my case, this American university asked only for my TOEFL scores and my high school grades. In addition to these, a Lebanese university asked me to take another three tests. The first was the English Entrance Exam, which is much harder than the TOEFL. The second was the Scientific Qualification Exam, which includes mathematics, physics, and chemistry. The results of the SQ exam decide whether a student is eligible to take the third test or not. Obviously, the difference is clear.

The second major difference between the two systems is the path that is followed in order to graduate. In America, every field of study has certain requirements that must be achieved. There are no restrictions on how or in how many years they are achieved. Whether a person takes one course at a time or more than that, he is free, as long as he passes them all. In contrast to this, a college degree in Lebanon consists of several years. Each year is made up of several courses and the failure to pass any two of these courses costs a student the whole year, which must then be repeated. If the student fails the same year for a second time, he is considered ineligible for a college degree and he must drop out.

Another major difference is the amount of work needed each semester. The number of hours studied in an American university per week has an upper limit of eighteen hours. A full-time student has a lower limit of twelve hours, but no such limit exists for a part-time student. In Lebanon, on the other hand, only one limit exists. Each student must take as many as thirty hours per week, which guarantees busy afternoons and weekends. Of course, there is no need to mention that there is no such thing as a part-time student. So a student in Lebanon must really be dedicated to studying. He must put aside his personal interests and habits and forget about his free time.

Even though both systems provide a good education, one system makes earning a college degree much easier than the other. Of course, this system is the American one. Perhaps the difficulty of the Lebanese system is the reason behind my finding the American one easy, but I think that the designers of the American system worked hard to make college degrees accessible to the majority of the American people and they succeeded.

—*Tammam Dandashi*

EXERCISE 7-7

On a separate sheet of paper, answer the following questions about "Two University Systems."

1. What is the thesis of the essay? What are its points of comparison?
2. Does the essay focus more on comparison or on contrast?
3. Which pattern of organization does the writer follow? Why was this pattern selected?
4. Does the essay have a topic sentence that states the controlling idea about the differences in university admissions requirements? If so, what is it?
5. What is the controlling idea about their differences in graduation requirements? Workloads?
6. Is the essay unified? Coherent?
7. Is the conclusion logical?
8. Make a detailed outline of the essay.

EXERCISE 7-8: WRITING ASSIGNMENT

Using the preceding essay as a model and the notes you made in Exercise 7-5, write a first-draft essay that compares and contrasts two educational systems or two products.

As you read the essay that follows, try to locate its thesis statement and determine its purpose—that is, why the author is writing about this topic. Before reading, however, you might need to look up some vocabulary words. For example, the writer uses the word ***branch*** to mean a "branch of a river," probably a small stream. Here are some other terms to check: ***medieval, pirate, bin, chute, instinct, honeysuckle, alligator, disrepair, graffiti, knight, adolescent, idyllic.***

MY OLD NEIGHBORHOOD

Several years ago I returned to Washington, D.C., and visited one of my old neighborhoods. I had not been on Nash Street for more than twenty years and as I walked along the street, my mind was flooded by waves of nostalgia. I saw the old apartment building where I had lived and the playground where I had played. As I viewed these once-familiar surroundings, images of myself as a child there came to mind. However, what I saw and what I remembered were not the same. I sadly realized that the best memories are those left undisturbed.

As I remember my old apartment building, it was bright and alive. When I was a child, the apartment building was more than just a place to live. It was a medieval castle, a pirate's den, a space station, or whatever my young mind could imagine. I would steal away with my friends and play in the basement. This was always exciting because it was so cool and dark, and there were so many things there to hide among. Our favorite place to play was the coal bin. We would always use it as our rocket ship because the coal chute could be used as an escape hatch out of the basement into "outer space."

All of my memories were not confined to the apartment building, however. I have memories of many adventures outside of the building, also. My mother restricted how far we could go from the apartment building, but this placed no restrictions on our exploring instinct. There was a small branch in back of the building where my friends and I would play. We enjoyed it there because honeysuckles grew there. We would go there to lie in the shade and suck the sweet-smelling honeysuckles. Our biggest thrill in the branch was the day the police caught an alligator there. I did not see the alligator and I was not there when they caught it, but just the thought of an alligator in the branch was exciting.

This is how I remembered the old neighborhood; however, as I said, this is not how it was when I saw it.

Unlike before, the apartment building was now rundown and in disrepair. What was once more than a place to live looked hardly worth living in. The court was dirty and broken up, and the windows in the building were all broken out. The once-clean walls were covered with graffiti and other stains. There were no medieval knights or pirates running around the place now, nor spacemen; instead, there were a few tough looking adolescents who looked much older than their ages.

As for the area where I used to play, it was hardly recognizable. The branch was polluted and the honeysuckles had died. Not only were they dead, but they had been trampled to the ground. The branch itself was filled with old bicycles, broken bottles, and garbage. Now, instead of finding something as romantic as an alligator, one would expect to find only rats. The once sweet-smelling area now smelled horrible. The stench from my idyllic haven was heart wrenching.

I do not regret having seen my old neighborhood. However, I do not think my innocent childhood memories can ever be the same. I suppose it is true when they say, "You can never go home again." —*Floyd Bonner*

EXERCISE 7-9

On a separate sheet of paper, answer the following questions about "My Old Neighborhood."

1. What is the thesis? Where is it stated?
2. What is the controlling idea about the apartment building as it was when the author was a child?
3. What is the controlling idea about the apartment building when he visited it twenty years later?
4. What is the controlling idea about the branch as it was when he was a child?
5. What is the controlling idea about the branch as he saw it twenty years later?
6. One of the paragraphs is only one sentence long. What function does that sentence serve?
7. What pattern of organization does the writer use? Why? Does he cover the same points in the first part as he does in the second?
8. What do you think the writer's purpose is in writing about this topic?
9. Is the essay coherent? Unified?
10. In a couple of places the author uses *would* when referring to the past. What kind of action does "*would* + verb" indicate when referring to the past time?
11. What are some of the expressions the author uses to indicate the change from the past to the present? Reread the essay and underline the expressions and phrases that clarify the changes. (For example, "The *once-clean walls* were covered with graffiti. . . .")
12. Make an outline of the essay.

EXERCISE 7-10: WRITING ASSIGNMENT

Choose one of the following writing assignments.

1. Have you ever visited a place you had left a long time ago and found it had changed considerably? Write an essay comparing and contrasting the "way it was" with the "way it is now." Try to formulate a controlling idea about the change. Have things changed for the better? The worse?
2. In "A Fable for Tomorrow" (pages 229–31), Rachel Carson describes an imaginary town that had undergone a serious change. If you are familiar with a similar situation, write an essay describing a place both before and after a disaster or major change of some type. It could be a house or area before and after a natural disaster like an earthquake or the effects of pollution.
3. Before you came to this country, you undoubtedly had certain ideas and expectations about the United States. After you had been here awhile, did any of those ideas change? Did you find certain things to be different from what you expected? Choose several aspects of your life and experiences in the United States and contrast the way you thought they would be with how you find them now.

COMPOSITION SKILLS

Coherence

Transitions for Comparison and Contrast

Transitional expressions give writing coherence; that is, they help to move smoothly from one idea to the next. In addition, a variety of transitions adds interest to an essay. In this lesson you will practice using transitions that will give a comparison–contrast essay both coherence and interest. Note the transitional expressions used in these sentences:

In contrast to American universities, Lebanese universities have stricter admissions requirements.

American and Lebanese universities *also differ* in graduation requirements.

In Lebanon, *on the other hand,* only one limit exists.

Whereas American students may go part-time, Lebanese students must attend school full-time.

Unlike before, the apartment building was now rundown and in disrepair.

Even though both systems provide a good education, one system makes earning a college degree much easier than the other.

There is quite a large number of transitions that can be used for comparison and contrast. They fall into the following three major groups. Study them carefully and note the necessary punctuation for each type.

1. TRANSITIONS IN PHRASES

All of the transitions in this group need to be followed by a ***noun***. The phrase in which they occur is often used at the beginning of a sentence and is generally followed by a comma. The following transitions indicate similarity: ***similar to, like***. The following indicate difference: ***different from, in contrast to, compared with, unlike***. Note the following examples.

Similar to New Orleans, San Francisco attracts many tourists.

Like this American university, a Lebanese university also asked for my high school grades.

Different from the Road Runner, the Speed Demon has comfortable seats.

Compared with New Orleans, San Francisco has a very cold climate. (This means that probably the climate in San Francisco is not really that cold; it is just that the climate in New Orleans is extremely hot.)

Unlike the Road Runner, the Speed Demon is quite economical.

2. COORDINATING CONJUNCTIONS AS TRANSITIONS

The coordinating conjunctions ***but*** and ***yet*** are often used as transitions to indicate the opposite of what was expected. Coordinating conjunctions occur between two complete sentences and are preceded (but not followed) by a comma. Study these examples:

San Diego is very dry, *but* Houston is not.

The Speed Demon 280 is cheaper than the Road Runner XL, *yet* it has a better air-conditioning system.

Note: Sometimes these conjunctions are used as transitions at the beginning of a sentence:

Several events contributed to my depression last year. *But* my greatest sadness was losing the mathematics contest.

3. TRANSITIONAL EXPRESSIONS BETWEEN SENTENCES

The transitions in this group generally occur between two independent clauses. When they do, they must be preceded by either a period or a semicolon.

Ecuador ships out a lot of bananas. *In addition,* it is an exporter of oil.

Ecuador ships out a lot of bananas; *in addition,* it is an exporter of oil.

Ecuador exports oil. *Moreover,* it is a coffee producer.

Ecuador exports oil; *moreover,* it is a coffee producer.

Occasionally, these transitional expressions are used in an independent clause. In this case, the expressions (except *also*) should be set off with commas:

Ecuador ships out a lot of bananas. It is, *in addition,* an exporter of oil.

Ecuador exports oil. It is, *moreover,* a producer of coffee.

Ecuador exports oil. It is *also* a coffee producer.

This group of transitions has the greatest number of words and phrases. Examine them in three parts:

a. Additive Transitions: ***first, next, besides, in addition, moreover, furthermore, also, then.*** We discussed most of the transitions in this group in Chapters 2 and 4. They can be used to indicate chronological order, to number or list examples, or to add more information to something that was just stated. In comparison–contrast, they can fulfill all these functions.

The tropical rain forest is a beautiful and fascinating place. *Besides,* it is extremely important to our ecosystem.

In addition, the tropical rain forest contains many important species of plants.

Moreover, valuable plant life is threatened.

The rain forest is *also* home to a wide variety of animals.

Also, the rain forest is home to a wide variety of animals.

b. Transitions to Indicate Similarity: ***likewise, similarly, in the same way.*** **These words are used to indicate a similarity between the items given in the two sentences.**

Smog is adversely affecting the trees in the mountains near Los Angeles. *Likewise,* acid rain is harming trees in the northeast.

New Orleans has a big seafood business. *Similarly,* a great deal of fishing and oyster farming is done around San Francisco.

c. Transitions to Indicate Difference: ***on the other hand, conversely, in contrast, however.*** **These words are used to indicate a difference or a contrast between the items given in the two sentences.**

Senator Smith wants to reduce the budget deficit by raising taxes. Jones, *on the other hand,* advocates making more cuts in spending.

New Orleans has hot, humid summers. *In contrast,* San Francisco's summers are cool and windy.

As I viewed these once familiar surroundings, images of myself as a child there came to mind. *However,* what I saw and what I remembered were not the same.

The expression *on the contrary* is also in this group, but it is very restricted in its use. It indicates that the two ideas being expressed cannot both be true. It is often confused with *on the other hand.* Compare the following:

Jose: It's rather hot today.
Hong: It is not very hot today. *On the contrary,* it is quite cool.
It is not very hot today. *On the other hand,* it is not cool either.

Jose: The Earth is the fifth planet from the Sun.
Hong: The Earth is not the fifth planet from the Sun. *On the contrary,* it is the third.
The Earth is not the closest planet to the Sun. *On the other hand,* it's not the farthest either.

Note that *on the contrary* really means "No, it isn't." Another transition that can sometimes be used in its place is *in fact.*

It is not very cold today; *in fact,* it's quite hot.

EXERCISE 7-11

Fill in the blanks with either *on the other hand* or *on the contrary,* whichever is appropriate.

1. **New Orleans does not have a harsh winter. ______________, it is quite mild.**

2. New Orleans does not have a harsh winter. __________, its summers are terrible.
3. New Orleans does not have a large population. __________, it is not a village.
4. Many people think that New Orleans is a large city. __________, it has quite a small population.
5. New Orleans was not originally settled by the Spanish; __________, its first European settlers were French.
6. New Orleans is a big seaport. __________, its manufacturing industry is quite small.

EXERCISE 7-12

Read the following paragraph about the writer Jorge Luis Borges.

> Jorge Luis Borges is one of the greatest modern writers in Spanish. Born in Argentina, he was educated in Europe, and in his early days he served as a municipal librarian in Buenos Aires. Borges has written a variety of works, including poetry, essays, film criticism, and short stories. He was at odds with the policies of the Peron government in Argentina in the 1940s and 1950s. After the Peron government was overthrown, Borges became a professor of literature at the University of Buenos Aires. Many of his works have been translated into English and other languages.

For each of the following items, write sentences, using the transitions given, comparing or contrasting Borges with the Japanese writer Yukio Mishima. The first one is done for you.

1. Yukio Mishima is considered one of the greatest modern Japanese writers.

   like Like Borges, Mishima is considered one of the greatest modern writers.

   also Borges is a great modern writer. Mishima is also considered a great modern writer.

   similarly Borges is a great modern writer. Similarly, Mishima is considered by many people to be a great modern writer.

2. Mishima was educated in his native country of Japan.

   unlike __________

   but __________

in contrast ______________________________

3. In his early days, Mishima worked for the Finance Ministry.

   in contrast to ______________________________

   whereas ______________________________

   however ______________________________

4. Mishima was a prolific writer, authoring short stories, poems, plays, essays, and novels.

   similar to ______________________________

   likewise ______________________________

   like ______________________________

5. Mishima was critical of the Japanese military policies.

   in the same way ______________________________

   similar to ______________________________

   similarly ______________________________

6. Mishima performed as an actor.

   unlike ______________________________

   but ______________________________

   in contrast ______________________________

7. Many of Mishima's works have been translated into English and other languages.

   like ______________________________

   similar to ______________________________

   likewise ______________________________

---

4. Adverbial Clauses of Comparison, Contrast, and Concession

For sentence variety and for even more smoothly flowing sentences, try to use adverbial clauses. Just as adverbial clauses of time are especially useful in narratives, adverbial clauses of comparison, contrast, and concession can be particularly useful in improving coherence in comparison–contrast writing.

• Adverbial Clauses of Comparison: *just as, in the same way that. Just as* (which means the same as *in the same way that*) indicates comparison. Observe:

Just as Borges and Mishima differ in nationality, they also differ in educational background.

So is often used in the main clause following the clause that contains *just as*. Note the inverted subject–verb order:

Just as "weasel words" are used to engender favorable impressions, *so are* euphemisms.

Just as Bill is a fine student, *so is* his sister.

Just as some people in the Northern Hemisphere are fortunate to see the northern lights, *so are* some people in the Southern Hemisphere, who can see the southern lights.

Just as I wrote a letter to the senator, *so did* Sharon.

• Adverbial Clauses of Contrast: ***while, whereas***. ***While*** and ***whereas*** are used to indicate contrast, and like most other adverbial clauses, they can occur at the beginning or at the end of a sentence.

Whereas the northern lights are called the aurora borealis, the southern lights are called the aurora australis.

The average male (gorilla) cranial capacity is 550 cc, *while that of the female is about 460 cc.*

Note: Unlike most other adverbial clauses that occur at the end of a sentence, ***while*** and ***whereas*** require commas before them. Also, note that ***whereas*** is the preferred subordinator to indicate contrast.

• Adverbial Clauses of Concession: ***although, though, even though***. An adverbial clause of concession is a clause that admits a contrast or an unexpected idea. The subordinators roughly mean "despite the fact that." This type of clause is useful for comparison and contrast papers to concede a point. For example, if you are emphasizing contrasts in a paper, it may be necessary to admit that there are similarities. If you are emphasizing similarities, it may be useful to admit that there are apparent contrasts. Observe:

Although both the Speed Demon 280 and the Road Runner XL are quite similar, I find they differ in safety features.

In this sentence, the writer is admitting that the two automobiles have similarities, but despite these similarities, they are different. Note these other examples of adverbial clauses of concession:

Although Grants Pass is a small town, it offers much to amuse summer visitors.

Although villages lack some services, they still provide a better environment to raise children in.

He refuses to retire, *even though he is now 70 years old.*

Even though not all tornadoes cause such massive devastation, if they touch down in populated areas, you can expect considerable damage.

Though she was quite tired, Mary continued to work hard.

As you may have guessed, *though* and *even though* are less commonly used than *although*. *Though* is more common in speech, and *even though* is usually used when the writer wants to be more emphatic than *although*.

Special Note: *even though* and *even*

Do not confuse *even though* and *even*. As you have seen, *even though* is a subordinator that introduces an adverbial (and therefore dependent) clause. *Even*, when used as an adverb, is a word used to intensify the meaning of another element in the sentence. It can be used to introduce an independent clause.

As an intensive word, *even* can be used to:

1. Emphasize a modifier (adjective or adverb):

   She looked tired, *even exhausted.*

2. Indicate something unexpected:

   Even John laughed at the joke. (Apparently John does not laugh much at jokes.)

3. Stress the comparative degree:

   My brother was *even more fanatical than I* about speaking English.

EXERCISE 7-13

Rewrite or, if necessary, combine the following sentences by including *even* or *even though* as appropriate.

1. San Francisco has a lot of tourism and good seafood. It has a mild winter.

   ____

   ____

2. Most houses in San Francisco have furnaces. San Francisco has a mild winter.

   ____

   ____

3. San Francisco is a beautiful city. Many people do not like it there.

   ____

   ____

4. Although New Orleans is a beautiful city, some people think that San Francisco is more beautiful.

____

____

5. All of the people of San Francisco gathered in the square for the celebration. The mayor was there, too.

____

____

6. I will never forget my happy times in San Francisco. I was poor when I was there.

____

____

EXERCISE 7-14

Read the following paragraphs about high school and college. Then write a sentence or two using the transitions given. The first one is done for you.

Most people like college better than high school. In high school, students have very little homework, maybe only a half hour a night. This means that they do not learn very much. In high school, students are constantly watched by the teachers and school officials. In order to go to the restroom, a student must get permission. If students do not attend classes, the principal will call their parents to check on them. Basically, students are treated as if they are children.

1. In college, students have a lot of homework.

   unlike Unlike high school, in college students have a lot of homework.

   while While students have very little homework in high school, they have quite a lot in college.

2. In college, nobody watches the students.

   different from _______________________________

   on the other hand _______________________________

   whereas _______________________________

3. Students do not need permission to go to the restroom.

   unlike _______________________________

   but _______________________________

   while _______________________________

4. No one calls the parents if students do not attend class.

in contrast ______________________________

in contrast to ______________________________

whereas ______________________________

5. **Basically, in college students are treated as adults.**

however ______________________________

whereas ______________________________

different from ______________________________

Some college students think college is no different from high school. In college they have to study very hard, sometimes even reading a whole book in one night. They enjoy going to college football and basketball games and cheering for their team. They also enjoy talking with their classmates, who are basically just like them.

6. **Students have to study hard in high school.**

just as ______________________________

7. **Students enjoy going to high school football and basketball games.**

just as ______________________________

8. **Students enjoy talking with their classmates in high school.**

just as ______________________________

For each of the following items, combine the two sentences by using *although* or *even though* as appropriate.

9. **High school students have very little homework. They learn a lot during their classes.**

____

10. **There are many rules in high school. They are meant to protect the students.**

____

11. **College students learn a lot. College students have to study hard.**

____

12. **College students can spend some time at football games. Most of the time they spend studying.**

____

____

EXERCISE 7-15: WRITING ASSIGNMENT

In the following essay, transitions have been omitted from the italicized parts. Rewrite the essay using a variety of transitional devices.

When scientists first examined the human brain, they found it to be divided into two halves, or hemispheres, which are nearly identical in appearance, mirroring each other just as the two sides of the body do. When Roger Sperry examined patients whose connection between the two hemispheres was severed—the corpus callosum—he found that the two sides of the brain seemed to have different functions. Many investigators have studied the differences between the functions of the two hemispheres and found their relationship to be quite complex. Unfortunately, however, most people have tended to overgeneralize. The left brain is supposed to be logical, rational, analytical; whereas the right brain is supposed to be creative and emotional. The brain's hemispheres are not so simplistically split into two neat divisions. In fact, both halves of the brain participate in almost all our mental activity.

To begin with, both sides of the brain are in operation when we reason. The left brain seems to dominate in the kind of reasoning it takes to translate symbols, recognize abstract differences, and handle algebra and geometry problems. *The left hemisphere may be dominant in these types of reasoning. The right hemisphere also reasons.* The right half functions to integrate information and draw conclusions. *The left hemisphere is dominant in recognizing abstract differences. The right hemisphere tends to recognize sameness.* For example, the right side is where we mediate facial recognition and recognize shapes.*

The two hemispheres act as partners in language and communication. It appears that the left hemisphere is dominant when it comes to understanding grammar and syntax, but when it comes to interpreting emotions in communication, the right brain excels. *The right brain can interpret tone of voice and facial expressions. Whenever we use language, both sides of the brain process the information.*

The brain is not totally divided about music. Many people assume that music is mediated solely in the right brain. *That is not so.* It is true that the right brain recognizes chords and melodies and seems to mediate pure and slow tones. *The left hemisphere is also involved* in music. Fast music, such as bluegrass, requires judgments about sequencing and rhythm, and for this the left hemisphere lends its services. When words are involved, again the left brain dominates.

Both halves of the brain are involved in our mental activities. The corpus callosum and other bridges between the two hemispheres obviously serve to integrate the functions of the two halves, which are in constant communication to make sense out of life.

EXERCISE 7-16: WRITING ASSIGNMENT

Read the following paragraphs. Revise the paragraphs in two ways. First rewrite them using Pattern B. Be sure to divide them into shorter paragraphs. Then rewrite them using Pattern A. Use appropriate transitions. Use the following thesis sentence for your essay.

*Information from Richard Thompson, *The Brain: An Introduction to Neuroscience* (New York: W. H. Freeman and Co., 1985) pp. 315–17 and Camille B. Wortman and Elizabeth F. Loftus, *Psychology* (New York: Alfred H. Knopf, 1985) pp. 84–89.

Thesis Sentence:

There are some interesting parallels between the Roman and Chinese empires even though these empires ended differently.

The Roman Empire ruled the Mediterranean world from about 500 B.C. to about 500 A.D. From a geographic base around Rome, it spread out to include North Africa, the Middle East, and Northern Europe. It developed a higher level of civilization than the areas surrounding it. It had a complex governmental structure and a bureaucracy, while the people surrounding it were barbarians and nomads. These barbarians were a constant threat to the Roman Empire. The leaders of the empire devised three ways to protect the empire. First, they conquered territory whose outer boundaries were natural barriers. Examples are the Rhine and Danube Rivers. They also built fortifications to keep out invaders. They built some, for example, between the Rhine and Danube and between Scotland and England. Third, they used precautionary buffer states, like colonies, which were midway between barbarism and civilization. These all helped to protect the base of the empire, Rome itself. However, toward the end of the empire's rule, some of the buffer states revolted. The final collapse occurred when the German and Slavic barbarians broke through the fortifications. In a short two hundred years, the Roman Empire fell to the power of the Germans.

The Chinese Empire grew and remained intact from 221 B.C. to 1911 A.D. From a geographic base around the Yellow River, it spread northward to Peking, west to the Central Plain, and south to Canton. It developed a higher level of civilization than the areas surrounding it. It became a center for art and philosophy, while the people surrounding it were nomads and barbarians. These barbarians, Huns and Mongols, were a constant threat to the empire. The leaders of the empire devised three ways to deal with them. First, they used natural boundaries like the Yellow and later the Yangtze Rivers. They built the incredible Great Wall of China, and they used buffer states that learned much from China, becoming civilized in the process. However, at times the barbarians broke through the fortifications and the buffer states. The barbarians did not destroy the Chinese Empire, however. Because the barbarians admired the superior culture of China, they set up dynasties imitating the Chinese way of life. Examples are the Chau, Yuan, and Manchu dynasties. In other words, the Chinese Empire absorbed its intruders and lived on. The one exception to this was a short rule by the Mongols, Genghis and Kublai Khan from 1215–1279. The subjugated Chinese dynasty reasserted itself shortly, however. The Chinese Empire continued to decline slowly until the Manchu dynasty ended in 1911 and a republic was declared.*

*Information from C. Harold King, *A History of Civilization: Earliest Times to the Mid-Seventeenth Century* (New York: Scribner's, 1964).

EXERCISE 7-17: WRITING ASSIGNMENT

Look again at the essays you wrote for Exercises 7-8 and 7-10. Can you make them more coherent by adding appropriate transitions? Rewrite your essays, trying to use a variety of coherence devices.

EXERCISE 7-18: WRITING ASSIGNMENT

Choose one of the following writing topics. Before you begin writing, decide on a controlling idea and thesis statement. Then choose the support. Decide whether to use organizational pattern A or B. Then write an essay.

1. Review the paragraphs about the Roman and Chinese empires in Exercise 7-16. Then write an essay comparing and/or contrasting two periods in your country's history.
2. Review "Columbus and the Moon" by Tom Wolfe on pages 232–36. Then write an essay comparing and/or contrasting two historical events that you are familiar with. You may want to get additional information from the library.
3. Review the information about the writers Borges and Mishima in Exercise 7-12. Write an essay comparing and/or contrasting two famous people—two political leaders, two artists, two performers, and so on. Be sure to include a thesis expressing your attitude about the two people.

GRAMMAR REVIEW

Comparisons

A comparison and contrast essay shows how things are alike or different. To do this, you need to use a number of grammatical constructions that show similarities and differences. Following are some of the most important ones to review.

Indicators of Equality or Similarity

1. The following constructions are used to indicate equality or similarity between two items. They are all a part of a complete sentence. Note carefully how they are used:

John's coat	resembles		Bill's coat.
	is	the same as	
	is	like	
	is	the same color (noun) as	
	is	similar to	

For those patterns using the verb *to be*, the two items being compared can be placed at the beginning of the sentence and the comparative adjectives put at the end. Note how the sentences change:

John's coat and Bill's coat *are* the same.
alike.
the same color (noun).
similar.

Note: The word *resemble* does not have an adjective form, so it cannot be used in this pattern.

Intensifiers are words that are used to emphasize or to show finer distinctions in comparisons. Except for *resemble* and *similar (to)*, the preceding comparisons often use the intensifiers *exactly* and *just*. They always follow the verb *to be:*

John's coat and Bill's coat are exactly the same.

2. The construction *as . . . as* is also used to indicate equality or similarity. It can be used in two ways. In the following sentences, two people are being compared:

(with adverbs)	Mark plays	as	forcefully	as Bill (does).
(with adjectives)	Mark is	as	strong	as Bill (is).
(with count nouns)	Mark has	as many	fine qualities	as Bill (does).
(with noncount nouns)	Mark has	as much	enthusiasm	as Bill (does).
(with adjective + noun)	Mark is	as good	an athlete	as Bill (is).

In the following sentences, two things about one person are being compared:

Mark plays tennis as well as *he plays* football.

Mark is as strong as *he is* tall.

Mark has as many tennis balls as *he has* footballs.

Mark has as much strength as *he has* courage.

In this pattern, the second subject and verb (italicized) are generally included for clarity. The intensifier *just* is common with the pattern *as . . . as*. It always precedes the first *as:*

Mark plays tennis *just* as well as he plays football.

All of these constructions can indicate inequality or dissimilarity by putting *not* in front of them. Study these examples:

Mary does *not resemble* her mother at all.

A computer programmer is *not the same* as a data clerk.

My mother is *not like* my Aunt Agatha.

John is *not the same height* as Tom.

This building is *not similar to* the Empire State Building.

These two books are *not the same.*

My two sisters are *not alike.*

These cars are *not the same size.*

New Orleans and New York City are *not similar.*

Mark does *not play* pool *as well as* Bill.

Sally is *not as pretty as* Margaret.

Billie Jean King does *not play as many tennis matches as* she used to play.

John never has *as much luggage as* his wife.

Bill can*not swim as well as* he can play pool.

The intensifiers ***nearly, exactly,*** and ***just*** are common with the patterns in the first group above. ***Resemble*** and ***similar*** are exceptions. The intensifier ***very*** is common with similar. The intensifier follows ***not:***

My mother is not *exactly* like my Aunt Agatha.

This building is not *very* similar to the Empire State Building.

The intensifiers ***nearly*** and ***quite*** are common with the patterns in the second group. The intensifier precedes the first ***as:***

Sally is not *nearly* as pretty as Margaret.

John never has *quite* as much luggage as his wife.

Indicators of Inequality

3. The following construction is used to show the difference between two items. It is also part of a complete sentence. Note its use:

John's coat is *different from* Bill's coat.

The comparative adjective can be placed at the end of the sentence:

John's coat and Bill's coat are *different.*

The intensifiers ***a little, somewhat, much,*** and ***completely*** are useful in this pattern. The intensifier precedes ***different:***

John's coat is *a little* different from Bill's coat.

Note: The noun ***difference*** can also be used for inequality. Note its use:

There is a major *difference* between your plan and mine.

The major *difference* between the two coats is length.

There is a great deal of *difference* between you and me.

4. The construction ***adjective/adverb + -er than*** is also used to show difference or inequality. ***Adjective/adverb + -er than*** (like ***like*** and ***as . . . as***) can be used in two ways: to contrast two people in reference to a quality or action or to contrast two qualities or actions in reference to one person. Use this pattern with the following kinds of adjectives and adverbs:

a. **Most one-syllable adjectives and adverbs:**

John is *older than* Bill (is).

John can kick the ball *harder than* Tom (can).

John can kick the ball *farther than* he can throw it.

b. **Two-syllable adjectives ending in *y* or *ow*:**

John is *lazier than* his sister (is).

The river is *shallower than* the lake (is).

The river is *shallower than* it is long.

Note: The following adjectives and adverbs have irregular comparative forms:

ADJECTIVES	ADVERBS
good — better	well — better
far — farther (further)	far — farther (further)
bad — worse	badly — worse

5. The construction ***more*** [adjective/adverb/noun] ***than*** is commonly used to show difference. Use this pattern with the following kinds of adjectives and adverbs:

a. **Most two-syllable adjectives and adverbs:**

Chemistry 101 is *more* basic *than* Chemistry 102 (is).

My history professor speaks *more* clearly *than* my math professor (does).

This train is *more* rapid *than* it is clean.

He plays *more* honestly *than* he does effectively.

b. **All adjectives and adverbs with more than two syllables:**

John is *more* successful *than* Bill (is).

John works *more* carefully *than* Bill (does).

John is *more* intelligent *than* he is sociable.

John works *more* consistently *than* he does efficiently.

c. **All adjectives derived from verbs:**

John is *more* demanding *than* Bill (is).

John is *more* bored with life *than* he is interested in it.

Use this pattern with count and noncount nouns:

John has *more* books *than* Bill (does).

John has *more* books *than* he has records.

John has *more* enthusiasm *than* Bill (does).

John has *more* enthusiasm *than* he has intelligence.

The intensifiers *much, a lot,* and *a little* are used with the adjective and

adverbs discussed in paragraphs 4 and 5. With the adjectives and adverbs in paragraph 4, the intensifier precedes the comparative adjective:

John is *much* older than Bill.

With the adjectives and adverbs in paragraph 5, the intensifier precedes *more:*

John is *much* more intelligent than he is sociable.

The intensifiers *many, a lot,* and *a few* are used with count nouns. The intensifiers *much, a lot,* and *a little* are used with noncount nouns. The intensifier precedes *more:*

John has *many* more books than Bill does.

John has *a little* more enthusiasm than Bill does.

Special Note: ***less*** and ***fewer***

To indicate a smaller amount or number, we can replace *more* with *less* for use with adjectives, adverbs, and noncount nouns. We can replace *more* with *fewer* for use with count nouns.

This is a *less* exciting movie *than* the one on television.

This class has *fewer* students *than* my history class.

Note: *Than* can also be followed by a clause in more complex sentences.

This is a *less* exciting movie *than* the one we saw last week.

This class has *fewer* students *than* I can ever remember.

He is *more* interesting *than* you had indicated.

EXERCISE 7-19

Read the following paragraph about gorillas and the list of statements about chimpanzees. For each item in the list, write a one-sentence comparison of the two animals. Use *same, like, alike, similar, different,* or *difference* as appropriate. The first one is done for you.

Gorillas belong to the highest order of mammals—the primates. Gorillas have a restricted range; they live either in the mountains of Zaire or in several countries along the west coast of equatorial Africa. A male gorilla averages about five feet in height and weighs between four hundred and five hundred pounds. Females are smaller than males. Gorillas live in family groups. At night the females and young sleep in a crude nest of twigs and leaves in the trees. Because of his weight, the male sleeps on the ground at the base of the tree. The gorilla's big toe is opposable; that is, it can move freely and pick up objects. Gorillas eat fruits, nuts, and vegetables.

1. **Chimpanzees are classified as primates.**

   The chimpanzee's classification is the same as the gorilla's classification.

   The classification of the chimpanzee and the gorilla is the same.

   The chimpanzee has the same classification as the gorilla.

2. The chimpanzee's range includes a lot of African countries.

   ____

3. An adult chimpanzee is about five feet tall.

   ____

4. An adult chimpanzee weighs up to 140 pounds.

   ____

5. Female and young chimpanzees sleep in a nest of twigs in a tree at night.

   ____

6. Male chimpanzees sleep in a nest of twigs in a tree at night.

   ____

7. The chimpanzee's thumb is opposable.

   ____

8. Chimpanzees eat fruit, nuts, and vegetables.

   ____

EXERCISE 7-20

Compare and contrast San Diego and Houston using the following information. Use the constructions *as . . . as* and *-er/more . . . than*. You can add *not* to both of these constructions. Write fifteen sentences on a separate sheet of paper.

		SAN DIEGO	HOUSTON
1.	Founded	1542	1836
2.	Population (1980)	1,015,190	1,728,910
3.	Land area	320 square miles	556 square miles
4.	Average annual precipitation	9.35 inches	45 inches
5.	Unemployment rate (1987)	4.2 percent	8.6 percent
6.	Per-capita income (1987)	$15,940	$15,053
7.	Average normal temperature	64°F	68°F
8.	Number of radio stations	27	45
9.	Number of hospitals	18	59
10.	Number of universities and colleges	8	27

Example:

San Diego is an older city than Houston.
San Diego is not as large as Houston.
Houston is warmer than San Diego.

EXERCISE 7-21: WRITING ASSIGNMENT

Use the following information or information you may already know to write one or two paragraphs contrasting New York City and Miami. Use as many of the transitions, expressions, and patterns that you have studied in this chapter as you can. Use the following topic sentence (fill in the blanks):

_____________ is a better city to live in than _____________.

		NEW YORK CITY	MIAMI
1.	Founded	1625	1870
2.	Population (metro area)	9,386,700	1,441,200
3.	Land area	320 square miles	34 square miles
4.	Average high temperature	84°F	89°F
5.	Average low temperature	26°F	60°F
6.	Average annual rainfall	41.61 inches	59.80 inches
7.	Natural disasters	Hurricanes—possible from the Atlantic Ocean.	Hurricanes—possible from the Atlantic and the Caribbean.
8.	Composition of population	Very cosmopolitan, many different ethnic groups—Greek, Chinese, Italian, Latin American. Home of United Nations.	Gateway to Latin America, large Latin American and Cuban population.
9.	Business/commerce	Financial headquarters of the United States. Many banks and businesses. Popular tourist city.	Main industry is tourism. Large hotels for popular semitropical beaches.

10. Recreation	Cultural capital of the United States. Broadway —home of famous theaters. Lincoln Center for the Performing Arts. Many artists of all kinds. Home of New York Yankees baseball team.	Sports are very important. Year-round horse racing. Home of Orange Bowl football game and Miami Dolphins football team. Many beautiful beaches. Sailing and water sports are popular.

EXERCISE 7-22: WRITING ASSIGNMENT

Choose one of the following writing topics. First decide on a controlling idea and thesis statement. Then decide on the support and determine whether pattern A or B should be used to organize the support. Write the essay. Be sure to use transitions and specific detail.

1. Write an essay comparing or contrasting two cities.
2. Write an essay comparing or contrasting two life-styles. You might choose a life-style in the United States and compare–contrast it to one in your country. You might choose two in the United States or two in your country.
3. Write an essay comparing or contrasting two different attitudes. For example, you might choose the attitude toward punctuality in the United States compared with the attitude toward punctuality in your country.
4. Write an essay comparing–contrasting your parents' attitude toward something with your attitude toward it.
5. Write an essay comparing human beings with another group of primates, such as gorillas.
6. Write an essay comparing–contrasting two products. You may choose two cars, two cameras, two stereo systems, two motorcycles, or the like.
7. Compare and contrast two teachers of the same subject.
8. Compare and contrast two planets in our solar system.

Comparison and Contrast Essay Checklist

1. The purpose of the comparison and contrast essay is to persuade, explain, or inform, not just to list differences or similarities. Is your thesis sentence persuasive? Does it express an attitude?
2. The points chosen for comparison or contrast should be the most significant, interesting, and insightful points to support your thesis. Have you been selective in choosing your points of comparison?
3. Most essays emphasize either comparison or contrast. Which one have you emphasized?
4. There are two basic patterns for organizing a comparison–contrast essay. Have you chosen one of these patterns? Is the organization of your essay logical and consistent?
5. Is your essay coherent; that is, does it flow smoothly?

Chapter 8

The Classification Essay

Readings: A Healthy Society

Of course, we all want to be healthy, but in today's society where many occupations do not involve physical activity, maintaining health is often difficult. People try to stay healthy in a variety of ways, including daily exercising, dieting, and for some trying to stop smoking. Yet maintaining one's health is not all that easy. Although health-conscious people may exercise or diet seriously for a certain length of time, many of them discontinue these activities due to a loss of motivation.

The following essays explore two common problems in our not-so-healthy society. In the first reading, "Three Kinds of Fatigue," Jane Brody discusses what causes certain types of fatigue. In the second, "A Very Short History of Some American Drugs Familiar to Everybody," Adam Smith points out the dangers of some common drugs—drugs that most all of us use—and he questions why such dangers exist in our society. Before you read the essays, consider the following questions:

1. What are the probable causes of fatigue?
2. What types of legal drugs are used commonly in the United States? In other countries?
3. Why do people use legal drugs?
4. In your opinion, what can people do to remain healthy?

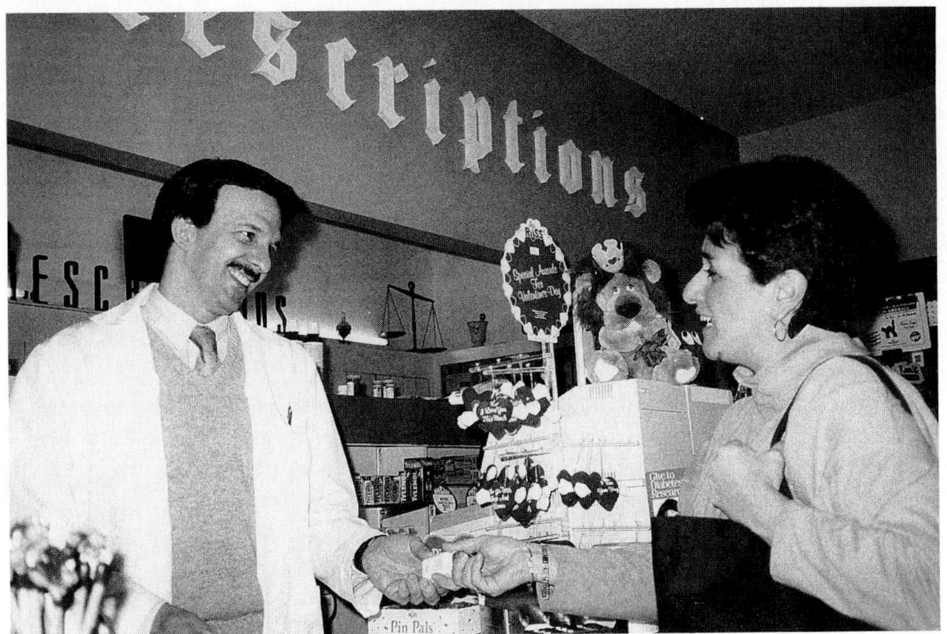

READING 1

THREE KINDS OF FATIGUE

JANE BRODY

Jane Brody has written much about health issues in recent years. She writes a "Personal Health" column for* The New York Times *and has written several books on health and nutrition. The following excerpt is taken from* Jane Brody's New York Times Guide to Personal Health *(1982). As you read the excerpt, try to answer these questions:

1. What are the three kinds of fatigue?
2. What causes each kind?

1 Fatigue is one of the most common complaints brought to doctors, friends, and relatives. You'd think in this era• of labor-saving devices and convenient transportation that few people would have reason to be so tired. But probably more people complain of fatigue today than in the days when hay was baled[1] by hand and laundry scrubbed on a washboard. Witness these typical complaints:

era: period of time

2 "It doesn't seem to matter how long I sleep — I'm more tired when I wake up than when I went to bed."

[1]**hay was baled** *dried grass was tied in bundles*

3 "Some of my friends come home from work and jog for several miles or swim laps. I don't know how they do it. I'm completely exhausted at the end of a day at the office."

4 "I thought I was weary because of the holidays, but now that they're over, I'm even worse. I can barely get through the week, and on the weekend I don't even have the strength to get dressed. I wonder if I'm anemic• or something."

anemic: reduction of red blood corpuscles or hemoglobin in the blood

5 "I don't know what's wrong with me lately, but I've been so collapsed that I haven't made a proper meal for the family in weeks. We've been living on TV dinners and packaged mixes. I was finally forced to do a laundry because the kids ran out of underwear."

6 The causes of modern-day fatigue are diverse and only rarely related to excessive physical exertion.• The relatively few people who do heavy labor all day long almost never complain about being tired, perhaps because they expect to be. Today, physicians report, tiredness is more likely a consequence of underexertion than of wearing yourself down with overactivity. In fact, increased physical activity is often prescribed as a *cure* for sagging energy.

exertion: energetic activity

7 There are three main categories of fatigue:

8 **Physical.** This is the well-known result of overworking your muscles to the point where metabolic• waste products —carbon dioxide and lactic acid—accumulate in your blood and sap your strength. Your muscles can't continue to work efficiently in a bath of these chemicals. Physical fatigue is usually a pleasant tiredness, such as that which you might experience after playing a hard set of tennis, chopping wood, or climbing a mountain. The cure is simple and fast: You rest, giving your body a chance to get rid of accumulated wastes and restore muscle fuel.

metabolic: the body's processes involving breaking food down into energy

9 **Pathological.** Here fatigue is a warning sign or consequence of some underlying physical disorder, perhaps the common cold or flu or something more serious like diabetes or cancer. Usually other symptoms besides fatigue are present that suggest the true cause.

10 Even after an illness has passed, you're likely to feel dragged out for a week or more. Take your fatigue as a signal to go slow while your body has a chance to recover fully even if all you had was a cold. Pushing yourself to resume full activity too soon could precipitate• a relapse and almost certainly will prolong your period of fatigue.

precipitate: to make happen before expected

11 Even though illness is not a frequent cause of prolonged• fatigue, it's very important that it not be overlooked. Therefore, anyone who feels drained of energy for weeks on end should have a thorough physical checkup. But even if nothing shows up as a result of the various medical tests, that doesn't mean there's nothing wrong with you.

prolonged: going on for a long period of time

12 Unfortunately too often a medical work-up ends with a battery• of negative test results, the patient is dismissed, and the true cause of serious fatigue goes undetected. As Dr. John Bulette, a psychiatrist at the Medical College of Pennsylvania Hospital in Philadelphia, tells it, this is what happened to a Pennsylvania woman who had lost nearly fifty pounds and was "almost dead—so tired she could hardly lift her head up." The doctors who first examined the woman were sure she had cancer. But no matter how hard they looked, they could find no sign of malignancy• or of any other disease that could account for her wasting away. Finally, she was brought to the college hospital, where doctors noted that she was severely depressed.

collection

cancer

13 They questioned her about her life and discovered that her troubles had begun two years earlier, after her husband died. Once treated for depression,• the woman quickly perked up, gained ten pounds in just a few weeks, then returned home to continue her recovery with the aid of psychotherapy.

feelings of hopelessness, inadequacy, and an inability to do anything

14 **Psychological.** Emotional problems and conflicts, especially depression and anxiety, are by far the most common causes of prolonged fatigue. Fatigue may represent a defense mechanism[2] that prevents you from having to face the true cause of your depression, such as the fact that you hate your job. It is also your body's safety valve[3] for expressing repressed emotional conflicts, such as feeling trapped in an ungratifying• role or an unhappy marriage. When such feelings are not expressed openly, they often come out as physical symptoms, with fatigue as one of the most common manifestations.• "Many people who are extremely fatigued don't even know they're depressed," Dr. Bulette says. "They're so busy distracting themselves or just worrying about being tired that they don't recognize their depression."

unfulfilling

signs

15 One of these situations is so common it's been given a name—tired housewife syndrome.[4] The victims are commonly young mothers who day in and day out face the predictable tedium• of caring for a home and small children, fixing meals, dealing with repairmen, and generally having no one interesting to talk to and nothing enjoyable to look forward to at the end of their boring and unrewarding day. The tired housewife may be inwardly resentful, envious of her husband's job, and guilty about her feelings. But rather than face them head-on, she becomes extremely fatigued.

boredom

16 Today, with nearly half the mothers of young children

[2]*behavior unconsciously used to protect against painful feelings or impulses*
[3]*mechanism to protect itself from harm*
[4]*set of characteristics identifying a type of condition*

working outside the home, the tired housewife syndrome has taken on a new twist: that of conflicting roles and responsibilities and guilt over leaving the children, often with an overlay of genuine physical exhaustion from trying to be all things to all people.

17 Emotionally induced• fatigue may be compounded by sleep disturbance that results from the underlying psychological conflict. A person may develop insomnia[5] or may sleep the requisite• number of hours but fitfully, tossing and turning all night, having disturbing dreams, and awakening, as one woman put it, feeling as if she "had been run over by a truck."

brought about

required

18 Understanding the underlying emotional problem is the crucial first step toward curing psychological fatigue and by itself often results in considerable lessening of the tiredness. Professional psychological help or career or marriage counseling may be needed.

19 There is a great deal you can do on your own to deal with both severe prolonged fatigue and those periodic washed-out feelings. Vitamins and tranquilizers are almost never the right answer, sleeping pills and alcohol are counterproductive,[6] and caffeine is at best a temporary solution that can backfire• with abuse and cause life-disrupting symptoms of anxiety. Instead, you might try:

having the opposite effect

20 **Diet.** If you eat a skimpy• breakfast or none at all, you're likely to experience midmorning fatigue, the result of a drop in blood sugar, which your body and brain depend on for energy. For peak energy in the morning, be sure to eat a proper breakfast, low in sugar and fairly high in protein, which will provide a steady supply of blood sugar throughout the morning. Coffee and a doughnut are almost worse than nothing, providing a brief boost and then letting you down with a thud.

small, inadequate

21 The same goes for the rest of the day: Frequent snacking on sweets is a false pick-me-up• that soon leaves you lower than you were to begin with. Stick to regular, satisfying, well-balanced meals that help you maintain a trim figure. Extra weight is tiring both physically and psychologically. Getting your weight down to normal can go a long way toward revitalizing• you.

something to give quick energy

give new life

22 **Exercise.** Contrary to what you may think, exercise enhances,• rather than saps, energy. Regular conditioning exercises, such as jogging, cycling, or swimming, help you to resist fatigue by increasing your body's ability to handle more of a work load. You get tired less quickly because your capability is greater.

improves

[5]*being unable to sleep*
[6]*having negative results*

23 Exercise also has a well-recognized tranquilizing effect, which helps you work in a more relaxed fashion and be less dragged down by the tensions of your day. At the end of a day exercise can relieve accumulated tensions, give you more energy in the evening, and help you sleep more restfully.

24 **Sleep.** If you know you're tired because you haven't been getting enough sleep, the solution is simple: Get to bed earlier. There's no right amount of sleep for everyone, and generally sleep requirements decline with age. Find the amount that suits you best, and aim for it. Insomnia and other sleep disorders should not be treated with sleeping pills, alcohol, or tranquilizers, which can actually make the problem worse.

25 **Know yourself.** Try to schedule your most taxing• jobs *difficult*
for the time of day when you're at your peak. Some are
"morning people" who tire by midafternoon; others do their
best work in the evening. Don't overextend• yourself, trying *take on too much*
to climb the ladder of success at a record pace or to meet
everyone's demands or expectations. Decide what you want
to do and what you can handle comfortably, and learn to say
no to additional requests. Recognize your energy cycles and
plan accordingly. Many women have a low point premen-
strually, during which time extra sleep may be needed and
demanding activities are particularly exhausting.

26 **Take breaks.** No matter how interesting or demanding
your work, you'll be able to do it with more vigor• if now and *energy, life*
again you stop, stretch, and change the scenery. Instead of
coffee and a sweet roll on your break, try meditation, yoga,
calisthenics, or a brisk walk. Even running up and down the
staircase can provide refreshment from a sedentary• job. If *sitting a lot*
your job is physically demanding, relax in a quiet place for a
while. The do-something-different rule also applies to vacation; "getting away from it all" for a week or two or longer can
be highly revitalizing, helping you to put things in perspective
and enabling you to take your job more in stride upon your
return.

EXERCISE 8-1: COMPREHENSION/ DISCUSSION QUESTIONS

1. Explain the first kind of fatigue that Brody describes (par. 8). What is its cause?
2. Explain the second kind of fatigue (par. 9). What is its cause?
3. Explain the third kind of fatigue (par. 14). What causes it?

4. According to the author, what is the "tired housewife syndrome"?
5. How can sleep disturbances be related to fatigue?
6. In what order does Brody present her three categories of fatigue? Why does she choose this order?
7. What is the author's main purpose in paragraphs 20–26?
8. Do you agree with Brody's classification of types of fatigue? Do you think there are other causes of fatigue? What are they?
9. What do you think of the author's list of advice? Is it sensible? Sufficient? Do you agree with it? Can you add to it?
10. What do you do to combat fatigue?

EXERCISE 8-2: VOCABULARY DEVELOPMENT

The following words are related to physical and psychological health. They are listed in a word-form chart. Rarely used forms and participial forms have been omitted (X). Fill in each blank with the correct form of the word.

	NOUN	VERB	ADJECTIVE	ADVERB
1.	X	X	physical (par. 8)	________
2.	________	X	anemic (par. 1)	________
3.	cure (par. 6)	________	X	X
4.	blood (par. 8)	________	________	________
5.	muscle (par. 8)	________	________	X
6.	________	X	pathological (par. 9)	________
7.	symptom	X	________	________
8.	malignancy (par. 12)	X	________	________
9.	________	X	psychological (par. 14)	________
10.	emotion (par. 14)	________	________	________
11.	________	X	anxious (par. 14)	________
12.	guilt (par. 16)	X	________	________

Fill in the correct form of the word in parentheses in each of the following sentences. The form given may or may not be correct.

1. (*Physical*) ________ fatigue is the result of heavy manual labor and exhausting work.

2. (*Anemic*) ____________ is a blood condition that results in fatigue.
3. His body is (*muscle*) ____________ because of his hard physical work.
4. Some fatigue has (*pathological*) ____________ causes.
5. Prolonged fatigue might be (*symptom*) ____________ of an underlying disease like cancer or diabetes.
6. Because the tumor was (*malignancy*) ____________, they operated immediately.
7. She is (*psychological*) ____________ a very healthy person.
8. (*Anxious*) ____________ can be a major cause of fatigue.

READING 2

A VERY SHORT HISTORY OF SOME AMERICAN DRUGS FAMILIAR TO EVERYBODY

ADAM SMITH

In the following excerpt from Powers of the Mind *(1975), Adam Smith classifies some common drugs used in our society. In particular, he points out how common these drugs and their effects are. Although Smith supports his writing with a great deal of factual information, he is making a statement about drugs as well. As you read the essay, try to answer these questions:*

1. What are the "okay" drugs in our society?
2. Why are some drugs okay but others are not?

1 Our attitude toward the word "drug" depends on whether we are talking about penicillin or heroin or something in-between. The unabridged three-volume Webster's• says a drug is "a chemical substance administered to prevent or cure disease or enhance physical and mental welfare" or "a substance affecting the structure or function of the body." Webster's should have added "mind," but they probably thought that was part of the body. Some substances that aren't drugs, like placebos, affect "the structure or function of the body," but they work because we *think* they're drugs.

a well-known dictionary

2 We are a drug-using society. We take, for example, twenty thousand tons of aspirin a day, almost one aspirin per person in the whole country. Aspirin is a familiar drug from a

family called salicylates, specifically, acetylsalicylic acid. It lowers body temperature, alleviates• some types of pain, and stimulates• respiration.

lessens
increases

3 Nicotine is a familiar and widely recognized drug, a stimulant to the central nervous system. It is addictive. The toxic• effects of nicotine have been detailed at great length by the Surgeon General. Americans smoke 600 billion cigarettes a year.

dangerous, poisonous

4 Alcohol is also a widely recognized drug. In the United States 70 million users spend $10 billion a year. Five million of the 70 million alcohol users are said to be addicts, that is, they have a physical dependence on the drug. Alcohol is unique, says the pharmacology[1] textbook, because it is "the only potent pharmacological agent[2] with which self-induced• intoxication is socially acceptable." Alcohol is so much a part of everyday life we do not think of it, on the rocks or straight up,[3] as a drug or a potent pharmacological agent.

bringing it on oneself

5 Then there is the family of drugs called the xanthines. Americans take xanthines at the rate of 100 *billion* doses per year. Xanthines are alkaloids which stimulate portions of the cerebral cortex.• They give you "a more rapid and clearer flow of thought, allay• drowsiness . . . motor activity is increased. There is a keener appreciation of sensory stimuli, and reaction time to them is diminished." This description, again from the pharmacology textbook, is similar to descriptions of cocaine and amphetamine.[4] Of course, the xanthine addict pays a price. He is, says Sir Clifford Allbutt, Regius Professor of Medicine at Cambridge, "subject to fits of agitation• and depression; he loses color and has a haggard• appearance. The appetite falls off; the heart suffers; it palpitates, or it intermits. As with other such agents, a renewed dose of the poison gives temporary relief, but at the cost of the misery."

part of the brain
make less
violent motion or stirring / worn out, tired

6 Xanthines are generally taken orally through "aqueous extracts"• of the plants that produce these alkaloids, either in seeds or leaves. In the United States the three most common methylated xanthines taken are called caffeine, theophylline and theobromine. The seeds of *Coffea arabica* contain caffeine, the leaves of *Thea sinensis* contain caffeine and theophylline, and the seeds of *Theobroma cacao* contain caffeine and theobromine. In America the three are known as "coffee," "tea" and "cocoa," and they are consumed daily, at the rate of billions of pounds a year. They are generally drunk as hot drinks, but Americans also drink cold drinks containing caffeine from the nuts of the tree *Cola acuminata*. The original

watery substances

[1] *study of the preparation, qualities, and uses of drugs*
[2] **pharmacological agent** *normally studied and legally used drug*
[3] **on the rocks or straight up** *two ways to drink alcohol—with or without ice cubes*
[4] **cocaine and amphetamine** *two kinds of illegal drugs*

drinks ended in the word "cola," but now there are many "colas" which do not bear that name in the title. The early ads for Coca-Cola said it gave you a lift.

7 Coffee, tea, cocoa and cola drinks are all drugs. Caffeine is a central nervous system stimulant, theophylline less so, and theobromine hardly at all. All xanthines increase the production of urine. Xanthines act on smooth muscles—relaxing, for example, especially in the case of theophylline, bronchi that may have been constricted. Like the salicylates—aspirin—xanthines can cause stomach irritation. Caffeine can cause sleeplessness, and researchers have found that it causes chromosome breaks.

8 Maxwell House, meet the Regius Professor of Medicine. Is the stuff good to the last drop,[5] or another dose of the poison? Is it a food, to be sold in supermarkets, or a stimulant to the central nervous system like the amphetamines? "The popularity of the xanthine beverages depends on their stimulant action, although most people are unaware of any stimulation," says the giant pharmacology text.

9 It is surprising to find substances we think of so cheerfully, perkin' in the pot,[6] listed as drugs. That's the point. In our society, there are some drugs we think of as okay drugs, and other drugs make us gasp.• A coffee drinker who drinks coffee all day and cannot function without it is just a heavy coffee drinker, but someone using a non-okay• drug is a "drug user" or an "addict."

be surprised

not legally or socially acceptable

10 *Consumer Reports*[7] asked: how did drugs with such potential hazard spread without arousing the legal repression and social condemnation• aroused by other drugs? They were domesticated,• it said. There was no illegal black market, the dosages were relatively small, and some people buffered the drug effect with cream and sugar.

disapproval

made an accepted part of society

11 The worst of what our society thinks of as "hard drugs"• comes from the unripe capsule of the opium poppy. In the nineteenth-century United States, you could buy opiates at grocery stores and drugstores, and by mail. Godfrey's Cordial—a molasses, sassafras and opium combination—was especially popular. Genteel• Southern ladies in lace and ruffles, smelling of verbena and other sweet things, sounding like Scarlett O'Hara,[8] were slugging down• daily a combination of opium and alcohol called laudanum. The first surveys of narcotics showed that women outnumbered men

illegal drugs, like heroin

refined, polite

drinking in one gulp, in an unrefined way

[5]**good to the last drop** *a well-known advertising slogan for Maxwell House coffee*
[6]**perkin' in the pot** *a pot of coffee being made*
[7]*popular magazine that analyzes products*
[8]*movie character who typifies the refined Southern lady and speaks with a refined Southern accent*

three to one, because "the husbands drank alcohol at the saloon, and the wives took opium at home."

12 The point of this capsule• history is not to warn people from the perilous xanthines. (I drink them all, *Coffea arabica* and *Thea sinensis*, sweetened, no cream, please, and *Theobroma cacao* on cold winter days, the *Cola acuminata* on warm summer ones, and I have to be paying attention to be aware of the stimulant action.)

short

13 Nor is it to diminish the danger of illegal narcotics. (Legal narcotics are part of legitimate medicine.) There is no comparison between legal, domesticated, mild, buffered drugs and illegal and undomesticated ones, but it is society that has produced the legalities and the domestication. Illegal narcotics, producing huge profits and employing the worst criminal elements, are merchandised• to the least stable• elements of society, producing tremendous social problems.

sold / undependable, unestablished

14 A Coke at snack time, a drink before dinner, a cup of coffee after dinner, a cigarette with the coffee—very relaxing. Four shots of drugs. Domesticated ones. It would be rather comic• to have addicts sneaking down dark alleys for a shot of coffee, but nicotine is so strong that when currencies fail—Germany right after World War II, for example—cigarettes become currency.

funny

15 In some Muslim countries, you can sit and smoke hashish• all day at a café, but possession of alcohol will land you in jail; in the United States, you can sit in a saloon ingesting alcohol all day, but possession of hashish will land you in jail.

drug similar to marijuana

16 Lysergic acid diethylamide [LSD] was invented by the Swiss. Curious to think of the Swiss, the symbol of sobriety• and industry, watch-making and cuckoo clocks, as having invented LSD, Librium and Valium, psychedelics and tranquilizers, the turn-ons and the turn-offs,[9] but then the Swiss have been in the drug business since Paracelsus of Basle, roughly a contemporary of Columbus.

sensible in their use of alcohol

EXERCISE 8-3: COMPREHENSION/ DISCUSSION QUESTIONS

1. In the first paragraph, Smith implies two large categories of drugs. What are they? What examples of each category does he give?

[9]**LSD, Librium and Valium, psychedelics and tranquilizers, the turn-ons and the turn-offs** *particular drugs or types of drugs intended to alter the mental state*

2. Explain the dictionary definition of the word *drug* given in the first paragraph.
3. In paragraphs 2–4, Smith discusses some familiar drugs. What are they? For each drug, give the effects and the statistics on usage.
4. What is unique about alcohol?
5. In paragraphs 5–7, Smith discusses a family of drugs called "xanthines." How many xanthines does he discuss? What are their common names?
6. What are some of the positive effects of using certain xanthines? The negative effects?
7. Paragraph 8 begins, "Maxwell House, meet the Regius Professor of Medicine." What are the references here? Explain the meaning of this sentence. Then of the paragraph.
8. In paragraph 9, Smith restates the major categories of drugs. What terms does he use for them here? Smith also states part of his thesis in this paragraph? What is it?
9. According to *Consumer Reports*, how did many xanthine drugs escape being considered socially unacceptable?
10. What is laudanum? Who used it? Was laudanum considered an "okay" drug when it was used heavily in the United States? How do you know?
11. Smith says there are two reasons that did *not* prompt him to write this essay. What are they?
12. What difference does the author see between xanthines and illegal narcotics?
13. Smith states another part of his thesis in paragraph 13. What is it?
14. In paragraph 14, he points up a difference between xanthines and nicotine. What is it?
15. What are Smith's points in paragraphs 15 and 16?
16. What is Smith's thesis in this essay? State it in your own words. Where does the author state it?
17. Do you think that Americans use too many soft drugs, like aspirin, caffeine, and alcohol? Be prepared to support your answer.
18. Compare the American use of drugs with consumption of drugs in your countries. Explain your comparison.
19. Do you think soft drugs, like aspirin, alcohol, caffeine, and xanthines, are harmful? Helpful? Why?

EXERCISE 8-4: VOCABULARY DEVELOPMENT

Smith makes a number of references to people or objects in American culture with which he expects his readers to be familiar. Study the following list and identify these references.

1. Webster's (par. 1) ______________________________

2. the Surgeon General (par. 3) ______________________
3. Coca-Cola (par. 6) ______________________
4. Maxwell House (par. 8) ______________________
5. *Consumer Reports* (par. 10) ______________________
6. Scarlett O'Hara (par. 11) ______________________
7. Columbus (par. 16) ______________________

Smith also expects his readers to be familiar with particular drugs or types of drugs. Study the following list of drug names and be prepared to explain each one.

1. penicillin (par. 1)
2. heroin (par. 1)
3. cocaine (par. 5)
4. amphetamine (par. 5)
5. opium (par. 11)
6. hashish (par. 15)
7. LSD (lysergic acid diethylamide) (par. 16)
8. Librium and Valium (par. 16)
9. psychedelics (par. 16)
10. tranquilizers (par. 16)
11. turn-ons (par. 16)
12. turn-offs (par. 16)

Writing

The patterns of exposition are really ways to organize thoughts, to develop ideas in an organized fashion so the reader can follow them easily. Some topics are best developed as example essays; others are best developed as comparison and contrast essay. This chapter pursues another common pattern of exposition: classification and division. This pattern, like process analysis and cause-and-effect analysis, is used for analyzing topics.

When analyzing a subject, you break it down into parts to study or determine the relationship of the parts or the nature of the parts. For example, analyzing an engine involves examining the parts to see how they make the engine run. If you were analyzing the United States government, you would probably begin by dividing the government into its three branches—the legislative, executive, and judicial—and then by studying how these branches operate to make up the government. If you were studying psychology and were interested in dreams, you would probably begin by sorting the dreams into categories that share common characteristics, and by so doing you might learn something about the various kinds of dreams. Taking one thing—such as the government—and breaking it down into parts is analysis by division; taking a large group of things—

such as governments—and separating the group into categories is analysis by classification. Since classification and division are very similar processes of analysis, and since as patterns of exposition they are even more similar, the general rhetorical term *classification* is used in this text to refer to the general pattern.

The Principle of Classification

When you classify, you divide the members of a group into categories whose members share similar characteristics. But on what basis do you assign the members to categories? When you classify, you need a principle of classification—a guideline for your classifying procedure. For example, the students in your English class might be classified according to the languages they speak natively: Spanish speakers, Vietnamese speakers, Japanese speakers, Dutch speakers, Arabic speakers, and so on. However, including a group such as "hard-working students" disrupts the classification by switching principles of classification. Members of the "hard-working" group could also be members of any of the other groups. Using more than one principle in this way causes categories to "overlap"; that is, the members of one category could also fit into one or more of the other categories. Just what principle of classification to choose is up to you. There are any number of principles available; the important thing to remember is to *use only one principle of classification* in an essay.

EXERCISE 8-5

Study the following classification groups. Underline the category that does not belong. The first one is done for you.

1. Automobiles: two-door, four-door, station wagons, economy.
2. Police officers: detectives, sergeants, lieutenants, captains.
3. Transportation: on land, by water, by air, by train.
4. Rivers: long, dangerous, short.
5. Drugs: stimulants, depressants, illegal.
6. Exercise: aerobic, muscle building, swimming.
7. Fiber: soluble, insoluble, fruit.
8. Languages: Semitic, Indo-European, ancient.
9. Teachers: well-prepared, easy graders, hard graders.
10. Clouds: high clouds, middle clouds, white clouds, low clouds.

Any number of principles of classification are available for a topic. To illustrate, consider the topic *students*. This topic could be classified according to:

1. How many credits the students have completed: first-year students, sophomores, juniors, seniors.
2. Age: under 18, 19–25, 26 and older.
3. Majors: biology, history, science, and so forth.
4. Level of intelligence: brilliant, intelligent, average, below average.
5. Where they sit in class: front row, back row, side walls, middle.
6. Attitude toward school: a place to improve one's general knowledge, a place to socialize, a place to learn a trade.
7. Style of dress: formal, semiformal, casual.

Most of the principles of classification are of three types: (1) *degree* (inferior to superior—for example, rating students from poor to excellent); (2) *chronology* (dividing the subject according to time periods); and (3) *location*. These are common types of principles, but not all principles are these types.

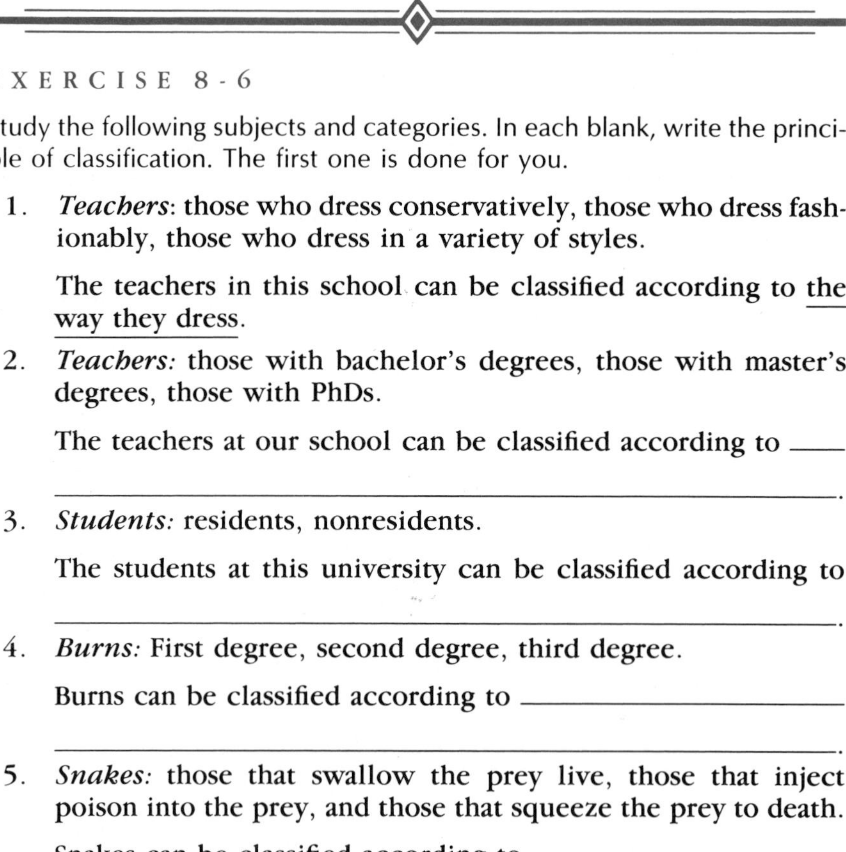

EXERCISE 8-6

Study the following subjects and categories. In each blank, write the principle of classification. The first one is done for you.

1. *Teachers*: those who dress conservatively, those who dress fashionably, those who dress in a variety of styles.

   The teachers in this school can be classified according to the way they dress.
2. *Teachers:* those with bachelor's degrees, those with master's degrees, those with PhDs.

   The teachers at our school can be classified according to ____________________.
3. *Students:* residents, nonresidents.

   The students at this university can be classified according to ____________________.
4. *Burns:* First degree, second degree, third degree.

   Burns can be classified according to ____________________.
5. *Snakes:* those that swallow the prey live, those that inject poison into the prey, and those that squeeze the prey to death.

   Snakes can be classified according to ____________________.
6. *Smokers:* Those who smoke because of nervousness, those who smoke to look sophisticated, those who smoke out of boredom.

   Smokers can be classified according to ____________________.
7. *Readers:* those who read voraciously, those who read regularly,

those who read sporadically, and those who read as rarely as possible.

People who read can be classified according to ____________.

8. *Readers:* those who read very difficult material, those who read moderately difficult material, those who read only light material.

Readers can be put into categories according to ____________.

9. *Drivers:* reckless, careless, careful, overly careful.

Drivers can be classified according to ____________________.

10. *Instructors:* professors, associate professors, assistant professors, instructors.

Instructors can be classified according to ____________________

____

Making the Classification Complete

Once you have decided on a principle of classification, check to see if the classification includes *all* members of the group. For instance, if you are classifying the students in a class, the categories might cover each and every one of the students in that class, if at all possible. If the students in a class were classified as brilliant or stupid, an obvious group—the average students—would be left out. To avoid omission of members and oversimplifying the analysis, then, it is generally a good idea to divide the group into more than two categories. For most college essays, three or four categories are the average.

When you divide a large group into categories whose members share common characteristics, there will be some members that do not fit perfectly into a category. For instance, you might classify politicians as liberals or conservatives, but since some politicians may be liberal concerning some issues and conservative concerning others, it would be wise to admit any variations or complications in the classification. It is also a good idea to note what the primary characteristics of the members are. For instance, do these politicians vote conservatively most of the time? If so, then placing them in the conservative category and mentioning that they vote liberally on some issues could be justified.

EXERCISE 8-7

Return to Exercises 8-5 and 8-6 and determine if the categories given there are complete.

EXERCISE 8-8: WRITING ASSIGNMENT

Evaluate television programming to determine the quality of the programs. Since the topic *television programming* is rather broad, narrow it down to a particular type of show, such as news programs, detective shows, or children's programs. Make a list of all the television shows in that group. Then sort through your list to find groups that share common characteristics. Rewrite the list, clustering the shows into groups. Make sure that a show that appears in one group cannot fit into another group. Write out the principle of classification. Remember to keep in mind your purpose in classifying these programs. If you prefer, choose radio programs, movies, or books.

Organizing the Classification Essay

After deciding on the principle of classification and dividing the group into categories, you need to discuss each of those categories. In the developmental paragraphs, it is useful to devote one paragraph to each category. When discussing the category, include the following points:

1. *Identify the group.* If it has a special name, identify it.
2. *Describe or define the category.* What are the general characteristics of the members of this category? Once you have established what the category is according to your classification, discuss the common characteristics of the members.
3. *Give examples:* Often it is helpful to illustrate the characteristics (which are generalizations, by the way) by giving one or two examples of *typical* members of the category.

In the second and subsequent developmental paragraphs, add another point:

4. *Distinguish this category from the other categories.* Discuss the characteristics of the second category by comparing and contrasting them with those of the first category. Doing this will help to distinguish between the categories. How does group 1 really differ from group 2? (For coherence, as in comparison–contrast, try to discuss the characteristics in the same order as the previous group.)

In these respects, classification papers are really a combination of example essays and comparison–contrast essays. Therefore, you will need the expository skills you have been developing.

Introducing the Categories

In an introductory paragraph, it is often a good idea to introduce the categories by mentioning the names of the groups. The thesis statement

for the classification essay can be one that simply introduces the classification and the categories:

> The teachers in this college can be classified according to the way they dress: those who dress formally, those who dress semiformally, and those who dress casually.
>
> There are basically three types of burns: first degree, second degree, and third degree.
>
> Drugs fall into three categories: stimulants, depressants, and hallucinogens.

Although there is no law that says the categories must be identified in the introduction, identifying them will help keep the essay organized.

When you name the categories in the introduction, express them in parallel structure; that is, express them in the same parts of speech. If you identify a category using a clause, then all of your categories should be identified using clauses.

> There are *those who like movies, those who hate movies,* and *those who are indifferent toward movies.* (clauses)
>
> There are basically three types of bus drivers: *friendly, indifferent,* and *mean.* (adjectives)
>
> The students in this class fit into the following categories: *the minis, the middies,* and *the maxis.* (nouns)
>
> Most people respond in one of three ways: *eagerly, indifferently,* or *reluctantly.* (adverbs)

As you read the following essay, determine whether it contains the characteristics of a good classification paper: a single principle, well-defined categories, good examples, categories expressed in parallel structure, and completeness.

COLD REMEDIES

Cold remedies have a long if not glorious history. Pliny the Younger, a first-century A.D. cold expert, advised "kissing the hairy muzzle of a mouse." Sixteen hundred years later, colonial Americans fought colds by applying kerosene plasters to the chest or by stuffing a dirty sock with salted pork and onion and then wrapping it about the neck. While today's remedies smell better, they still do not cure the common cold. However, they are an improvement over past cold remedies and can relieve some of the symptoms. But the cold sufferer should beware. Most of the cold products contain up to seven different drugs. Since people differ greatly in their cold symptoms, users of these multidrug remedies often end up paying for unnecessary drugs that increase the risk of side effects. Thus, it may be a good idea for cold sufferers to look for effective single-ingredient drugs. These drugs can be classified according to the symptoms they are targeted to alleviate.

The first type of cold remedy is for congestion, which is the most common cold symptom. Decongestants reduce the swelling of the mucous membranes in the nose, resulting in easier breathing and better drainage. There are two kinds of decongestants: topical and oral. Topical decongestants, which include sprays and drops, work rapidly, but there is a potential problem. If used too much, they can cause "rebound congestion," which means worse congestion than there was originally, so they should be used sparingly. Examples of topical decongestants include Dristan and Neo-Synephrine, which contain the active ingredient phenylephrine; Afrin, which contains oxymetazoline; and Neo-Synephrine II, which contains xylometazoline. Oral decongestants, such as Sudafed and Oramyl, both of which contain pseudoephedrine, take longer to be effective but don't produce rebound congestion. However, potential side effects include dry mouth, sleep disturbances, and an increase in blood pressure.

While most cold sufferers have congestion, only a little over a third suffer from the aches and pains so often mentioned in commercials; in fact, only about 25 percent suffer from headaches, 10 percent from muscle pain, and 1 percent from mild fever. The three standard pain-relieving ingredients for aches and pains include aspirin, acetaminophren, and ibuprophen. Products whose primary ingredient is aspirin include Bayer, Bufferin, Norwich, and St. Joseph aspirin. There is one caution about aspirin. Studies have shown a link between aspirin and Reye's syndrome, a rare but potentially fatal illness that strikes children and teenagers. Therefore, children and teens should not be given aspirin when they have cold symptoms. Alternatives to aspirin include acetaminophren, which is the main ingredient in Datril and Tylenol, and ibuprofen, which is the active ingredient in Advil and Nuprin.

About half of cold sufferers also have a cough. Cough remedies approach this symptom in different ways. Suppressants act on the brain to depress the cough reflex. For this purpose, products such as Benylin DM and Pertussin 8-Hour Cough Formula contain dextromethorphan. Another active ingredient used is diphenhydramine, found in Benylin. However, since this is an antihistamine, it can cause drowsiness. The main problem with cough suppressants is that it may not be wise to suppress the cough, particularly for people with lung ailments. Medicated lozenges, on the other hand, act locally on the throat to ease coughs. Lozenges, such as N'Ice Sugarless Cough Lozenges, which contain more than 5 milligrams of menthol, may help. Expectorants, in contrast to suppressants, supposedly help liquefy and loosen phlegm, making it easier to cough up. Guaifenesin is the active ingredient in Robitussin.

Finally, the last major symptom of the cold is the one that occurs first—the sore throat. About 50 percent of cold sufferers get a sore throat. There are many medicated lozenges and sprays available for such relief: Chloraseptic Sore Throat Spray, which contains phenol compounds; Spec-T Sore Throat Anesthetic Lozenges, made with benzocaine; Sucrets, made with Hexylresorcinol; and N'Ice Sugarless Cough Lozenges, whose active ingredient is menthol. Since a sore throat is also symptomatic of other illnesses, if the sore throat persists one should see a doctor.

While it may be easier to purchase a cold remedy that contains multiple ingredients, it may not be wise. The prudent cold sufferer should consider remedies targeted for specific single symptoms. Nevertheless, all sufferers should remember that there is no cure for the common cold; it will still have to run its course. Finally, when in doubt, people with colds should always consult their physicians. —Adapted from "Cold Remedies: Which Ones Work Best?" *Consumer Reports*, January 1989, pp. 8–11.

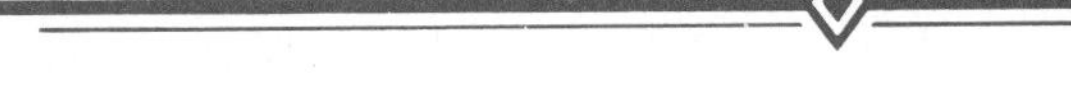

EXERCISE 8-9

On a separate sheet of paper, answer the following questions about the essay "Cold Remedies."

1. What is the thesis?
2. What seems to be the writer's purpose for writing about these kinds of cold remedies?
3. What is the principle of classification?
4. What are the characteristics of the decongestants?
5. What is the controlling idea about the cough remedies?
6. What are the characteristics of cough remedies?
7. Do the examples the writer uses to illustrate the categories seem appropriate?
8. Does the conclusion appear to be logical?
9. Write an outline of this essay.

EXERCISE 8-10: WRITING ASSIGNMENT

In Exercise 8-8, you were asked to make some notes about television programs. Using the preceding essay as a model, make the first draft of an essay on that topic.

COMPOSITION SKILLS

Introductory Paragraphs

The Turnabout

In Chapter 5, you learned how to compose one of the most common types of introductory paragraphs, what is often called the "Funnel." This approach to opening essays is a good one, but of course it is not the only way writers can introduce their essays. Another common approach is what we call the "Turnabout." This type of introduction opens with a few sentences summarizing a point of view that is actually the opposite of the writer's own thesis. By the end of the introduction, the writer makes a complete turnabout and presents his or her thesis—the opposite of what he or she started out with. This technique is useful when the writer's purpose in the essay is to argue a point or to clear up a commonly held misconception.

Like the Funnel, the Turnabout opens generally and congenially, but unlike the Funnel, the Turnabout has this dramatic shift in ideas. In other words, in the Turnabout the writer sets up the opponent's view for attack. You have already seen some examples of this type of introduction, such as the introductory paragraph by Habeeb Al-Saeed on page 171 in Exercise 5-4. In the following introductory paragraph from Exercise 5-3, the writer opens with a statement about the generally held view that watching television is a worthwhile pastime, but by the end of the paragraph, she presents the opposing view for her thesis.

> We live in an era where television is the national pastime. Since the invention of the television set, people have been spending more of their free time watching television than doing anything else. Many of the television addicts feel that this particular pastime is not a bad one; indeed, they argue that people can learn a great deal watching television. I am sure that if you look long and hard enough, you can probably find some programs that are educationally motivating. But, for the most part, I say that watching television is a waste of time.
>
> —*Pamela Moran*

Professional writers often use the Turnabout introduction as well. Study the following introduction to an article in a popular magazine:

> In the struggle for existence, individual animals that are best adapted to their environment are more likely to survive and procreate. Their offspring inherit the adaptive traits, which after many generations spread throughout the species. That, in a nutshell, is Darwin's theory of evolution by natural selection. But for some years now there has been evidence that a struggle for existence also takes place on a completely different level, one that Darwin couldn't have dreamed of: the level of individual genes. While eggs or sperm are being formed, some genes seem to outmaneuver others and thus manage to appear in more than their fair share of the offspring. Because this behavior benefits the genes themselves, and not necessarily the organisms that carry them, the genes are called selfish.
>
> —From "Killer Gene," *Discover the World of Science* December 1988: p. 15.

EXERCISE 8-11: WRITING ASSIGNMENT

1. For the draft essay you composed for Exercise 8-10, revise the introduction to make it a Turnabout.
2. Select one of the essays you wrote for an exercise in an earlier chapter. Rewrite your introduction using the Turnabout approach.

Coherence

Transitions for Classification

A classification essay is really a combination of the example and comparison–contrast essays. Therefore, expect the transitions for this type of essay to be generally the same as those for the example and comparison–contrast essays. Review the following transitions:

1. **TRANSITIONS TO INTRODUCE CATEGORIES.** These are generally additive transitions: *first, second, next, last, another, in addition.*

The *first* group includes those students who dress formally.

The *next* group includes those who dress semiformally.

The *last* category includes those who dress casually.

And *finally*, there is the type that everyone dreads: the negative teacher.

In addition to these two groups, there is another group: the dunces.

2. **TRANSITIONS TO SHOW SIMILARITIES AND DIFFERENCES.** In a classification paper it is important to clarify the distinctions between the categories; therefore, make use of the transitions that show similarities and differences (see Chapter 7).

Unlike the positive teachers, the neutral teachers are not very agreeable.

However, *like* the positive teacher, the neutral teacher allows for questions.

Their classes tend to be *more boring than* the positive teachers' classes because they allow *less time* for discussion.

Expectorants, *in contrast to* suppressants, supposedly help liquefy and loosen phlegm, making it easier to cough up.

3. **TRANSITIONS TO INTRODUCE EXAMPLES.** Chapters 3 and 5 discuss how to use transitions to introduce examples. The same transitions are used for the classification essay.

A good example of a positive teacher is my French teacher, Monsieur Poirrot.

An excellent example of a negative teacher is Dr. Wollen.

One day, *for example*, when one student asked him to repeat his explanation, he became quite angry.

Professor Hilton is *typical* of the neutral teacher.

4. **TRANSITIONS TO SHOW THE IMPORTANCE OF THE CATEGORY.** It is a good idea to indicate if an example or a category is more or less significant than the others. Indicate, too, the relative size.

Of the three types of teachers, the negative teachers are the *least* agreeable.

Fortunately, this group is *in the minority*.

EXERCISE 8-12: WRITING ASSIGNMENT

Study the following essay. The original version contained transitions that have been omitted from this version. Rewrite the essay to include transitions wherever necessary.

KINDS OF HOTELS

Hotels are found in every country and city of the world and even in communities with few inhabitants. That's why the hotel industry ranks high among the largest worldwide industries. Today, the lodging industry offers many new alternatives for the traveling public. Some properties offer luxury accommodations; others offer budget accommodations; while still others accommodate the need of travelers to be away from home. Whatever the reason, there are many different kinds of hotels and they can be classified according to their size, facility, type, price, or service. Generally, we can classify these hotels into three large groups based on location.

Airport hotels accommodate the air traveler. Because air travel has become more common, this kind of hotel has become more popular. The principal distinction is that it is located near airports. It is very convenient to the traveler. Its guests include passengers with short stay overs or cancelled flights and travelers who are in business. The length of stay is between one to three days for the guests. These kinds of hotels provide a limited level of service and the rates are usually between low to medium. The Hilton, the Marriott, and the Holiday Inn are large chains that have hotels near airports. Best Western and the TraveLodge are among the smaller hotel chains.

Downtown hotels, also called commercial hotels, are located near large office complexes and retail stores in the major metropolitan areas. Their primary markets are in the business industry. The downtown hotels are near business destinations for daytime activities and are close to the city's entertainment centers for nighttime activities. This combination is attractive to people attending meetings and conventions. Although the primary market for these hotels is the business traveler, many tourists use them as well. The length of stay for the guests is between three to five days and rates can run between medium to high depending on the hotel. The downtown hotels have a variety of services such as room service, a coffee shop, a formal dining room, laundry services, a gift shop and a swimming pool. The downtown Hyatt-Regency is a well-known hotel in this category.

There are also the resort hotels located near the beaches, mountains, or spas. Resort hotels are destinations or parts of a destination complex and their primary clients are vacationers and recreation-minded people. Guests in these resorts can spend from one week to an entire season. The resort hotels must provide guest entertainment. Because the resort guests expect to be entertained right on the premises, they are willing to pay higher rates. The level of service is much higher than what an airport or downtown hotel offers. These complexes are designed with the family and children in mind. The most famous of these is the Walt Disney World Resort, which includes not only the theme park but also all varieties of water sports, campgrounds, and golf courses.

There may be a few other general areas where hotels are located, such as along the interstate highways, but most of them are located near airports, in the downtown areas, and in resort areas.

—*Adapted from an essay by Carlos Palacio*

EXERCISE 8-13: WRITING ASSIGNMENT

What is the thesis of the essay "Kinds of Hotels"? Make an outline of the essay.

EXERCISE 8-14: WRITING ASSIGNMENT

Using the preceding essay as a model, write an essay classifying some other type of building or business for another purpose, such as banks, hospitals, restaurants, or gas stations. Be sure to include transitions and examples.

GRAMMAR REVIEW

Correlative Conjunctions

Coordinating conjunctions (*and, but, yet*) can be used as transitions to give writing coherence. Correlative conjunctions can also connect two sentences together, just as regular conjunctions do.

The correlative conjunctions include

both . . . and	*either . . . or*
neither . . . nor	*not only . . . but also*

Note how these pairs of words are used in the following sentences:

The Rabbit and the Chevette differ *not only* in ride *but also* in mileage.

Both Nhan *and* Hung want to do good things for human beings.

You can take the test *either* on Monday *or* on Wednesday.

It has *neither* a good price *nor* good gas mileage.

Correlative conjunctions add clarity and coherence to writing by signaling the relationship between the two ideas in the sentence. When reading the first one of the pair, the reader immediately knows the second one is to follow and what the relationship between the two ideas is. However, with a regular conjunction in a compound sentence, this relationship is not clear until the reader reaches the second part of the sentence. Compare:

That professor is not a good lecturer, *and* he is not a fair grader.

That professor is *neither* a good lecturer *nor* a fair grader.

The position of the correlative conjunctions in the sentence is important. Each conjunction comes just before the item it is comparing. Further, the grammatical elements that follow correlative conjunctions should be parallel—that is, they should both be verbs, nouns, infinitives, and so on. Study these examples:

Both . . . and

Both *John* and *I* love to ski. (nouns)
John loves both *to ski* and *to dance.* (infinitives)
John both *loves* to ski and *hates* to dance. (verbs)

Either . . . or

Either *Bill* or *his cousin* will give the party. (nouns)
Bill will either *take out* the trash or *wash* the dishes. (verbs)
Bill will take out either *the trash* or *the old newspapers.* (nouns)

Not only . . . but also

Not only is Bill rich, but *his wife* is rich also. (nouns)
He is not only *rich,* but he is also *talented.* (adjectives)

Note: ***Not only*** **can come at the beginning of the clause for emphasis. When it starts a clause, a form of the verb** ***to be*** **or an auxiliary verb immediately follows it. The preceding example can be emphasized like this:**

Not only *is* he rich, but he is also talented.

Mozart composed not only *for piano,* but also *for violin.* (prepositional phrases)
Mozart not only *composed* for piano, but also *wrote* for violin. (verbs)
Not only did Mozart *compose* for piano, but he also *wrote* for violin.

Neither . . . nor

I have read neither *the book* nor *the short story.* (nouns)
I have neither *read* the book nor *seen* the movie. (verbs)

Note: ***Nor*** **can come at the beginning of the clause for emphasis. When it starts a clause, a form of the verb** ***to be*** **or an auxiliary often follows it. The preceding example can be restated like this:**

I have neither read the book, nor *have* I seen the movie.

Pay attention to subject–verb agreement with ***neither . . . nor, either . . . or,*** and ***not only . . . but also.*** With a compound subject the verb agrees with the nearer part of the subject. Study these examples:

Neither John nor Bill *is* excited about the party.

Either the boys or their sister *is* feeding the dog.

Neither John nor his brothers *are* interested in this book.

Not only Bill but also Mary *is* intending to go with us.

EXERCISE 8-15

Combine the two sentences into one using the correlative conjunctions given. Pay special attention to the position of the verb *to be* or to the auxiliary with *not only* and *nor.*

1. The first type of student is quiet. The second type of student is quiet.
   a. Not only is the first type ______________________________
   ____

2. The first type of student is quiet. The first type of student is smart.
   a. The first type of student is not only ______________________________
   ____
   b. Not only is the first ______________________________
   ____

3. The second type of student hates sports. The second type of student hates music.
   a. The second type of student hates ______________________________
   ____
   b. The second type of student not only ______________________________
   ____
   c. Not only does the second ______________________________
   ____

4. The students can be classified according to where they live. The students can be classified according to how they get to school.
   a. The students can be classified not only ______________________________
   ____

b. The students can not only ______________________

____

c. Not only can the students ______________________

____

5. John does not like this type of teacher. John will not take his classes.

   a. John neither ______________________________

   ____

6. This type of teacher does not prepare properly. This type of teacher does not grade fairly.

   a. This type of teacher neither ______________________

   ____

7. This type of teacher should not be hired. This type of teacher should not be paid.

   a. This type of teacher should neither ________________

   ____

EXERCISE 8-16

Combine the two sentences in each item using the correlative conjunction given.

1. (*both . . . and*) Physics is classified as a physical science. Chemistry is classified as a physical science.

   ____

2. (*neither . . . nor*) We cannot classify mathematics as a biological science. We cannot classify psychology as a physical science.

   ____

3. (*not only . . . but also*) Botany and zoology are normally considered biological sciences. They are generally requirements for a B.S. degree.

   ____

4. (*either . . . or*) All liberal arts majors have to take two physical science courses. Instead, all liberal arts majors could take two biological science courses.

   ____

5. (*not only . . . but also*) In order to graduate, all students in college must take certain required

courses. They have to take some electives.

---

6. (*both . . . and*) Nicotine is a drug. Alcohol is a drug.

---

7. (*neither . . . nor*) Nicotine is not healthy for the body. Alcohol is not healthy for the body.

---

8. (*not only . . . but also*) Nicotine can be addictive. Alcohol can be addictive.

---

9. (*not only . . . but also*) Nicotine and alcohol are in the category of acceptable drugs in our society. Caffeine is in the category of acceptable drugs.

---

10. (*either . . . or*) Users of acceptable drugs should stop using those drugs. Users of acceptable drugs should be extremely moderate in their drug intake.

EXERCISE 8-17: WRITING ASSIGNMENT

1. Using some of the transitions mentioned in this chapter as well as correlative conjunctions if they fit logically, revise your classification essay of television programs. (See Exercise 8-10.)
2. The following essay lacks coherence. Using all of the coherence devices you have studied so far, rewrite it. You will need to add transitions and conjunctions and repeat key words and phrases. You will also need to rewrite some sentences to make them flow smoothly.

Everyone makes excuses. Who hasn't said, "Oh, it's so hot. I just can't go outside and wash the car," or "It was really John's idea. He made me do it," or "I had a terrible headache." It seems as we all, at one time or another, feel the need to explain why something happened or didn't happen, to assign blame. Because we all do it, making excuses may seem innocent enough. Certain excuses, sometimes called "little white lies," perform a social function of smoothing over a potentially disagreeable situation. No one is truly deceived and perhaps no harm is done. Most excuses are not so innocent. They are intended to deceive. While it may seem we intend to deceive others, it is really ourselves that we are deceiving. Making excuses is a way of not taking responsibility for our actions. It is a way of assigning blame to something else, someone else, or even our mental or physical state so that we do not have to look at ourselves.

We can escape blame by pointing the finger at forces or circumstances outside ourselves. You may say, "I couldn't possibly write a good essay. It was ninety degrees in the room. There was no air conditioning. It was just too hot." Since you have no control over the heat, you are exonerated. It's not your fault. Perhaps you've heard someone say to the teacher, "I'm sorry I missed class today, but my car ran out of gas on the freeway." The person is not responsible, right? There are forces outside our control that intervene and prevent us from doing something. There are floods, fires, and "acts of God." These might be valid reasons for why something was or was not accomplished. They might not be excuses. The important thing is to look at the circumstances and determine our own attitude and reaction. Are we blaming a force outside ourselves for our own inability? If so, we are making an excuse.

We can blame other people. This type of excuse lets you off the hook because you are not responsible; someone else is. Typical examples include: "Well, it wasn't my idea to cheat on the test. Bill suggested it and I just went along with him." "I got a bad grade in that course because the teacher doesn't make it interesting." "I didn't get a raise because my boss is so stingy." "I know my child is naughty but his mother spoils him so." The person making the excuse is not taking his or her responsibility. Passing the buck is a special kind. This kind of excuse making often occurs in large companies and government bureaucracies. Let's say a company loses a million dollars because of a bad investment. The president of the company blames the vice-president who advised him. The vice-president passes the buck to one of her analysts who had done the research. The analyst says, "It wasn't my fault. The research was erroneous," or even "The typist typed it wrong." The blame gets passed from person to person and maybe to the computer, with no one ever taking responsibility for the error. It is easier to look outside ourselves and assign blame than to look at ourselves and our true capabilities.

Excuses closest to home are those in which we blame our own mental or physical state but at the same time do not accept responsibility for them. It is as if our body and mind are separate from us and can be blamed. Here you have the psychosomatic excuses: "I had such a headache I couldn't write my report." "Every time I jog I get a terrible stomachache. I guess I just won't exercise any more." "My eyes burn if I read too much." At times we are truly sick. The problem is in determining when we use our physical state as a way of avoiding something we consider unpleasant. We blame our inaction or inability on our mental state. "I was so depressed about my family I didn't study for the exam." "I wasn't in the mood to go to that party and see all those strangers." "I was so excited I just didn't think about the consequences." Excuses allow us to avoid looking at ourselves and the problems that we face.

We all make excuses. They are not necessarily healthy for us. When we look at ourselves, at circumstances, or at our own physical and mental state, we do not have to look at ourselves and see something unpleasant. We do not take responsibility for ourselves and our actions. Our physical and mental health depends on our ability to solve problems. If we are to solve the problems that confront us, we must look through our excuses and see ourselves.

Adjective Clauses Reduced to Participial Phrases

Adjective clauses connect two sentences by replacing a noun with a relative pronoun (*who*, *which*, *that*, and so on). Certain adjective clauses can be reduced to participial phrases. To reduce an adjective clause—relative clause—to a participial phrase, delete the relative pronoun that is acting as a subject and the form of the verb *to be* that follows the pronoun. This should leave a present participle (an *-ing* word) or a past participle (an *-ed/-en* word). To see how this works, first underline the adjective clauses in the following sentences:

I know the man who John is picking up.

I know the man who teaches at this school.

I know the man who is standing over there.

I know the man who was taken to jail.

I know the man who was being charged with the crime.

Note that in the first two sentences, adjective clauses *cannot be reduced.* In the first one, the relative pronoun is not the subject of the clause. In the second one, we do not have a form of the verb *to be* or the present participle. A reduction here would result in an incorrect sentence:

Incorrect:

I know the man teaches at this school.

(Often, in this type of sentence, the verb can be changed to a present participle and we can have the following: "*I know the man teaching at this school.*")

Note the correct sentences when *who* + *is/was* is deleted:

I know the man standing over there.

I know the man taken to jail.

I know the man being charged with the crime.

The sentence with the present participle is reduced from an active verb, whereas the sentences with the past participle (*-ed/-en*) are reduced from passive verbs. Do not confuse the simple past tense verbs with passive. Note this sentence:

The man who walked down the street was a thief.

This sentence does not have a form of the verb *to be*, so it cannot be reduced. Reduction would result in this incorrect sentence:

Incorrect:

The man walked down the street was a thief.

However, the sentence that follows is passive, so it has a form of the verb *to be*:

The car that was returned to me was not mine.

It can be reduced thus:

The car returned to me was not mine.

Sometimes the reduction of a clause will leave just the participle after the noun. When the participle tells "which," it remains after the noun:

The woman who is singing is my sister.
= The woman singing is my sister.

The man who was accused is angry.
= The man accused is angry.

However, when the participle tells "what kind of," it is placed in front of the noun. Study these sentences:

Countries that are developing need capital.
= Developing countries need capital.

Plays that are unpublished are often performed.
= Unpublished plays are often performed.

Finally, we should note that both restrictive and nonrestrictive adjective clauses can be reduced. (For a review of restrictive and nonrestrictive clauses, see Chapter 3.) Note these examples:

The man giving the lecture is Mr. Brown.

Mr. Brown, giving a lecture on economics, paced back and forth.

A city founded one hundred years ago is quite young by European standards.

New York City, founded over a hundred years ago, is one of the oldest American cities.

EXERCISE 8-18

Review the rules for punctuating restrictive and nonrestrictive adjective clauses on pages 110–12. The same rules apply to participial phrases reduced from adjective clauses. Punctuate the following sentences, inserting commas where necessary.

1. Scientists working in the field of genetic engineering are very excited about its future.
2. The young hikers tired and worn out decided to take a rest.
3. Robots run by computers are being used in some automobile factories.
4. The convict planning his escape requested to work in the fields.
5. The Chinese New Year celebrated by millions of Asians all over the world is a grand event.
6. The airline pilot fighting off fatigue drank another cup of coffee.
7. The band playing in the Superdome tonight is one of the most famous in the world.
8. The tightrope walker cheered by the crowds below made his way by rope from the top of one skyscraper to the top of the other skyscraper.
9. The athlete wearing the blue shorts is competing in the 50-yard dash.
10. That swimmer practicing in the pool is planning to swim the English Channel.

EXERCISE 8-19

In the following paragraph, underline the relative clauses and determine if any of them can be reduced to participial phrases. Then rewrite the paragraph using participial phrases where possible.

In order to be healthy, we all need a daily balanced diet. A balanced diet includes eating some foods each day from each of the four major food groups, which include dairy foods, meats, vegetables and fruits, and breads and cereals. The first group, which is dairy foods, obviously includes milk. Other dairy foods that are able to supplement milk to fulfill our daily needs are cheese and ice cream. Although dairy foods are high in animal fat, which is a substance to be avoided, they are widely available in low-fat forms such as skim milk and ice milk. The second major group that is needed for good health is meats, which are used by our bodies to provide protein. Meat can be obtained in a variety of ways, which include beef, pork, fowl, and fish. In recent years, we have been warned to avoid red meats, which are beef and pork, and to concentrate on eating the leaner fish and fowl. Some people avoid all or some of these meats for religious reasons. These people must obtain their protein in other ways.

EXERCISE 8-20

Now complete the paragraph in Exercise 8-19 by writing about the two final food groups: (1) vegetables and fruits and (2) breads and cereals. Add as much information and detail as you can. Use participial phrases wherever possible.

EXERCISE 8-21

Write an essay classifying types of exercise programs, diets, or diseases. Be sure to have a thesis statement and clear topic sentences.

Articles for Classification

As you learned in Chapter 4, the most common use of the article ***a*** is to indicate a nonspecific item, whereas the most common use of the article ***the*** is to indicate a specific item. We also noted times when no article is used. In this chapter, we study another possible use of ***a***, ***the***, and the plural noun without the article, and this is for classification.

As you know, classification is the process of putting nouns in categories. You want to identify a member, or a smaller class, as part of a larger class. Often you use a single member of the class to represent the smaller class. It is a symbol or representative of the entire smaller class. Both the articles *a* and *the* can be used to indicate the representative member:

MEMBER/SMALLER CLASS		LARGER CLASS
The cat	is	a mammal.
A cat	is	a mammal.

However, the most common way to classify nouns is with the plural noun:

Cats are mammals.

There is a difference in emphasis among the three sentences. With *the*, emphasis is on the class and on the *idea* of the class. With *a*, emphasis is on an unidentified, individual representative of the class. In the preceding sentence, *a* means *any* cat. The plural noun emphasizes all the representatives of the class. In our example it means *all* cats.

Note that the larger class is indicated by the article *a* or the plural noun, depending on what was used to indicate the smaller class.

In giving definitions or in scientific classifications, all three patterns are possible. Note the classification of insects, birds, plants, animals, elements, and instruments:

A mosquito is a common carrier of disease.

Sparrows are seed eaters.

The magnolia is a common tree in the southern part of the United States.

An atom is a part of a molecule.

The piston is a necessary part of an engine.

Note that we also classify people:

The computer scientist has an important function in our everyday life.

The typical American is married.

With proper names and noncount nouns, no article is used with the member of the class:

John F. Kennedy was a president of the United States.

Hydrogen is a gas.

EXERCISE 8-22

Match the member or smaller class listed in column A with the larger class listed in column B. Write a complete sentence for each one. Be sure to use the article or plural noun correctly.

A	B
lever	common city bird
apple	famous general
oxygen	means of transportation
starling	fairly large insect
rose	fruit
motorcycle	microscopic organisms
dragonfly	simple machine
bacteria	element
Milky Way	sweet-smelling flower
Napoleon	galaxy

EXERCISE 8-23

In the following passages, underline each article + noun or plural noun that is a member or a smaller class in a classification. Circle the noun that is the larger class.

1. The cougar is a big-game hunter. Usually it spends the day sleeping in some rocky cavern or sunning itself on a high, warm ledge. After dark the cougar leaves its lair and sets forth on a silent hunt. More than once it has been seen swimming across rivers at least a mile wide. It may range twenty miles through the night.

   This big cat's natural prey are the deer and sometimes the elk, but it will track down other animals like the skunk, and its victims often include domestic stock—cattle, sheep, horses, and pigs. Stalking the doomed animal in the shadows, the cougar approaches soundlessly for the final rush. Now it gathers its feet under its body and humps its back. The taut muscles burst into action. In one, two, or three quick bounds, the cougar is upon its quarry, hurling it to the ground and piercing its throat or neck with long, murderous fangs. —Frederick Drimmer, *The Animal Kingdom*, vol. 1 (New York: Greystone Press, 1954), p. 573.

2. There are four kinds of poisonous snakes in the United States. Rattlesnakes, copperheads, and cottonmouth moccasins are pit vipers. The other poisonous snake is the coral snake. The pit vipers have a pit on each side of the head between the eyes and the nostrils. The coral snake, found along the coast and lowlands of the Southeast, is small; it chews rather than bites and cannot readily attach to large surfaces, such as the forearm and calf. Its potent venom affects the nervous system, whereas that of the pit vipers affects the blood circulatory system. —American Red Cross, *First Aid Textbook*, 4th ed. (Garden City: Doubleday, 1957), pp. 148–49.

EXERCISE 8-24

In the following passages, insert *a*, *an*, or *the* wherever you think it is required. Before you do this exercise, review the discussion of articles in

Chapter 4, pages 152–59. Rewrite the paragraphs on another piece of paper.

1. Sometimes, if you aren't getting enough calcium from foods, your physician will recommend calcium supplement. Wide variety of calcium tablets are available. However, they can be added expense, and some people forget to take them regularly or find tablets hard to swallow.

   Calcium carbonate is type of calcium most commonly found in calcium supplements. Some antacids contain calcium and fall into this category. Calcium carbonate is safe when taken in recommended doses. Oyster shell calcium is essentially calcium carbonate, with addition of some naturally occurring trace elements. However, calcium carbonate tablets that contain aluminum may lead to loss in body calcium.

   Calcium glucomate or calcium lactate are less widely available but are found in some vitamin and mineral supplements. However, they contain relatively low amounts of calcium. This could mean having to swallow many tablets every day to meet your RDA of calcium.

   Bonemeal and dolomite are also forms of calcium but some have been known to contain lead or other impurities. Because purity of these supplements has been questioned, you may wish to consult your physician before buying them. —Adapted from *The Calcium Book*, Proctor & Gamble, June 1987.

2. There are three types of honey bees: queens, workers, and drones. Each has its own role in life of hive, and to perform its functions properly each must be able to communicate with other individuals and to respond correctly to their communications.

   There is only one queen in colony. She is larger than other bees and is only fertile female. Her sole function is laying eggs. Except for brief period in her early adult life, when she leaves hive on few brief nuptial flights and mates with several males, she remains permanently within hive.

   Workers are also female, but they are sterile and are smaller then queen. As their name implies, they perform everyday chores around hive—gathering food, feeding larvae and queen, storing surplus food, building hive and adding to it as more cells are needed for new eggs or more food, keeping hive and its inhabitants clean, and defending it against bees from other colonies.

   Third type of honeybee is male bee, or drone. Drones have only one function: to mate with queen. They do little else, and except for their participation in mating flight, they lead idle life. During spring and summer, when drones still have some potential use, workers tolerate them, but as autumn approaches, workers drag them out of colony and leave them to die. No new drones are produced until following spring.

   Three types of honeybee ensure perpetuation of species.

Queen and drones attend to reproduction, and workers do housekeeping and care for eggs, larvae, pupae, queen, and drones. For all this to work properly, each bee must "know" what is needed from it. Some information comes to bee in its heredity—whether it is male or female—and this information is already present in egg. Other information comes from bee's environment. What it sees, smells, tastes, hears, or feels determines how it will act at given moment. —Adapted from Joan E. Rahn, *Biology: The Science of Life*, 2d ed. (New York: Macmillan, 1980), p. 39.

3. Fragments of genes from extinct animal, relative of zebra and horse, have been found and reproduced in the laboratory, scientists of University of California at Berkeley report. They said gene fragments are first to be extracted from any vanished animal species. Genetic material, DNA, was extracted from scrap of dried muscle tissue found inside skin of animal called quagga. Skin, preserved 140 years ago, had been kept at Mainz Museum of Natural History in West Germany. Species died out about century ago. —"Parts of Extinct Animal's Genes Cloned," *Times-Picayune States Item*, 11 June 1984, sec. 7, p. 2.

EXERCISE 8-25: WRITING ASSIGNMENT

The following topics are for a classification essay. After making a list of items, try to find a logical principle around which you can formulate a thesis statement. In the development, be sure to use specific examples to illustrate the classes, transitions, correlative conjunctions if appropriate, and participial phrases reduced from adjective clauses. (Have no more than four categories.)

1. If you are taking a course in another discipline, use information from that course to develop a classification. For example, if you are taking an engineering course, you might classify types of bridges or roads. If you are taking a business course, you might classify types of retail stores. If you are in computer science, you might classify types of computers or computer programs. Be sure to have a principle of classification and an interesting thesis. Write an essay describing your classification.
2. You have received a letter from a friend back home asking you about your American friends. In your response, you have decided to classify your friends.
3. In your psychology class your professor has decided to have you analyze your own dreams in a report that will be a part of a larger report by the entire class on dreams. Write an essay classifying your dreams. What types of dreams do you have?
4. Write an essay classifying jobs in the computer field. This essay can be written for an article in the school newspaper.
5. Choose one of these topics for a classification essay:
   a. Types of lies people tell.

b. Types of excuses students make up for missing class.
c. Types of sciences.
d. Your neighbors.
e. The books you read.

Classification Essay Checklist

1. A classification essay analyzes a subject by breaking it down into its parts to study the nature or relationship of the parts. Does your essay break a subject down into parts?
2. To classify, you must have one principle of classification. What is the principle of classification in your essay?
3. Your classification should include all the members of the group. Is your classification complete?
4. In organizing your classification essay, you need to identify each group, describe or define it, give examples, and distinguish it from the other groups. Is your essay well organized and sufficiently developed?
5. Have you used an interesting introduction for your essay?
6. Is your essay coherent?

Chapter 9

The Process Analysis Essay

Readings: The World of Work

Work is love made visible. And if you cannot work with love but only with distaste, it is better that you should leave your work and sit at the gate of the temple and take alms of those who work with joy. —*Kahlil Gibran*

All work, even cotton spinning, is noble; work is alone noble. . . . A life of ease is not for any man, nor for any god. —*Thomas Carlyle*

I don't like work—no man does—but I like what is in work—the chance to find yourself. Your own reality—for yourself, not for others—what no other man can ever know. —*Joseph Conrad*

Whether we find work noble, enriching, or boring, for most of us work is a part of life. A major part of our lives is taken up with work—whether we are students, parents, engineers, farmers, or television personalities. Because we work throughout most of our lives, it is easy to see work as a process—something that started and continues through time.

In the following readings, the writers present descriptions of two different people at work. As you read the selections, ask yourself these questions:

1. What is the attitude of each worker toward his work?
2. What is the attitude of other people toward the worker and his work?
3. What do you like or dislike about work?

READING 1

FROM *THE DARK CHILD*

CAMARA LAYE

Camara Laye, originally from French Guinea in West Africa, was studying engineering in Paris when he wrote The Dark Child *(1954), from which this reading is taken. In this book, Laye describes his early life, his family, and the village he lived in. In the excerpt that follows, Laye describes his father, a goldsmith and metal worker, making a piece of jewelry for a customer. Note that while the reading describes the process of making the trinket, it also has a clearly stated thesis. As you read, try to answer these questions:*

1. What kind of man was the writer's father? What was the attitude of other people toward him?
2. What are the steps in the process of making a piece of gold jewelry?
3. What is the writer's attitude, or thesis, about the process of making the gold jewelry?

1 Of all the different kinds of work my father engaged in, none fascinated me so much as his skill with gold. No other occupation was so noble, no other needed such a delicate touch. And then, every time he worked in gold it was like a

festival—indeed it *was* a festival—that broke the monotony of ordinary working days.

2 So, if a woman, accompanied by a go-between, crossed the threshold of the workshop, I followed her in at once. I knew what she wanted: she had brought some gold, and had come to ask my father to transform it into a trinket. She had collected it in the placers• of Siguiri where, crouching over the river for months on end, she had patiently extracted grains of gold from the mud.

flat dishes used for mining

3 These women never came alone. They knew my father had other things to do than make trinkets. And even when he had the time, they knew they were not the first to ask a favor of him, and that, consequently, they would not be served before others.

4 Generally they required the trinket for a certain date, for the festival of Ramadan or the Tabaski or some other family ceremony or dance.

5 Therefore, to enhance• their chances of being served quickly and to more easily persuade my father to interrupt the work before him, they used to request the services of an official praise-singer, a go-between, arranging in advance the fee they were to pay him for his good offices.•

make better, improve

service

6 The go-between installed• himself in the workshop, tuned up his *cora*, which is our harp, and began to sing my father's praises. This was always a great event for me. I heard recalled the lofty deeds of my father's ancestors and their names from the earliest times. As the couplets• were reeled off it was like watching the growth of a great genealogical tree• that spread its branches far and wide and flourished its boughs and twigs before my mind's eye. The harp played an accompaniment to this vast utterance of names, expanding it with notes that were now soft, now shrill.

established, set up

two successive lines of poetry

a diagram of one's ancestors

7 I could sense my father's vanity• being inflamed,• and I already knew that after having sipped this milk-and-honey[1] he would lend a favorable ear to the woman's request. But I was not alone in my knowledge. The woman also had seen my father's eyes gleaming with contented pride. She held out her grains of gold as if the whole matter were settled. My father took up his scales and weighed the gold.

pride / excited, increased

8 "What sort of trinket do you want?" he would ask.

9 "I want. . . ."

10 And then the woman would not know any longer exactly what she wanted because desire kept making her change her mind, and because she would have liked all the trinkets at once. But it would have taken a pile of gold much larger than she had brought to satisfy her whim, and from then

[1]**sipped this milk-and-honey** *been made agreeable by compliments and praise*

on her chief purpose in life was to get hold of it as soon as she could.

11 "When do you want it?"

12 Always the answer was that the trinket was needed for an occasion in the near future.

13 "So! You are in that much of a hurry? Where do you think I shall find the time?"

14 "I am in a great hurry, I assure you."

15 "I have never seen a woman eager to deck herself out[2] who wasn't in a great hurry! Good! I shall arrange my time to suit you. Are you satisfied?"

16 He would take the clay pot that was kept specially for smelting• gold, and would pour the grains into it. He would then cover the gold with powdered charcoal, a charcoal he prepared by using plant juices of exceptional purity. Finally, he would place a large lump of the same kind of charcoal over the pot.

melting, refining

17 As soon as she saw that the work had been duly• undertaken, the woman, now quite satisfied, would return to her household tasks, leaving her go-between to carry on with the praise-singing which had already proven so advantageous.

without too much delay, at the right time

18 At a sign from my father the apprentices[3] began working two sheepskin bellows.[4] The skins were on the floor, on opposite sides of the forge,[5] connected to it by earthen pipes. While the work was in progress the apprentices sat in front of the bellows with crossed legs. That is, the younger of the two sat, for the elder was sometimes allowed to assist. But the younger—this time it was Sidafa—was only permitted to work the bellows and watch while waiting his turn for promotion to less rudimentary tasks. First one and then the other worked hard at the bellows: the flame in the forge rose higher and became a living thing, a genie• implacable• and full of life.

supernatural being, spirit / unchangeable

19 Then my father lifted the clay pot with his long tongs and placed it on the flame.

20 Immediately all activity in the workshop almost came to a halt. During the whole time that the gold was being smelted, neither copper nor aluminum could be worked nearby, lest some particle of these base metals fall into the container which held the gold. Only steel could be worked on such occasions, but the men, whose task that was, hurried to finish what they were doing, or left it abruptly to join the apprentices gathered around the forge. There were so many, and they crowded so around my father, that I, the smallest

[2]**deck herself out** *beautify, get dressed up*
[3]*people learning the trade*
[4]*device for blowing air*
[5]*place for the fire, where the smithy does his work*

person present, had to come near the forge in order not to lose track of what was going on.

21 If he felt he had inadequate working space, my father had the apprentices stand well away from him. He merely raised his hand in a simple gesture: at that particular moment he never uttered a word, and no one else would: no one was allowed to utter a word. Even the go-between's voice was no longer raised in song. The silence was broken only by the panting of the bellows and the faint hissing of the gold. But if my father never actually spoke, I know that he was forming words in his mind. I could tell from his lips, which kept moving, while, bending over the pot, he stirred the gold and charcoal with a bit of wood that kept bursting into flame and had constantly to be replaced by a fresh one.

22 What words did my father utter? I do not know. At least I am not certain what they were. No one ever told me. But could they have been anything but incantations•? On these occasions was he not invoking the genies of fire and gold, of fire and wind, of wind blown by the blast-pipes of the forge, of fire born of wind, of gold married to fire? Was it not their assistance, their friendship, their espousal[6] that he besought•? Yes. Almost certainly he was invoking• these genies, all of whom are equally indispensable[7] for smelting gold.

special words and formulas in magic spells and rituals

was looking for / asking for help

23 The operation going on before my eyes was certainly the smelting of gold, yet something more than that: a magical operation that the guiding spirits could regard with favor or disfavor. That is why, all around my father, there was absolute silence and anxious expectancy. Though only a child, I knew there could be no craft greater than the goldsmith's. I expected a ceremony; I had come to be present at a ceremony; and it actually was one, though very protracted.• I was still too young to understand why, but I had an inkling• as I watched the almost religious concentration of those who followed the mixing process in the clay pot.

drawn out, long

idea

24 When finally the gold began to melt I could have shouted aloud—and perhaps we all would have if we had not been forbidden to make a sound. I trembled, and so did everyone else watching my father stir the mixture—it was still a heavy paste—in which the charcoal was gradually consumed. The next stage followed swiftly. The gold now had the fluidity of water. The genies had smiled on the operation!

25 "Bring me the brick!" my father would order, thus lifting the ban that until then had silenced us.

26 The brick, which an apprentice would place beside the fire, was hollowed out, generously greased with Galam butter. My father would take the pot off the fire and tilt it carefully, while I would watch the gold flow into the brick, flow like

[6] *bringing together, marrying*
[7] *necessary, cannot do without*

liquid fire. True, it was only a very sparse trickle of fire, but how vivid, how brilliant! As the gold flowed into the brick, the grease sputtered and flamed and emitted• a thick smoke that caught in the throat and stung the eyes, leaving us all weeping and coughing. *gave off*

27 But there were times when it seemed to me that my father ought to turn this task over to one of his assistants. They were experienced, had assisted him hundreds of times, and could certainly have performed the work well. But my father's lips moved and those inaudible, secret words, those incantations he addressed to one we could not see or hear, was the essential part. Calling on the genies of fire, of wind, of gold and exorcising• the evil spirits—this was a knowledge he alone possessed. *dispelling, getting rid of*

28 By now the gold had been cooled in the hollow of the brick, and my father began to hammer and stretch it. This was the moment when his work as a goldsmith really began. . . .

29 The woman for whom the trinket was being made, and who had come often to see how the work was progressing, would arrive for the final time, not wanting to miss a moment of this spectacle—as marvelous to her as to us—when the gold wire, which my father had succeeded in drawing out from the mass of molten gold and charcoal, was transformed into a trinket.

30 There she would be. Her eyes would devour• the fragile gold wire, following it in its tranquil and regular spiral around the little slab of metal which supported it. My father would catch a glimpse of her and I would see him slowly beginning to smile. Her avid attention delighted him. *eat up, look at hungrily*

31 "Are you trembling?" he would ask.

32 "Am I trembling?"

33 And we would all burst out laughing at her. For she would be trembling! She would be trembling with covetousness• for the spiral pyramid in which my father would be inserting, among the convolutions, tiny grains of gold. When he had finally finished by crowning the pyramid with a heavier grain, she would dance in delight. *greed, want very much*

34 No one—no one at all—would be more enchanted than she as my father slowly turned the trinket back and forth between his fingers to display its perfection. Not even the praise-singer whose business it was to register excitement would be more excited than she. Throughout this metamorphosis• he did not stop speaking faster and ever faster, increasing his tempo, accelerating his praises and flatteries as the trinket took shape, shouting to the skies my father's skill. *transformation, change in form*

35 For the praise-singer took a curious part—I should say rather that it was direct and effective—in the work. He was drunk with the joy of creation.• He shouted aloud in joy. He *making something*

plucked his *cora* like a man inspired. He sweated as if he were the trinket-maker, as if he were my father, as if the trinket were his creation. He was no longer a hired censer-bearer, a man whose services anyone could rent. He was a man who created his song out of some deep inner necessity. And when my father, after having soldered• the large grain of gold that crowned the summit, held out his work to be admired, the praise-singer would no longer be able to contain himself. He would begin to intone the *douga*, the great chant which is sung only for celebrated men and which is danced for them alone. . . .

fused together

36 At the first notes of the *douga* my father would arise and emit a cry in which happiness and triumph were equally mingled; and brandishing• in his right hand the hammer that was the symbol of his profession and in his left a ram's horn filled with magic substances, he would dance the glorious dance.

waving, shaking

37 No sooner had he finished, than workmen and apprentices, friends and customers in their turn, not forgetting the woman for whom the trinket had been created, would flock around him, congratulating him, showering praises on him and complimenting the praise-singer at the same time. The latter found himself laden with gifts—almost his only means of support, for the praise-singer leads a wandering life after the fashion of the troubadours[8] of old. Aglow with dancing and the praises he had received, my father would offer everyone cola nuts, that small change• of Guinean courtesy.

typical indication

38 Now all that remained to be done was to redden the trinket in a little water to which chlorine and sea salt had been added. I was at liberty to leave. The festival was over!

EXERCISE 9-1: COMPREHENSION/ DISCUSSION QUESTIONS

1. In the first part of the reading, Laye describes a typical woman who came to her father to have a piece of jewelry made. What are the woman's characteristics? Is she clever? In a hurry? Decisive?
2. Early in the selection, Laye gives an account of a particular process—a woman trying to get the goldsmith to make a piece of jewelry for her. What are the steps in this process?
3. Throughout most of the essay, Laye describes the process of making a piece of jewelry. What are the steps in the physical process of making the trinket?

[8]singers who wandered from one place to another

4. In addition to the physical process of making the gold trinket, Laye describes a mystical or spiritual process that accompanies it. For each step in the physical process you described in question 3, give the accompanying mystical element or step (if there is one).
5. According to Laye, the praise-singer took a "direct and effective" part in the process. What part does the praise-singer play in the process of making the piece of jewelry?
6. What is the attitude of the people toward the goldsmith? Support your answer with examples from the text.
7. What is Laye's attitude toward the gold-working process? In which paragraph or paragraphs does he state his thesis?
8. Although the process of requesting a piece of jewelry to be made and the process of making it occur in all cultures, which elements of Laye's description of these processes are particular to the West African culture? Which are universal?
9. What is the attitude of people in your culture toward a skilled craftsperson? Support your answer with examples.
10. If you wanted to ask someone to make something for you—for example, a piece of jewelry, a suit, or a dress—what process would you go through in order to accomplish this?

EXERCISE 9-2: VOCABULARY DEVELOPMENT

Following are some idiomatic expressions used in the reading passage. Read the sentence containing the expression and write a word or short phrase that means approximately the same thing as the italicized words. Then write an original sentence using the idiomatic expression.

1. broke the monotony (par. 1)
   And then, every time he worked in gold it was like a festival—indeed it was a festival—that *broke the monotony* of ordinary working days.

   ____

   ____

2. lend a favorable ear (par. 7)
   I could sense my father's vanity being inflamed, and I already knew that after having sipped this milk-and-honey he would *lend a favorable ear* to the woman's request.

   ____

   ____

3. deck herself out (par. 15)
   I have never seen a woman eager to *deck herself out* who wasn't in a great hurry!

   ____

   ____

4. in progress (par. 18)

While the work was *in progress* the apprentices sat in front of the bellows with crossed legs.

____

____

5. to lose track of (par. 20)
There were so many, and they crowded so around my father, that I, the smallest person present, had to come near the forge in order not *to lose track of* what was going on.

____

____

6. shouting to the skies (par. 34)
Throughout this metamorphosis he did not stop speaking faster and ever faster, increasing his tempo, accelerating his praises and flatteries as the trinket took shape, *shouting to the skies* my father's skill.

____

____

READING 2

PORTRAITS OF A COP

N. R. KLEINFIELD

In this essay, the writer presents an account of an unusual but interesting occupation. As you read, try to answer these questions:

1. What is the meaning of the title of the essay?
2. What are the steps in the process described?
3. What makes this essay interesting?

1 A pencil poking out from behind his ear, Arthur Hagenlocher fidgets• on his high-legged chair in his box-like office in the old Loft's candy factory at 400 Broome St. in the New York City Hall area. Staring at him are an uncompleted sketch• and all manner of pencils and soft erasers. Tacked• up on the walls are sketches he and his colleagues have drawn. Except for one of Richard Nixon and another of Alfred E. Newman ("What, me worry?"), the sketches resemble no one recognizable, and Mr. Hagenlocher himself doesn't have any idea who they are supposed to be.

fidgets: moves nervously
sketch: drawing
Tacked: Pinned

2 "They're just faces to me," he says. "I don't know what their names are, what their occupations are, where they live.

To be frank, I haven't any notion• who they are. With most of them, I never will."

idea

3 Arthur Hagenlocher makes a career of sketching people he has never met. Told by other people what they look like, he sketches them plainly, without much fine detail or embellishment.• When he sketches them well enough, they will look, at best, like any one of several thousand or several million people; at worst, they will look like no one. Every so often, however, his sketches lead to the apprehension• of a criminal, which, in fact, is what they are intended to do. Arthur Hagenlocher is a police artist, and everyone he draws is a suspected criminal. . . .

decoration
arrest

4 When a crime that is witnessed occurs and a detective wishes a sketch, he calls an artist as quickly as possible (one artist is always on call). Either the detective will bring witnesses to the artist's office, or else the artist will hustle• to the scene of the crime and work there.

hurry

5 First off, Mr. Hagenlocher buttonholes• all available witnesses, and weeds out• those who, by his judgment, are unreliable. Almost always, Mr. Hagenlocher prefers to deal with just one reliable witness, rather than with many conflicting voices that simply befuddle• him. All too often when he works with several witnesses, there is a clash of facts. "The more witnesses there are, the more confusing it gets," the artist says.

gets a hold of
eliminates
confuse

6 Determining who makes the most reliable witness in-

volves perception,• interrogation• and luck. "There's a lot of psychology involved," Mr. Hagenlocher says. "You can sort of feel a good witness. If someone hesitates, or changes his mind, he's no good. If you have to pull things out of someone, he's no good. If the person just starts telling you about mouths and ears right away, then he's good."

understanding / questioning

7 Usually, the younger the witness, the better. "Fourteen-year-old kids make great witnesses," Mr. Hagenlocher says. "They remember everything. Old ladies make terrible witnesses. They can't remember anything. You ask a child about a nose, and he'll tell you about a nose. You ask an adult about a nose, and he'll start telling you about the color of the person's socks." Youngsters also tend to draw their own sketches to help out.

8 Initially, Mr. Hagenlocher tries to put witnesses at ease so they trust him, rather than barging up• and identifying himself as a police officer. When questioning someone, the artist tries to exact as much detail as possible about the suspect, though he can get by on remarkably few facts. As a rule, he looks for five features: shape of face, hair, eyes, ears, and mouth. Distinguishing scars,[1] birthmarks,[2] beards, and mustaches are an artist's dream for producing a useful sketch, but they don't often crop up.•

move clumsily and rudely

come along

9 Mr. Hagenlocher always carts along• 150 to 200 of the 900,000 mug shots• the police force keeps. Witnesses are asked to leaf through these to try to find a similar face, and then subtle• changes can be made in the sketch. "You could use just one photo and work from that," Mr. Hagenlocher says. "Using that as a base, you have the witness compare the hair—is it longer or shorter?—the mouth—is it thinner or wider?—and so forth. But that's harder and takes more time. It's usually much quicker to show him a lot of photos and have them pick one that's close."

carries with

pictures of the faces of suspects

slight, small

10 "But I remember one time," the artist goes on, "when a girl flipped through a mess• of photos and finally picked one. 'That looks exactly like him,' she said, 'except the hair was longer, the mouth was wider, the eyes were further apart, the nose was smaller and the face was rounder.' She was a big help."

a lot of, bunch of

11 Besides the five basic features, Mr. Hagenlocher also questions witnesses about a suspect's apparent nationality and the nature of the language he used. This can be of subtle assistance in sketching the suspect, but it can also sometimes link several sketches together. For instance, if over a short period of time three suspects are described as soft-spoken, in addition to having other similar traits,• then chances are they

characteristics

[1]*permanent marks left after wound or burn*
[2]*skin blemishes present at birth*

are the same person. It is also a good idea to ask a witness if a suspect resembled a famous person. Suspects have been compared to Marlon Brando, Rod Steiger, Winston Churchill, Nelson Eddy, Jack Palance, Jackie Gleason, Mick Jagger and a Greek god.

12 After Mr. Hagenlocher completes a sketch, he shows it to the witness or witnesses for their reaction. Usually, there will be lots of minor, and sometimes not too minor, changes to be made. When it's finished, the sketch isn't intended to approach the polished form of a portrait. "We're just trying to narrow down the possibilities," Mr. Hagenlocher says. "If you've just got a big nose and a thin mouth to go with, then at least you've ruled out all the people with small noses and thick mouths. There are still millions of people still in the running, but millions have also been eliminated."

13 From time to time, Mr. Hagenlocher produces no sketch at all. This happens when he receives too many conflicting reports from witnesses, or when a witness can't make up his mind or can't supply sufficient detail. "The whole point is to completely satisfy the witness," Mr. Hagenlocher says. "If the witness isn't satisfied, then I don't turn in a sketch. Some women have cried when they saw my sketch. Others have said, 'No way, no way. That's nothing like him.'" . . .

14 Once a sketch is completed, two photographs are taken of it. These go to the detective who requested the sketch, who can then order copies that can be distributed among police precincts• and other forces• and departments. The sketch itself, designated by an identification number, the case number, the date drawn and the artist's initials, is filed away in the sketching room. When a suspect is apprehended, the sketch is filed in a different place. Though they are supposed to, detectives don't always notify artists when culprits• are caught because they are tied down with new cases. . . .

divisions / police forces

guilty people

15 For the time being, Mr. Hagenlocher is content with turning out sketches of people he doesn't know. "There's a tremendous satisfaction," he says. "If you can take a picture of a person after he's apprehended and have it look like your sketch, you say, 'Wow, I can't believe I did that.' But you did."

EXERCISE 9-3: COMPREHENSION/ DISCUSSION QUESTIONS

1. **What is the process described in this essay?**
2. **In which paragraph is the process made clear?**

3. Why does Kleinfield wait until then to make the topic clear?
4. What are the steps that Mr. Hagenlocher goes through to sketch a particular suspect?
5. How does Hagenlocher determine which witness to use for his information?
6. What features of the human face does Hagenlocher look for?
7. What is Kleinfield's point in paragraph 10?
8. Besides the basic features of the face, what other information does Hagenlocher ask his witness for? Why?
9. What finally happens to Hagenlocher's sketches?
10. Do you think Mr. Hagenlocher likes his job? Support your answer with examples from the text.
11. Is there a clearly stated thesis? If so, what is it and where does it appear? If not, where and how is it implied?
12. What makes this essay interesting?

EXERCISE 9-4: VOCABULARY DEVELOPMENT

Kleinfield uses a number of colloquial, or informal, words and expressions in his essay. These words help to give the essay an informal, conversational tone, as if the writer is actually talking with the reader. These informal words also help to make the essay interesting because they are specific. Although colloquial expressions are appropriate in informal writing, they are often inappropriate in formal academic writing.

Some of the informal words and expressions that Kleinfield uses in his essay are given here. For each one, write a short definition and then write an original sentence.

1. fidgets (par. 1)

   ____

2. hustle (par. 4)

   ____

3. buttonholes (par. 5)

   ____

4. weeds out (par. 5)

   ____

5. befuddle (par. 5)

   ____

6. barging up (par. 8)

   ____

7. crop up (par. 8)

   ____

8. carts along (par. 9)

   ____

9. mess of (par. 10)

____

____

Writing

A process is a series of actions leading to an expected or planned outcome. There are two types of process essays: those that instruct or direct and those that explain or analyze. ***Directional process essays*** tell how to do something. For example, a directional process might explain how to fix a flat tire. The purpose of this type of essay is to clarify the steps in the procedure so that the reader can re-create the steps and the results. An ***informational process essay*** explains or analyzes a process—it tells how something works, how something happened, or how something is or was done. For example, you could explain how World War II began or how hurricanes form. The informational process essay has a purpose different from a directional process essay. Its main purpose is to inform, explain, or analyze. The reader is gaining an understanding of the process; he or she does not necessarily expect to be able to recreate the process.

Although process essays that explain or instruct have different purposes, they can be developed using the same pattern of development and organization. In this chapter, then, our concentration is on developing and organizing the process essay.

Planning the Process Analysis Essay

When you are planning your essay, you should bear in mind the following advice:

• *Be aware of the audience.* When you are planning a process essay, your first question should be, "What do my readers know about my topic?" Identifying the audience is important in deciding what to include and what to omit in the essay. For instance, suppose that you decided to explain how to paint a room to an inexperienced audience—people who have never before painted a room. You would have to be very specific and assume that the readers know little or nothing about the process. However, if your audience is made up of professional or experienced painters, you would have to approach the assignment differently. In this case, you would probably explain a special technique that your audience may not be aware of.

In general, though, you should assume that readers know little about the topic being explained, but have the same general knowledge you do. For instance, it can be assumed that most people know what a paintbrush is, but it cannot be assumed that your readers know which kind of brush is best to use with a certain type of paint.

• ***Order the steps chronologically.*** Since a process paper describes a sequence of steps leading to some preconceived end, it is important that the steps be discussed in the order that they occur; in other words, the steps should be arranged in chronological order. This principle of organization is the same as the one used for narration (see Chapter 2). In a process essay, ordering ideas chronologically is vital, especially if readers are to be able to re-create the process. The only time to break from chronological order is when you explain some unfamiliar term or give some word of advice or caution.

EXERCISE 9-5

Think of a process topic such as "How to Get a Visa," "How to Develop a Photograph," or some other process you are interested in. Make a list of all the steps in that process. Be sure that the steps are arranged chronologically.

• ***Make sure that the process is complete.*** Whether you are explaining how to do something or how something was done, make sure to include *all* the steps in the process. Obviously, if you are explaining how to do something and leave out one of the steps, your readers will not be able to re-create the process and get the same result. A good way to test the thoroughness of the steps of a process is to have someone follow each step exactly as explained.

Let us say, for example, that you wanted to write an essay for the campus International Student Association's newsletter about how to get a driver's license. You can assume that the audience is the international student who has probably recently arrived in the United States and does not yet have a driver's license. You might list the steps as follows:

1. Go to the Motor Vehicle Department in your area.
2. At the Motor Vehicle Department, the first thing you will do is take a vision test.
3. After that, you will take a written test.
4. Then you will take a driving test.
5. Finally, you will pay the fee.

Is this list complete? Certainly, these are the major steps involved, but there are many other things that the reader will need to know to get a driver's license. The following is an example of the expanded list of steps.

1. First obtain a pamphlet with the driving rules from the Motor Vehicle Department. You can do this by telephoning them at 555-3333 and asking them to mail you the pamphlet.
2. Study the pamphlet carefully.

3. Before you go to the Motor Vehicle Department, be sure that your car is in proper working order.
4. Take your birth certificate or your passport with you.
5. Take $10 in cash.
6. Have a friend drive you to the MVD on Main Street and Vine Avenue. You can park at the rear of the building.
7. Get in the line marked "Driver's License Exam."
8. Fill out the information on the card they give you.
9. Take the vision test.
10. Then take the written exam.
11. If you pass, then you will take the driving test.
12. If you pass that, you can pay the fee of $10.

This version is certainly more thorough than the original list, but it is still incomplete. For example, it would be a good idea to give the reader some more instructions about taking the written and the driving tests. Can you think of any other specific steps that should be included?

EXERCISE 9-6

Using the list of steps you made for Exercise 9-5, test its thoroughness by having someone follow the steps you have outlined. Now revise the list to make it more complete.

• *Be sure to define new or unfamiliar terms.* This is especially true for process essays that give instructions. Sometimes a process description may introduce a word or phrase that the reader might not understand. Since it makes little sense to have the reader attempt to complete a process without understanding the particular terms involved, always define what he or she might not know. If you are explaining how to repair a flat tire, for example, you might have to describe or define what a lug wrench is; otherwise, the reader would not know which tool is being discussed and could not continue with the process. In the example of the process of getting a driver's license, it might be necessary to explain the meaning of a few terms that will be used during the test, for example "oncoming traffic" or "Class A License":

> When you are filling out the form, check the box that says "Class A." A Class A license is for those who want to drive automobiles—not trucks or motorcycles.

• *Warn your reader of difficulties in the process.* When planning a process essay, try to anticipate what problems the reader might have in understanding or re-creating the process. If one step is particularly difficult, warn the reader of this. Be sure to warn the reader of what *not* to do as well. For example, if you are explaining how to get a driver's license, it is a good idea to warn the reader about some of the tricky things that might come up during the driving test. Perhaps you should warn your reader to practice parallel parking before going to take the driving test, or advise the reader to fill out the forms carefully and to ask questions if he or she is confused. You might also advise the reader what to do if the car stalls.

EXERCISE 9-7

Go back over the list you revised for Exercise 9-6. Add definitions of new or unfamiliar terms and warnings of difficulties in the process.

• *Explain the purpose of a step when necessary.* A process essay is more than just a list of steps. Expect that the reader wants to understand the process, whether he or she will attempt to re-create it or merely to read it. Therefore, you should explain the rationale behind the steps when the rationale is not obvious. In other words, try to explain—if only briefly—the purpose of the step. This kind of explanation is especially useful when the reader may skip the step because he or she thinks that it does not serve any real purpose. For example, in step 3 of the driver's license process (page 319), explain why the reader should see to it that the car is in proper working order (for example, the driver may get a citation for having a brake light out).

• *Try to make your thesis statement persuasive.* A thesis statement for a process essay does not have to have a strong central idea; in fact, it can be as simple as "There are three major steps involved in changing a flat tire." However, since the essay has as its underlying purpose more than just a listing of steps (those steps should be explained and analyzed), it is a good idea to have a thesis that contains a strong central idea. The thesis statement might be, "Changing a flat tire is really quite easy." This statement will require showing that the process is indeed easy. However, if the thesis is "Changing a flat tire is a horrible experience," it would be necessary to show how horrible the process is.

EXERCISE 9-8

Go back over the list of steps you have been working on in the three preceding exercises. Formulate a thesis statement that contains a central idea about the process you are describing.

Organizing the Process Analysis Essay

One of the more difficult aspects of writing a process essay is deciding where to divide the essay into paragraphs. Generally speaking, most processes break down into a beginning, middle, and end. Here are a few pointers for dividing process steps logically into paragraphs:

1. *Introduction.* The introductory paragraph should introduce the topic and establish the purpose for writing the process. The reader should understand why the process is being described and in what situations the process is used.
2. *Developmental paragraphs.* The actual description of the process usually begins in the first developmental paragraph. However, if you are describing how to do something and the process requires that the reader obtain some items first, then you may need to point out in the first developmental paragraph what items are needed.

   The actual steps of the process usually can be divided into three or four major steps. For example, if you were explaining how to change a flat tire, the first section could deal with getting the car jacked up; the next section could deal with removing and replacing the tire; and the last section could deal with removing the jack. In most cases, each major section can be described in a separate paragraph. Note, too, that the topic sentence in a process essay is often implied rather than stated directly.
3. *Conclusion.* How to conclude a process essay depends on the type of process being described. Often the conclusion discusses the results of the process. Take special note of the conclusions in the model process essays in this chapter.

EXERCISE 9-9

Think of a persuasive thesis for the driver's license process. Then break down the steps on pages 318–19 into logical groups.

EXERCISE 9-10

Using the process you have been working on in the preceding exercises, break down the steps into logical groups.

Now that you are familiar with some of the major points concerning process essays, let us look at the following process essay. Observe the paragraphing, locate the thesis, and determine if there is a central idea and if that idea is carried out in the process. Also, try to find explanations,

examples, warnings, and definitions in the essay. Finally, note if the process description is complete.

STUDYING MATH

Math is probably the most difficult course for most people. However, I think that what makes math difficult is the power that the term *mathematics* has upon people's minds. Most students are afraid of not passing because of the reputation the course has of being hard. The study of math needs lots of concentration and practice, but it isn't really hard; it just deals with the relationship and symbolism of numbers and magnitudes. What is the most difficult part of math? Working problems progressively probably. How should students study math in general? They should follow some guidelines, like the ones I have prepared, in order to feel less nervous about the subject.

Concentration is the first thing that a student should acquire before even trying to think about studying math. Full concentration is needed to study math as well as to be free of any thoughts outside the study of math. Preparing to study starts the concentration because at that moment the student starts to think about what he or she is going to cover or what he or she will need in order to solve some problems. Also, a student should be completely rested, because if a student is tired he or she may end up taking a lot longer to accomplish what he is supposed to.

In order for the student to understand the material involved, the student should read all sections completely. I think the most appropriate way of doing this is by reading a section completely first. Then, the student should analyze that section and he or she should take all the formulas and write them down on a separate sheet in order to memorize and analyze them completely. Right after this, the student should take a break of about ten minutes in order to be relaxed to work some of the problems given in the section. Most students do all the problems at once, but I don't think that is the appropriate way. A student should only do the problems he can figure out. If he can't do one of the problems in the section, he should leave it and go on to the next one. Then the student should take another short break. After that, he is ready to read the next section and follow the same procedure.

Right after a student has read all sections, he or she should look at the problems that he or she couldn't do. The student should try again to work them out, but only to a limit. The student shouldn't have to think more than five or ten minutes to figure out what is going on. Instead, a student should take those problems to the professor in order to get a complete understanding of the problems. If a student takes too much time to do a problem, he or she will get burned out and will end up hating the material.

Then right after the student has finished all sections, he should start doing the problems in the review section in order to have a better understanding and to increase his or her speed while working out a problem. At this stage, the student should find a partner to work with. Believe it or not, working with a partner helps a lot, because if a problem comes into action there are two minds that will solve the problem easily.

Math can be difficult if an individual thinks that it is difficult. But if a student follows some of my guidelines, I'm sure that he or she will do well and will like the material.
—*Igor Gonzalez*

EXERCISE 9-11

On a separate sheet of paper, answer the following questions about "Studying Math."

1. What is the thesis? The central idea?
2. Does the author establish a need for this process? If so, where?
3. Look at the paragraph divisions. Why does the author divide up the steps as he does?
4. What is the controlling idea for paragraph 2?
5. Is there a topic sentence for each paragraph? If not, is it implied?
6. Why should you take frequent breaks?
7. Is this essay unified? Coherent?
8. Are the steps clearly explained? Is the process complete?
9. Who is the audience?
10. Is this essay a directional or informational process explanation?
11. What verb tenses are used in this essay? Underline them in the essay.
12. Outline this essay.

EXERCISE 9-12: WRITING ASSIGNMENT

Using the notes you started in Exercise 9-5, write the first draft of your process essay.

Now let us look at a different kind of process essay. As you read "Cognitive Development," try to determine whether it's an informational or directional process explanation. Also, take note of the verb tenses used by the author. If you are not familiar with the meaning of the word *cognitive*, refer to your dictionary before reading the essay.

COGNITIVE DEVELOPMENT

When I was talking to my three-year-old niece on the telephone, I asked her if she liked pre-school. I heard nothing. I asked her again but still there was no response. Then her mother took the telephone and told me that my niece had been nodding her head to indicate "yes." At age three, my niece was not able to understand that I could not see what she could see or do while she was on the phone talking to me. This kind of observation of children led the great Swiss psychologist Jean Piaget to conclude that children are not born with a cognitive structure. He argued that children's cognitive understanding of the world emerges with experience; in other words, it develops. Knowledge, then, is a process rather than a "state." A child knows or understands an object by interacting with it, and from this interaction he expands his ability to comprehend. According to Piaget, just as all children grow and mature physically in the same basic sequence, they also develop cognitively in a process that is the same for all children, regardless of cultural upbringing.

Piaget called the first stage that children go through the sensorimotor period, which extends from birth to around age two. The child develops a "sense" of the objects around her by her "motor," or physical, action on the objects. Her understanding of the world is limited to her physical actions on the objects in her world. For example, newborns have certain reflexes, such as sucking and grasping a finger that touches their hand. From these reflexes the infant begins to learn about and recognize objects, and she can generalize to other objects. At about eight to twelve months, the infant is able to act intentionally and even plan her actions. If she kicks hard enough the rattle in the crib will make the noise she wants to hear. An important developmental milestone during this stage is what Piaget terms object permanence. By the end of this stage, the infant recognizes that an object continues to exist even when she cannot see it or touch it. For instance, a person who walks behind a screen is still there even though the infant cannot see her.

Object permanence is the beginning of the child's awareness that people and objects exist independent from him, but this is only the beginning. The achievements of the sensorimotor stage just prepare him for the next stage, called the preoperational period, lasting from about age two to seven. During this stage, a child perceives and interprets the world in terms of self. He cannot comprehend that another person sees objects differently. He thinks other people see and hear what he does. Thus, my three-year-old niece nodded her head to indicate "yes" because she assumed I could see her. During this stage, Piaget describes children as being rigid in thought. They base their conclusions on one obvious factor or feature of an object. For instance, if a bowl of water is poured into a tall jar, the child will conclude that the tall jar has more water because its level is higher. But toward the end of this period, the child is beginning to learn about objects in a new way. For instance, he begins to understand that water poured from the bowl into the tall jar is still the same water; that is, an object can change its shape but still be the same basic object. A good example is that a child now understands that if a person puts on a mask he or she is still the same person. The child is developing representational thought.

This increasing flexibility prepares the child for what Piaget called the concrete operational period. From about seven to eleven years old, a child makes great strides in her cognitive development. She develops the ability to make mental transformations with regard to concrete objects. A child begins to comprehend the concepts of reversibility, compensation, and addition and subtraction. Piaget uses the concept of conservation to illustrate this development. If you pour the water back from the tall jar to the bowl, during this stage the child can understand that the amount of water that was in the jar is the same as what's in the bowl, even though the water levels are different. She can understand that the width of the bowl makes up—or compensates—for its lack of height. The child also understands that no water has been removed or added.

In the next stage, called the formal operational period, from about eleven to fifteen years old, the child develops more sophisticated reasoning abilities. He can reason now; he can see more logical relationships between objects and can think more systematically before acting. In other words, he can think in more abstract terms; he can use information from the past to predict consequences. One game that requires such skills is chess. During this stage of development, a child can learn not only the rules and movements involved but also can use strategies.

Refinement of cognitive skills continues on into adulthood, but Piaget felt that the development of structure of thought is achieved by about age fifteen. After that, the content and quality of thought may develop. Although not all researchers in cognitive development agree with Piaget's scheme and all of his conclusions, he can be credited for having a tremendous impact on our understanding of how children develop their understanding of the world around them. Children are not miniature adults who reason as adults do; they understand and interpret their environment in terms of their cognitive development. This is important to realize if we want to understand our children—and ourselves—better.*

EXERCISE 9-13

On a separate sheet of paper, answer the following questions about "Cognitive Development."

1. What kind of process is being analyzed in this essay?
2. What is the central idea about the process of cognitive development?
3. What is the topic of paragraph 2?
4. What does Piaget mean by object permanence? Can you give another example?
5. During which stage does the child make a lot of progress?
6. What do you think the writer's purpose is for writing this essay?
7. Does the conclusion logically follow?
8. What verb tense is used frequently? Is it active or passive?
9. Make an outline of this essay.

---

*Information from Patricia H. Miller, *Theories of Developmental Psychology* (New York: W. H. Freeman, 1983), pp. 30–66.

Here is another example of this type of process essay, originally printed in a popular science magazine. If you are not familiar with the following words, check their meaning in a dictionary or a chemistry book: *crystal, silicon, photovoltaic, lattice, electron, dopant, boron, phosphorous.*

HOW DO SOLAR CELLS MAKE POWER?

While often criticized for their expense and inefficiency, solar cells are unique among power generators in producing electricity indefinitely without wearing out. One solar cell, made from a single crystal of the element silicon, typically weighs about six grams and has a four-inch diameter. It is within this tiny package that the direct conversion of light to energy—the photovoltaic process—occurs.

A single silicon crystal is composed of trillions of atoms that are lined up neatly in a lattice structure. Each is connected to the next by four electrons orbiting its shell. Added to this tidy crystal structure are small amounts of dopants, boron and phosphorous. At the back of the cell, boron atoms bond with silicon atoms. Since boron has only three electrons, a vacancy—or instability—in each bond is created.

The other dopant, phosphorous, takes up just a fraction of an inch at the cell's surface. Since phosphorous atoms have five outer electrons, one is left over after each atom bonds with a neighboring silicon atom. Many of these extra electrons flow toward the holes in the boron-silicon lattice.

As the vacancies fill up with these electrons in the boron layer, an electrical field—a region of negative and positive charges—is built up between the phosphorous and boron. It is created because the electrons carry a negative charge to the boron and leave behind a positive charge in the phosphorous when they move to fill in the "holes."

When sunlight strikes the solar cell, trillions of energy particles called photons bombard the silicon and boron atoms, knocking their electrons loose. Many of the electrons are then swept into the electrical field. In the field, each electron picks up an energy potential. As they become energized, the electrons quickly penetrate the phosphorous layer and then travel through a wire, on the outside of the cell, to a light bulb. A typical cell generates half a volt. After passing through the bulb, the electron stream returns, via a wire in the back of the cell, to the boron layer to be used again. In this way, solar cells never run out of electricity.

—*Science Digest* July 1984: p. 80.

EXERCISE 9-14

On a separate piece of paper, answer the following questions about the preceding essay.

1. What is the process being analyzed? What type of process is it?
2. What is the controlling idea of the essay? Where is it stated?
3. What is the function of the dopants in the process?
4. What is the function of sunlight in the process?

5. What verb tense is used throughout? Why?
6. Make an outline of the essay.

COMPOSITION SKILLS

Introductory Paragraphs

The Dramatic Entrance

The two types of introductions that you have been writing, the Funnel and the Turnabout, are good approaches to beginning essays. However, as your writing skills improve, you should strive not only for sentence variety but also for variety in essay openings as well. A dramatic, humorous, or otherwise interesting opening will generate interest in the reader. It is important, after all, to capture the reader's attention. The type of introduction that serves this purpose can be called the "Dramatic Entrance."

There are various ways to make a Dramatic Entrance. One way is to describe a scene that introduces your reader to the subject of your essay. Note how this writer opens an article on carbohydrates and depression:

> On May 16, 1898, the intrepid Arctic explorer Frederick A. Cook made the following notation in his journal: "The winter and the darkness have slowly but steadily settled over us. . . . It is not difficult to read on the faces of my companions their thoughts and their moody dispositions. . . . The curtain of blackness which has fallen over the outer world of icy desolation has also descended upon the inner world of our souls. Around the tables . . . men are sitting about sad and dejected, lost in dreams of melancholy from which, now and then, one arouses with an empty attempt at enthusiasm. For brief moments some try to break the spell by jokes, told perhaps for the fiftieth time. Others grind out a cheerful philosophy; but all efforts to infuse bright hopes fail."
>
> We now know that the members of the Cook expedition were suffering from classic symptoms of winter depression, a condition related to a recently described psychiatric disorder, known as seasonal affective disorder, or SAD. —Richard J. Wurtman and Judith J. Wurtman, "Carbohydrates and Depression," *Scientific American* Jan. 1989: p. 68.
>
>

For process papers, it is often useful to begin with a description of a scene that establishes the need for a process explanation. Observe here how one student uses a description to set up a process paper:

> The rain pours down as if running from a faucet, lightning streaks across the dark restless sky, and thunder pounds the roof and walls of the house. All of a sudden the wind kicks up. Trees sway madly back and forth; loose objects are picked up and thrown all around. The house creaks and moans with every gust of wind. Windows are broken by pieces of shingle from a

neighbor's roof or by loose objects picked up by the wind. Power lines snap like thread. The unprepared house and its occupants are in grave danger as the awesome hurricane approaches. Had they prepared for the hurricane, they might not be in such danger. Indeed, careful preparation before a hurricane is essential to life and property. —*Donald Landry*

EXERCISE 9-15

On a separate sheet of paper, answer the following questions about Donald Landry's introductory paragraph.

1. How is this description organized? Is it organized chronologically, spatially, or both? Why has the writer selected this pattern of organization?
2. What is the process that will be explained?
3. Does the introduction establish a need for the process?

EXERCISE 9-16

Study the following process topics. Select one and write an introduction that is a Dramatic Entrance.

1. How to do a particular job.
2. What to do in case of an accident.
3. How to study for a particular course.
4. How something is made (you choose).
5. How something works.
6. The life cycle of an insect.
7. How to repair something.
8. How to prepare for a natural disaster (such as a flood, storm, or the like).

EXERCISE 9-17: WRITING ASSIGNMENT

In exercise 9-16, you were asked to write a dramatic introduction. Now complete the essay.

Coherence

Participial Phrases

In Chapter 8, we learned that adjective clauses can sometimes be reduced to participial phrases:

> The man *who is* riding the bicycle is my brother.
>
> The man *riding the bicycle* is my brother.

Reducing an adjective clause to a phrase in this way helps to eliminate unnecessary words, making your writing more precise and coherent. In this chapter, we discuss participial phrases reduced from adverbial clauses of time to achieve coherence in process writing.

Since process analysis essays are organized chronologically, like narrations, many of the transitional devices discussed in Chapter 2 are used: sequence markers (*first, next, after that,* and so forth) and adverbial clauses of time. To achieve even more coherence in chronologically developed essays, participial phrases can be used to indicate the sequence of actions between clauses. Participial phrases not only make writing more coherent, they also add variety in sentence structure, thus improving the writing.

Adverbial clauses of time are used to clarify the time relationship between the action in one clause and the action in another. Adverbial clauses of time are used when you combine two independent clauses, making one subordinate, or dependent. Adverbial clauses of time can be reduced to participial phrases when the subject of the adverbial clause is the same as the subject of the independent clause. Study the following examples:

First I went to the store. Then I went home. (TWO INDEPENDENT CLAUSES)

After I went to the store, I went home. (ADVERBIAL CLAUSE + INDEPENDENT CLAUSE)

After going to the store, I went home. (PARTICIPIAL PHRASE + INDEPENDENT CLAUSE)

Having gone to the store, I went home. (PARTICIPIAL PHRASE + INDEPENDENT CLAUSE)

The three most common types of participial phrases that can be used to reduce adverbial clauses of time to participial phrases are (1) the present participle (verb + *ing*), (2) the perfect participle (***having*** verb + *ed*), and (3) the passive perfect participle (***having been*** verb + *ed*). The type of participial phrase used depends on the sequence of actions in the clauses and the verb tenses. Study the following examples of uses of participial phrases reduced from adverbial clauses of time.

THE PRESENT PARTICIPLE (VERB + ***ing*****).** This participle can be used to indicate that the action in the participle takes place before, after, or at the same time as the action in the main clause. *After, before*, and *while* can appear before the participial phrase to clarify the time relationship.

Before John went to the store, he went to the bank.

Before *going* to the store, John went to the bank.

After he goes to the bank, he goes to the store.

After *going* to the bank, he goes to the store.

While John was going to the store, he saw an automobile accident.

While *going* to the store, John saw an automobile accident.

When John arrived at the bank, he saw a hold-up in progress.

Arriving at the bank, John saw a hold-up in progress.

After he goes to the service station, he will go home.

After *going* to the service station, he will go home.

THE PERFECT PARTICIPLE (*HAVING* VERB + *ed*). This participle is used to introduce phrases in which the action occurs before the action in the main clause. It is not necessary to introduce the phrase with the adverbial *after*. Notice also that cause is sometimes implied in these phrases.

After John made a withdrawal at the bank, he went home.

Having made a withdrawal at the bank, John went home.

After John finishes with his chores, he will feel good.

Having finished with his chores, John will feel good.

THE PASSIVE PERFECT PARTICIPLE (*HAVING BEEN* VERB + *ed*). This participle is used when the original clause was in the passive voice. It indicates that the action in the participial phrase precedes the action in the main clause. Again, note that it can also indicate cause.

After the candidate was nominated for the office, he took out a loan.

Having been nominated for the office, the candidate took out a loan.

The students were scared away after they were warned about cheating.

Having been warned about cheating, the students were scared away.

After he was given the chance to reform, the young man robbed a bank anyway.

Having been given a chance to reform, the young man robbed a bank anyway.

Sometimes these clauses can be further reduced by leaving off ***having been*** and starting the clause with the past participle. (These are often called ***absolute constructions.***) Compare these sentences with those preceding:

Nominated for the office, the candidate took out a loan.

Warned about cheating, the students were scared away.

Given a chance to reform, the young man robbed a bank anyway.

Finally, note that if the subject of the sentence first appears in the adverbial clause, it is transferred to the main clause when the adverbial clause is reduced.

The monument was built in 1881. It honored the soldiers.

Built in 1881, *the monument* honored the soldiers.

EXERCISE 9-18

Reduce the following adverbial clauses to participial phrases and rewrite the sentences in the blanks. Remember to include the subject of the sentence in the main clause. The first one is done for you.

1. Before the female monarch butterfly lays her eggs, it finds a milkweed plant.
   Before laying her eggs, the female monarch butterfly finds a milkweed plant.
2. After the young monarch caterpillar is hatched, it eats the milkweed.
   ____
3. While the caterpillar eats the plant, it continues to grow.
   ____
4. As the caterpillar grows constantly, it sheds its skin several times.
   ____
5. After the caterpillar has been nourished by the milkweed for about three weeks, it spins a chrysalis.
   ____
6. After the green chrysalis has been spun, it is attached to a green leaf.
   ____
7. After the caterpillar has spent a week inside the chrysalis, an exciting transformation takes place.
   ____
8. When the caterpillar emerges from the chrysalis, it is no longer a caterpillar, but a beautiful monarch butterfly.
   ____
9. After the butterfly has been born, it begins to search for flowers in order to sip their nectar.
   ____
10. After the life cycle of the monarch butterfly has been completed, it will begin again.
    ____

EXERCISE 9-19

The following paragraphs about how to get a job are not as coherent as they should be because they lack participial phrases for transitions. Rewrite the paragraphs, using participial phrases at major transitional points.

You are about to graduate from college and you want to get a job. How do you go about finding the right job for you? Here is one way to begin your job hunt. First, you need to prepare a resumé. A resumé is a one- or two-page document that lists brief personal information, the type of job you are looking for, your educational background, your job experience, your interests and hobbies, and your references. You can do your resumé yourself on a typewriter or computer or have it done professionally. So, now you have done your resumé. Next, you need to decide which prospective employers you are going to send it to. Of course, this depends on your particular job interests. If you are a business major, for example, and want to work in a bank, you will want to make a list of the banks for which you would like to work. And you go ahead and make your list. Then, you will need to draft a generic cover letter to send with your resumé to the banks on your list. The cover letter should point up your strongest qualities and present you in a favorable light. It and your resumé are your representatives to the prospective employers on your list.

It is a good idea at this point to collect all the supplies you will need for the actual mailing out; these will include the correct number of envelopes, stamps, and good quality paper. You now have your supplies, your resumé, your cover letter, and the addresses of your prospective employers. You can now begin the actual work of preparing each letter. If you have your cover letter in a computer, you can quickly print up the cover letters with the correct inside address on each one. You may find it easier to do the envelopes on a typewriter. You have printed all the resumés and cover letters that you need and you have typed all the addresses on the envelopes. Now you simply need to stuff the envelopes. When you stuff the envelopes, be sure to get the correct letters in the correct envelopes and be sure to include a resumé in each one. Finally, you lick and stamp the envelopes and drop them off at the Post Office. Now comes the hardest part—the long wait.

EXERCISE 9-20: WRITING ASSIGNMENT

Now that you have practiced participial phrases, take the essay that you wrote for Exercise 9-17 and revise it using participial phrases.

GRAMMAR REVIEW

In writing process essays, infinitives and gerunds as subjects are very useful (review them on pages 210–16). You will also find that the passive is common with process essays (review the passive voice on pages 92–94).

Imperative/ You*/Modals*

As is evident from the preceding model essays, writers often uses the imperative mood when writing a process essay. The imperative mood is a direct command or order to someone; it is a sentence with a command verb in which the subject *you* has been deleted:

> *Put* the fish on the hook.
>
> *Don't forget* to board up the windows.

The imperative mood is best for a process essay. Sometimes, however, in process essays, the *you* is included in the sentence. Note this example:

> Before putting the putty on the window, *you* remove the old putty.

In this case, *you* does not necessarily refer to a specific person. It means anyone who is doing the job. Often *a person* or *one* is used instead of the less formal *you*. However, these words can sound awkward at times, especially if they're overused. Unless your teacher objects, go ahead and use *you* in a process composition.

Certain modals are also common in process essays. The most useful are ***should, might, must,*** and ***can***. First, these are used to be less direct than the imperative and hence more polite. Second, they are used to add the specific meaning that each modal has. For instance, ***should*** is often used to give advice about some step in the process; ***might*** and ***can*** are used to offer possibilities; and ***must*** is used to show that something in the process is necessary. Note the following examples:

> You *should begin* getting these things together when you hear the first warning.
>
> You *might ask* for advice about paint from the salesperson.
>
> You *must prepare* the room before painting.
>
> You *can begin* to paint.

EXERCISE 9-21

Choose either topic A or B and write a sentence for each item in the list. Write some of the sentences with the imperative and some with *you*. Use a modal where appropriate. Also use transitional words like *first, next,* and *then* in some of the sentences, and articles where necessary. Write your sentences in the form of a paragraph.

A. How to Find Information on the Space Shuttle in the Library

1. Find the *Reader's Guide*/other index.
2. If you do not know, ask.

3. Look in the *Reader's Guide* under "space," "space travel," "transportation."
4. Jot down possible articles.
5. Check the library listing of periodicals—which periodicals are available.
6. Cross out periodicals not available.
7. Write down call numbers of periodicals available.
8. Check library floor plan—where periodicals are kept.
9. Find periodicals.
10. Find articles.
11. Scan articles/determine if helpful.
12. Duplicate articles if helpful.

B. How to Apply to Graduate School

1. Begin the process the summer before your senior year.
2. Obtain a list of schools with your major.
3. Send for applications in August.
4. In August, send for the Graduate Record Examination (GRE) bulletin at the Educational Testing Service, P.O. Box 6000, Princeton, N.J. 08541–6000, if the test is required.
5. Return the application and fee for the GRE in August or as soon as possible.
6. Prepare applications for graduate studies in September.
7. Request letters of recommendations from faculty, if required.
8. Take the GRE in October, if required.
9. GRE results come in usually near the end of November.
10. If GRE scores are poor, you can retake the GRE in December.
11. Mail in your applications and fees by the deadline set by the university, or earlier if possible.

Expressions of Purpose

In writing process compositions it is often necessary to include the purpose for a particular step or action. That is, it is necessary to tell why or for what purpose something should be done. There are several grammatical patterns that are used to state purpose.

INFINITIVES OF PURPOSE. The phrase ***in order*** plus an infinitive is often used to show purpose. Note these examples:

Light the fire *in order to boil* the water.

Touch the wheel lightly with your hand *(in order) to slow* it down.

Note that ***in order*** can often be left out and the meaning remains the same.

Light the fire to boil the water.

ADVERBIAL CLAUSES OF PURPOSE. Two conjunctions that introduce adverbial clauses of purpose are *so that* and *in order that*. Study these examples:

> Wear gloves *so that* you will not cut your hands.
>
> Put it away immediately *in order that* you will not forget it.

These two conjunctions are used in the same way and have the same meaning. However, *in order that* is more formal than *so that*.

It is important to note that a modal normally follows *so that* and *in order that*. Notice that in the preceding examples the modal *will* is used. This modal is usual in imperative sentences. However, in nonimperative sentences *would* and *could* are the most common:

> He saved his money *so that* he *could* buy a new car.
>
> He did his work early *so that* he *would* not miss his favorite program.

EXERCISE 9-22

Answer each of the following questions with two complete sentences. Write one sentence with *in order to* and the other with *so that*. The first one is done for you.

1. For what purpose should you think about your intended major?
   You should think about your intended major in order to choose a university that is well qualified and staffed in your major. You should think about your intended major so that you can choose the best university with that major.
2. For what purpose should you send for catalogues from different universities?
   ____
   ____
3. For what purpose should you think about your financial situation?
   ____
   ____
4. For what purpose should you find out about financial aid?
   ____
   ____
5. For what purpose should you find out about part-time jobs?
   ____
   ____

6. For what purpose should you find out about living arrangements?

____

____

7. For what purpose should you talk to your high school advisor or principal?

____

____

8. For what purpose should you talk to alumnae of various schools?

____

____

9. For what purpose should you think about the climate in a particular area of the country?

____

____

Conditionals

REAL CONDITIONS. In writing a process essay you often need to tell the reader what might happen if a particular step is not followed. In other words, you need to give advice or warning. To state this warning, you often use a clause beginning with *if:*

> *If you do not stir the white sauce,* it will burn.
>
> The new putty will not hold *if you do not scrape the old putty off first.*
>
> *If the glass breaks,* buy another one.

Note that these real conditions are ones that are possible to be realized; they could really happen. Notice also that the *if* clause uses the present tense. In the first two examples, *will* is used in the main clause to indicate future time. In the third example, the imperative is used.

The words *unless* and *otherwise* are also used often to indicate conditions. *Unless* means "if . . . not":

> *If* you do *not* bandage the cut, it will get infected.
>
> *Unless* you bandage the cut, it will get infected.

Note that *otherwise* is equivalent to the entire *if* clause and is used as a transition between two complete sentences:

> Give me the money. *If you don't give me the money,* I will sue you.
>
> Give me the money. *Otherwise,* I will sue you.

EXERCISE 9-23

The following are steps to follow when someone faints.* Give a warning about each of the steps using *if*, *unless*, or *otherwise*. The first one is done for you.

1. Leave the victim lying down.
   If you leave the victim lying down, he may be able to breathe more easily.
2. Loosen any tight clothing and keep crowds away.

   ____

   ____
3. If the victim vomits, roll him onto his side or turn his head to the side and, if necessary, wipe out his mouth with your fingers, preferably wrapped in cloth.

   ____

   ____
4. Maintain an open airway.

   ____

   ____
5. *Do not* pour water over the victim's face because of the danger of aspiration; instead, bathe his face gently with cool water.

   ____

   ____
6. *Do not* give any liquid unless the victim has revived.

   ____

   ____
7. Examine the victim to determine whether or not he has suffered injury from falling.

   ____

   ____
8. Unless recovery is prompt, seek medical assistance. The victim should be carefully observed afterward because fainting might be a brief episode in the development of a serious underlying illness.

   ____

   ____

*American National Red Cross, *Standard First Aid and Personal Safety* (New York: Doubleday, 1973), p. 174.

EXERCISE 9-24: WRITING ASSIGNMENT

Choose one of the following topics for a process analysis essay. First, decide if you want to write a directional process or an informational process. Then make a list in chronological order of the steps involved. Make sure the process is complete. Define any unfamiliar terms and give the reader appropriate warnings. Be sure to use appropriate transitions.

1. Choose a simple process from one of the sciences. For example, explain how to make a slide, how to use a particular kind of microscope, or how to use a Bunsen burner.
2. Choose a simple process from one of the arts. For example, explain how to learn to read music, how to prepare a canvas for painting, or how to take or develop a photograph.
3. Choose a life cycle of a particular animal. Explain the stages.
4. Choose one of the topics suggested in Exercise 9-16.

Process Analysis Essay Checklist

1. A process analysis essay either tells how to do something or explains how something happens. Have you chosen an appropriate subject—process—for your essay?
2. In writing a process analysis essay, you need to be aware of your audience, to order the steps of the process chronologically, to make sure your explanation of the process is complete, and to define any new or unfamiliar terms for your readers. Have you accomplished these tasks in your essay?
3. Your process analysis essay should warn your reader of difficulties in the process, explain the purpose of a step where necessary, and make a persuasive thesis statement. Does your essay perform these functions?
4. Does your essay have an interesting introduction?
5. Is your essay coherent?

Chapter 10

The Cause-and-Effect Analysis Essay

Readings: Men, Women, and the Family

The family is a basic unit of society. Our mother, father, siblings, and relatives help orient us to the world and to our place within it. Although each particular family may have its own unique characteristics, overall the family serves to familiarize us with basic cultural assumptions about the world as well as our roles as men and women within society. From this perspective, we spend our lives trying to fit these roles, understand them, and perhaps even change them.

The following essays investigate the roles of the family and of men and women in society. As you read them, ask yourself these questions:

1. What effect have the individual members of your family had on you?
2. What is the role of women in the world? Of men?
3. Do you want to be different from your parents in your relationship to your family? In your relationship to those of the opposite sex?

READING 1

LIFT YOUR FEET

ANDREW WARD

Born in Chicago in 1946, Andrew Ward is the author of a number of books and articles and has been a contributing editor of Atlantic Monthly. *In the following essay, taken from* Fits and Starts: The Premature Memoirs of Andrew Ward

(1970), Ward describes the effects of one of his mother's personal traits on the family. As you read, try to answer these questions:

1. **What behavioral characteristic of Ward's mother causes the effect described in his essay?**
2. **What effect does this characteristic have on the members of his family?**
3. **What is Ward's attitude toward his subject? How does he feel about his mother?**

1 All her life, my mother wanted busy children. Nothing infuriated• her more than the sight of one of her offspring lying around, staring into space. But she had a conflicting ambition which proved paramount:• that her house remain at all times tidy and hygienic,• that it exhibit, in effect, as little evidence of human activity as possible.

made her angry

of great importance / without germs, clean

2 You could turn your back for a moment in my mother's house, leave a half-written letter on the dining room table, a magazine open on the chair, and turn around to find it had been "put back," as my mother phrased it, "where it belonged."

3 My wife, on one of her first visits to my mother's house, placed on an end table a napkined packet of cheese and crackers she had made for herself and went to the kitchen to fetch a drink. When she returned, she found the packet had been removed. Puzzled, she set down her drink and went back to the kitchen for more cheese and crackers, only to return to find that now her drink had disappeared. Up to then she had guessed that everyone in my family held onto their drinks, sometimes with both hands, so as not to make water rings on the end tables. Now she knows better. . . .

4 These disappearances had a disorienting• effect on our family. We were all inclined to forgetfulness, and it was common for one of us, upon returning from the bathroom and finding that every evidence of his work-in progress had vanished, to forget what he'd been up to. "Do you remember what I was doing?" was a question frequently asked, but rarely answered, for whoever turned to address himself to it ran the risk of having his own pen, paper, book, tatting,• suddenly disappear into the order of my mother's universe. . . .

cause to lose one's place, confusing

kind of needlework

5 My mother's cleaning seems to have come to a head while I was in college. She started to get terrible headaches and psychosomatic[1] digestive problems. Pretty soon, she hired some cleaning women to come in every week. They were Teutonic,[2] like her grandmother, and did a good job,

[1]physical disorder aggravated or caused by one's emotional state

[2]Germanic (based on the stereotype of the German homemaker who has a passion for cleanliness)

and she was delighted to find that she didn't have to clean up after them half so much as she had cleaned up after her family. My sister has developed a second-hand passion for clean windows, and my brother does the vacuuming in his house, perhaps to avoid having to be the one to lift his feet. I try not to think about it too much, but I have latterly• taken to cleaning the baseboards once a week. I figure if you don't keep after them they'll just get filthy, and then where will we be?

at this later time

EXERCISE 10-1: COMPREHENSION/ DISCUSSION QUESTIONS

1. What behavioral characteristic of Ward's mother causes the effect described in the essay?
2. What is the effect of the mother's ambition on the writer's wife?
3. What is the effect of the mother's ambition on the family?
4. What have been the long-term effects on members of Ward's family?
5. What is Ward's attitude toward his subject? Is he serious, lighthearted, hurt, angry?
6. How does Ward feel about his mother? Is he criticizing her? Praising her?
7. What is the author's purpose in this essay? To inform? Analyze? Entertain? How do you know?
8. What reaction does Ward expect from his readers? Explain your answer.
9. Do you have a family member or friend with an idiosyncrasy that has an effect on the rest of the family? Be prepared to explain the peculiar habit and its effects.

READING 2

WOMEN AND PHYSICS

K. C. COLE

K. C. Cole's writings on science have appeared in Newsday, *the* New York Times, *and other publications. In the following essay, she explores the causes of the lack of women in science-related fields. As you read it, try to answer the following questions:*

1. In your opinion, why are there so few women in scientific fields?
2. Do you believe, according to "popular opinion," that there is "an innate difference in the scientific ability of boys and girls"? Does the writer?
3. What causes for the lack of women in science does Cole give?
4. Is the evidence that Cole gives to support her position convincing?

1 I know few other women who do what I do. What I do is write about science, mainly physics. And to do that, I spend a lot of time reading about science, talking to scientists and struggling to understand physics. In fact, most of the women (and men) I know think me quite queer• for actually liking physics. "How can you write about that stuff?" they ask, always somewhat askance.• "I could never understand that in a million years." Or more simply, "I hate science."

strange

with suspicion

2 I didn't realize what an odd• creature a woman interested in physics was until a few years ago when a science magazine sent me to Johns Hopkins University in Baltimore for a conference on an electrical phenomenon known as the Hall effect. We sat in a huge lecture hall and listened as physicists talked about things engineers didn't understand, and engineers talked about things physicists didn't understand. What *I* didn't understand was why, out of several

strange, queer

hundred young students of physics and engineering in the room, less than a handful were women.

3 Sometime later, I found myself at the California Institute of Technology reporting on the search for the origins of the universe. I interviewed physicist after physicist, man after man. I asked one young administrator why none of the physicists were women. And he answered: "I don't know, but I suppose it must be something innate.• My seven-year-old daughter doesn't seem to be much interested in science." *inborn, existing from birth*

4 It was with that experience fresh in my mind that I attended a conference in Cambridge, Mass., on science literacy,• or rather the worrisome lack of it in this country today. We three women—a science teacher, a young chemist and myself—sat surrounded by a company of august• men. The chemist, I think, first tentatively raised the issue of science illiteracy in women. It seemed like an obvious point. After all, everyone had agreed over and over again that scientific knowledge these days was a key factor in economic power. But as soon as she made the point, it became clear that we women had committed a grievous• social error. Our genders• were suddenly showing; we had interrupted the serious talk with a subject unforgivably silly. *ability to read and write* *respected* *terrible, unfortunate / sex*

5 For the first time, I stopped being puzzled about why there weren't any women in science and began to be angry. Because if science is a search for answers to fundamental questions then it hardly seems frivolous• to find out why women are excluded. Never mind the economic consequences. *silly, not worth doing*

6 A lot of the reasons women are excluded are spelled out by the Massachusetts Institute of Technology experimental physicist Vera Kistiakowsky in a recent article in *Physics Today* called "Women in Physics: Unnecessary, Injurious and Out of Place?" The title was taken from a nineteenth-century essay written in opposition to the appointment of a female mathematician to a professorship at the University of Stockholm. "As decidedly as two and two make four," a woman in mathematics is a "monstrosity,"• concluded the writer of the essay. *unnatural*

7 Dr. Kistiakowsky went on to discuss the factors that make women in science today, if not monstrosities, at least oddities. Contrary to much popular opinion, one of those is *not* an innate difference in the scientific ability of boys and girls. But early conditioning• does play a stubborn and subtle role. A recent *Nova* program, "The Pinks and the Blues," documented how girls and boys are treated differently from birth—the boys always encouraged in more physical kinds of play, more active explorations of their environments. Shelia *repeated behavior that comes to seem natural*

Tobias, in her book, *Math Anxiety*, showed how the games boys play help them to develop an intuitive• understanding of speed, motion and mass.

unconscious

8 The main sorting out of the girls from the boys in science seems to happen in junior high school. As a friend who teaches in a science museum said, "By the time we get to electricity, the boys already have had some experience with it. But it's unfamiliar to the girls." Science books draw on boys' experiences. "The examples are all about throwing a baseball at such and such a speed," said my stepdaughter, who barely escaped being a science drop-out.

9 The most obvious reason there are not many more women in science is that women are discriminated• against as a class, in promotions, salaries and hirings, a conclusion reached by a recent analysis by the National Academy of Sciences.

to show prejudice against

10 Finally, said Dr. Kistiakowsky, women are simply made to feel out of place in science. Her conclusion was supported by a Ford Foundation study by Lynn H. Fox on the problems of women in mathematics. When students were asked to choose among six reasons accounting for girls' lack of interest in math, the girls rated this statement second: "Men do not want girls in the mathematical occupations."

11 A friend of mine remembers winning a Bronxwide mathematics competition in the second grade. Her friends—both boys and girls—warned her that she shouldn't be good at math: "You'll never find a boy who likes you." My friend continued nevertheless to excel in math and science, won many awards during her years at the Bronx High School of Science, and then earned a full scholarship to Harvard. After one year of Harvard science, she decided to major in English.

12 When I asked her why, she mentioned what she called the "macho mores"• of science. "It would have been O.K. if I'd had someone to talk to," she said. "But the rules of comportment• were such that you never admitted you didn't understand. I later realized that even the boys didn't get everything clearly right away. You had to stick with it until it had time to sink in.• But for the boys, there was a payoff in suffering through the hard times, and a kind of punishment—a shame—if they didn't. For the girls it was O.K. not to get it, and the only payoff for sticking it out was that you'd be considered a freak."•

male code of behavior in which one does not show weakness / behavior

be understood

odd or strange person

13 Science is undeniably hard. Often, it can seem quite boring. It is unfortunately too often presented as laws to be memorized instead of mysteries to be explored. It is too often kept a secret that science, like art, takes a well-developed esthetic• sense. Women aren't the only ones who say, "I hate science."

sensitivity to beauty

14 That's why everyone who goes into science needs a little help from friends. For the past ten years, I have been getting more than a little help from a friend who is a physicist. But my stepdaughter—who earned the highest grades ever recorded in her California high school on the math Scholastic Aptitude Test—flunked calculus in her first year at Harvard. When my friend the physicist heard about it, he said, "Harvard should be ashamed of itself."

15 What he meant was that she needed that little extra encouragement that makes all the difference. Instead, she got that little extra discouragement that makes all the difference.

16 "In the first place, all the math teachers are men," she explained. "In the second place, when I met a boy I liked and told him I was taking chemistry, he immediately said: 'Oh, you're one of those science types.' In the third place, it's just a kind of a social thing. The math clubs are full of boys and you don't feel comfortable joining."

17 In other words, she was made to feel unnecessary, and out of place.

18 A few months ago, I accompanied a male colleague from the science museum where I sometimes work to a lunch of the history of science faculty at the University of California. I was the only woman there, and my presence for the most part was obviously and rudely ignored. I was so surprised and hurt by this that I made an extra effort to speak knowledgeably and well. At the end of the lunch, one of the professors turned to me in all seriousness and said: "Well, K.C., what do the women think of Carl Sagan?" I replied that I had no idea what "the women" thought about anything. But now I know what I should have said: I should have told him that his comment was unnecessary, injurious and out of place.

EXERCISE 10-2: COMPREHENSION/ DISCUSSION QUESTIONS

1. What is the purpose of the first five paragraphs of the essay?
2. What are Cole's reactions to the lack of women in science (paragraphs 1–5)? Does she present her reactions in a logical progression? Why does she become angry?
3. What is the first cause Cole gives for the lack of women in science? In what paragraph or paragraphs is it discussed? How is it developed?
4. One of the basic issues in this cause is whether there is "an

innate difference in the scientific ability of boys and girls." What is Cole's position on this issue? What is your position?

5. Are the causes given in paragraphs 9–10 two different causes or both part of the same cause?
6. How does Cole support the idea that young girls and women are made to feel out of place in science?
7. What does Cole mean by the "macho mores" of science (paragraph 12)? According to your experience, is this an accurate description?
8. What point is Cole making with her last example in paragraph 18?
9. Is the evidence that Cole gives to support her position convincing? Support your answer.
10. Drawing from your own experience, do you think that ability in science and math depends on social conditions and encouragement? Is this ability innate? Support your position.

EXERCISE 10-3: VOCABULARY DEVELOPMENT

For each of the following adjectives from the reading, first write the adverb form and then write an original sentence using either the adjective or the adverb.

1. odd (par. 2) ____________________
2. innate (par. 3) ____________________
3. grievous (par. 4) ____________________
4. august (par. 4) ____________________
5. frivolous (par. 5) ____________________
6. fundamental (par. 5) ____________________
7. intuitive (par. 7) ____________________
8. esthetic (also spelled "aesthetic") (par. 13) ____________________

____

Writing

When we classify and divide, we are attempting to impose order on—or perhaps find order in—the world around us, thereby hoping to understand the world we live in. When we analyze a process, we are also seeking to understand something, in this case how a sequence of events leads to an expected outcome. Similarly, when we analyze causes, we are attempting to understand the relationship of events that brought about an outcome, but in this case one that was probably unexpected and not likely to be repeated in exactly the same way. When we analyze effects, we consider the results of some action. Unlike process analysis, the relationship among events in cause-and-effect analysis is not chronological; it is *causal*: Something causes something else, or many things cause something; something results from something else, or many things result from one thing.

Every day we try to figure out the causes for something. When a problem arises, we start to examine the cause for it. For example, if police cars burst into flames in a large metropolitan police department, officials would immediately investigate to establish the reasons for the incidents. When any significant change in our lives occurs, such as the success of someone or something, we try to look at the factors that contributed to that change. When we identify an emotional problem, psychologists and other concerned people attempt to understand the causes. Understanding causes is not an idle pastime. We need to know why the police cars burst into flames in order to prevent the recurrence. We would like to know what it takes to be successful, so that we can try to be successful. We try to learn the causes of mental disorders so that we can cure the problem the person has. Understanding causes, therefore, is an important analytical process.

Likewise, we try to analyze—or, if the situation warrants it, predict—results, or *effects*. When a legislative body considers a tax-cut proposal, for example, it must examine the probable results the tax cut will have in the area. Too, as more tropical rain forests are destroyed, observers, scientists, and politicians are becoming increasingly concerned about the magnitude of the problems that the clearing is causing and will cause for the ecology of the world.

In short, then, cause-and-effect analysis is an important analytical skill to develop. Writing the essay that analyzes causes and effects will require examining the topic carefully in order to be complete and logical. In this chapter, then, our focus is the approaches to writing the cause-and-effect essay.

Since student essays are ordinarily between 300 and 500 words in length, generally speaking these essays can only deal effectively and thoroughly with an analysis emphasizing one or the other—causes *or* effects. And since most topics have more than one cause or effect, our focus here is on cause-and-effect essays that analyze more than one cause or effect. We discuss three types of cause-and-effect papers.

Multiple Causes → Effect

When we analyze the causes of something, we usually find that there are numerous contributing factors, or *multiple causes*; just how many factors depends on the complexity of the problem. Each cause may or may not be sufficient to produce the effect. Usually, however, we find that it is a combination of the causes that produces the result. Take, for example, the problem of obesity. Obesity is a complex problem, for it does not mean simply overweight. A person is considered obese if he or she weighs 20 percent above the generally accepted desirable weight for his or her height and age, in addition to having a certain amount of excess body fat. A person can be overweight because he or she has large bones, for example, but he or she is not considered obese. What causes obesity? Usually there is not a single cause; rather, a combination of factors leads to obesity:

Hereditary influences
Lack of exercise
Slow metabolic rate
Overeating
→ Obesity

In this example we might find that for some people, only overeating and a lack of exercise lead to obesity; for others a slow metabolic rate might suffice; for still others hereditary influences might be the culprit. Of course, in the discussion of overeating, one might find that behind it lies a deeper cause: emotional problems. A person might overeat to satisfy emotional deprivation. Or perhaps some people overeat because they have a deficiency in a certain enzyme that researchers believe is a factor in signaling the body to stop eating when it has had enough. And true, a further examination of the topic might yield even more causes, such as social or environmental factors.

In writing your analysis of this topic, then, you could plan to spend about one paragraph on each of the causes; each paragraph, too, would have to provide an explanation of the cause to show how it contributes to the effect. To illustrate, look at how a paragraph explaining the factor of lack of exercise might be developed:

> A lack of exercise is one of the major factors contributing to obesity. When we eat, we consume energy (measured as calories). When we exercise, we expend energy—or burn up calories. For example, when we run for an hour, we burn up approximately 450 calories, depending on our body size. When the number of calories we consume exceeds the number we burn up, the excess energy is stored in the body in the form of fat. If a person is inactive, it is more likely that he will not burn up all the calories consumed, so obesity can result. Moreover, studies have shown that inactivity can cause an obese person to expend less energy during a certain activity than a nonobese person. This is because inactivity lowers the basal energy rate (the basic minimum rate at which the body burns up energy). Therefore, if an obese person and a nonobese person try to run one mile, the obese person unused to activity will expend less energy because he has a lower basal energy rate.

EXERCISE 10-4

On a separate sheet of paper, answer the following questions about the preceding paragraph.

1. What is the topic sentence? The controlling idea?

2. What kind of support does the writer use to explain the factor?

EXERCISE 10-5

Study the paragraphs that follow. Each one attempts to explain a reason, but not all of the paragraphs are successful. Circle the number of each paragraph that does *not* adequately explain the reason given in the topic sentence. Explain your choices.

1. One reason I came to the United States was to learn English. English is the most important language in the world. It is the language spoken at the United Nations; it is also the official language of diplomacy. In addition, English is useful in many occupations. For example, air-traffic controllers all over the world must be able to speak English. Since English is so important, I decided to come to the United States.
2. Another reason I came to the United States was to go to college. In my country only a very small percentage of the applicants to the universities get accepted. Since I was unable to get accepted at a university at home, I had to go to a college outside of my country. I chose this university not only because I was able to get accepted at it, but also because it offers a program that I want to pursue: computer science.
3. One of the reasons for anxiety among American men is their changing role in society. In the past, it was simple. Men were strong, tough, and aloof. The models for these masculine qualities were movie stars like John Wayne, Humphrey Bogart, and Clint Eastwood. Today, however, most women want men to be more sensitive, more gentle, more understanding—more like Robert Redford, Dustin Hoffman, and Alan Alda. So men who grew up following the old role model are suddenly told that they are not right, not good enough. They should be different. They are being asked to change the way they think about themselves and their concept of manhood, and they are being asked to change in their relationships with women. This shift in expectations calls into question men's sense of who they are and how they relate to others, giving rise to self-doubts and problems of identity. Of course, this uncertainty about their role in society can cause men serious anxiety.
4. The major reason for anxiety among American men is their changing role in society. According to all accounts, this anxiety is pervasive. It is particularly so among men in their 30s and 40s, but it can also affect men in their 50s. One psychologist tells of a 56-year-old man who originally supported his wife's desire to go back to work and get a job. But, when she was promoted to a managerial position and began to travel a lot, the husband began to have anxiety attacks. Many men respond to this anxiety by refusing to commit themselves in marriage or by taking refuge in the new "macho

man," the man who thinks women really do want the strong silent type and he will be that man.

EXERCISE 10-6: WRITING ASSIGNMENT

Select one of the paragraphs in Exercise 10-5 that does not explain the reason adequately. Rewrite the paragraph and explain the reason.

EXERCISE 10-7: WRITING ASSIGNMENT

Choose one of the following topics and write three or four causes for the effect. Write complete sentences.

1. What causes people to emigrate to the United States?
2. What caused you to come to the United States?
3. Choose a disease that you are familiar with. What factors cause it?
4. Select a bad habit that you have. Why do you have that bad habit?
5. Select an idiosyncrasy of a family member or friend. Why does she or he have that peculiarity?

EXERCISE 10-8: WRITING ASSIGNMENT

Select one of the causes that you wrote in Exercise 10-7 and use it as a topic sentence for a paragraph. Write the paragraph by explaining the cause. Give enough detail and support for your generalization. Use the paragraph on lack of exercise as a model (page 348).

Organizing the Causal Analysis Essay

When you are discussing multiple causes for an effect, you need to be aware of the types of causes you are analyzing. The causes may be unrelated to each other, but all are related to the effect. These types of causes are often called *factors*; they are not causally related to each other, but they do work to contribute to the effect. When discussing these kinds of causes, as in the case of the obesity example, arrange the paragraphs (causes) according to your own preference. However, the most common principles are *order of familiarity* (obvious to less obvious) and *order of interest* (less interesting to more interesting). These two principles are useful when the causes are of equal significance. When one cause is more significant, order the paragraphs according to *importance*, with the most important last. Remember to identify the most important cause as the most significant.

Causes are not always unrelated, however. Sometimes a cause could not have brought about an effect unless certain *conditions* existed. In this case, the causes are related to each other. For example, the incident that launched Europe into World War I was the assassination of the Austrian heir to the throne, Archduke Franz Ferdinand, on June 28, 1914, by a young Serb nationalist. However, it is generally felt that this incident alone would not have caused the war if certain other conditions had not existed in Europe at that time: economic rivalries, heightened nationalism, imperialism, and so forth. In this kind of causal analysis, the causes that directly precede the effect are called *immediate* causes (sometimes called *direct* causes), and those causes that are further removed in time from the effect are called *remote* causes (sometimes called *indirect* causes). In the case of World War I, the immediate cause was the assassination but the remote causes were the conditions mentioned earlier, such as heightened nationalism.

Although remote causes are also often the most important ones (as in the case of the World War I example), they are not always the most important or the most reasonable ones. For instance, you might blame the overcrowded conditions in the public schools on overpopulation and overpopulation on the failure of the government to encourage birth control (remote), but a more reasonable explanation might be on the failure of the local officials to provide adequate educational facilities (immediate).

When you are analyzing causes that are not of equal importance or that are immediate and remote, it is generally a good idea to organize the paragraphs beginning with the immediate and proceeding to the remote, or from the less important to the most important.

EXERCISE 10-9

Following are two sets of causes that are given in no particular order. For each set, decide which of these causes are immediate and which are remote. Then organize them into an outline for an essay.

A. Causes for My Fear of the Water

1. I can't swim.
2. When I was a child, my mother wouldn't let me go near the water.
3. I don't like the feel of being immersed in water.
4. My mother had an unreasonable fear of the water.
5. My eyes are very bad. When I take off my glasses in the water I can't see.
6. I don't trust the water. I don't think it will hold me.
7. I associate the water with being disciplined by my mother.
8. When I was ten years old, I saw someone drown.

B. Causes for Air Pollution in Los Angeles

1. There are a lot of cars.
2. There are a lot of factories and oil refineries.

3. Weak legislation for antipollution devices in factories and refineries exists.
4. People remove antipollution devices from their cars.
5. The life-style requires that people live in suburbs a long distance from their work and commute to work.
6. Air is trapped between the mountains, not allowing the winds to disperse it.
7. Los Angeles is built in and around hills, so the suburbs are very spread out.

The Thesis Statement for the Causal Analysis Essay

In a causal analysis essay, the thesis statement does not have to be persuasive, since a topic is being analyzed and the central idea is found in that analysis. A thesis statement for a causal analysis can simply state briefly the causes to be discussed, or it may express the most significant cause. Consider this example:

> Conflicts over money, interfering relatives, and career problems all contributed to the demise of their relationship.

The topic is ***the demise of their relationship*** and the central idea is *reasons for its demise*.

Now study the following causal analysis essay. As you read, try to determine whether the author is discussing causes of equal significance, causes of unequal significance, or immediate and remote causation.

CAUSES OF MENTAL RETARDATION

A couple who is expecting a baby looks forward to the birth of their child with high hopes and expectations. Fortunately, most babies are born in good health, with their brains and bodies intact. Sometimes, of course, a baby is born with physical and/or mental defects. One such defect is mental retardation. There is no single cause of mental retardation, but researchers have uncovered several causes, some of which are preventable.

Brain damage due to genetic conditions is a well-known cause of mental retardation. Most people are familiar with Down's syndrome, which occurs more often in babies whose mothers are over 35 years old. Down's syndrome is caused by the formation of an additional chromosome. The normal number of chromosomes for people is 46; babies born with Down's syndrome have 47. Another chromosome-related cause of mental retardation is a malformation of the X-chromosome. Evidently, the X-chromosome breaks in two, thereby altering the normal development of the fetus. There are also several recessive-gene diseases that result in mental retardation. For example, an infant born with the recessive-gene disease called phenyleketonuria will end up with profound mental retardation because this disease affects the transmittal of information between the cells in the brain, particularly the neurons in the frontal lobes. Fortunately, blood tests can detect this problem at birth and immediate measures can be taken to limit the damage. Another disorder caused by recessive genes is Tay-Sachs disease, which is found primarily among Jewish families of northeastern Europe ancestry. This disease also affects the nerve cells, though not in the same way as phenyleketonuria. But there are blood tests that can detect carriers, so it can be prevented.

Not all brain damage resulting in mental retardation occurs because of problems in the genetic makeup of the infant. Certain infectious diseases that the mother may contract during pregnancy can adversely affect the developing brain of the baby, particularly if the mother catches these diseases during the first three months of her pregnancy. The most commonly known diseases include rubella (German measles), herpes simplex, and syphilis. Because these diseases are infectious, to a certain extent they are preventable.

Another preventable cause of mental retardation in newborns relates to what the pregnant woman ingests. Certain drugs are known to hinder the development of the baby's brain. In the early 1960s, for instance, some pregnant women suffering from pregnancy-related nausea were prescribed a drug called thalidomide. This drug interfered with the development of the embryo and resulted in physical deformations and mental deficits. These women had no way of knowing at the time what this drug could cause, but now we know that many drugs can adversely affect the development—both physical and mental—of the fetus. The most easily preventable cause of mental retardation is fetal alcohol syndrome. Drinking as little as one or two glasses of wine during the first three months of pregnancy can result in physical and intellectual impairments in the infant. The mother's diet is also important during her pregnancy. Researchers find mental retardation more common among babies whose mothers were malnourished during pregnancy.

Once the child is born other factors can cause mental retardation, such as head injuries and environmental pollutants, such as mercury and lead. But even before the child is born the damage may already have been done. Fortunately, much of this damage can be prevented by the pregnant woman. Genetic counseling, caution to avoid infectious diseases, avoidance of drugs, including alcohol, and proper diet can increase the chances that a woman will bear a child whose intellectual functioning will be in the normal range.*

EXERCISE 10-10

On a separate sheet of paper, answer the following questions about "Causes of Mental Retardation."

*Information from Gerald C. Davison and John M. Neale, *Abnormal Psychology: An Experimental Clinical Approach*, 4th ed. (New York: Wiley, 1986), pp. 407–15.

1. What is the thesis statement?
2. What is the controlling idea of paragraph 2; in other words, what is the reason discussed in that paragraph?
3. What are the controlling ideas in the next paragraphs?
4. Is the writer discussing immediate and remote causes, or are the causes of equal significance?
5. Does the conclusion follow logically?
6. How does the role of the pregnant woman contribute to the prevention of mental retardation?
7. Make an outline of this essay.

A Problem in Reasoning

When discussing causes and effects, be certain that your analysis is logical. One of the logical fallacies—errors in reasoning—to avoid is called *post hoc ergo propter hoc*, a Latin phrase meaning "after this, therefore because of this." This problem in logic occurs when the writer assumes that an incident that precedes another is the *cause* of that incident: "President X was elected in January. Three weeks later our nation suffered a severe depression. Therefore, President X caused that depression." This is an example of *post-hoc* reasoning. In this example, the illogic is clear, but be careful not to confuse chronological order with cause and effect; in addition, be certain to explain clearly the cause-and-effect relationship.

EXERCISE 10-11

Study the following groups of sentences. If the relationship is solely chronological, put "Time" in the space provided; if the relationship is also causal, put "C/E" (for cause/effect) in the blank.

1. ____________ Every time I ride my moped to school it rains. I am not going to ride it today, so it won't rain.
2. ____________ Chemicals were dumped in the Love Canal area of New York. People who lived in Love Canal have a high rate of cancer.
3. ____________ The sun came out. The dew on the grass dried.
4. ____________ A meteor was seen in the sky over Los Angeles. An earthquake occurred the next morning.
5. ____________ Last winter an unusually small amount of snow fell in the mountains. This summer the water supply in the plain below dried up.

6. ____________ It rained last Tuesday. Now I have a cold.

7. ____________ A strong hurricane formed in the Gulf of Mexico. Tidal waves hit the coast of Texas.

8. ____________ There was a severe drop in car sales. Several workers were laid off.

9. ____________ I touched a dead fish. The next day I developed pain in my fingers.

10. ____________ Ten movies shown in movie theaters this year showed adultery. There is an increase in adultery in our society.

EXERCISE 10-12: WRITING ASSIGNMENT

Following are some topics for a causal analysis essay. After you choose a topic, decide on the causes. Are they multiple causes or factors? Can you distinguish immediate and remote causes? Using this information, decide on the organizational pattern. Be sure to support the causes with details and examples.

1. Complete the essay that you started in Exercise 10-6.
2. Choose another of the topics in Exercise 10-7.
3. Give the causes for your particular fear of something.
4. Give the causes for pollution in a particular area or city (either in the United States or in your country).
5. Give the causes for a recent social condition or change (for example, a change in men's roles, women's roles, divorce rates, family size, number of smokers versus nonsmokers, amount of stress in children).

Cause → Multiple Effects

Just as an effect can have multiple causes, so can a cause have ***multiple effects***. For example, several years ago most people thought that processed sugar (such as granulated sugar) was a relatively harmless sweetener that produced a pleasant taste, provided a small burst of energy, and perhaps contributed to tooth decay. There was little concern about the seemingly minor effects of eating sugar. But in recent years our consumption of sugar has increased tremendously; in addition, we have begun to uncover some unpleasant and serious effects of eating so much sugar. Although sugar may not be the sole cause of some of the following more remote effects, research has shown it can contribute to them:

Excessive Consumption of Sugar
- Blood Sugar Imbalances
- Tooth Decay
- Hyperactivity in Children
- Weight Gain

When an analysis is primarily of effects, as in this case, expect to devote a paragraph to each effect. The paragraph would have to explain the relationship between the cause and the effect. Note how the effect of tooth decay is explained in the following paragraph.

One of the major effects of eating too much sugar is a high incidence of tooth decay. When we eat something with sugar in it, particularly refined sugar, enzymes in the saliva in the mouth begin to work immediately to change that sugar into a type of carbohydrate. As one eats, particles of the sugary food get lodged between the teeth and around the gums. As the food changes its chemical composition, the resultant carbohydrate produces bacteria that begin to eat away at the enamel on the outside of our teeth. This is actually the decaying of the tooth. Now, if this process happens each time we eat sugar, we can see that eating excessive amounts of sugar causes more and more tooth decay. It is true that some tooth decay can be avoided with immediate brushing after eating, dislodging all the particles of food trapped in the teeth. However, sweets are often eaten as snacks between meals and during the day, times when people generally do not brush after eating. Therefore, the dangerous process of tooth decay is allowed to continue.

EXERCISE 10-13

On a separate sheet of paper, answer the following questions about the preceding paragraph.

1. **What is the topic sentence?**
2. **Does the paragraph show how eating too much sugar can result in tooth decay?**
3. **Is the paragraph unified? Coherent?**

EXERCISE 10-14: WRITING ASSIGNMENT

Select one of the following topics and write out three or four effects stemming from the cause. Write complete sentences.

1. **What are some of the effects of drinking products that contain caffeine, such as cola and coffee?**
2. **What are some of the effects of smoking cigarettes?**
3. **Have you ever witnessed a disaster, such as an earthquake, a hurricane, or a severe storm? What were some of the effects of that disaster?**
4. **In what ways has coming to the United States affected you?**

EXERCISE 10-15: WRITING ASSIGNMENT

Select one of the causes listed in Exercise 10-14 and use it as a topic sentence for a paragraph. Write a paragraph explaining an effect. Use the preceding paragraph about tooth decay as a model.

Organizing the Effect Analysis Essay

The principles for organizing an effect paper are much the same as those for organizing a causal analysis. Like causes, effects can be unrelated (causally) to each other even though they all stem from the same cause. For instance, when a killer hurricane hits, several effects result: death, property damage, energy failures, and so on. These effects are not necessarily related causally; they were all just caused by the same thing—the killer hurricane. Although effects can be of equal value or importance, usually some are more important than others. In this case, like causes, organize the paragraphs dealing with effects according to order of importance (though focus should be on the more important—or major—ones).

Effects, too, like causes, can be immediate or remote. In the example of excessive sugar consumption, an immediate effect of eating sugar is a boost in energy, but more remote are the blood sugar problems and tooth decay. In this case, the remote effects happen to be the most important. An immediate effect of the earthquake in Soviet Armenia, in 1988, was the death of thousands of people; a more remote effect will be, perhaps, buildings constructed under a safer and more stringent building code. In this case, although the immediate effect is the most important, the remote effect is still worth discussing.

If an analysis, then, is of effects that occur relatively in the same time relationship, with the cause—in other words, they are all basically immediate or remote—it is a good idea to order the effects according to importance. However, if the discussion is of immediate and remote effects, it is a good idea to begin with the immediate and continue to the remote. Reminder: Identify the quality of the effect (immediate, major, and so on) to the reader to clarify the type of effect being discussed.

EXERCISE 10-16

Following are two sets of effects that are given in no particular order. For each set, decide which of the effects are immediate and which are remote. Then organize them into an outline for an essay.

A. The Effects of Watching Television

1. More people get eyestrain.

2. There is more violent crime in our cities.
3. People get fat.
4. There are more divorces.
5. Husbands and wives do not talk to each other anymore.
6. People do not enjoy reading anymore.
7. People are more afraid of each other.
8. People are lonely.

B. The Citizens of This City Have Passed Legislation to Lower Property Taxes. (First divide effects into negative and positive.)

1. Many city employees will lose their jobs.
2. Police patrols in the suburbs and downtown area will be reduced.
3. Citizens will have more money to spend on consumer items.
4. There will not be money for street repair.
5. The school budget will be reduced.
6. New business will be attracted to the city.
7. The park service will not be able to plant new trees along the highways.
8. The garbage will be picked up only once a week instead of twice a week.
9. More jobs will open up.
10. The local high schools will no longer have football teams.

The Thesis Statement for the Effect Analysis Essay

Like a causal analysis essay the thesis statement for an effect analysis essay does not have to be persuasive. The thesis statement can have a more simply stated central idea:

The tax increase will bring benefits to our city.

Here, of course, the topic is ***tax increase*** and the central idea is that it will ***bring benefits*** to the city.

Now read the following essay, which analyzes effects. As you read, locate the thesis and determine whether the writer has clarified the type of effects being discussed.

DO IT!

Some do it to music, some while watching television; others do it in the privacy of their own homes, others in gyms. For some, they do it in the morning, others at night. But no matter where or when, millions of people all over the world do it—and that is exercise. But, unfortunately, millions of people do not get enough exercise. The benefits of regular aerobic exercise are so great that it's a wonder everybody doesn't start on a program today.

Probably the most well-known effect of aerobic exercise can be achieved in a relatively short period of time, and that is improved cardiovascular and pulmonary functions. When a person exercises long and hard enough, the heart pumps faster and blood is circulated well throughout the body. Since the heart is a muscle, exercise serves to strengthen it. As the heart becomes stronger, a person's stamina improves as well as her energy level. The same is true of the lungs. It doesn't take long to reap these benefits. A person can get such results within a few weeks just by walking briskly for 30 minutes three or four times a week.

Another physical benefit of regular aerobic exercise takes longer to achieve, but it is well worth the effect, particularly for women. Exercise can help prevent the crippling bone degeneration called osteoporosis. Osteoporosis is a gradual process of bone loss that occurs naturally as people age, but it can be halted by regular aerobic exercise. Exercise actually helps increase bone mass, and is said to be the best preventive measure to take to avoid osteoporosis.

Just as regular exercise can help people achieve cardiovascular and skeletal fitness, it can also help people improve their emotional fitness. One of the good things about exercise is that it reduces stress. It does this in different ways. By improving one's overall fitness, aerobic exercise makes a person more capable of handling stress because he is less tense. When exercising, blood circulation improves and people burn off the adrenalin that stress causes the body to produce. Another way that exercise helps people handle stress is that after sufficient aerobic exercise, the body produces beta-endorphins, which are natural stress-relieving chemicals. In addition to helping people cope with stress, exercise can also help to alleviate depression.

There are no doubt many other benefits of regular aerobic exercise. It doesn't require that much time or effort to become a healthier person within weeks. Instead of watching television so much, people would be better off cycling or walking.

EXERCISE 10-17

On a separate sheet of paper, answer the following questions about "Do It!"

1. **What is the thesis?**
2. **Does the writer establish a need or purpose for writing this paper?**
3. **Which kind of effect does the writer begin with?**
4. **What is the controlling idea in the third paragraph?**
5. **Why did the writer discuss the emotional fitness last?**
6. **Make an outline of this essay.**

EXERCISE 10-18: WRITING ASSIGNMENT

Choose one of the following topics for an essay that analyzing effects. Be sure to distinguish between major and minor causes or between immediate and remote causes, whichever is appropriate.

1. Complete the essay that you started in Exercise 10-15.
2. Choose another of the topics in Exercise 10-14.
3. Analyze the effects of a change in your life. For instance, how has living away from home for the first time affected you?
4. Every family has problems. Perhaps, for example, a family member is unemployed, homesick, depressed, ill, angry, an alcoholic, or physically or mentally disabled. Problems like these affect the other family members. Discuss the effects of a family member's problem on your family.
5. Discuss the effects of a political or social change in your country.

The Causal Chain

Another type of cause-and-effect analysis is the *causal chain*. Unlike the multiple cause-and-effect analyses, the causes and effects in a causal chain are always directly related; in fact, they are linked. In the causal chain, one effect can become a cause of another effect, which, in turn, can become a cause of another effect, and so on. For example, suppose an overweight smoker is inactive because of shortness of breath. The doctor told her to quit smoking and she did. Soon she was able to breathe more easily; as a result, she felt better physically. She started an exercise program and as a result of this increased activity, she lost weight. This domino-like chain might be diagramed as follows:

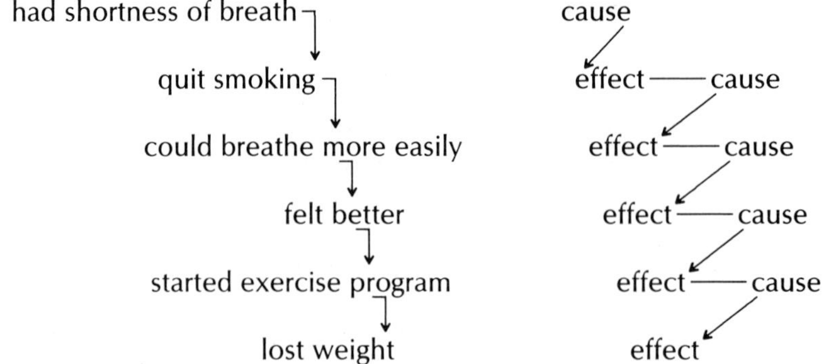

There are two major uses of the causal chain. First, it is sometimes useful for explaining one of the causes in a multiple-cause essay. For instance, in the example of obesity, the cause of overeating could be explained as follows:

The most obvious cause of obesity is overeating. But why do people overeat? One reason is emotional problems. For example, consider the case of Debbie. When Debbie was a child, her parents rewarded her for good behavior with candy and other sweet things. As she grew older, she began to reward herself quite regularly. As a result, she began to gain weight. By the time she was a teenager, Debbie had become rather heavy. Her weight then became a target for the other young people at school. They teased her unmercifully, as youngsters will do. She was teased so much that she started feeling sorry for herself and consoled herself by eating more and more. She gained more weight, and the vicious cycle continued until her self-image was so bad that she could not really perceive herself as anything but fat; therefore, diets were unsuccessful because she would inevitably get depressed during or after a diet and go on an eating binge to soothe her feelings.

EXERCISE 10-19

On a separate sheet of paper, make a causal chain diagram of the preceding paragraph.

The other major use of the causal chain is used in science to analyze various kinds of cycles, such as biological or chemical chains. Study the following essay, which analyzes a causal chain. Determine if the cause–effect relationship is clarified and explained.

UPSETTING THE BALANCE OF NATURE

The members of a living community exist together in a particular, balanced relationship, or ecosystem. One animal species eats another animal species which in turn eats another. Over years, a balance is worked out among the plants and animals in a community and it remains basically stable. It is like a huge puzzle with all of the pieces in their proper places. However, at times this balance in nature is disturbed, resulting in a number of possibly unforeseen effects. Perhaps a disease results in the near extinction of one species, leaving another species with no natural predator. The result can be a terrific increase in that one species' population. This could further result in the devastation of a shared food supply, which could in turn affect another species. It is possible for the disruption in the balance of nature to have natural causes: disease, drought, fire. Sometimes, however, human beings intervene in a natural environment, perhaps only slightly and with good intentions. The result is the same. The balance of nature becomes unbalanced and results in an entire chain reaction of unforeseen and unwanted effects.

A good example of this occurred in the Antilles in the 1870s. Sugar cane was a major crop there, but rats were eating and nesting in the cane, causing a great deal of damage. The mongoose, a one-and-a-half-foot-long mammal of the East Indies, was known to be an excellent rat hunter. Several males and females were imported in 1872, and laws were established that forbade the killing of them or their offspring. The mongoose flourished in the Antilles. After ten years it had multiplied abundantly and had significantly reduced the rat population. Consequently, damage to the cane fields was greatly reduced. It seemed that the scheme to add another piece to the ecological puzzle in the Antilles had been successful.

However, that is not the end of the story. The influence of the mongoose did not stop there. As the rat population decreased and the mongoose population increased, the mongoose needed to enlarge its menu. It attacked young pigs and goats, game, poultry, and began to destroy bananas, maize, and pineapples. Because the mongoose could not be hunted, its numbers increased rapidly, and it became a terrible pest. All of the indigenous animals suffered damage. The mongoose learned to enjoy the native birds, snakes, lizards, and turtles and their eggs. Now, it was specifically these animals that kept the local insect population in check. There were in the ecosystem of the Antilles a number of beetles, borers, and other insects that lived on and in the sugar cane. Until that time, they had not caused significant damage to the cane, because they were the natural food of so many local animals that kept their numbers down. However, as the birds, snakes, lizards, and turtles disappeared, the insect population began to increase. With no natural predators to keep them in check, the insects began to do more and more damage to the cane fields.

Finally, the people of the Antilles realized that the introduction of the mongoose had caused a finely and delicately balanced system to go awry. The law against killing the mongoose was rescinded, and the mongoose population was reduced. Gradually, the different members of the plant and animal community came back into balance with each other and equilibrium was reestablished. However, the human members of the community would not soon forget that a single change in an ecosystem can cause a chain reaction that results in completely unforeseen and sometimes unwanted effects.

—Adapted from Karl von Frisch, *Biology: The Science of Life* (New York: Harper & Row, 1964).

EXERCISE 10-20

On a separate sheet of paper, answer the following questions about "Upsetting the Balance of Nature."

1. **What is the topic of the essay? What is the central idea?**
2. **What is the incident in the Antilles an example of?**

3. Is this causal chain logical; that is, is the relationship among the causes and effects clearly and logically presented?
4. Does the conclusion logically follow?
5. Make an outline of this essay.

EXERCISE 10-21

Following are two sets of information, each giving the steps in a causal chain. What is the causal chain in each one? Devise a topic sentence for each set of information and write a paragraph explaining the causal chain. (You may need to add steps.)

A. Disaster in Southern California

1. Summers are hot and dry.
2. In fall, high winds come from the desert.
3. Forest fires begin and spread.
4. In spring, heavy rains fall.
5. In spring, mudslides and floods occur.

B. Poverty

1. People lack capital.
2. They buy items on credit.
3. They pay high interest on credit accounts.
4. This reduces their capital and puts them in debt.
5. They buy more items on credit.
6. This reduces their capital even more; it puts them further in debt.

EXERCISE 10-22: WRITING ASSIGNMENT

Choose one of the following topics for an essay that develops a causal chain. First, think through the chain carefully. Do not leave out any important steps. Develop a thesis sentence and outline. Then write an essay.

1. Choose a chain from one of the sciences; for example, a biological food chain.
2. Reread the preceding essay on the balance of nature. Write an essay describing an upset in the balance of nature that you are familiar with.
3. Choose a chain from geography. What has happened to the land in a particular area?
4. Choose a social problem like alcoholism, poverty, divorce, overpopulation, or teenage pregnancy, or teenage drug use.

COMPOSITION SKILLS

Introductory Paragraphs

The Dramatic Entrance

In Chapter 9, we learned how a description of a scene can be used to open an essay. There are, of course, other approaches to use for a Dramatic Entrance. For instance, your essay can begin with a particularly interesting example that illustrates your thesis or is pertinent to your topic; or it can open with an effect if your paper is analyzing causes or with a cause if it is analyzing effects. Note how the writer, Anastasia Toufexis, uses interesting examples in the following opening to her essay on mother-and-son relationships.

> Industrialist Andrew Carnegie's mother begged him not to marry until after she died; he waited one year after her death and finally wed at fifty-two. Dwight Eisenhower interrupted planning of the Allied invasion of France in May 1944 to send a Mother's Day greeting to Ida Eisenhower in Kansas. When Franklin Roosevelt was quarantined with scarlet fever at boarding school, his distraught mother Sara climbed a ladder each day to peer through the window of his room to check on his recovery. Actor James Dean explained his troubled life this way: "My mother died on me when I was nine years old. What does she expect me to do? Do it all alone?"
>
> The cord that unites mother and son may be Western society's most powerful bond, yet attitudes toward the relationship are either murky or coated over with cliché. "We think we're comfortable with it, but culturally what we get are caricatures," argues Carole Klein, a longtime observer of the dynamics of family relationships. . . .
>
> —Anastasia Toufexis,
> *"The Most Powerful Bond of All,"*
> *Time* 1 Oct. 1984: p. 86.

When you are writing an essay that analyzes causes, you might consider opening with an effect, or vice versa. Look at how student writer Carolyn Udell opens her essay in which she analyzes the causes and effects of her fear of cockroaches; she describes a dream—one of the effects of her fear.

ROACHES

[1] Roaches crawling all over the walls, all over the floor, pouring into the bedroom door, where can I run? I jump on top of the bed. They follow me up. Oh, my God, they're starting to fly all around me. . . . "Oh, it was just a dream." Vile and repugnant are two of the best words used to describe the most despicable creature on earth, the roach. The Bible portrays the devil as a serpent in the Garden of Eden. However, I am sure that God meant the roach to play the part. My feelings for these creatures are of spasmodic disgust, but especially fear.

[2] I am not sure when this fear started, somewhere back in my early childhood. As far back as I can remember, I have never had the desire to

touch a roach. The first thing I think of when a person says the word *roach* is its abhorrent looks. Their prehistoric appearance makes me cringe. The dark brown color reminds me of something dirty and gives me a feeling of disgust, which is exactly what a roach is — disgusting, with its long, skinny, black feelers protruding from its head, always moving and twitching in an erratic way, no matter if it is squatting still or scurrying away beneath your feet. This is certainly an immediate cause of my fear.

[3] Maybe the fear stems from the fact that they will eat anything, including the dead body of another animal, humans not excluded. This fact makes them seem disease-ridden. Every disease ever known to man or imagined by man can be caught from a roach, or so it seems.

[4] Granted, some of the fear I have for these parasites might be learned from my mother. You would think you could call good ole Mom to the rescue when you spot a big two-inch roach on the wall and count on her to take care of it for you, but this is not so with my mother. Oh, she may come when you call her all right, but when she spots the two-incher on the wall, she hands me the can of Raid and runs for cover.

[5] Another thing about roaches is that they are nocturnal insects. This may be an indirect cause of my fear of them, but maybe not. A psychiatrist might evaluate it this way. Roaches are nocturnal creatures. People are afraid of the night and associate it with evil things. Therefore, I, ultimately, am afraid of roaches. Now, I do not know how valid this is, because I am not afraid of roaches because of the night. It is more like I am afraid of the night because of roaches. I do not know why, but roaches seem to be scarier at night.

[6] Anyway, it all comes down to this. This nightmare I recounted earlier is just an example of the many bad dreams I have had as a kid, and still do have, occasionally. These dreams are a direct result of my fear of roaches. I imagine them crawling on my bed and all over me. These dreams leave me wide awake, scared to death, and unable to go back to sleep.

[7] I can't walk into a dark room without some trepidation. I could not stand to touch one of these things. This would leave me a mental case. The only way I can kill a roach is with Raid. This kind of apprehension makes life very difficult for me when I am roughing it or camping out. I'll lie there in my sleeping bag in my tent and I will not budge, with my can of Raid by my side and a light on, of course. An actual encounter with a roach, and I lose my sense of logic. I become unable to function in a controlled manner. I remember one time when I was down in the French Quarter in New Orleans, and if roaches are manufactured somewhere, that's the factory. Anyway, I was walking through a doorway when this big black roach crossed my path. He started flying — right from the floor into midair — at me! I almost died. I did not know whether to run backward or make a dive for the floor. This would have gone on, running backward contemplating a dive for the floor, until I was all the way to Baton Rouge, had not the roach decided to divert its course.

[8] In a controlled situation, such as that of a classroom, I am mentally as well as physically agonized. I saw a roach in a class once, about a chair ahead of me. I did not want to make a scene and start screaming, especially

since the roach was not that big. My mind was telling me to get up calmly and casually stroll away. However, my body was wanting to jump up and run. It was a terrible strain on me. I did manage to walk a far enough distance back without making a scene.

[9] There is one way and only one way to overcome this fear. And that is to walk up boldly to the biggest, blackest roach I can find and grasp it with both hands, and hold it firmly. It would only take a minute. Then, all the bad dreams would stop. I would have confidence when I entered a dark room. And my mental and physical state of being would bear no strain. . . . "Oh, no! A roach! Quick! Raid!"

—*Carolyn Udell*

EXERCISE 10-23

On a separate sheet of paper, answer the following questions about the essay "Roaches."

1. What is the writer's purpose in analyzing this topic?
2. What is the thesis statement? Is it stated directly or is it implied?
3. Is the essay primarily a causal analysis, an effect analysis, or both?
4. Why is "Oh, it was just a dream" in quotation marks (paragraph 1)?
5. Is the introduction inviting; that is, does it make you want to read the rest of the essay? Explain.
6. What is the topic of paragraph 2? The controlling idea?
7. Does the writer focus on immediate or remote causes?
8. What purpose or function does paragraph 6 serve?
9. What is the topic of paragraph 7?
10. What does the example of the incident in New Orleans illustrate?
11. Does the writer discuss immediate or remote effects primarily?
12. Does there seem to be any hope that the writer will overcome her fear of roaches?
13. Does the writer seem to be serious about this topic? What clues do we get that she has a sense of humor about her fear?
14. What does "granted" at the beginning of paragraph 4 refer to?
15. Make an outline of this essay.

The Relevant Quotation

Another frequently used approach to opening essays is what we call the Relevant Quotation. An essay with this type of introduction opens with a quotation by an authority on the topic or by someone who says something relevant to what is discussed in the essay. Sometimes writers begin with a famous quotation and then work it into their topic. Observe how this writer uses a quotation to introduce an article about the harvesting of saffron in Spain:

> "The saffron is an arrogant flower," begins an old Spanish zarzuela named for this lush, purple blossom. "It is born with the sunrise and dies at sunset." For a couple of weeks in October of every year, in Spain's La Maucha region, the arrogant crocus is harvested frenetically, as fast as it flowers.
>
> For saffron is the world's most precious spice, often rivaling, ounce for ounce, the cost of gold. A pound of its tiny threads—the stigmas, or female organs, of *Crocus sativus*, an autumn crocus—currently costs well over $2,000. There is such a demand for these little fibers the Spanish call "red gold" that virtually all that is grown will be sold. —Diane Raines Ward, "Flowers Are a Mine for a Spice More Precious Than Gold," *Smithsonian* Aug. 1988: p. 105.

In the following introduction, the author uses a quotation by a famous Englishman to introduce an article about the United States Constitution:

> It took an Englishman, William Gladstone, to say what Americans have always thought: "The American Constitution is, so far as I can see, the most wonderful work ever struck off at a given time by the brain and purpose of man." From this side of the water, however, the marvel has not been so much the unique system of government that emerged from the secret conclave of 1787 as the array of ordered and guaranteed freedoms that the document presented. "Every word of [the Constitution]," said James Madison, the quintessential Founding Parent, "decides a question between power and liberty." —H. B. Zobel, "How History Made the Constitution," *American Heritage* Mar. 1988: p. 54.

EXERCISE 10-24: WRITING ASSIGNMENT

Select one of the following topics and use a Dramatic Entrance or a Relevant Quotation for your introduction. Assume that your essay will discuss causes.

1. An unreasonable fear you have (such as a fear of roaches, flying, heights, or the like).
2. A particular like or dislike you have (such as a passion for a certain sport).
3. The causes of something tragic (such as a hotel fire, a bomb explosion, an accident, or the like).

Coherence

Transitions and Expressions for Cause and Effect

Transitions are important for coherence. In writing cause-and-effect essays, transitions are necessary to introduce causes and effects. In addition to the transitions studied in earlier chapters, there are other transitions that are particularly useful in cause-and-effect essays. Pay close attention to the punctuation required for each type of transition.

TRANSITION IN PHRASES. The transitions in this group must be followed by a *noun*. If the phrase containing the transition comes at the beginning of the sentence, it is usually followed by a comma. The following transitions indicate cause: ***because of*** and ***as a result of***. Study these examples:

> *Because of* the possibility of fetal brain damage, pregnant women should not consume alcohol.
>
> *As a result of* exercising regularly, a person can handle stress better.

EXPRESSIONS IN SENTENCES. The transitions in this group are verbs that express cause or effect. The following transitional verbs indicate cause: ***caused by*** and ***results from***. Study these examples:

> Premature aging of the skin *results from* too much exposure to the sun.
>
> Her fear of roaches was *caused by* an early childhood trauma.

The following transitional verbs indicate effect: ***cause*** and ***result in***. Study these examples:

> Lack of exercise can *cause* obesity.
>
> Walking regularly can *result in* improved health.

Special Note: *the reason is that . . .*

The expression ***the reason is that*** is often used to introduce a cause. It must be followed by a complete sentence. Note this example:

> Why do people exercise? *The reason is that* they are trying to stay healthy.

COORDINATING CONJUNCTIONS AS TRANSITIONS. The coordinating conjunctions *so* and *for* are often used as transitions. *So* indicates a result. However, it is somewhat colloquial and is usually avoided in formal writing. *For* indicates a cause and is quite formal. Study these examples and note the punctuation for coordinating conjunctions:

> The mongoose was protected by law, *so* it increased in number rapidly.
>
> We stopped at a restaurant, *for* we had not eaten since early morning.

TRANSITIONAL EXPRESSIONS BETWEEN SENTENCES. The transitions in this group usually occur between two complete sentences. They must be preceded by either a period or a semicolon. They cannot be preceded by a comma, but a comma often follows them. The following transitions indicate an effect or result: ***thus, therefore, consequently, as a result, for this reason***.

Mathematics and science teachers do not encourage young girls to study science; *thus*, there are not many female scientists.

She perceived herself as fat; *therefore*, diets were unsuccessful.

It significantly reduced the rat population. *Consequently*, damage to the cane fields was reduced.

Debbie ate constantly. *As a result*, she became rather heavy.

The students were protesting against the food served in the cafeteria. *For this reason*, the president cancelled classes and closed the university.

Note: These transitions can also occur within an independent clause. When they do, they are set off by commas:

He had exceeded the speed limit. He was, *therefore*, charged a fine.

Adverbial Clauses of Cause and Result

ADVERBIAL CLAUSES OF CAUSE. Both ***because*** and ***since*** can be added to sentences to make adverbial clauses of cause. The adverbial clause can come at the beginning or the end of the sentence. When the clause comes at the beginning, it is followed by a comma.

Because these diseases are infectious, to a certain extent they are preventable.

I did not speak to him *since* I did not remember his name.

EXERCISE 10-25

Following are four reasons for liking the study of biology. Write a sentence for each of the transitions given. The first one is done for you.

1. Biology systematically classifies living things.

because of	I like the study of biology because of its systematic classification of living things.
so	Biology classifies living things in a systematic way, so I find it satisfies my need for order.
thus	Biology has a systematic classification of living things. Thus, I find it useful in knowing the names of things.

2. Biology explains the characteristics of living things.

because of	____________________

for ______________________________

therefore ______________________________

since ______________________________

3. Biology explains the interdependence of living things.

because of ______________________________

so ______________________________

as a result ______________________________

since ______________________________

4. Biology encourages curiosity and research.

since ______________________________

consequently ______________________________

for this reason ______________________________

because ______________________________

ADVERBIAL CLAUSES OF RESULT. Adverbial clauses of result are made by connecting two sentences with *so/such . . . that*. Note how the two sentences are connected in this example:

> That building is tall. I cannot climb to the top.
>
> That building is *so* tall *that* I can't climb to the top.

Note carefully the kind of word or phrase that must follow *so/such*:

> She is *so afraid that* she hands me the can of Raid and runs for cover. [*so* + adj + *that*]
>
> That elevator goes *so slowly that* I cannot wait for it. [*so* + adverb + *that*]
>
> Johanne likes *so many things that* he cannot decide what to do next. [*so* + *few/many* + plural noun]
>
> This car requires *so much gas that* I have decided not to buy it. [*so* + *much/little* + noncount noun]
>
> He gave me *such good advice that* I passed the test easily. [*such* + adjective + noncount or plural count noun]
>
> It was *such a powerful movie that* I could not forget it. [*such* + *a/an* + adjective + singular count noun]

Note: The adverbial clause of result always comes at the end of the sentence, so no comma is needed.

EXERCISE 10-26

Fill in the blanks with *so, such,* or *such a.*

1. Ramon stayed up ____________ late last night that he got up late this morning.
2. He left the house ____________ quickly that he forgot his briefcase.
3. He had ____________ many important papers in it that he had to return home for it.
4. There was ____________ heavy traffic on the freeway that he did not get back to the office until 11 A.M.
5. He was in ____________ terrible mood that he snapped sharply at his colleagues.
6. He had ____________ much work to do that he did not have time for lunch.
7. By the time he got home, he was ____________ exhausted that he fell asleep immediately.
8. He had had ____________ bad day that he dreamed about it all night long.

EXERCISE 10-27

Rewriting the following sentences to use the *so/such . . . that* pattern. The first one is done for you.

1. None of the planes could take off because the snowstorm was terrible.
   <u>The snowstorm was so terrible that none of the planes could take off.</u>
2. Because there were many people trapped in the airport, some of them slept on the floor.

   ____

   ____
3. Some of the people did not care about the snowstorm because they were having a good time.

   ____

   ____
4. However, some of the people demanded their money back because they were angry.

   ____

____

5. They said that they would never fly again because the airlines were giving bad service.

____

____

6. The airline officials explained that because it was snowing hard, the pilots could not see.

____

____

EXERCISE 10-28

Fill in the blanks with the appropriate transitions and expressions of cause and effect. Pay careful attention to the punctuation given.

CAUSES OF TEENAGE SMOKING

A 13-year-old boy, standing in the doorway of his school, puffs on a cigarette. He holds it carelessly, like an adult, yet in plain view. He looks around to make sure that the other guys are watching. If you ask how long he has smoked, you will find out that he started when he was eleven. By now, he is an addicted smoker. If you ask him why he smokes, he will probably say that he enjoys it. ____________ you wonder if that is really the reason. It seems to me that the causes for teenage smoking are more complex. More specifically, they have more to do with the ambiguous role of teenagers in society. Teenage smoking is ____________ by personal insecurity, a desire to be like adults, and peer pressure.

The ____________ cause of teenage smoking is the personal insecurity young people often feel. They are at a difficult age. They are no longer children, ____________ the ways in which they have behaved in the past are inappropriate. On the other hand, they are not yet adults; ____________, they do not know the ways of the adult world. This conflict can ____________ feelings of insecurity. ____________, if children want attention from their parents or a toy or sweet, they can cry to draw attention to their desires. For teenagers, ____________, crying will be labeled childish and they will be told to "act their age." Often, ____________, the teenager does not know how to act his or her age. ____________ teenagers do not know what to do, they often turn to smoking as a way to hide their nervousness and insecurities.

As we have just seen, teenagers need to learn how to behave as adults. They of course realize this and spend time emulating adults. ____________ they try to adopt more adult attitudes and manners. They pay attention to their dress and the opposite sex. One thing that young teenagers perceive as "very adult" is smoking cigarettes. Perhaps a boy sees his father or older brother smoke. He thinks of his father as a man and ____________ he wants to be "a man" like his father, he starts to smoke, ____________ beginning a habit that most adults know is unhealthy.

While it is true that teenagers are attempting to become adults, this effort is often not fully conscious. ____________, they often see the adults closest to them, their parents and teachers, as enemies. ____________, they turn to their peer group for support. We are all familiar with the teenagers who want to look, act, and dress exactly like all of the other teenagers in their peer group. This peer group can exert ____________ pressure ____________ often teenagers do things in the group that they would not normally do. One of these things is smoking cigarettes. Imagine a group of guys playing pool together after school. One says to the others, "I'm going to buy a pack of cigarettes. Do you want to smoke one with me?" The peer pressure here is ____________ great ____________ most normal boys will succumb.

We can see that personal insecurity, desire to be like adults, and peer pressure can cause many teenagers to start something that they will later regret.

GRAMMAR REVIEW

Unreal Conditions

At times in writing about effects, you may want to make a prediction about an effect or a possible effect. For example, you may decide to explain what could have happened or what might have happened if a particular law had not been passed. To make predictions, you may find unreal conditional clauses useful. Let us review them briefly.

Unreal conditions are either impossible to realize or not likely to be realized. In these sentences, a contrary-to-fact condition exists. Study these examples:

Present Time:

If this *was allowed* to happen, the dam *would collapse.*

If the dam *collapsed,* many acres of good farm land *would* disappear.

Past Time:

If this *had* not *been allowed* to happen, the dam *would* not *have collapsed.*

Past Time with Present or Future Result:

If the law *had* passed, the economy *would be* in better shape now.

Note that for present time, ***was*** (singular) and ***were*** (plural) are used in the ***if*** clause, and ***would*** or ***could*** + verb is used in the main clause. For past time, ***had*** + past participle is used in the ***if*** clause and ***would/could have*** + past participle is used in the main clause. Note the combination of the two when the ***if*** clause is past time but the main clause is the present or future result.

EXERCISE 10-29

The following sentences tell something *real.* Change them to indicate something *unreal.* The first one is done for you.

1. Some television programs are violent. They can result in increased violence among some viewers.
   If television programs were not violent, they would not result in increased violence among some viewers.
2. We have the international Olympic Games. Therefore, we do not have more international violence.
   ____
3. We allowed the oil company to build this refinery. Therefore, we have oil pollution now.
   ____
   ____
4. We did not stop the construction of this dam. We destroyed miles of natural wilderness along the river.
   ____
   ____
5. We pay taxes. Our schools are not closed.
   ____
6. We voted for Smith for president. We are in a terrible mess now.
   ____

7. This university does not have more student housing. It does not attract more international students.

____

____

8. We have to deal with a computer when we pay our bills. Our business transactions have become impersonal.

____

____

9. Cigarette smoking is not against the law. Many people get sick from it.

____

____

10. The government did not deal with the crisis properly. Inflation has continued at high levels.

____

____

EXERCISE 10-30

According to one anthropologist, soap operas are so popular in part because they deal with family problems. Read the following plot of the soap opera "Days of Our Lives," which tells the story of the characters Bob, Phyllis, and Julie. Assume that this is *real* information and that it took place in the past. Then, using this information, write three sentences using *unreal* conditions.

> Bob and Phyllis were happily married for many years but now Bob has fallen in love with Julie. Bob decides he must leave Phyllis for he no longer loves her. Phyllis becomes distraught; she thinks about killing Julie. Bob proposes marriage to Julie and she eventually accepts, even though she does not love him, for he can provide her with social and financial security. Can their marriage be successful if Julie does not love Bob (and in fact is in love with another)?
>
> —Susan S. Bean, "Soap Operas: Sagas of American Kinship," *Anthropology for the Eighties*, ed. Johnnette B. Cole (New York: Free Press, 1982), p. 163.

Example:

If Bob hadn't fallen in love with Julie, maybe he wouldn't have left Phyllis.

1. ____
2. ____
3. ____

The following plot is from another soap opera, "Another World." Again, assume that this is real information and write three sentences using unreal conditions.

> Steven and Alice are married. They are blissfully happy for a while. They would like to have a family but Alice is unable to have children. Steven decides to be more of a father to his natural son, Jamie, with whom, until this time, he has had little contact. He arranges to contribute to Jamie's support and to spend time with him. Rachel, Jamie's mother, is delighted, seeing this as an opportunity to get closer to Steven through their child. Alice is jealous of Steven's relationship with his natural son. Rachel arranges for Alice to discover her alone with Steven in suspicious circumstances. Alice, sure that Steven is involved with Rachel, becomes distraught and disappears with no explanation. Rachel succeeds in her plot. After a time Steven decides to marry her, mainly so that he can be a real father to his son. Eventually Alice returns. Steven and Alice realize they still love each other. With great resistance from Rachel, Steven manages to get a divorce. Steven and Alice remarry. Disputes over the custody of Jamie begin. Jamie is torn between his love for his mother and his love for his father.
>
> —Susan S. Bean, "Soap Operas: Sagas of American Kinship," *Anthropology for the Eighties*, ed. Johnnette B. Cole (New York: Free Press, 1982), pp. 166–67.

1. ______________________________

2. ______________________________

3. ______________________________

____

Articles

In Chapters 4 and 8, we reviewed some of the uses of articles. Here we review two final uses of articles.

Some nouns can be both countable and noncountable, especially those that come from verbs. The noncount noun indicates the act or thing itself. No article is used with a noncount noun:

Many of us seek a lifetime of *pleasure*.

The count noun refers to the product or result of the action. In this case, the article *a* can be used with a count noun:

It is *a* pleasure to meet you.

EXERCISE 10-31

Fill in the article *a/an* if the noun is used in a countable sense.

1. Joyce hates ____________ authority.

2. Professor Remby is ____________ authority on the Middle East.
3. A parrot learns to speak through ____________ imitation.
4. That vase is ____________ imitation of an antique French vase.
5. ____________ life is often difficult.
6. John has ____________ difficult life.
7. "____________ possession is nine-tenths of the law."
8. He considers his violin ____________ valuable possession.
9. There is ____________ revolution in that country right now.
10. Sometimes ____________ revolution is necessary to change governments.

It is also possible to use noncountable abstract nouns that have adjective modifiers with the article ***a/an***. In these sentences, ***a/an*** usually means "a type of" or "a kind of." Note this example:

She had a *beauty* not often found in one so young.

Do not confuse this use of ***a*** with the use of ***the*** followed by an adjective modifier:

The beauty that he spoke of was not apparent to me.

EXERCISE 10-32

Fill in either *a/an* or *the* in the blanks as appropriate.

1. She enjoys ____________ atmosphere of gaity and friendliness.
2. ____________ atmosphere at the party was lively and free.
3. ____________ distrust he felt after his friend abandoned him was understandable.
4. He feels ____________ distrust of people that is inexplicable.
5. ____________ popularity of that new song is due to its subject matter.
6. That song has ____________ popularity that is hard to explain.
7. Generally, ____________ advice he gives is worth listening to.
8. He felt ____________ loneliness that almost overwhelmed him.
9. ____________ loneliness that she felt was overwhelming.

10. Professor Rankin has ____________ inexhaustible knowledge of that subject.

EXERCISE 10-33

Add the articles *a/an* and *the* wherever you think they belong in the following paragraphs. You may want to review the explanation of articles in Chapter 4, pages 152–54, and in Chapter 8, pages 298–99.

1. Researchers suspect it's not so much social conditioning as it is basic hormonal difference that makes women cry four times more often than men.

   Chemical breakdown of emotional tears reveals several substances, including hormone prolactin, that aren't contained in reflex tears, kind you shed when you cut onions or when bit of dust gets in your eye. And women have 60 percent more prolactin circulating in their blood than men do. Prolactin levels in young girls, on other hand, are same as those in boys. And, sure enough, girls don't cry any more than boys do.

   Higher level of prolactin in women may stimulate tear glands to secrete tears in much same way that it signals women's mammary glands to make milk. Another hormone may play just opposite role in men. Experiments with lab rats have shown that tear production is reduced when animals are given high levels of androgen—sex hormone that helps boys develop into men.

   Most people who shed emotional tears feel better afterward. One theory suggests that emotional tears remove harmful chemicals that build up in body during stress. If so, crying may be sign not of emotional weakness, but of good health. —Adapted from "House Calls," *Hippocrates,* Jan./Feb. 1989: p. 100.

2. Many arthritis sufferers swear they can sense approach of bad weather in their swollen joints. In 1960s, scientists invited dozen arthritic test subjects into climate chamber and found that, indeed, rising humidity and falling barometric pressure—conditions associated with storms—did cause their joints to ache.

   What causes pain? Some researchers speculate that another symptom of rheumatoid arthritis—increased cell permeability—may hold the key. Because blood vessel walls are more permeable in arthritis sufferers—and because blood is always under higher pressure than surrounding body tissues—more of blood's fluids are forced out into tissues of someone with arthritis. That movement would be greatest when pressure of surrounding environment is lowest, as it is just before storm. With joints already stiff, inflamed, and swollen, force of this added fluid may well trigger extra pain. —Adapted from "House Calls," *Hippocrates,* Jan./Feb. 1989: p. 100.

EXERCISE 10-34: WRITING ASSIGNMENT

Choose one of the following topics for a cause–effect essay. Be sure to think through the causes and effects carefully. Write a thesis sentence and an outline. Use transitions and specific detail in the essay.

1. Complete the essay you started in Exercise 10-24.
2. Choose another topic from Exercise 10-14, 10-18, 10-22, or 10-24.
3. Discuss the effects of watching television often.

Cause-and-Effect Analysis Essay Checklist

1. A cause-and-effect essay most often focuses on either the causes or the effects of some event or situation. Does your essay focus on either causes or effects?
2. If your essay focuses on causes, have you analyzed the causes sufficiently and in enough detail? If your essay focuses on effects, is your analysis insightful and sufficient? If your essay focuses on a causal chain, are the links in the chain clear?
3. Some common principles of organization for the cause-and-effect essay are order of familiarity, order of interest, and order of importance. Does your essay follow a logical pattern of organization?
4. The thesis statement for a cause-and-effect essay should contain the central idea of the essay. Does your essay have an effective and succinct thesis statement that expresses your central idea?
5. Does your essay have an interesting introduction?
6. Is your essay coherent?

Chapter 11

The Argumentative Essay

Readings: Problems, Issues, and Solutions

Although we cannot deny the magnitude and seriousness of the problems facing us today, as humans we have the understanding, the energy, and the will to solve them. Certainly, one aspect of solving both the world's and our own personal problems is to look at them carefully, analyze them, and evaluate all sides of complex issues before we draw conclusions.

The three essays that follow discuss contemporary problems or issues. In each one the author takes a clear stand on an issue and suggests or presents solutions. As you read the essays, try to answer these questions:

1. What is the problem or issue being discussed in the essay?
2. What is the writer's position on the problem or issue?
3. Does the writer support his or her point convincingly?
4. Do you agree with the writer? Explain.

READING 1

BILINGUALISM'S GOAL

BARBARA MUJICA

The United States is a country of immigrants, and so the relationship between a person's "old" and "new" culture is sometimes complex. The old melting pot theory has given way to a new concern for ethnic identity. This change has resulted in bilingual education programs, some of which do not have universal support. In the following essay, which

first appeared in the New York Times ***(1984), Barbara Mujica takes a stand on this issue.***

1 Mine is a Spanish-speaking household. We use Spanish exclusively. I have made an effort not only to encourage use of the language but also to familiarize my children with Hispanic culture. I use books from Latin America to teach them to read and write, and I try to maintain close contacts with Spanish-speaking relatives. Instilling in my children a sense of family and ethnic identity• is my role; it is not the role of the school system.

identity: feeling of belonging to a particular racial or cultural group

2 The public schools, supported by public funds, have the responsibility to teach skills needed in public life—among them the use of the English language. They also must inculcate• an appreciation of all the cultures that have contributed to this country's complex social weave. To set one ethnic group apart as more worthy of attention than others is unjust, and might breed resentment against that group.

inculcate: to impress upon the mind

3 I differ with educators who advocate bilingual education programs whose goal is to preserve the Spanish language and culture among children of Hispanic families. These professionals argue that in an English-speaking environment, Spanish-speaking children often feel alienated• and that this causes them to become withdrawn and hostile. To prevent

alienated: left out, apart

this reaction, they say, the home environment must be simulated• at school.

duplicated

4 Imagine how much more alienated these youngsters will feel, however, if they are kept in special bilingual programs separate from the general student body, semester after semester. How much more uncomfortable they will feel if they are maintained in ghettos• in the school. Youngsters feel a need to conform. They imitate each other in dress and in habit. To isolate Spanish-speaking children from their English-speaking peers may prove more psychologically damaging than hurling them into an English-speaking environment with no transition courses at all.

areas where people of one particular racial, social, or cultural group live

5 The purpose of bilingual education must be to teach English to non-English-speaking youngsters so that they will be able to function in regular classes.

6 The term "bilingual education" encompasses• a huge variety of programs ranging from total immersion• to special classes for foreigners to curricula that offer courses in mathematics and history in the child's native language. The most effective bilingual education programs have as their goal the gradual incorporation of non-English-speaking students into regular programs in which English is used.

takes in

the student's entire course of study

7 Not all children of Spanish-speaking parents need bilingual education. Many Spanish-speaking parents oppose the placement of their children in special programs; the wishes of these parents should be respected. Furthermore, very young children are able to learn a foreign language rapidly; bilingual programs for the nursery, kindergarten and early primary years should be kept to a minimum. Older children who have done part of their schooling in a foreign country often need to be eased into an English-speaking curriculum more gently. For them, it is helpful to offer certain subjects in their native tongues until they have learned English; otherwise, they may feel so lost and frustrated that they will drop out of school. High school dropouts have less chance than others of finding satisfying careers and are more likely to find themselves in trouble and unemployed.

8 Hispanics are now the fastest-growing minority• in the United States. According to the Population Reference Bureau, a private organization, Hispanics, counted at 14.6 million in the 1980 census, may well number 47 million by the year 2020. Yet, they are notoriously• underrepresented in the arts, sciences, professions and politics. Economically, as a group, they tend to lag behind non-Hispanics. According to March 1983 Federal figures, the median income for Hispanics is $16,227; for non-Hispanics, $23,907. Certainly, part of the remedy is educational programs that give young people the

a racial or cultural group smaller than the majority

well known

preparation and confidence necessary to pursue satisfying careers.

9 To get better jobs, young people must be fluent in English. Without English, they will be stuck in menial• positions. Without English, they will be unable to acquire advanced degrees. Without English, they will be unable to protest to the proper authorities if they are abused. Non-English-speaking individuals are vulnerable• to not only economic but also political exploitation.• Too often, politicians who speak their language claim unjustly to represent their interests.

unimportant, low-paying

subject to

to be used by someone for that person's gain

10 The primary goal of bilingual education must be the mainstreaming of non-English-speaking children through the teaching of English. But while the schools teach my children English, I will continue to teach them Spanish at home, because Spanish is part of their heritage. Ethnic identity, like religion, is a family matter.

EXERCISE 11-1: COMPREHENSION/ DISCUSSION QUESTIONS

1. What is the major issue discussed in this essay?
2. What is Mujica's position on the issue? In which sentence of paragraph 1 does the author take a stand?
3. What is Mujica's point in paragraph 2?
4. The author describes several types of bilingual education programs. Which type is mentioned in paragraph 3? According to some people, what are the benefits of this type of program?
5. What is Mujica's position on the type of program mentioned in paragraph 3? In which paragraph does she explain her position?
6. What type of bilingual program does Mujica favor? In which paragraphs is it discussed?
7. What is the author's main point in paragraph 7? How does it relate to the type of program described in paragraphs 5 and 6?
8. What is the point of paragraphs 8 and 9? How does it relate to the writer's overall argument?
9. Summarize Mujica's position on bilingual education and give her main support.
10. What is your position on this issue? Support your answer.
11. Have you ever been enrolled in a bilingual education program? If so, did you find it effective? Be prepared to describe your experience to the class.

READING 2

THE BOUNTY OF THE SEA

JACQUES COUSTEAU

In the following essay, Jacques Cousteau, the famous French oceanographer and researcher, makes clear his position on the conservation of the world's oceans. As you read the essay, take special note of the cause–effect chains that Cousteau uses to support his thesis.

1 During the past thirty years, I have observed and studied the oceans closely, and with my own two eyes I have seen them sicken. Certain reefs that teemed• with fish only ten years ago are now almost lifeless. The ocean bottom has been raped by trawlers.• Priceless wetlands have been destroyed by landfill. And everywhere are sticky globs of oil, plastic refuse, and unseen clouds of poisonous effluents.• Often, when I describe the symptoms of the oceans' sickness, I hear remarks like "they're only fish" or "they're only whales" or "they're only birds." But I assure you that our destinies• are linked with theirs in the most profound and fundamental manner. For if the oceans should die—by which I mean that all life in the sea would finally cease—this would signal the end not only for marine life but for all other animals and plants of this earth, including man.

full of

fishing boats

waste materials, discharges from sewers and factories

future, fate

2 With life departed, the ocean would become, in effect, one enormous cesspool.• Billions of decaying bodies, large and small, would create such an insupportable stench• that man would be forced to leave all the coastal regions. But far worse would follow.

tank or hole for sewage

smell, stink

3 The ocean acts as the earth's buffer.• It maintains a fine balance between the many salts and gases which make life possible. But dead seas would have no buffering effect. The carbon dioxide content of the atmosphere would start on a steady and remorseless• climb, and when it reached a certain level a "greenhouse effect" would be created. The heat that normally radiates outward from the earth to space would be blocked by the CO_2, and sea level temperatures would dramatically increase.

go-between, stabilizer

without pity

4 One catastrophic effect of this heat would be melting of the icecaps at both the North and the South Poles. As a result, the ocean would rise by 100 feet or more, enough to flood almost all the world's major cities. These rising waters would drive one-third of the earth's billions inland, creating famine, fighting, chaos, and disease on a scale almost impossible to imagine.

5 Meanwhile, the surface of the ocean would have

scummed over with a thick film of decayed matter, and would no longer be able to give water freely to the skies through evaporation. Rain would become a rarity, creating global drought and even more famine.

6 But the final act is yet to come. The wretched remnant• *remains, last ones*

of the human race would now be packed cheek by jowl• on the remaining highlands, bewildered, starving, struggling to survive from hour to hour. Then would be visited upon them the final plague, anoxia (lack of oxygen). This would be caused by the extinction of plankton algae• and the reduction of land vegetation, the two sources that supply the oxygen you are now breathing.

very closely

microscopic plant life that floats on ocean waters

7 And so man would finally die, slowly gasping out his life on some barren hill. He would have survived the oceans by perhaps thirty years. And his heirs[1] would be bacteria and a few scavenger[2] insects.

EXERCISE 11-2: COMPREHENSION/ DISCUSSION QUESTIONS

1. What is Cousteau's thesis? Where in the essay is it stated?
2. Where does Cousteau give his credentials for writing about this topic? Is he an authority on the topic? Do his credentials help to make his argument convincing?
3. What is the "greenhouse effect"?
4. How does Cousteau support his main idea?
5. Cousteau develops his essay in two cause–effect chains. The first chain is explained in paragraphs 2–4. Explain the cause–effect chain presented here. The second chain is given in paragraphs 5–6. Explain it.
6. Does Cousteau support his thesis convincingly?
7. Cousteau does not give specific conservation measures that should be undertaken to preserve the oceans. What are some solutions to the problems he presents? Are any of these being done today? Can or should individuals do anything regarding marine conservation?
8. Do you think marine conservation is a serious problem? Why, or why not?

[1]*those who inherit his property and belongings*
[2]*animals that eat decaying matter or garbage*

READING 3

THERE'S NO WAY TO GO BUT AHEAD

ISAAC ASIMOV

Isaac Asimov, a noted essayist and science fiction writer, discusses the problems of growing industrialization and technology. But unlike those who find them responsible for many of the world's problems, the author tells why he sees them as part of the solution.

1 We are all now aware that some new scientific or technological advance, though useful, may have unpleasant side effects. More and more, the tendency is to exert caution before committing the world to something that may not be reversible.•

reversible: return to earlier way

2 The trouble is, it's not always easy to tell what the side effects will be. In 1846, Ascanio Sobrero produced the first nitroglycerine. Heated, a drop of it exploded shatteringly. The Italian chemist realized in horror its possible application to warfare and stopped his research at once. It didn't help, of course. Others followed up, and it and other high explosives were indeed being used in warfare by the close of the 19th century.

3 Did that make high explosives entirely bad? In 1867, Alfred Nobel learned how to mix nitroglycerine with diatomaceous earth to produce a safer-to-handle mixture he called "dynamite." With dynamite, earth could be moved at a rate far beyond that of pick and shovel and without brutalizing• men by hard labor. It was dynamite that helped forge the way for railroads, that helped build dams, subways, foundations, bridges, and a thousand other grand-scale constructions of the industrial age.

brutalizing: to be cruel, savage

4 A double-edged sword[1] of good and evil has hung over human technology from the beginning. The invention of knives and spears increased man's food supply—and improved the art of murder. The discovery of nuclear energy now places all the earth under threat of destruction—yet it also offers the possibility of fusion power as an ultimate solution to man's energy problems.

5 Or think back to the first successful vaccination in 1796 and the germ theory of disease in the 1860s. Do we view medical advance as dangerous to humanity, or refuse to take advantage of vaccines and antitoxins, of anesthesia and asepsis, of chemical specifics and antibiotics? And yet the side

[1]**double-edged sword** *sword having two sides*

effects of the last century's medical discoveries have done more to assure civilization's destruction than anything nuclear physicists have done. For the population explosion today is caused not by any rise in average birth rate but by the precipitous• drop—thanks to medicine—in the death rate.

sharp

6 Does that mean science should have avoided improving man's lot through medicine and kept mankind a short-lived race? Or does it mean we should use science to correct the possibly deleterious• side effect, devise methods that would make it simpler to reduce the birth rate and keep it matching the falling death rate? The latter, obviously!

harmful, causing injury

7 Science and technology are getting a bad press• these days. Increasingly scornful of the materialism of our culture, young people speak about returning to a simpler, pre-industrial, pre-scientific day. They fail to realize that the "good old days" were really the horribly bad old days of ignorance, disease, slavery and death. They fancy themselves in Athens, talking to Socrates, listening to the latest play by Sophocles—never as a slave brutalized in the Athenian silver mines. They imagine themselves as medieval[2] knights[3] on armored chargers•—never as starving peasants.

bad publicity, spoken ill of

horses covered with metal armor

8 Yet, right down to modern times, the wealth and prosperity of a relative few have been built on the animal-like labor and wretched existence of many—peasants, serfs and slaves. What's more, nothing could be done about it. Slavery and peonage were taken for granted. Not until science became prominent• did slavery come to be recognized as a dreadful wrong, to be abolished.• It was the scientist, supposedly cold and concerned with things rather than ideals, who brought this about. His investigations made possible the harnessing of the energy of the inanimate• world. With steam, electricity and radio beams to do our work for us, there was less need for the comparatively weak and fumbling human muscle—and slavery began to vanish.

important

done away with

not living

9 It is also a fact that, before modern technology, the full flower of art and human intellect was reserved for the few. It was the technical advances of printing that scattered books widely, made universal literacy practical. It was the movies, radio, the record player and television that brought many of the marvels of mankind (along with much of the refuse•) to even the poorest.

garbage

10 Yes, science has helped create problems, too—serious ones. And we must labor to solve them—in the only way history tells us problems have been solved: by science. If we were to turn away now, if a noble young generation abandoned• the mainstream of an industry, what would hap-

left behind

[2]*period of European history, 500–1500 A.D.*
[3]*noblemen bound to do good deeds*

pen? Without the machinery of that industry, we would inevitably drift back to slavery.

11 In these days of urban decay and energy crisis, there is a constant longing to return to the land and flee back to a simpler way of life. But it can't be done. We have a tiger by the tail[4] and we can't go home again.[5] We never could.

12 When mankind learned how to make use of fire some 50,000 years ago, it meant protection against predators, and more and better food. It also meant that man could venture out of the tropics into colder climates. Do you suppose this didn't bring problems? When the fire went out in the cave on a winter night and could not be relighted, there was the danger of freezing. Or the smoke would ruin one's lungs.

13 Why not give up fire, then, go back to the tropics and the simpler, carefree ways? Ah, one could not. Extending his range, man had increased his numbers. Returnees would find the tropics full, and there would be a catastrophic struggle for the smaller supply of food. So, having once learned to use fire, people either endured its discomforts—or did away with them by further technological advance. They learned better ways of making fire, heating dwelling places, handling smoke.

14 No fundamental technological advance has ever been given up willingly by any society. There has been no way to do it.

15 About 8000 B.C., mankind invented agriculture. Again it made possible an increase in numbers. People had never eaten so well, but it meant they had to give up the free, nomadic life and remain bound to the soil. It meant hard labor. It meant banding together to fight off surrounding tribes who, still food gathering, might help themselves to your crops. It also meant the risk of crop failures.

16 Where irrigation was introduced to make harvest more dependable, it meant the formation of a large political unit, the social tyranny[6] of a king, an aristocracy,[7] a priesthood.[8] And, even if the land grew prosperous and populous, any infectious• disease that got started ran through the crowded population like wildfire.

passed from one person to another

17 Why not, then, go back to the wilder, freer ways of hunting and food gathering? Wouldn't that mean less work and worry, less war, less pestilence?

18 But you can't! Abandon agriculture and, out of every 10,000 people, only 100 survive. No, the problems to which agriculture gave rise could be solved only by moving forward

[4]**tiger by the tail** *in charge of a powerful force*
[5]**can't go home again** *can't return to a simpler life*
[6]*oppressive, unjust government*
[7]*noble, high-born class*
[8]*religious class*

with additional advances in technology—the use of oxen in place of men, horses in place of oxen, crop rotation, fertilizer, etc.

19 So it is now with our industrial age, which has once again increased man's numbers and his range—and brought new problems. If there is a shortage of gasoline, can't we in a pinch abandon our automobiles and go back to horse-and-wagon? Give up our oil furnace for the fireplace? Give up electric lights and use candles?

20 No, we can't. There are no longer enough horses to move us about, or enough wood to warm us, or enough candles to light our way. Besides, if we try it for long, we will quickly find that the simple life just won't do.

21 In 1800, when the earth was still supported almost entirely by nonindustrial methods, the population of the planet was 900 million. Now it is pushing four billion. Where does the food come from to support the extra three billion? It comes from the industrialization of the farm: from the use of high-energy machinery to plow and seed the weed and reap. It comes from fertilizers and insecticides produced by sophisticated• high-energy chemical factories. *complex*

22 We can't abandon industrialization, if only because our food supply depends on it. You can talk about "natural" food all you want, but if everyone decided to grow food without chemical fertilizers or insecticides or machinery, it would mean that only one quarter of the world population could be fed.

23 Can we abandon some of our industrial technology and hold onto the rest? That would be very difficult, since it all hangs together.• *is interrelated*

24 We can save, conserve, cut out waste, but what we have we must keep. The only solution, as always in the history of mankind, is to solve problems by still further advances in technology.

EXERCISE 11-3: COMPREHENSION/ DISCUSSION QUESTIONS

1. What is the main point of the first six paragraphs?
2. What are the four examples Asimov uses in the first six paragraphs to prove his main point?
3. What does Asimov think of the idea of returning to a simpler life? What would happen? Why?
4. What was life like before technology? How did technology change things?
5. How was science responsible for the abolition of slavery?

6. What point is Asimov making in his discussion of the invention of fire? The invention of agriculture?
7. How does the discussion of the invention of fire and agriculture help to prove Asimov's main point?
8. Do you agree with Asimov's main point? Explain.
9. Does the essay have a stated thesis sentence? If so, what is it? If not, what is the main point of the essay?
10. How does Asimov support and develop his argument? Does he use any of the modes of development studied earlier (cause–effect, comparison–contrast, and so forth)?
11. Is the author's support effective? Are you convinced? Could he have used any other kinds of support that would have been as effective or more effective?
12. Can you find any weak points in his argument? How would you argue against Asimov?

EXERCISE 11-4: VOCABULARY DEVELOPMENT

The following words are used in the Asimov essay.

Part A
Fill in the blanks with the best word from the list.

brutalizing	horrified	reversible
cautioned	forge	precipitously
deleterious	wretched	fundamental
sophisticated		

1. We were ____________ against moving too fast on the icy streets.
2. This jacket is ____________. It can be worn with either side out.
3. One of the ____________ beliefs of science is observation of natural phenomena.
4. We were ____________ when we saw the destruction that the fire had caused.
5. We need to ____________ ahead if we are going to finish our work today.
6. The cliffs rise ____________ from the valley floor.
7. The poor, ____________ peasants sat huddled together in front of the fire.
8. She is a world traveler, having rich, influential, ____________ friends.

Part B
Fill in the blanks with the best word from the list.

prominent	inanimate	refuse
predators	flee	catastrophic
aristocracy	tyranny	pestilence

1. Kings, queens, and nobles formed the ____________ in European countries in the eighteenth and nineteenth centuries.
2. The effects of the earthquake were ____________ to the poor mountain villages in Italy.
3. He threw the ____________ into the garbage can.
4. She is a ____________ physician and scientist; everyone knows her reputation.
5. During the Middle Ages, ____________ and disease were common among the poor.
6. Because of the ____________ of the aristocracy, many countries abolished monarchy and set up republics.
7. Cats are ____________ of mice.
8. Many people had to ____________ their homes when the country was overrun with guerillas.

Writing

Thus far you have been writing essays that are primarily expository, in which the main purpose is to explain or analyze. You have found, too, that narration and description can aid in this kind of writing as support. In this chapter, we focus on another type of essay, one that has a somewhat different purpose: to convince or persuade. This is the *argumentative essay*.

An argument ensues when two parties disagree about something. One party gives an opinion and offers reasons in support of it and the other party gives a different opinion and offers reasons in support of its stand. However, people can disagree about many things that cannot be argued effectively. For example, two people might argue that one flavor of ice cream tastes better than another, but there is no way that either party could convince the other party to change his or her *preference*. It could, however, be argued that one flavor seems to be more popular; in this case, facts about sales could be cited. Two people might also disagree about the existence of God, but again, it is unlikely that one person could convince the other person to change his or her belief, for religious belief is based on *faith*, not on logic or verifiable facts. Moreover, two people might disagree about who won the national soccer match in 1990, but if they do some research, the argument would be settled using a *fact*. Therefore, arguments of preference, belief or faith, and fact are not the type of arguments one can effectively and logically deal with in the formal argumentative essay.

The kind of argument that can be argued logically is one based on an opinion that can be supported by evidence such as facts. For example, when the Three Mile Island nuclear power plant broke down in 1979, debate ensued concerning the whole issue of nuclear power. Those in favor of continuing the construction of nuclear power plants argued against those who wanted to ban further construction of the plants. The issue was whether or not the United States should ban further construction. The proponents (those in favor of the issue—banning further construction) said yes and gave their reasons; the opponents (those against banning construction) said no and gave their reasons. There were definitely two sides to that issue, but more importantly, it was an issue that was arguable: It was *not* an argument of belief or faith, preference, or fact.

The Argumentative Thesis: Taking a Stand

Most writing, of course, is improved by having a persuasive edge to the thesis, but for analysis and exposition, that "edge" need not always be sharp. For example, a thesis such as "My first experiences with Americans were traumatic" has a central idea—*traumatic*—but it is not really strongly persuasive, and it is certainly not argumentative. An argumentative essay, however, is one that attempts to *change* the reader's mind, to convince the reader to agree with the point of view or opinion of the writer. Therefore, the argumentative essay attempts to be highly persuasive and logical.

What is the difference, then, between a thesis with a strong central idea and an argumentative thesis? To begin with, the argumentative thesis takes a side of an issue; frequently, too, it proposes a course of action (often expressed, by the way, with the modal *should*). In the argument concerning the Three Mile Island nuclear power plant, the thesis for a paper on this topic might be, "The United States should ban further construction of nuclear power plants." Of course, someone else might argue, "The United States should continue building nuclear power plants."

EXERCISE 11-5

Study the following thesis statements. Put an "A" in the blank if the statement is argumentative. Be careful! A statement having *should* as part of the verb is not automatically argumentative.

1. ______________ The earthquake in Soviet Armenia was one of the most devastating in history.
2. ______________ Prospective parents should be required to get licenses in order to have children.
3. ______________ The building codes in Las Vegas, Nevada, are inadequate.
4. ______________ Most of the Americans I have met are quite hospitable.

5. ____________ Students should have a say in the hiring and firing of teachers.
6. ____________ Pornographic books ought to be banned from the library.
7. ____________ State University should not have a football team.
8. ____________ There are many complex reasons for the failure of the police to respond quickly to alarms.
9. ____________ The citizens of this state should be allowed to carry guns.
10. ____________ The U.S. government ought to allow more immigrants into this country.

The Opposition: Knowing What You Are Up Against

When you write an argumentative paper, more so than with expository or analytical essays, you must be acutely aware of your audience—the reader. Remember, the purpose of an argumentative essay is to convince the reader that your position is the better one. To begin with, assume that the reader disagrees with you. After all, if he or she did not, there would be no cause to argue. Next, remember that although the reader disagrees with you, that does not mean he or she is any less intelligent than you. Therefore, avoid attacking the reader with such statements as, "Anyone who believes we should ban nuclear power plants must be ignorant or out of touch with reality." Indeed, address your reader by writing objectively, logically, and respectfully.

The most important thing to consider about the members of your audience is why they hold their opinion. What reasons do you think they might use to support their opinion? Trying to identify and understand your opponent's point of view is important; if you do not understand your opponent's reasons and you just argue your own reasons, you are not likely to convince the reader at all. For example, let us say that you felt we should continue building nuclear power plants and you give the following reasons:

1. They produce energy at a relatively low cost.
2. They provide renewable sources of energy.
3. They reduce our dependence on foreign sources of energy.
4. They provide immediate jobs.

Your reasons might be very good ones, but these points are probably not the points on which your opposition bases its argument; in fact, your opponents will probably agree with you on these points! At the heart of your opponents' argument is the issue of safety. If you do not address that issue and convince your opponents that nuclear power plants are safe, then you cannot expect to convince them that we should build more nuclear power plants. Once you have argued to the points the opposition holds, then you can further support your case by adding the other reasons mentioned earlier.

EXERCISE 11-6

Read the following thesis statements and think of the reasons in support of the thesis ("pros") and the reasons against ("cons") it. Supply two reasons on both sides. Then circle the letter of the reason that you think is the crucial one—the one at the heart of the issue. The first one is done for you.

1. Marijuana smoking should be legalized.

PRO	CON
a. It is a harmless, enjoyable relaxer.	a. It is dangerous to health.
(b.) The government should not have the right to tell us what we can or cannot consume.	b. The government should not allow harmful drugs to circulate without control.

2. A basic core curriculum of liberal arts courses should be required for all students graduating from college.

a. ____________________	a. ____________________
b. ____________________	b. ____________________

3. Governments of Third World countries should dictate to their young people what majors in college the young people should have.

a. ____________________	a. ____________________
b. ____________________	b. ____________________

4. When a U.S. industry is in financial trouble, the government should restrict competitive foreign imports of that industry.

a. ____________________	a. ____________________
b. ____________________	b. ____________________

5. The United States should not restrict immigration or have immigration quotas.

   a. ______________________ a. ______________________

   ______________________ ______________________

   b. ______________________ b. ______________________

   ______________________ ______________________

Arguing Your Case: The Logic Behind Your Reasons

It is necessary to know why your opponent holds his or her opinion so that you can deal with those reasons; in other words, so you can "prove" that you are right and the opponent is wrong. But how can you convince someone who disagrees with you? First, you need to understand what points need to be argued; that is, you must be sure that you understand the "heart" of the issue. As you saw in the last section, this step comes by thinking of both sides of the issue and determining what the most important points are. If you know your stand on the issue and you know what point or points you have to prove, then you are well on your way toward constructing a logical argument.

All formal arguments are based on logic. There are two kinds of formal logical reasoning: *inductive* and *deductive*. *Induction* refers to the process of examining particular details and arriving at a conclusion based on that evidence. Let us say that you were an investigative newspaper reporter and you were asked to look into the causes of a famous hotel fire. After some research, you learned that the fire was due to faulty electrical wiring and you found out that Eee-Zee Wire Company had installed the wiring. Curious, you decided to do some investigation of Eee-Zee Wire Company. After further research, you discovered that 60 percent of the buildings that were wired by Eee-Zee Wire Company caught fire within two years, and of those fires, 85 percent were due to faulty electrical wiring. From this data, then, you could reasonably conclude:

Buildings wired by Eee-Zee Wire company are likely to have faulty wiring.

Note that you cannot reasonably conclude that all buildings wired by this company have faulty wiring, because your evidence does not support that conclusion: *all*. This inductive process is really what you have been doing throughout this textbook. Whenever you formulate a generalization, you do so after examining evidence—whether consciously or unconsciously.

Deduction, on the other hand, refers to the process of arriving at a conclusion about a particular case based on a generalization. In other words, in deduction you begin with a generalization and apply it to a specific case. Take the case of Eee-Zee Wire Company. As you continue your investigation, you discover that the elegant Statler Hotel was wired by Eee-Zee Wire Company. Having already concluded that "Buildings wired by Eee-Zee Wire Company are likely to have faulty wiring," you could logically conclude:

The Statler Hotel probably has faulty wiring.

The logic of deductive arguments can be checked by breaking the argument down into its *syllogism*. The initial generalization is called the *major premise*, the specific case the *minor premise*, and the resultant statement *the conclusion*.

Major Premise:

Buildings wired by Eee-Zee Wire Company are likely to have faulty wiring.

Minor Premise:

The Statler Hotel is a building that was wired by Eee-Zee Wire Company.

Conclusion:

The Statler Hotel is likely to have faulty wiring.

Although induction is sometimes used as a way to organize essays, it is more often considered a thought process; the evidence one accumulates in the inductive process can often be used in the deductive argument as support. Deduction, on the other hand, is more commonly used to argue a side of an issue.

How does the syllogism apply in an argumentative essay? The syllogism is really the superstructure behind the reasons. When you plan an argumentative essay, it is often a good idea to begin the argument at a point where you and your opponent both agree. (This point of agreement, by the way, can be arrived at inductively.) For example, suppose you wanted to argue that Eee-Zee Wire Company should have its business license taken away. Why? Because they do not install safe wiring. Whether you realize it or not, your major premise here is that only electrical companies that install safe wiring should have licenses. Sometimes the major premise is obvious, but it often should be stated. Here is the argument in a syllogism:

Major Premise:

Only electrical companies that install safe wiring should have licenses.

Minor Premise:

Eee-Zee Wire Company does not install safe wiring.

Conclusion:

Eee-Zee Wire Company should not have a license.

The major premise, then, is a generalization that you and your reader can both agree on, whether it is a generally accepted statement or whether you had already proved it earlier in the argument. The minor premise, then, becomes the part that needs to be proved in your argument.

Sometimes the issue is more complex and requires more than one premise to be proved. Take the case of nuclear power plant construction. Let us say that you want to argue in favor of constructing nuclear power plants. You know that your opponent's most formidable point is the safety issue, so you will have to argue to that point. You can begin with the major premise:

Only safe sources of energy should be developed.

This is a reasonable assumption. You can expect most people to agree with that. Now you have to prove:

Nuclear power plants are safe sources of energy.

This minor premise is what you have to prove. If you do so effectively, your conclusion is logical:

Therefore, nuclear power plants should be constructed.

Let us suppose that you want to add reasons to support your side of the issue further now that you have dealt with your opponent's most formidable point. Each time that you assert another reason, consider it as another minor premise. Note that you want to come to the same conclusion: "Nuclear power plants should be constructed." Look at this example:

> Another reason we should construct nuclear power plants is that they provide renewable sources of energy.

We can break down this reason into another syllogism:

Major Premise:

All safe, renewable sources of energy should be developed.

Minor Premise:

Nuclear power plants are a safe source of renewable energy.

Conclusion:

Nuclear power plants should be constructed.

Note that in the major premise here, *safe* is included, since that point was established in the previous section. And if you wanted to add still another reason, you could build on the previous arguments:

> And finally, we should consider the expense. Not only are nuclear power plants safe, renewable sources of energy, they are relatively inexpensive sources of energy.

Major Premise:

All safe, renewable, inexpensive sources of energy should be developed.

Minor Premise:

Nuclear power plants are safe, renewable, and inexpensive sources of energy.

Conclusion:

Nuclear power plants should be constructed.

Since *safe* and *renewable* were proved previously, your task in this section would be to prove *inexpensive*.

EXERCISE 11-7

Study the following statements and construct syllogisms from them. The first one is done for you.

1. One reason that we should not construct nuclear power plants is that they are in fact not inexpensive.

Major Premise:

Only inexpensive sources of energy should be developed.

Minor Premise:

Nuclear power plants are not inexpensive sources of energy.

Conclusion:

Nuclear power plants should not be constructed.

2. Another reason that we should not construct nuclear power plants is that they are unsafe.

Major Premise: ______________________________

Minor Premise: ______________________________

Conclusion: ______________________________

3. We should increase taxes because the additional revenue will allow more police officers.

Major Premise: ______________________________

Minor Premise: ______________________________

Conclusion: ______________________________

4. A reduction in taxes would stimulate investments.

Major Premise: ______________________________

Minor Premise: ______________________________

Conclusion: ______________________________

5. If you reduce taxes by 33 percent, vital city services would suffer.

Major Premise: ______________________________

Minor Premise: ______________________________

Conclusion: ______________________________

6. We should hold the convention in Merchantville because it has a huge modern convention center.

Major Premise: ______________________________

Minor Premise: ______________________________

Conclusion: ______________________________

7. Vote for Mr. Ballou because he is honest.

Major Premise: ______________________________

Minor Premise: ______________________________

Conclusion: ______________________________

EXERCISE 11-8

Now take the reasons that you stated in Exercise 11-6 and turn them into syllogisms.

There are, of course, ways that the deductive reasoning process can break down. To avoid being illogical, keep the following points in mind.

1. *The major premise and the minor premise must be true if the conclusion is to be valid.* As indicated earlier, you can begin your argument at a point where you and your audience both agree. This point can be a generally accepted truth, or a point that you proved earlier in your argument. There are certain things that you can assume most of your readers agree on, and your duty is to make sure that your major premise is

agreeable. When arguing to someone of a different culture, making assumptions for your major premises can be difficult. For example, earlier we cited the premise: "Only safe sources of energy should be developed." This premise, of course, was based on an assumption: that we do not want dangerous sources of energy. What you assume depends on your audience. Let us consider this argument:

Major Premise:

All people like to suffer.

Minor Premise:

Johnny is a person.

Conclusion:

Johnny likes to suffer.

The major premise here is based on an assumption that is not necessarily one that most people would agree with. Therefore, before the argument could continue, the writer would have to prove that "all people like to suffer."

In short, whenever you make a statement such as, "I think we can all agree that . . . ," you had better be certain that we can *all* agree on that point! A good way to check your assumption is to ask someone of a different culture or opinion.

In addition to unacceptable or faulty premises, an argument can go wrong when the information in the premises is untrue. For example, if you argue that buildings that have a certain kind of wiring are bad and that the ABC Building has that kind of wiring, if that building does not indeed have that kind of wiring, your conclusion "The ABC Building is bad" would be invalid.

2. *The major and minor premises must be set up to follow the correct logical structure.* There can be two true statements in the premises, but if they are not set up properly in the argument form, the conclusion will not follow logically (even though coincidentally it may be true, too). The correct structure of the syllogism is as follows:

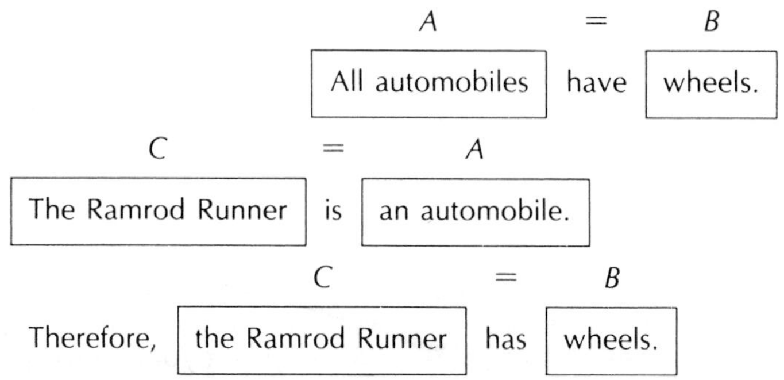

Symbolically, this syllogism is as follows:

$$A = B$$
$$C = A$$
$$\therefore C = B$$

A faulty version of this argument is as follows:

All automobiles have wheels.		All $A = B$
The Ramrod Runner has wheels.	=	$C = B$
Therefore, the Ramrod Runner is an automobile.		$\therefore C = A$

This is illogical, though the conclusion is perhaps coincidentally true. In fact, the Ramrod Runner may be a motorcycle or a wagon.

3. *The terms in one premise must be used the same way in the other premise.* Note the following ways this problem can occur:

a. Some vegetarians eat eggs.
John is a vegetarian.
∴ John eats eggs.

In this syllogism, the major premise introduces the class "some vegetarians," but in the minor premise "a vegetarian" is not the same as "some vegetarians." John may, indeed, not eat eggs at all. For this syllogism to be logical, the major premise would have to say, "All vegetarians eat eggs."

b. All citizens have rights.
John is a citizen.
∴ John is right.

In this syllogism, *right* is used in two ways; in addition, there has been a shift from *have* to *is* in the conclusion.

EXERCISE 11-9

Study the following syllogisms. If the syllogism is logical and the conclusion valid, write *logical* in the blank. If not, write *illogical* and explain why.

1. ____________ The sun is bright.
Mary is bright.
Mary is the sun.

____

2. ____________ People who cheat are fair.
Sally cheats.
Sally is fair.

____

3. ____________ All football players are strong.
Bill is strong.
Bill is a football player.

---

4. ____________ All Americans speak English.
George is a South American.
George speaks English.

---

5. ____________ All mammals are warmblooded.
Cats are mammals.
Cats are warmblooded.

---

6. ____________ All cars use gasoline.
The Electrocar uses a battery.
The Electrocar is not a car.

---

7. ____________ Some teachers are tall.
Cindy is a teacher.
Cindy is tall.

---

8. ____________ All astronauts have been men.
John is a man.
John must have been an astronaut.

---

9. ____________ Peace is good for man.
Jill is not a man.
Peace is not good for Jill.

---

10. ____________ All people who are taking History 101 are students.
Steve is taking History 101.
Steve is a student.

EXERCISE 11-10

Now take the syllogisms that you wrote for Exercise 11-8 and determine if they are logically reasoned.

There are a variety of other ways to break down the logic of inductive and deductive reasoning. See Appendix XIII (pages 487–89) for additional examples.

Explaining and Supporting the Reasons

There is no one particular pattern of organization for an argumentative paragraph. Since the purpose is to convince or persuade, you can use whatever type of organization and support that is suggested by the reason you give. For instance, if you believe that there should be stricter controls over the dumping of chemical wastes and one of the reasons you give is the pollution that irresponsible dumping has caused, you could discuss the effects of dumping; in addition, you could give examples of dumping grounds that have polluted the environment. You might even explain the process of pollution—that is, how dumping pollutes.

No matter what underlying pattern of development you use, at all times you must be certain to show the progression of your logic from the major premise to the conclusion. Just as it is necessary to explain an example to show its relevance to the generalization, it is necessary to explain the reason to show how it supports the thesis. Look at how a paragraph supporting the thesis "Universities should continue to give football scholarships" is developed:

> Giving football scholarships is really just a wise investment on the part of the university. What the university really needs and wants is money in the form of football ticket sales, contributions, and endowments from alumni, and allotments and grants from the state legislature. By giving football scholarships, many smaller, struggling universities, Notre Dame for example, can attract talented, sought-after football players. These players build a winning football team and the university builds a reputation. The university's football games may be on television and the team may be asked to play in a bowl game. With this publicity, fans and alumni are eager to attend the games, thus boosting ticket sales. Rich alumni, who are proud of their school, give endowments and grants. And for state schools, members of Congress and representatives at the state Capitol are pleased with the publicity the school, and thus the state, receives. As a result, the state's coffers are a little more open and the money flows, enabling the university to pay its faculty, build new buildings, and maintain the quality of its teaching. Yes, the football scholarship is a small investment from which the university hopes to reap big gains.

EXERCISE 11-11

On a separate sheet of paper, answer the following questions about the preceding paragraph.

1. What is the topic sentence for the paragraph? Where is it located?
2. What is the reason the author gives for universities spending funds on football scholarships?

3. What underlying pattern of development does the author use to support his or her reason — examples, cause, effect?
4. Do you think the writer could improve this paragraph by giving some details?
5. Outline the logic of this writer in a deductive syllogism.

Undoubtedly, the paragraph about football scholarships could be improved with the use of details and examples. The author could, for instance, give some dollar amounts of revenue that certain schools earn from football. However, the author does develop his or her reason logically and clearly.

At all times, however, you should strive to use details and examples as support. Your best support is *facts*. Facts include data that have been objectively proved and are generally accepted, such as historical facts, scientific data, statistics, and so forth. Obtaining facts may require some research, but their strength as support is well worth it.

Special Note

Avoid using as "facts" statements from religious books such as the Bible or the Koran. Although those whose faith is based on either of these (or other) books regard them as containing the truth, using them as support would be ineffective in an argumentative paper, since your reader, who may have a different religious belief, may not accept your data as fact; he or she may not accept the premise on which it is based. For example, if you said we should not build nuclear power plants because the deity forbids it, you would have a difficult time persuading a nonbeliever. Or, if you said that we should continue building the plants because if God did not want us to He would not have made us capable of building them, you again would have an even more difficult time persuading your possibly atheist reader. Moreover, even if your reader did have the same religious belief, there is no guarantee he or she would accept that premise. Remember: Assume that your reader disagrees with you!

Note how factual details assist in this argumentative paragraph. Here this writer is arguing that the use of pesticides should be restricted and controlled.

One of the reasons the use of pesticides in farming should be severely restricted and controlled is that pesticides kill "good" and "bad" insects indiscriminately. You may think the more dead insects the better, but some insects are actually beneficial to farmers. By spraying their fields with toxic pesticides, they destroy the good with the bad. One example of a good insect is the ladybug. The ladybug actually eats insects such as aphids and scale that do damage to plants. In fact, some farmers are beginning to use ladybugs instead of the dangerous pesticides for insect control. Another example of a useful insect is the honeybee. In the United States, nearly 100 crops with a farm value of $1 billion annually depend on the honeybee for pollination. Another $3 billion worth of crops benefit from bee pollination because of higher and better-quality yields. However, honey bees gather poison as they forage for pollen. As a result, they are steadily being exterminated by the very people they are helping. Today there are 20 percent fewer honeybee colonies in the United States than there were ten years ago. And scientists predict that their population will continue to decline. You might argue that farmers can get along with smaller yields. However, the world's population is continuing to increase and higher food production is becoming a global priority. Farmers agree that honeybees are the most efficient way to pollinate their crops. Yet with their use of pesticides, they are surely eliminating their best friends. If we are to have enough food in the future, we should protect our friends the honey bees by controlling dangerous pesticides.*

EXERCISE 11-12

On a separate sheet of paper, answer the following questions about the preceding paragraph.

1. What is the author's main reason for restricting the use of pesticides?
2. What major premise is this reason based on?
3. What kind of support is given for this reason?

A less effective, though sometimes acceptable, type of support includes examples drawn from personal experience (yours or someone else's). It is fine to use examples, especially if the topic is rather narrow and concerns something you are close to, but the danger is in drawing hasty generalizations from too few examples. Always remember that examples should be typical, selected from a sufficient number of examples to prove the case. (See Chapters 4 and 6.) For instance, you can argue that a street light should be put in on a street because that intersection is dangerous; as your support, you can give eyewitness accounts of accidents and near accidents, and you can discuss how difficult it is for pedestrians to cross that street because of the heavy traffic.

* Information from Joseph M. Winski, "Bees and Ecology," *The Writer's World*, ed. George Arms et al. (New York: St. Martin's, 1978), pp. 361–62.

EXERCISE 11-13

Study the following sentences, which give reasons. For each one, decide what kind of development you would use to explain the reason. For example, would you explain with the use of examples and/or factual detail? Would you explain a process? Would you discuss causes or effects? Would you compare and contrast?

1. One reason that we should legalize marijuana is that we could benefit from taxation on its sale.

   ____

2. One reason we should not legalize marijuana is that it is a dangerous drug.

   ____

3. We should not build nuclear power plants because of the potentially devastating effects they could have if they break down.

   ____

4. Requiring parents to get licenses in order to have children would help reduce child abuse.

   ____

5. One of the advantages of having a football team is that it boosts student morale.

   ____

6. One major problem with this type of power plant is that it can break down easily.

   ____

7. We should not allow a bar in our neighborhood because it will destroy the historic beauty of the area.

   ____

8. One reason we should not build the Number One missile is that it is too expensive.

   ____

9. One reason we should build the Number One missile is that it can defend us against our enemy's Number Two missile.

   ____

10. An important reason that we should increases taxes is that our parks department will fold without more revenue.

    ____

EXERCISE 11-14: WRITING ASSIGNMENT

Using one of the reasons from Exercises 11-6 or 11-13, write a paragraph explaining and supporting that reason.

Planning the Argumentative Essay

As you plan an argumentative essay, keep in mind that it should contain the following characteristics.

1. *The argumentative essay should introduce and explain the issue or case.* This point is obvious; clearly the reader needs to understand the issue being argued. In addition, it is often necessary to *define any ambiguous terms* that are key to the discussion. For example, if you were arguing that the government should not cut funding of basic research, it would no doubt be useful for your audience to define what you mean by "basic research." Part of good arguing is clear communication, and clear communication requires that each party understand the terms being used.

2. *The essay should offer reasons and support for those reasons.* In other words, the essay should prove its point.

3. *The essay should refute opposing arguments.* It is this characteristic that is more particular to the argumentative essay than to expository essays. Since there are two sides to the issue, and since you—the writer—want to convince the reader that you are right, not only must you prove your own case, but you should also prove that the opponent is wrong, or at least that your points are more valid or significant. *Refute* means to prove wrong by argument or to show that something is erroneous. In short, you will have to deal with the opponent's reasons and show that yours are more valid or superior.

The following paragraphs demonstrate this concept of refutation. The argument proposed in the first paragraph is refuted in the second paragraph.

> One reason people over 75 should not be allowed to drive is that they are a hazard on the road. By that age most people's vision and hearing have deteriorated; thus, they cannot see cars, pedestrians, and traffic signs as well as they could in their youth. In addition, they have slower reaction times. This is particularly problematic because while driving one must be constantly on the alert to the need to stop or swerve suddenly to avoid a collision. These physical and mental impairments lead to a lot of accidents. In fact, if we compare on a per-mile basis the elderly with other age groups of drivers, it turns out that the elderly are involved in 25 accidents per 100 drivers. This is second only to the group aged 24 and under.

Now observe how this point is refuted:

> My opponents argue that people over 75 should not be allowed to drive because they are a hazard on the road. While it is true that the accident rate per mile driven is high for the elderly, the fact is that the elderly simply do not drive as much as those in other age groups; consequently, the actual number of accidents in this age group is the lowest among all the younger age groups. Moreover, while it is also true that their abilities to see, hear,

and react are not as sharp as they were when they were younger, this does not necessarily have to make them hazardous on the road. In fact, elderly drivers can be trained to compensate for their deficiencies by taking special driver's education courses designed for them.

Now note how this writer states an opposing argument on a different topic and then refutes it:

> Execution—preferably in public—should be a solemn ritual of great significance—a ritual that powerfully announces to all its citizens that the state so values human life that it must mark its violation with the most awful penalty available.
>
> Those who assert that capital punishment is wrong because the state should not itself take on the guilt of murder completely miss the point. For by failing to take the life of those who murder their fellow men, the state becomes a passive accessory after the fact.
>
> The state says, in effect, that murder is no more serious an offense than embezzlement or shoplifting. When children grow up in a state that often releases even the most sadistic murderer after a relatively short prison sentence, or, in the extreme, no sentence at all, how can these children fail to get the message: that neither their elders nor their society gives great weight to human life—or its destruction. —Nettie Leef, "Respect for Life—and Capital Punishment, Too," *New York Times* 30 June 1975.

EXERCISE 11-15

On a separate sheet of paper, answer the following questions about the passage by Nettie Leef.

1. This passage is from a longer essay by Nettie Leef on capital punishment. What do you think is the thesis of the essay?
2. What is the opponent's point that the author addresses and refutes?

EXERCISE 11-16: WRITING ASSIGNMENT

For Exercise 11-6, you wrote out the opponent's reasons. Choose one of those reasons and refute it in one or two paragraphs.

---

4. *If an opponent does have a valid point, concede that point.* It does little good in an argument to ignore any valid points the other side may have. You can concede them and then go on to show that your points are more important anyway.

Although it is true that we have had no real damage from any nuclear power plant breakdowns, the potential for devastation still exists. . . .

5. *The conclusion should logically follow from the argument.* As discussed in earlier chapters, the conclusion can summarize the main points and reassert the thesis. In an argumentative essay, however, the conclusion often makes a demand for some action. For example, an argument against the construction of nuclear power plants might conclude with a demand that all plants in construction now be closed down. Another way to wrap up an argument is to offer alternatives. In your antinuclear power plant essay, for instance, you might suggest that the funds now used for those plants be used for an alternative source of energy, such as nuclear fusion or solar power.

Organizing the Argumentative Essay

Although there is no set pattern for organizing the argumentative essay, there is a basic, workable approach that is commonly used:

1. *Introduction.* Sometimes writers break down the introductory material into two paragraphs: the first one introducing the problem and the thesis and the second one explaining additional information, providing definitions, and giving background information necessary for the argument.
2. *Reasons.* It is a good idea to spend one paragraph on each reason. Two or three reasons are typical.
3. *Refutation.* Depending on how many points the writer wishes to address, the refutation can take from one to three paragraphs.
4. *Conclusion.*

It is not uncommon, however, to see arguments in which the refutation comes before the reasons section.

Read the following essay. Note if the writer clearly states the case or issue under discussion; locate the thesis; evaluate the support and the argument. Is it convincing?

SCIENCE: WHO NEEDS IT?

At our school all students are required to take a minimum of six courses in the natural sciences: three in the biological sciences and three in the physical sciences, regardless of the student's major. Students majoring in the humanities often have to struggle to get through these demanding courses and their grade-point averages usually suffer as a result. It has been suggested that the requirements be modified, reducing the number of natural science courses required so that students can take more courses directly related to their majors. As a humanities major, I admit this would make college life a lot easier for me, but I still oppose the measure because natural science courses provide us with a crucial part of our education.

Students majoring in the humanities usually object to taking such science courses because they claim the courses are irrelevant to their majors. "What good will physics do me when I'm teaching Spanish?" a friend of mine asked. It's true that physics, chemistry, biology, and the like may not have a direct application to most careers in the humanities, but this objection ignores one of the key issues of a university education. A university is not simply a training facility; it is an institution of higher learning where students are educated, not merely trained. Even the term *university* implies that it's a place to obtain a general knowledge base; a university education means the student has been educated in many subjects. Since part of our universal knowledge is science, it is and logically should be a part of the university curriculum.

Humanities students might accept this argument and agree that they should take some natural science, but not as many courses as are now required. They might suggest a one-semester course in biological science and a one-semester course in physical science, along with perhaps one semester of math for non-majors. This, they argue, would expose them sufficiently to the universe of science. If the point of a university education were merely to expose students to a variety of subjects, then I might agree. But a university education implies more than mere exposure. After all, people can be exposed to subjects by watching television. Again, the purpose of going to a university is to get an education. What does that mean? It means more than just training and exposure; it means that students learn enough to become critical thinkers in the various disciplines. It means that they should gain enough understanding of the sciences, humanities, social sciences, and the arts to be able to discuss issues in these areas intelligently and to be able to question other people's views rather than just accept what people tell them.

One or two semesters of general science cannot sufficiently educate students in this field. What one learns in natural science courses is more than mere factual information. One learns to think critically, to approach problems logically, to use reasoning. And this takes time. It takes work. It takes studying different areas of science and applying the general principles in laboratory situations.

Developing a critical ability in science is important, but why? In addition to providing the student with a universe of knowledge, an understanding of science is vital in our highly technological society. We are all confronted with issues involving nuclear waste, chemical pollutants, medical advances, exploration in space, and so forth. In order to make intelligent decisions—in fact, even to be involved in the decision-making process—people need to have an understanding of these issues that goes beyond mere "exposure." Otherwise, the uneducated become mere puppets who, out of ignorance, can but nod in agreement with anyone who professes expertise.

Finally, I contend that science courses do have relevance to the humanities, and this is through the critical thinking approach of the scientific method. The scientific method is an approach to solving problems, an approach that has been tried and proven. It is an approach that demands that the researcher obtain support for his or her hypotheses. Courses in the humanities demand critical thinking as well. Students of literature must support their interpretations with "evidence" from the literary work; art majors must test their ideas—or hypotheses—by experimenting and drawing conclusions. True, in these fields one does not follow the formal scientific method, but it is the practice with that way of thinking that can benefit students in other fields.

Science courses, then, provide us not only with knowledge that is crucial for intelligent functioning in our society, but they also provide us with the opportunity to develop our critical, logical reasoning skills. Although these courses are difficult for the nonscience majors, they are well worth the effort. The knowledge and thinking skills gained from these courses make us less vulnerable to charletans and politicians as we more intelligently and critically evaluate the propositions offered to us.

EXERCISE 11-17

On a separate sheet of paper, answer the following questions about "Science: Who Needs It?"

1. What is the issue discussed by the writer?
2. What is the thesis statement?
3. What is the topic of paragraph 6?
4. What is the major premise of the essay?
5. Where does the refutation begin in the essay? What is the first point that the writer refutes?
6. Does the writer refute all possible objections to the thesis? Can you think of any someone might make?
7. Is the argument convincing? Why, or why not?
8. Does the conclusion logically follow?
9. Does the writer concede any points? Should some points be conceded? What points?
10. Make an outline of this essay.

EXERCISE 11-18: WRITING ASSIGNMENT

Choose one of the topics from Exercise 11-6 and write your first draft of an essay.

One of the major problems we face today is the use of illegal drugs. The writer of the following essay argues in support of a highly controversial solution to this problem. [There are a few terms you should know before you read the essay. "Prohibition" refers to the Eighteenth Amendment of the U.S. Constitution, which made the sale, manufacture, and transportation of alcoholic beverages ("intoxicating liquors") illegal. The amendment went into effect in January 1920 but was repealed in December 1933. The term "Demon Rum" refers to rum and loosely to other alco-

holic beverages that prohibitionists believed were evil, or made people do bad things.]

PROHIBITION AND DRUGS

[1] "The reign of tears is over. The slums will soon be only a memory. We will turn our prisons into factories and our jails into storehouses and corncribs. Men will walk upright now, women will smile, and the children will laugh. Hell will be forever for rent."

[2] This is how Billy Sunday, the noted evangelist and leading crusader against Demon Rum, greeted the onset of Prohibition in early 1920. We know now how tragically his hopes were doomed. New prisons and jails had to be built to house the criminals spawned by converting the drinking of spirits into a crime against the state. Prohibition undermined respect for the law, corrupted the minions of the law, created a decadent moral climate—but did not stop the consumption of alcohol.

[3] Despite this tragic object lesson, we seem bent on repeating precisely the same mistake in the handling of drugs.

[4] On ethical grounds do we have the right to use the machinery of government to prevent an individual from becoming an alcoholic or a drug addict? For children, almost everyone would answer at least a qualified yes. But for responsible adults, I, for one, would answer no. Reason with the potential addict, yes. Tell him the consequences, yes. Pray for and with him, yes. But I believe that we have no right to use force, directly or indirectly, to prevent a fellow man from committing suicide, let alone from drinking alcohol or taking drugs.

[5] I readily grant that the ethical issue is difficult and that men of goodwill may well disagree. Fortunately, we need not resolve the ethical issue to agree on policy. *Prohibition is an attempted cure that makes matters worse—for both the addict and the rest of us.* Hence, even if you regard present policy toward drugs as ethically justified, considerations of expediency make that policy most unwise.

[6] *Consider first the addict.* Legalizing drugs might increase the number of addicts, but it is not clear that it would. Forbidden fruit is attractive, particularly to the young. More important, many drug addicts are deliberately made by pushers, who give likely prospects their first few doses free. It pays the pusher to do so because, once hooked, the addict is a captive customer. If drugs were legally available, any possible profit from such inhumane activity would disappear, since the addict could buy from the cheapest source.

[7] Whatever happens to the number of addicts, the individual addict would clearly be far better off if drugs were legal. Today, drugs are both incredibly expensive and highly uncertain in quality. Addicts are driven to associate with criminals to get the drugs, become criminals themselves to finance the habit, and risk constant danger of death and disease.

[8] *Consider next the rest of us.* Here the situation is crystal-clear. The harm to us from the addiction of others arises almost wholly from the fact that drugs are illegal. A recent committee of the American Bar Association

estimated that addicts commit one-third to one-half of all street crime in the U.S. Legalize drugs, and street crime would drop automatically.

[9] Moreover, addicts and pushers are not the only ones corrupted. Immense sums are at stake. It is inevitable that some relatively low-paid police and other government officials—and some high-paid ones as well—will succumb to the temptation to pick up easy money.

[10] Legalizing drugs would simultaneously reduce the amount of crime and raise the quality of law enforcement. Can you conceive of any other measure that would accomplish so much to promote law and order?

[11] But, you may say, must we accept defeat? Why not simply end the drug traffic? This is where experience under Prohibition is most relevant. We cannot end the drug traffic. We may be able to cut off opium from Turkey—but there are innumerable other places where the opium poppy grows. With French cooperation, we may be able to make Marseilles an unhealthy place to manufacture heroin—but there are innumerable other places where the simple manufacturing operations involved can be carried out. So long as large sums of money are involved—and they are bound to be if drugs are illegal—it is literally hopeless to expect to end the traffic or even reduce seriously its scope.

[12] In drugs, as in other areas, persuasion and example are likely to be far more effective than the use of force to shape others in our image. —Milton Friedman, "Prohibition and Drugs," *Newsweek* 1972.

EXERCISE 11-19

Answer the following questions about Milton Friedman's essay.

1. The author opens with a quotation by a Prohibitionist. Is this an effective opening? What purpose does it serve?
2. How does Prohibition relate to the situation Friedman is discussing?
3. What is the thesis of the essay?
4. What is the topic of paragraph 4?
5. What does Friedman say about the "ethical issue"?
6. Why does Friedman not argue the ethical issue?
7. What does he choose to argue instead of the ethical issue?
8. What is the basic type of support in paragraph 6 (comparison/contrast, examples, causes, effects)?
9. What is the "reason" discussed in paragraphs 8, 9, and 10?
10. Does the author refute opposing arguments? If so, where?
11. Does the author concede any points in the essay? If so, where exactly?
12. Is the argument persuasive?
13. Can you think of any reasons Friedman may have left out that would help his case?
14. Can you think of any reasons an opponent might give that the author did not address?

15. Make an outline of this essay.

EXERCISE 11-20: WRITING ASSIGNMENT

Write an essay in opposition to the side that Friedman takes in "Prohibition and Drugs."

COMPOSITION SKILLS

Coherence Review

Good writing must be coherent; that is, one idea must follow logically and smoothly from the previous one. A number of ways to achieve coherence have been noted earlier. In writing essays, whether they are expository or argumentative, always strive to use a variety of techniques for achieving coherence. Let us review them briefly.

1. *Repetition of key words, synonyms, and pronouns.*

2. *Coordinating conjunctions and correlative conjunctions.* The coordinating conjunctions *and, but, or, for, nor, yet,* and *so* join two independent clauses and are usually preceded by a comma.

We went to the game, *but* we did not get good seats.

The correlative conjunctions *not only . . . but also, either . . . or, neither . . . nor, both . . . and* also join two independent clauses.

Not only do we object to what he said, *but* we *also* object to how he said it.

3. *Subordinate clauses.* Subordinate clauses (adverbial, adjective, and noun clauses) use a subordinating conjunction at the beginning of a subordinate clause to join the subordinate clause to an independent clause. Subordinate clauses effectively show the relative importance of the two sentences. A number of subordinate clauses were discussed:

a. Adjective clauses using *who, whom, which, that, whose, when,* and *where*:

The boy *whose* father is a doctor sits behind me in class.

b. Adverbial clauses of time using *while, as, when, whenever, before, after, until, as soon as, since, from the moment that:*

From the moment that I saw her, I was infatuated.

c. Adverbial clauses of comparison–contrast using *while* and *whereas*:

Maria is interested in dancing, *whereas* Sonia is interested in gymnastics.

d. Adverbial clauses of concession using ***although, though, even though:***

Although nuclear power is dangerous, it is necessary to provide us with enough electricity to meet our needs.

e. Adverbial clauses of purpose using ***so that:***

We arrived early *so that* we could get a good seat.

f. Adverbial clauses of condition using ***if:***

If the pump breaks, you will need to go to the service station.

g. Adverbial clauses of cause using ***because*** and ***since:***

We went to the concert *because* we were curious.

h. Adverbial clauses of result using ***so/such . . . that:***

The letter was *so* illogical *that* I could not understand it at all.

4. *Transitional words and phrases.* For the most part, transitional words and phrases are attached to the beginning of a sentence and are preceded by a period or semicolon. They do not really join two sentences together, but indicate the relationship between the two sentences. Note the relationship that the transitions denote:

Chronological Order:

first	after
second	that
next	last
	finally

Example:

for example
for instance
to illustrate

Addition:

also	in addition
furthermore	besides that

Conclusion:

in conclusion	to conclude
finally	in summary

Comparison – Contrast:

likewise	conversely
similarly	in contrast
in the same way	however

on the other hand	on the contrary	
similar to	different from	} *followed by*
like	in contrast to	} *noun phrase*

EXERCISE 11-21: WRITING ASSIGNMENT

The following paragraphs are not coherent. Rewrite them using any of the coherence devices that we have studied.

Women should not be drafted for combat duty. It is not practical. The army would need to set up two facilities for everything. It would need to set up two sleeping quarters, two sets of showers, and two latrines. The actual amount of work and supplies involved in setting up camp would double. More supplies and equipment in the field would slow down troop movement considerably. Our troops would lose any advantage they would have for surprise attack. We need an incredible amount of backup support for men. It is not practical to double that in wartime.

Women are not strong enough emotionally. Women are not strong enough physically. It takes a lot of strength and courage to be in actual physical combat. You need to be strong enough to kill people without any pangs of regret. Women could be strong. Women are sheltered. They are not taught to be strong. Men are taught to be strong. Women could not stand to see their best buddy get hit by a shell and die in front of their eyes. Women are not strong enough to handle killing and dying. Maybe they could be strong enough emotionally. They are not strong enough physically. Most women could not throw ninety-pound ammunition cases into a truck all day. Most women could not win in close hand-to-hand combat against a man. Women do not have the strength for combat duty.

EXERCISE 11-22: WRITING ASSIGNMENT

You have written two drafts of essays thus far; using this review of coherence devices, go back and revise those essays.

GRAMMAR REVIEWS

Subjunctive Noun Clauses

An argumentative paper often concludes with a suggestion or recommendation for future action. A good sentence construction to use for this is a noun clause beginning with *that*. Although noun clauses were discussed on pages 218–24, the noun clause pattern that recommends and suggests requires special attention. After certain verbs and adjectives that express the idea of requesting, advising, or urging, the simple verb form (or infinitive without *to*) is used. Note that this form is used regardless of the tense of the main verb:

I recommend that John *go* to the doctor immediately.

They advised that the government *pass* a law dealing with gun control.

We are requesting that all students *take* the test.

It has been suggested that the president *be* responsible for his actions.

Here is a list of the most common verbs used in this pattern:

advise	desire	urge	propose
ask	forbid	demand	recommend
beg	request	insist	stipulate
command	require	move	suggest

There are two other patterns that also advise and suggest, but these are used in more informal situations. The first one is with ***should.***

They recommend that we *should arrive* on time.

The second pattern uses the infinitive after a noun phrase. It can be used after the following verbs:

advise	command	request
ask	desire	require
beg	forbid	urge

I strongly urge you *to take* math before chemistry.

We asked him *to consider* his position.

Note that these structures usually include an object for the verb. The subjunctive also occurs after certain adjectives:

advisable	vital
essential	desirable
imperative	good (better, best)
mandatory	important
requisite	necessary
urgent	crucial

Note the following examples:

It is advisable that she not *drive* this car until it is fixed.

It is urgent that Mr. Philo *get* my message today.

Like for verbs, there are two other patterns using adjectives that can be used to advise and suggest in informal situations. The first one is ***should:***

It is necessary that he *should* become aware of the situation.

The other—and more commonly used—alternative involves the form *for . . . to:*

It is important *for him to be* on time to class.

It is vital *for us to understand* the world situation.

Note that *for* is followed by an objective pronoun or a noun phrase.

EXERCISE 11-23

Read the following situations and write sentences in which you use the words in parentheses to give advice. The first one is done for you.

1. You are a government inspector for a road-building project. During your inspection, you found that the All-Right Construction Company was using poor quality concrete. You also found that tiny cracks were appearing in portions of the road built only a month ago. You observed that the company was not using enough reinforcing rods in the road bed. Finally, you learned that some of the workers were not being paid the minimum wage. Write your suggestions in a report to your supervisor.

a. (*advise*) I advise that the All-Right Construction Company use a better grade of concrete.

b. (*recommend*) ______

c. (*urge this construction company to*) ______

______

d. (*necessary*) ______

e. (*essential for . . . to*) ______

______

2. You are a psychologist specializing in family problems. You have just had an hour-long session with Rob and Betty Blodge and their two children, Michael, 10, and Tammy, 7. Mr. Blodge complained that his wife did not have dinner ready for him when he came home from work. He also said that she spoiled the children by giving them anything they wanted. Mrs. Blodge complained that her husband ignored her and the children entirely. She said that he only wanted to watch television and get drunk. The children said that their parents fought all the time. Write sentences of advice for this family.

a. (*ask Mr. Blodge to*) ______

______

b. (*suggest*) ______

______

c. (*advisable for . . . to*) ________________________________

____

d. (*propose*) ________________________________

____

e. (*important*) ________________________________

____

EXERCISE 11-24: WRITING ASSIGNMENT

Now go back and revise your two essays, making sure that your subjunctive noun clauses are correct.

EXERCISE 11-25: WRITING ASSIGNMENT

Choose one of the following writing topics for an argumentative essay. As you write your essay, be sure to include the characteristics of an argumentative essay discussed on pages 408–10. Also, use subjunctive noun clauses when appropriate.

1. Select one of the topics in Exercise 11-6 that you did not choose earlier.
2. In Exercise 11-21 are two paragraphs giving two reasons why women should not be drafted. Write an essay in which you argue for or against the drafting of women into military service.
3. In Exercise 11-5 you identified thesis statements for argumentative essays. Select one of those thesis statements and write an essay. You may take the side of the issue given, or you may take the opposite side.
4. In the editorial section of the newspaper editors express their own opinions on topical issues, and in letters to the editor readers express their opinions. Write an essay that argues against the opinion expressed either in an editorial or in a letter to the editor. In your introductory paragraph, summarize the article you are arguing against ("In his article on inflation, Mr. X contends that. . . ."). You may wish to review the discussion of indirect speech and noun clauses in Chapter 6.

Argumentative Essay Checklist

1. An argumentative essay attempts to convince or persuade the reader. The subject for an argumentative essay should be an opinion that can be argued logically and supported by evidence. Have you chosen an appropriate argumentative subject? Have you explained the issue or case sufficiently?
2. The thesis of the argumentative essay should take a clear stand on the issue. Does your thesis express your stand clearly?
3. An argumentative essay should attempt to refute opposing arguments. Does your essay do so?
4. An argumentative essay should offer logical reasons and support for the writer's opinion. Does your essay do so?
5. Is your essay logically organized?
6. Is it coherent?

APPENDIXES

Appendix I

The Definite Article with Place Names

USE *THE* WITH:	DO NOT USE *THE* WITH:
All plural names: the United States, the Canary Islands the Sierra Nevada Mountains, the Great Lakes All names containing *of:* the Gulf of Cadiz, The University of Illinois, the Republic of South Africa	The names of continents: Europe, Asia, South America
The names of these countries: the Congo, the Sudan The names of countries containing the words *Union, United,* and *Commonwealth:* the Soviet Union, the British Commonwealth	The names of countries: Japan, Venezuela, Haiti, Australia
The name of this city: the Hague	The names of cities and states: Seoul, Caracas, Louisiana, Florida
Groups of Islands (see the first section above): the British Isles, the Aleutian Islands (The word *islands* may be omitted — the Philippines.)	The name of a single island: Victoria Island, Long Island
Most bodies of water (rivers, seas, oceans, channels, canals, gulfs, straits): the Saint Lawrence River, the China Sea, the	The names of lakes and bays: Lake Michigan, Manila Bay

USE *THE* WITH:	DO NOT USE *THE* WITH:
Atlantic Ocean, the Persian Gulf, the Bering Strait (the words *river, sea,* and *ocean* may be omitted — the Pacific)	
The names of mountain ranges: the Rocky Mountains (the word *mountain* may be omitted — the Alps)	The name of a single mountain: Mount Everest, Bald Mountain
The names of peninsulas: the Iberian Peninsula	
Distinct geographic areas using *north, south, east,* and *west:* the East, the Midwest, the Far East	
The names of libraries and museums: the Louvre, the Confederate Museum	The names of universities and colleges (unless part of the actual name): Harvard University, Rocky Mountain College, BUT: The Ohio State University
	The names of avenues, streets, and boulevards: Fifth Avenue, Main Street, Pontchartrain Boulevard
	The names of parks: Central Park, Audubon Park

EXERCISE AI-1

Fill in the word *the* wherever necessary in the following sentences.

1. He left ____________ Soviet Union to come to ____________ United States. He traveled by way of ____________ Europe and ____________ Danish Peninsula.
2. ____________ Africa includes ____________ Kenya, ____________ Tanzania, and ____________ Republic of South Africa.
3. After they left ____________ Egypt, they went down ____________ Nile River to ____________ Sudan.
4. ____________ Union of South Africa is now called ____________ Republic of South Africa.

5. After we left __________ Honolulu, which is on __________ island of Oahu in __________ Hawaiian Islands, we sailed for __________ Galapagos Islands off the coast of __________ Chile in __________ South America.
6. __________ Mississippi River flows into __________ Gulf of Mexico in __________ state of Louisiana.
7. __________ Tampa Bay in __________ Florida is the site of both __________ Clearwater and __________ Tampa.
8. __________ Gulf of Panama is on __________ Pacific side of __________ Panama Canal.
9. __________ Strait of Hormuz connects __________ Persian Gulf with __________ Gulf of Oman.
10. __________ Mount Fuji is a famous mountain in __________ Japan in __________ Far East.
11. __________ Formosa Strait connects __________ East China Sea with __________ South China Sea.
12. __________ Singapore is located on __________ Malay Peninsula.
13. After she left __________ University of Massachusetts, she went to __________ Ball State in Indiana.
14. We went down __________ Avenue of the Americas to __________ City Park Boulevard.
15. When we visited __________ South, we stopped at __________ Civil War Museum in __________ Atlanta.

The Definite Article with Other Proper Nouns

USE *THE* WITH:	DO NOT USE *THE* WITH:
	The names of holidays: Christmas, New Year's Day, Easter
All names containing *of:* the President of the United States	
Title of officials: the king, the	Titles of officials when the name

USE *THE* WITH:	**DO NOT USE *THE* WITH:**
secretary of state, the prime minister	accompanies the title: President Bush, King Hussein, Prime Minister Thatcher
Names of historical periods or events: the Middle Ages, the Civil War, the Manchu Dynasty, the Second World War	
Official documents and acts: the Monroe Doctrine, the Louisiana Purchase, the Magna Carta, the Equal Rights Amendment	Names with roman numerals: World War II
Branches of the government and political parties: the Judicial Branch, the Republican party	
Names of organizations and foundations: the United Nations, the Carnegie Foundation, the YMCA	
Law enforcement groups: the army, the navy, the marines	

EXERCISE AI-2

Fill in the word *the* wherever necessary in the following sentences.

1. At ____________ Christmas, ____________ Republican party held a conference with ____________ prime minister.
2. During ____________ First World War, ____________ German army invaded France.
3. ____________ President Nixon resigned from ____________ Executive Branch of the government.
4. ____________ King Hussein gave an address to ____________ United Nations.
5. After ____________ World War II, ____________ United Nations was formed.
6. Before ____________ Middle Ages, ____________ king signed ____________ Magna Carta in England.

7. Currently, ____________ Congress is debating ____________ Equal Rights Amendment.
8. ____________ Senate is dominated by ____________ Democratic party.

Appendix II

Punctuation Problems

Fragments

A fragment is a part of a sentence that has been punctuated as a complete sentence. It is usually a dependent clause or a phrase.

The man who is coming over to fix the washer and dryer this morning. (adjective clause)

Whether the legislature passes the bill or not. (noun clause)

The woman singing the lovely, haunting refrain. (participial phrase)

The beauty of the lake, the quiet solitude, the starlit night, and the lovely smell of the pine trees. (nouns and phrases)

A fragment can be corrected by attaching the dependent phrase or clause to an independent clause.

The man who is coming over to fix the washer and dryer this morning is charging $50 an hour.

I do not care whether the legislature passes the bill or not.

The woman singing the lovely, haunting refrain walks in the park every evening.

I was enthralled with the beauty of the lake, the quiet solitude, the starlit night, and the lovely smell of the pine trees.

EXERCISE AII-1

Find the fragments in the following sentences and correct them. Some of the sentences may be correct as written.

1. The bomb hidden in the church and waiting to explode.
2. Because the tennis court was occupied. Therefore, we decided to play football.
3. He responded slowly. Taking his time to think of the best answer.
4. She was convinced that she should buy a Rolls Royce. A car that she had dreamed of for twenty years.
5. Which car did she want? That was the big question.
6. Tired from his work at the office and wanting a cold beer. Mr. Osgood waited impatiently for the subway.
7. With his son and daughter always taking care of him and looking after his every need.

Comma Splices and Run-on Sentences

A comma splice occurs when two independent clauses are joined by a comma. A run-on sentence occurs when two independent clauses are written as one sentence with no punctuation at all.

The local tire plant shut down for the holiday, as a result, everyone had two weeks off.

We walked over to the waterfall slowly then we sat down to admire the beauty of the falls.

Comma splices and run-ons can be corrected in four main ways:

1. Use a period to make two complete sentences.
2. Use a semicolon between the two clauses.
3. Use a comma and a coordinating conjunction.
4. Use a subordinator to make a dependent clause; attach it to the independent clause.

The local tire plant shut down for the holiday. As a result, everyone had two weeks off.

The local tire plant shut down for the holiday; as a result, everyone had two weeks off.

We walked over to the waterfall slowly, and then we sat down to admire the beauty of the falls.

After we walked over to the waterfall slowly, we sat down to admire the beauty of the falls.

EXERCISE AII-2

Use any of the four ways to correct comma splices and run-ons in these sentences. Some may be correct as written.

1. There are several ways to prepare for a hurricane, here is one of them.
2. While trying to decide which road to take, we made a wrong turn then we were completely lost.
3. Nuclear power plants can be run safely this is what many people think.
4. We could not decide whether to go to the movie or the concert, we finally went to the concert.
5. One of the worst effects is on the underground water supply it can easily be contaminated. However, that was not the problem in this case.
6. Although television programs are often boring, we watch them anyway. What does that say about us?
7. While my father hates music, my mother enjoys it I find that curious.
8. No one would take responsibility for the accident, therefore, they were all arrested.

Rules for Punctuation

The Period

1. Use a period at the end of a statement or command.

   The government has promised to reduce inflation.

   Pick up the lug wrench.

2. Use a period after abbreviations.

   A.M. Mr. U.S. B.C.

The Comma

1. Use a comma to separate independent clauses joined by a coordinating conjunction.

   We went to the campsite as soon as we arrived, but it was already full.

   Note: If the clauses are quite short, the comma may be omitted.

   He studied hard and he passed the test.

2. **Use a comma to separate words, phrases, or clauses in a series.**

   We took our tent, our sleeping bags, food, and fishing poles.

   He drinks milkshakes in the morning, in the afternoon, and in the evening.

   We enjoyed ourselves before we took the boat ride, while we were on the boat ride, and after we left the lake.

3. **Use a comma after introductory phrases or clauses.**

   Because we had wanted to see all of the interesting sights in the city, we agreed to spend our entire vacation there.

   With the worst of the winter over, the people began to make plans for spring.

   Note: If the clauses or phrases are quite short, the comma may be omitted.

   After we arrived we had a beer.

4. **Use a comma after transitional words and phrases, mild interjections, and *yes* and *no*.**

   On the other hand, no effort has been made to help the stranded people.

   Oh, I do not think that is the answer.

   Yes, he said he was coming.

5. **Use commas to set off nonrestrictive clauses and phrases and appositives.**

   President John F. Kennedy, who was assassinated in 1963, was an eloquent speaker.

   The boat, tied securely to the dock, rode out the storm well.

   Mr. Benninger, a well-known physicist, received the key to the city.

6. **Use commas to set off contrastive elements or elements that interrupt a sentence.**

   We chose the moderately priced one, not the most expensive one, because we were short of funds.

   It is a good idea, therefore, to study this book thoroughly before the test.

7. **Use commas to set off absolute constructions. (An absolute phrase is a noun followed by a modifier. It modifies a whole sentence, not a particular element in the sentence.)**

   Night falling, the lights of the town slowly began to appear.

8. **Use commas in direct address and quotations.**

   He said, "Mary, did you steal the money?"

9. **Use commas with degrees, titles, dates, places, addresses, and numbers.**

   Mr. Ross Charleston, M.F.A., is the chairman of the English Department.

   Mr. Cyrus Leary, chairman of the board, made a number of changes in policy.

   We decided to have the wedding reception on Friday, October 8, because of our vacation.

   We arrived in this country in May of 1979.

   We arrived in this country in May, 1979.

   We arrived in this country in May 1979.

   The water in Chicago, Illinois, comes from Lake Michigan.

   They sold over 100,000 pounds of rice in 1979.

   Please send it to Mr. Harold Bobbs, 1230 Smith Place, New Orleans, Louisiana 70124.

   Note: As in the preceding example, there is no comma placed between the state and the zip code.

10. **Use a comma to prevent misreading.**

    Inside, the building was beautiful.

    Before eating, the dog barked three times.

EXERCISE AII-3

Add commas and periods wherever necessary in the following sentences.

1. Even after the museum displayed his work the artist was not confident that it was good.
2. We arrived in Athens Greece on May 12 1980 and toured the Acropolis the Plaka and the main square.
3. He said "What do you want Jerry?"
4. The governor hired William Touro M A for the job in Lansing Michigan
5. The Sphinx a famous monument in Egypt was built many centuries ago.
6. They habitually work all morning sleep all afternoon and party all evening.
7. After buying a dog we also had to buy a doghouse dog food and a long chain
8. Please send it to Ms Robin Smith 134 Main Street Nashua Iowa 50658.

The Semicolon

1. Use a semicolon between two main clauses that are not joined by a coordinating conjunction.

   This floor polish does not work; I have already tried it.

2. Use a semicolon between coordinate elements with internal commas.

   After we arrived, Mr. Buris, the manager of the plant, showed us the main assembly lines; but he neglected to show us the warehouse where most of the products, waiting to be shipped overseas, are stored.

3. Use a semicolon between items in a series when the items themselves contain commas.

   Present at the meeting were Charles Jones, chairperson; Lydia Jones, vice-chairperson; and Roger Smaltz, treasurer.

The Colon

1. Use a colon between two independent clauses when the second one explains the first.

   There is only one thing to say: He did not deserve it.

2. Use a colon to introduce an appositive.

   "There are three sources of belief: reason, custom, inspiration."
   —Blaise Pascal

3. Use a colon to formally introduce a quotation.

   Kennedy eloquently reminded us: "Ask not what your country can do for you; ask what you can do for your country."

4. Use a colon in a time reference, after the salutation of a formal letter, in biblical references, and in bibliographical entries.

   1:30 A.M.
   Dear Dr. Runch:
   Genesis 6:2
   New York: Macmillan, 1980

Note: Do not use a colon after a linking verb or preposition.

Incorrect:

Present at the meeting were: Mr. Jones, Mr. Osgood, and Ms. Blake.

Correct:

Present at the meeting were Mr. Jones, Mr. Osgood, and Ms. Blake.

The Dash

1. **Use a dash to indicate a sudden interruption in thought.**

He confessed to the crime—but why?

2. **Use a dash to set off abrupt parenthetical elements (particularly ones containing commas).**

He took the letter angrily—or was he really happy?—when the letter carrier arrived.

We saw him—huffing, puffing, and snorting—trying to break loose.

3. **Use a dash to set off an appositive or a brief summary.**

There is one poem I love more than any other—*The Wasteland.*

Persistence, agility, and strength—all of these are needed to learn tennis.

Parentheses

1. **Use parentheses to enclose a loosely related comment or explanation.**

The car (it had been purchased only the day before) needed new brakes, a tune-up, and new tires.

2. **Use parentheses to enclose figures numbering items in a series.**

The government tried to (1) increase employment, (2) reduce inflation, and (3) cut taxes.

Brackets

1. **Use brackets to enclose editorial corrections or additions in a quotation.**

Dirkson reports: "When we came upon him [General Lee], we found that he had been badly wounded in the leg."

2. **Note that the word *sic* in brackets means that the preceding word is an error and that the error appeared in the original.**

The editor asserted: "When I read the Bibel [sic], I was enlightened."

Quotation Marks

1. **Use double quotation marks to enclose a direct quotation.**

He said, "I cannot study anymore."

Note: Indirect speech is not put within quotation marks.

He said that he could not study anymore.

2. Use single quotation marks to enclose a quotation within a quotation.

   May reported, "When Bob said, 'I cannot see you anymore,' my sister was heartbroken."

   Smith argues that, "Hamlet's 'to be or not be be' has an entirely different meaning."

3. Use quotation marks to set off titles of songs, poems, short stories, articles, essays, chapters in longer works, paintings, and statues.

   My favorite song is "Raindrops Keep Falling on My Head."

   He recites "Mending Wall" for each of his classes.

   Have you read "The Blue Stocking" yet?

   Note: Quotation marks are essentially used to enclose short works of art. For longer works of art use italics (underlining).

4. Use quotation marks to denote a special meaning of a word.

   Her "pet" was a small round stone.

5. Put commas and periods inside quotation marks.

   He answered, "I cannot watch television tonight."

   Although he answered with a "yes," he did not seem enthusiastic.

6. Put colons and semicolons outside quotation marks.

   I am always sad when I see "The End"; it means the movie is over.

7. Put question marks, dashes, and exclamation points that are part of a quotation inside the quotation marks. Put question marks, dashes, and exclamation points that are not part of a quotation outside the quotation marks.

   Her father asked, "What time will you be home?"

   Did he just say, "We will not have school tomorrow"?

   He shouted, "Help! I cannot get out!"

   Do not shout "help"!

Italics

Italics are a special kind of print found in most publications. The letters in italics slant to the right. In handwritten or typed papers, use underlining for italics.

1. Use italics for the titles of books, magazines, newspapers, periodicals, plays, motion pictures, longer musical compositions, and other works published separately.

   The Grapes of Wrath (book)

   the *Atlantic Monthly* (magazine)

the *New York Times* (newspaper)
TESOL Quarterly (periodical)
Rocky (motion picture)
The Iceman Cometh (play)
The Rite of Spring (musical piece)

2. **Use italics for ships, trains, and airplanes.**

the *Queen Elizabeth* (ship)
the *Zephyr* (train)
the *Spirit of St. Louis* (airplane)

3. **Use italics for foreign words and phrases that have not yet been accepted into English.**

The *pièce de résistance* was his poached fish with hollandaise sauce.

4. **Use italics to call attention to words as words and letters as letters.**

The word *fluffy* reminds me of a cloud.
The teacher said, "Now put the letter *X* in the margin."

Note: This is an ineffective method of emphasis if it is overused.

The Apostrophe

1. **Use the apostrophe to indicate possessive.**

a. **For all proper nouns, add apostrophe and *s*.**

the girl's book	Jesus's birth
Charles's house	Kansas's weather

b. **For plural nouns, add apostrophe after the plural *s*.**

The boys' books

c. **For compound words, use the apostrophe after the last word.**

his mother-in-law's house   everyone's concern

d. **For joint possession, use the apostrophe after the last noun. For individual possession, use the apostrophe after both nouns.**

Charley and Bill's car   Sheila's and May's cameras

2. **Use the apostrophe to form the plural of letters.**

Only two A's were given in the class.

Note: Omit the apostrophe to form the plural of numerals and words referred to as words.

There were three 12s in the average.
Her two-page essay included twenty-five *of courses*.

Note: Omit the apostrophe when forming the plural of abbreviations, numbers, and periods of time expressed in years.

SATs VCRs fours 1990s

3. Use the apostrophe to indicate the omission of a letter or number.

wouldn't
Jack-o'-lantern
the '60s

The Hyphen

1. Hyphenate a compound of two or more words when it is used as a modifier before a noun.

He is a well-liked politician. He is well liked.

Note: Do not use the hyphen when the first word of the group is an adverb ending in *ly*.

a half-eaten apple a partly eaten apple

Note: Certain words are permanent compounds. They always use a hyphen. Consult your dictionary to determine which words are permanent compounds.

She is old-fashioned.

2. Hyphenate spelled-out compound numbers from *twenty-one* through *ninety-nine*.

sixty-four eighty-three

3. Hyphenate words of more than one syllable when they occur at the end of a typewritten line, when necessary. Hyphenate according to accepted syllabication. Consult your dictionary to determine where the syllable breaks are. Do not divide words of only one syllable and do not set off single letters. Do not divide words that already contain a hyphen elsewhere. Attempt to hyphenate in the approximate middle of the word.

Correct:

satis-faction water-melon

Incorrect:

bou-ght prett-y

Numbers

1. **Spell out numbers that can be written in one or two words.**

   one million   forty-three

2. **Use figures for other numbers.**

   145   2½ $456

3. **Use numerals for figures in a series and for tabulations and statistics.**

   Bill weighed 180 pounds; Steve, 150 pounds; and John, 100.

   He bought 125 pencils, 30 erasers, and 6 pens.

4. **Use figures for street numbers, page references, dates, percentages, money, and hours of the day with A.M. and P.M.**

	But:
101 Main Street	Tenth Street
Look at page 45.	I have twenty pages ready.
The interest was 15 percent.	
We paid $15 for the tickets.	
He gets up at 7:30 A.M.	He got up at seven o'clock.
We arrived on January 10, 1980.	

Note: Do not use figures to begin a sentence. Spell out the number or rephrase the sentence.

Appendix III

Rules for Capitalization

1. **Capitalize the first word in a sentence.**

    Where did he go?

2. **Capitalize the pronoun *I*.**

    Although he said so, I did not believe him.

3. **Capitalize proper names and nouns used as proper names.**
    a. **Capitalize a title preceding a proper noun.**

    President Bush
    Dr. Gonzalez

    b. **Capitalize the names of people and races.**

    Bob Luis Marcos Oriental Caucasian African-American

    Note: Do not capitalize the words ***black*** and ***white***.

    The blacks and whites in our neighborhood are well integrated.

    c. **Capitalize the names of religions, deities, and sacred terms.**

    Catholic Moslem Buddhist God

    d. **Capitalize geographic locations.**

    New York Mont Blanc the Ohio River

e. Capitalize the words *north, south, east,* and *west* when they refer to a section of the country usually considered to constitute a region.

the Midwest   the South

f. Capitalize nationalities and names of languages.

Vietnamese   Spanish   French   Japanese

g. Capitalize the complete names of specific churches and buildings.

the Statler Hotel   the First Baptist Church

h. Capitalize the days of the week, months, and holidays.

Wednesday   August   the Fourth of July

i. Capitalize the specific names of college courses (as the name would appear in the college catalogue).

I am taking French, American History 102, and a science course.

j. Capitalize all the words in a title except articles, prepositions, and conjunctions. Capitalize articles, prepositions, and conjunctions if they are the first or last word in the title or if they are of five or more letters in length.

Gone with the Wind   *We're Through with Heartache*   "He Comes In"

k. Capitalize nouns, adjectives, and prefixes in temporarily hyphenated compounds.

The Twentieth-Century Ideal   ***But:*** Twenty-five Brave Men

l. Capitalize the names of documents, historical events, and organizations.

The Bill of Rights
the Vietnam War
the National Organization for Women

Note: Do not capitalize the names of the seasons: spring, summer, fall, winter.

Appendix IV

Noun Plurals

Most nouns in English become plural by adding an *s* to the singular form:

SINGULAR	PLURAL
girl	girls
boy	boys

Some words, however, become plural by adding *es* to the singular form. This is generally true for words ending in *s, sh, ch, ss, zz,* or *x*. Note these examples:

SINGULAR	PLURAL
plus	pluses
ash	ashes
watch	watches
class	classes
buzz	buzzes
ax	axes

Words that end in a consonant plus *y* make the plural by changing the *y* to *i* and adding *es*.

SINGULAR	PLURAL
industry	industries
company	companies
city	cities
baby	babies

However, words that end in a vowel—*a, e, i, o,* or *u*—plus *y* form their plural by adding *s* only.

SINGULAR	PLURAL
boy	boys
highway	highways

Words ending in one *z* often make the plural by doubling the *z* and adding *es*.

SINGULAR	PLURAL
quiz	quizzes

For words ending in a consonant plus *o*, usage varies. Some words make the plural by adding *es* only.

SINGULAR	PLURAL
veto	vetoes
hero	heroes
tomato	tomatoes

Other words become plural adding *s* only.

SINGULAR	PLURAL
auto	autos
memo	memos
pimento	pimentos

And some words can be made plural in either way.

SINGULAR	PLURAL
motto	mottoes *or* mottos
zero	zeroes *or* zeroes

Words ending in *f* or *fe* form their plurals by changing *f* to *v* and adding *es*.

SINGULAR	PLURAL
wife	wives
half	halves
knife	knives

The following are exceptions to this rule.

SINGULAR	PLURAL
belief	beliefs
roof	roofs

Some nouns have special plural forms. They do not add *s* or *es* to form the plural. Note the following examples.

SINGULAR	PLURAL
man	men
woman	women
child	children
tooth	teeth
foot	feet
mouse	mice
goose	geese
ox	oxen
person	people (or persons)

Some words do not conform to any of the English rules for forming plurals but form their plurals in other ways. Note the following examples.

SINGULAR	PLURAL
medium	media
criterion	criteria
datum	data
crisis	crises
axis	axes

Some words do not change form in the plural. The form for singular and plural is the same.

SINGULAR	PLURAL
sheep	sheep
fish	fish
deer	deer
moose	moose

Some words that always end in *s* are singular in meaning. These words are considered singular, not plural. They include:

news	politics
economics	athletics

EXERCISE AIV-1

In each of the following sentences, write the correct plural form for the italicized word.

1. In these (*city*) ____________, pollution is not a problem but crime is.

2. I bought six (*ashtray*) ____________ at the market yesterday.
3. He sewed some colorful (*patch*) ____________ on his jacket.
4. As they say, "Nothing is certain but death and (*tax*) ____________."
5. Why don't you put (*pimento*) ____________ and (*tomato*) ____________ in the salad?
6. The (*wife*) ____________ have organized into a union to demand more money.
7. If you don't stand up for your (*belief*) ____________, you may be oppressed.
8. These (*datum*) ____________ must be incorrect; (*fish*) ____________ don't respond that way.
9. Most of the (*woman*) ____________ need to have a job.
10. How many (*zero*) ____________ are on that check?

EXERCISE AIV-2

In the following sentences, correct any errors in plural or singular noun forms. Some of the sentences may be correct as written.

1. The men and woman in my country like to eat dinner late.
2. In most city, the center part contains office building.
3. How many quizes have we had this week?
4. Kim's parent are pretty old, so they live with his cousin.
5. When I went to Germany, I bought some watch and a clock.
6. When I came to the United State, I listened to the news in order to learn English.
7. The company that are renting this building are complaining about the noise.

Appendix V

Subject–Verb Agreement

The verb of a sentence must agree in number with its subject. Singular subjects take singular verbs and plural subjects take plural verbs. The agreement pattern for the present tense is as follows:

	SINGULAR		PLURAL	
First person	I want	to go to a movie.	We want	to go to a movie.
Second person	You want		You want	
Third person	He wants She wants It wants		They want	

As you can see, the form of the verb is the same for all persons except for the third-person singular. Here the verb adds an *s* (or *es* in some cases) in order to agree with the subject. In addition to the pronouns given, the subject could be any singular noun for which you could substitute those pronouns. Exceptions to this pattern are the verbs *to be* and *have*, which change in other persons as well.

	TO BE		***HAVE***	
	SINGULAR	**PLURAL**	**SINGULAR**	**PLURAL**
First person	I am	We are	I have	We have
Second person	You are	You are	You have	You have
Third person	He is She is It is	They are	He has She has It has	They have

In order to make the verb agree in number with its subject, you must first determine which noun or pronoun is the subject of the sentence. There are several instances when the subject may not be apparent.

1. Sometimes the subject is separated from the verb by intervening words, phrases, or clauses.

   a. Prepositional phrases often follow the subject but never contain the subject.

   s v
   The student *by the window* likes to talk.

   s v
   The cars *in the parking lot* have their windows open.

   b. Adjective clauses often come between the main subject and verb of a sentence. Note that there are instances of subject–verb agreement in this case. The main subject and verb of the sentence must agree and the verb in the adjective clause must agree with its antecedent, or the word before, the relative pronoun.

MAIN SUBJECT	RELATIVE PRONOUN	VERB	MAIN VERB
The girls	that	live in the dorm	like to eat.

2. Sometimes subjects and verbs are reversed.

   a. Sentences beginning with ***there*** have reversed word order.

   v s
   There are a lot of students here for the test.

   v s
   There is a man waiting to see you.

   b. Sometimes subjects and verbs are reversed for stylistic purposes.

   v s
   Here comes the plane!

   v s
   Hardest hit by the tragedy was the mother of the family.

After you have determined which noun in the sentence is the subject, you must decide if it is singular or plural. Most nouns in English become plural by adding an *s* to the noun:

SINGULAR	PLURAL
girl	girls

1. Some nouns change their form in order to indicate plural:

SINGULAR	PLURAL
man	men
woman	women
child	children

The plural forms of these nouns — ***men, women, children, people*** —agree like this:

S V
The *people* **dislike** the commercials on television.

2. Some nouns, called collective nouns, are usually considered singular, but may, in some cases, be considered plural. These nouns take a singular verb when they refer to a group as a unit. Note the collective nouns (*italic*) and the singular verbs (**bold**) in the following sentences.

   My *family* **writes** to me every month.

   Our *class* **wants** to go to the museum.

   The *team* for our school **wears** red and white jerseys.

   The *faculty* **elects** a senate every year.

   The *committee* **needs** to have another meeting.

   These nouns may take plural verbs when they refer to individuals or parts of the group. However, this is more formal and less common usage. Note these examples:

   The *faculty* **disagree** on certain parts of the issue.

   The *committee* **argue** among themselves concerning the best course of action.

   Note: You can clarify these sentences by using the word ***members*** as the subject:

   The *members* of the faculty **disagree** on certain parts.

   The *members* of the committee **argue** among themselves concerning the best course of action.

3. Nouns that are plural in form but singular in meaning take singular verbs. These nouns include ***news, politics, economics, electronics, physics,*** and ***athletics***.

   The *news* on television **is** not very complete.

   Economics **is** an interesting field of study.

4. When words such as ***each, either, neither, one, everybody,*** and ***everyone*** are used as subjects, they take singular verbs.

   Neither **wants** to finish the work.

   Each of us **has** a good idea.

   Everybody in our class **wants** to go to the play.

   One of them **has** to do it.

5. When words such as ***all, any, half, most, none,*** and ***some*** are used as subjects, they can take either singular or plural verbs depending on the context.

   All of the people **dislike** the new tax.

   All of the money **is** gone.

6. A sentence that has two subjects joined by ***and*** requires a plural verb.

   My sister *and* my father **watch** television every night.

   The company *and* the bank **disagree** about the loan.

7. Singular subjects joined by ***or, either . . . or***, or ***neither . . . nor*** usually take a singular verb.

   John *or* Paul **buys** groceries for the family every week.

   Either the president *or* the vice-president **answers** every letter.

   Neither anger *nor* happiness ever **shows** on his face.

   If one of the subjects is singular and the other is plural, the verb agrees with the one closest to the subject.

   Mr. Smith *or* his sons **go** every day to pick up the mail.

   Neither the students *nor* the teacher **understands** the new schedule.

EXERCISE AV-1

Circle the correct form of the verb in each of the sentences that follow.

1. The difference between John and his brother (*is, are*) remarkable.
2. The athletes that (*win, wins*) most of the games (*is, are*) those who practice.
3. There (*is, are*) a great deal of controversy about the new president.
4. Here (*is, are*) the pair of shoes I lost last year.
5. My family (*live, lives*) in Manila.
6. The committee (*act, acts*) quickly on its business.
7. The members of the team (*do, does*) not like each other.
8. The politics of this country (*is, are*) confusing.
9. Each of the girls (*write, writes*) an editorial for the school newspaper every week.
10. Half of the money (*is, are*) gone.
11. All of the people (*want, wants*) to know the outcome of the election.
12. The chief of police and the mayor (*is, are*) scheduled to appear on the program.
13. Neither the owner of the restaurant nor the employees (*understand, understands*) the new fire regulations.
14. Either my mother or my father (*is, are*) coming to pick me up.
15. One of the books that the teacher assigns each semester (*is, are*) dull.

Appendix VI

Principal Parts of Irregular Verbs

SIMPLE FORM	PAST FORM	PAST PARTICIPLE FORM
be	was, were	been
bear	bore	born
beat	beat	beat
become	became	become
begin	began	begun
bend	bent	bent
bet	bet	bet
bind	bound	bound
bite	bit	bitten
bleed	bled	bled
blow	blew	blown
break	broke	broken
breed	bred	bred
bring	brought	brought
build	built	built
burst	burst	burst
buy	bought	bought
catch	caught	caught
choose	chose	chosen
come	came	come
cost	cost	cost
creep	crept	crept
cut	cut	cut
do	did	done
dig	dug	dug

SIMPLE FORM	PAST FORM	PAST PARTICIPLE FORM
draw	drew	drawn
drink	drank	drunk
drive	drove	driven
eat	ate	eaten
fall	fell	fallen
feed	fed	fed
feel	felt	felt
fight	fought	fought
find	found	found
fit	fit	fit
flee	fled	fled
fly	flew	flown
forbid	forbade	forbidden
forget	forgot	forgotten
forgive	forgave	forgiven
freeze	froze	frozen
get	got	gotten
give	gave	given
go	went	gone
grind	ground	ground
grow	grew	grown
hang	hung	hung
have	had	had
hear	heard	heard
hide	hid	hidden
hit	hit	hit
hold	held	held
hurt	hurt	hurt
keep	kept	kept
know	knew	known
lay	laid	laid
lead	led	led
leave	left	left
lend	lent	lent
let	let	let
light	lit	lit
lose	lost	lost
lie	lay	lain
make	made	made
mean	meant	meant
meet	met	met
pay	paid	paid
put	put	put
quit	quit	quit
read	read	read
ride	rode	ridden
ring	rang	rung

SIMPLE FORM	PAST FORM	PAST PARTICIPLE FORM
rise	rose	risen
run	ran	run
say	said	said
see	saw	seen
seek	sought	sought
sell	sold	sold
send	sent	sent
set	set	set
shake	shook	shaken
shine	shone	shone
shoot	shot	shot
shut	shut	shut
sing	sang	sung
sink	sank	sunk
sit	sat	sat
sleep	slept	slept
slide	slid	slid
speak	spoke	spoken
speed	sped	sped
spend	spent	spent
spin	spun	spun
split	split	split
spread	spread	spread
spring	sprang	sprung
stand	stood	stood
steal	stole	stolen
stick	stuck	stuck
sting	stung	stung
strike	struck	struck
swear	swore	sworn
swim	swam	swum
swing	swung	swung
take	took	taken
teach	taught	taught
tear	tore	torn
tell	told	told
think	thought	thought
throw	threw	thrown
understand	understood	understood
wake up	woke up	woken up
wear	wore	worn
weave	wove	woven
weep	wept	wept
win	won	won
wind	wound	wound
wring	wrung	wrung
write	wrote	written

Problem Verbs

Some verb forms are particularly troublesome. Note carefully the following forms:

begin	began	begun
choose	chose	chosen
fall	fell	fell
feel	felt	felt
throw	threw	thrown
write	wrote	written

The following sets of verbs have similar forms but are used in different ways.

1. *Lie/lay/lain/lying* means "to recline." It is intransitive, so it takes no object.

   I *lie* down every afternoon.

   I *lay* down yesterday.

   I *have lain* down many times.

2. *Lay/laid/laid/laying* means "to put." It is transitive, so it needs an object.

   Lay the book over there.

   He *laid* it there yesterday.

   He has *laid* it there before.

3. *Sit/sat/sat* means "to sit down." It is intransitive (takes no object).

   I sit in the same chair every day. I sat here yesterday.

4. *Set/set/set* means "to put something down." It is transitive, so it needs an object.

   Set the dishes on the table.

   He *set* the books over there.

5. *Lose/lost/lost* means "to misplace." It is transitive.

   I always *lose* my shoes.

   I *lost* them two weeks ago.

6. *Loosen/loosened/loosened* means "to relax something." It is transitive.

   He *loosened* his shoes.

   Note: The term *loose* is an adjective.

   I like *loose* clothing.

EXERCISE AVI-1

Fill in the correct form of the verb in each of the following sentences.

1. She has not (*begin*) ____________ yet.
2. Last week, he (*choose*) ____________ Mary to be his partner.
3. He (*fall*) ____________ out of the tree and hurt his leg.
4. She (*feel*) ____________ sad yesterday.
5. She has (*throw*) ____________ away all his old clothes.
6. Have you (*write*) ____________ the letter yet?

EXERCISE AVI-2

In these sentences, fill in the correct form of either verb in parentheses.

1. (*lie/lay*) He is ____________ down on the bed.

   Cheryl ____________ on the floor to listen to the stereo.

   Yesterday, he ____________ his gloves on the dresser.

   Today they are ____________ carpet in the dining room.

   She has ____________ out in the sun all afternoon.

   Please ____________ it over there.

2. (*sit/set*) He is ____________ in the brown chair.

   Do not ____________ the vase on the stereo.

   She ____________ in the same chair every day.

   He ____________ some tomato plants out yesterday.

3. (*lose/loosen*) He ____________ his tie in order to be more comfortable.

   Did you ____________ your wallet?

   She should not ____________ the bandage on her arm.

Appendix VII

Verbs and Their Complements

Verb Followed by an Infinitive

This (S) man happens (V) to be (INF) my husband.

agree	hope
appear	intend
arrange	learn
ask	manage
attempt	mean
beg	need
care	plan
choose	promise
decide	refuse
desire	request
endeavor	seem
expect	tend
fail	threaten
get	try
guarantee	used
happen	want
have	wish

Special Expression

I *can(not) stand* **to sit** here like this!

We *can(not) bear* **to see** him suffer.

Verb Followed by a Noun Phrase + Infinitive

S V NP INF
I do not want you to go now.

advise	engage	persuade
allow	expect	phone (*also* telephone)
appoint	forbid	pick
ask	force	prefer
assign	get	prepare
authorize	hate	push
beg	help	raise
call	hire	rely on
cause	inspire	remind
challenge	instruct	request
choose	intend	require
command	invite	select
contract	lead	send
convince	like	teach
dare	love	tell
depend on	meant	tempt
desire	name	train
direct	need	trust
drive	notify	urge
elect	oblige	want
employ	order	warn
enable	pay	wire
encourage	permit	write

EXERCISE AVII-1

Complete the following sentences using an infinitive or a noun phrase + infinitive, whichever is appropriate.

1. We have all agreed ____________________
2. The chair of the board refuses ____________________
3. The president depends on ____________________
4. The reluctant father promised ____________________
5. The enemy threatened ____________________
6. We all expect ____________________
7. The earthquake caused ____________________
8. "Oh, I am so happy! I get ____________________"

9. Lazy people cannot stand ______________________________

10. The millionaire hired ______________________________

____

Verb Followed by a Gerund

S V GER
Children enjoy learning new things.

admit	enjoy	picture	resent
advise	escape	postpone	resume
appreciate	feel like	put off	resist
avoid	finish	protest	risk
can't help	get around to	practice	save
confess	get out of	quit	stop
consider	imagine	recall	succeed in
debate	include	recommend	suggest
delay	keep on	regret	take up
deny	mention	relate	welcome
discuss	mind	remember	work at
dislike	miss	report	understand

Verb Followed by a Gerund or an Infinitive

S V INF
He continued to serve the Queen.
S V GER
He continued serving the Queen.

(can) afford	dread	regret
attempt	forget	remember
begin	hate	(can) stand
bother	intend	start
choose	like	stop
continue	neglect	try
deserve	prefer	

Special Note

Some verbs change their meaning when they are followed by a gerund or an infinitive:

John stopped *to pet* the dog. (John's intention in stopping was to pet the dog.)

John stopped *petting* the dog. (He ceased the action of petting.)

I remember *to lock* the doors each night. (The action of locking comes after the action of remembering.)

I remember *locking* the doors last night. (The action of locking comes *before* the action of remembering.)

EXERCISE AVII-2

Fill in the blank with the appropriate form of the complement: a gerund or an infinitive.

1. The youngster admitted _______________ (commit) the crime.
2. We will endeavor _______________ (work) harder.
3. Even when we are tired, we should keep on _______________ (try).
4. Not wanting to go to the dentist, the child delayed _______________ (get) in the car.
5. I used _______________ (ride) a horse when I was a child, but I do not anymore.
6. People cannot help _______________ (fall) for gimmicks like that.
7. The convict attempted _______________ (escape) but failed.
8. If you do not want to study, then I suggest _______________ (go) home.

Verbs Followed by a Noun Phrase + Gerund

S V NP GER
The broadcasters reported the spaceship's landing.

admit	hate	recall
applaud	imagine	recommend
appreciate	like	regret
approve	mention	remember
concede	mind	report
deny	miss	risk
disapprove	picture	save
enjoy	prefer	salute
forget	protest	welcome
depend on		

Verb–Preposition Combination Followed by a Gerund or Noun Phrase + Gerund

S V PREP NP GER
The officer forgot about John's breaking the law.

S V PREP GER
John forgot about breaking the law.

admit to	cry about	look forward to
agree on	decide against	object to
allude to	decide on	pay for
approve of	depend on/upon	plan on

argue about
argue against
ask about
balk at
begin with
believe in
care about
center on
confess to
count on
dream about/of
end with
fight about
figure on
forget about
hear about
inquire about
insist on
laugh about
lie about
refer to
rely on
speak about/of
start with
talk about/of
tell about
think about/of
warn against/of/about
wonder about
worry about

Special Note

As a general rule, most verb–preposition combinations are followed by a gerund. Beware, however, of confusing the infinitive *to* with the verb–preposition combination requiring *to* as part of the verb.

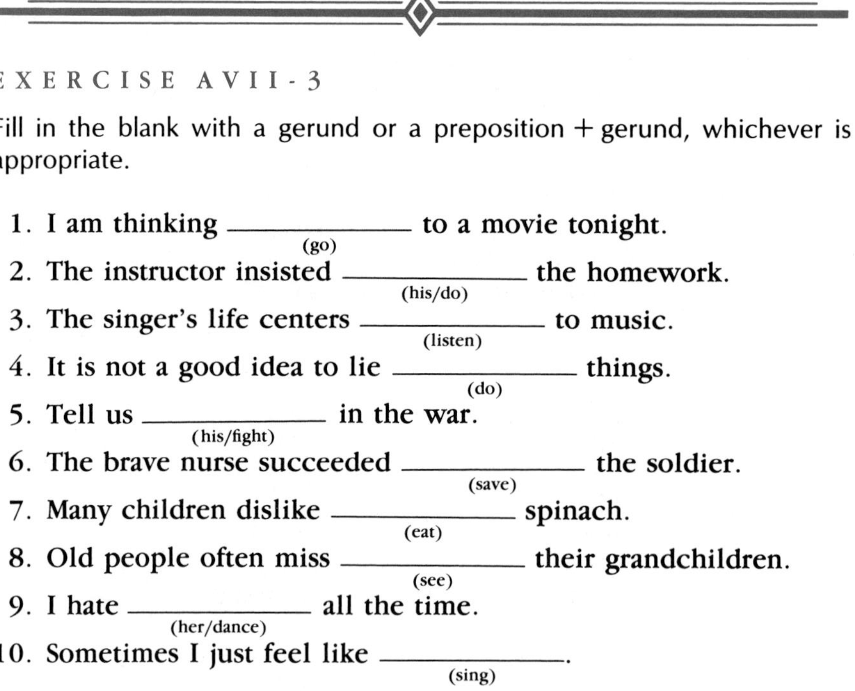

EXERCISE AVII-3

Fill in the blank with a gerund or a preposition + gerund, whichever is appropriate.

1. I am thinking __________ (go) to a movie tonight.
2. The instructor insisted __________ (his/do) the homework.
3. The singer's life centers __________ (listen) to music.
4. It is not a good idea to lie __________ (do) things.
5. Tell us __________ (his/fight) in the war.
6. The brave nurse succeeded __________ (save) the soldier.
7. Many children dislike __________ (eat) spinach.
8. Old people often miss __________ (see) their grandchildren.
9. I hate __________ (her/dance) all the time.
10. Sometimes I just feel like __________ (sing).

Adjective–Preposition Combination Followed by a Gerund

S V ADJ PREP GER
We are sick of sailing.

Special Note

When an adjective is followed by a preposition, it is usually followed by a gerund.

accustomed to	cynical about	proud of
addicted to	delighted about	resigned to
afraid of	disappointed about	sad about
amazed at	disturbed about	satisfied with
angry about	excited about	sick of
annoyed about/with	famous for	slow at/about
anxious about	fond of	sold on
ashamed about	glad about/of	sorry about
aware of	good at	successful at
bad at	good about	superb at
bored with	happy about	surprised at/about
capable of	hesitant about	tired of
careful about	impressed with	unaccustomed to
clever at	interested in	undecided about
confident of	new at	upset about
confused about	opposed to	used to
concerned about	pleased about	worried about
conscious of		

Adjective Followed by an Infinitive

S V ADJ INF
I am delighted to go with you.

able	fun	reluctant
afraid	glad	sad
anxious	good	slow
apt	happy	smart
ashamed	hard	sorry
bound	inclined	stupid
careful	kind	strange
certain	likely	supposed
delighted	nice	sure
depressing	pleased	surprised
disturbed	possible	terrible
eager	predicted	welcome
easy	prepared	willing
expected	qualified	wise
foolish	quick	wonderful
free	ready	wrong

Special Note

Some adjectives occur with *it* as the subject.

It is nice to stay at home on weekends.
It is nice of him to stay with the family.

Adjectives in this group include the following:

depressing	kind	stupid
easy	likely	strange
expected	nice	supposed
foolish	possible	sure
free	predicted	terrible
fun	sad	wise
good	smart	wrong
hard		

EXERCISE AVII-4

Insert the gerund or infinitive in the blank as appropriate. Add a preposition if necessary.

1. **Julio was undecided __________ (go) to college.**
2. **I am disturbed __________ (hear) about your problem.**
3. **The principal is opposed __________ (let) students vote for teachers.**
4. **The weather forecaster was anxious __________ (give) a good weather report.**
5. **Most people are willing __________ (give) new things a try.**
6. **They are surprised __________ (Roberto's/go) away.**
7. **He is certain __________ (win) the prize.**
8. **The student was interested __________ (see) the new film.**
9. **She was sad __________ (leave) home.**
10. **The old man is quite fond __________ (play) chess.**

Verb That Can Be Followed by a Noun Clause

S V NC
He declared *that he* loved her.

acknowledge	discover	maintain	retort
admit	doubt	mean	reveal
advise*	estimate	mention	say
agree	expect	note	see
announce	explain	notice	sense
answer	fear	notify	shout
anticipate	feel	order*	show
argue	forbid*	point out	signify
arrange*	forget	predict	state
ask*	gather	prefer*	suggest*
assert	guarantee	presume	suppose
assume	guess	pretend	suspect
believe	hear	promise	swear
charge	hint	protest	teach
claim	hope	prove	tell
comment	imagine	read	think
conclude	imply	realize	trust
decide	indicate	recall	understand
declare	infer	recommend*	urge*
demand*	inform	regret*	vow
demonstrate	insist*	relate	whisper
deny	know	remember	write
determine	learn	request*	

EXERCISE AVII-5

Complete the following sentences with noun clauses. Be careful of tense and watch out for subjunctive noun clauses.

1. My boss guaranteed ______________________________
2. I fear ______________________________
3. They request ______________________________
4. We all understand ______________________________
5. I sense ______________________________
6. Jose told us ______________________________
7. The sergeant said ______________________________
8. I vow ______________________________
9. He suggests ______________________________
10. My mother insists ______________________________

____

*Subjunctive noun clauses: The verb stays in the base form and does not change for conjugation or tense.

Appendix VIII

Prepositions

A preposition is a word that precedes a noun phrase; the preposition combined with the noun phrase can function as an adverbial or an adjectival phrase. In other words, prepositional phrases can indicate when, where (location or direction), how (by what means, by what agent, or in what way), how long or how much, and purpose; they can also modify a noun, describing a state or condition.

Prepositions Indicating When or How Long (Time) [See Chapter 2]

about	It was *about* three o'clock when the game began.
after	It was *after* six o'clock when the game ended.
at	The party began *at* 7:30 P.M.
before	No one arrived at the party *before* seven o'clock.
by	However, everyone was there *by* 7:30.
during	The wife of the soccer star cried *during* the game.
for	That means that she cried *for* over three hours.
from	In other words, she cried *from* 3:00 to after 6:00 P.M.
in	*In* the fall, *in* November, I like to go walking *in* the early morning rain.
on	I like to get home every Monday in time for the football game, for it always begins *on* time—at exactly 5:30.
past	He stayed well *past* the hour when everybody else had left.
since	She has been crying *since* three o'clock.
to	He danced until a quarter *to* 4:00.
until	He danced *until* midnight with Marie-Claire.

Prepositions Indicating How (By What Means, by What Agent, in What Way)

by Agnes likes to travel any way she can: *by* bus, *by* car, *by* train, or *by* plane.
However, she does not like to travel *by* herself.
By traveling with someone, she enjoys everything more.
She earns her money for the trip *by* working hard.
Once, however, she was robbed *by* a young man.

from Actually, the robbery resulted *from* her carelessness.

in It all happened *in* a minute, maybe two.
The thief appeared to take pride *in* snatching her purse when she was not looking.
He left the station *in* a hurry.
But when he saw that her name was engraved *in* gold, he decided to throw the purse away.

like By that time, he felt *like* a cad.

on He had stolen the purse because he had lived *on* almost nothing for too long.

with Unfortunately, Agnes had summoned the police. *With* guns in their hands and *with* anger on their faces, they chased him.

Prepositions Indicating How Much and How Long

for The police chased the thief *for* ten minutes.
He purchased his new car *for* only $8,500.

by We used to buy gasoline *by* the gallon, but it is common now to buy it *by* the liter.

Preposition Indicating Purpose

for Everything that I have done, I have done *for* you.
We searched the lot *for* the clue, but we could not find it.
We went to San Francisco *for* a good time, but we did not enjoy ourselves.
I respect you *for* your intelligence.

Prepositions Indicating Where (Location or Direction) [See Chapter 3]

about The man with amnesia wandered *about* the room.

around The dog did not want to confront the cat, so he walked *around* the yard to avoid it.

at She lives *at* 3540 Dumaine Street. However, she is not always *at* home.
She might be *at* school, *at* her mother's house, or *at* her favorite café.
She likes the restaurant because no one bothers to look *at* her.

beneath The diver remained *beneath* the surface of the water for two hours.
The prince married *beneath* his social status.

down The ball slowly rolled *down* the hill into the water puddle.
They are from *down* south.

from We are leaving *from* Boston and driving to Portland, Oregon.
I cannot wait to get away *from* here!

in She has been *in* college a year now. She spends much of her time *in* the library. She lives *in* the dormitory. Her parents live *in* Maine.

inside The SWAT team knew that the murderer was *inside* the house.
The new employee was nervous about going *inside* the huge skyscraper.

next John lives *next* door to Mary.

of Pierre and Anne live just north *of* here.

off Take the tablecloth *off* the table, please.

on He lives *on* the south side of town.
Place the model *on* the desk so we can observe it.
Put the package *on* the train for her, or else we will have to put it *on* the bus.

out Get *out* of here!
The sad lover stayed *out* in the cold.

outside Bill lives just *outside* of Denver.

through People enjoy honking their horns when they drive *through* a tunnel.
I once read a story about a man who could walk *through* walls.

to Bill goes *to* the university, but his brother goes *to* high school.
Send the package *to* me immediately.

under Cousteau does a lot of exploring *under* the water. (also *underwater*)
The cat hid *under* the table.

up They live *up* the river from us.
They moved *up* north.
They climbed *up* the mountain.

with John decided to go *with* them.

within The well-trained dog stayed well *within* the confines of the yard.

Prepositions That Modify Nouns (Describing States or Conditions)

at I am *at* school now.

by I prefer to live *by* myself; that is, I prefer to live alone.

in He is *in* a hurry.
The man *in* the gray coat just robbed the fast-food restaurant on the corner.
Many people died because they were *in* a state of panic and did the wrong thing.

next The woman *next* in line for the job is his niece.

of The man *of* my dreams must be very intelligent.

on The police force will now be *on* duty all during the parade.
She feels *on* top of the world.
Marie is *on* edge about the appointment.
The ring *on* her left finger was given to her by a famous celebrity.

with The man *with* the gray coat on his arm is a spy.

The woman *with* blond hair is a famous movie star.
Who is that person *with* the cane?
The child, *with* tears in his eyes, made his mother feel bad.

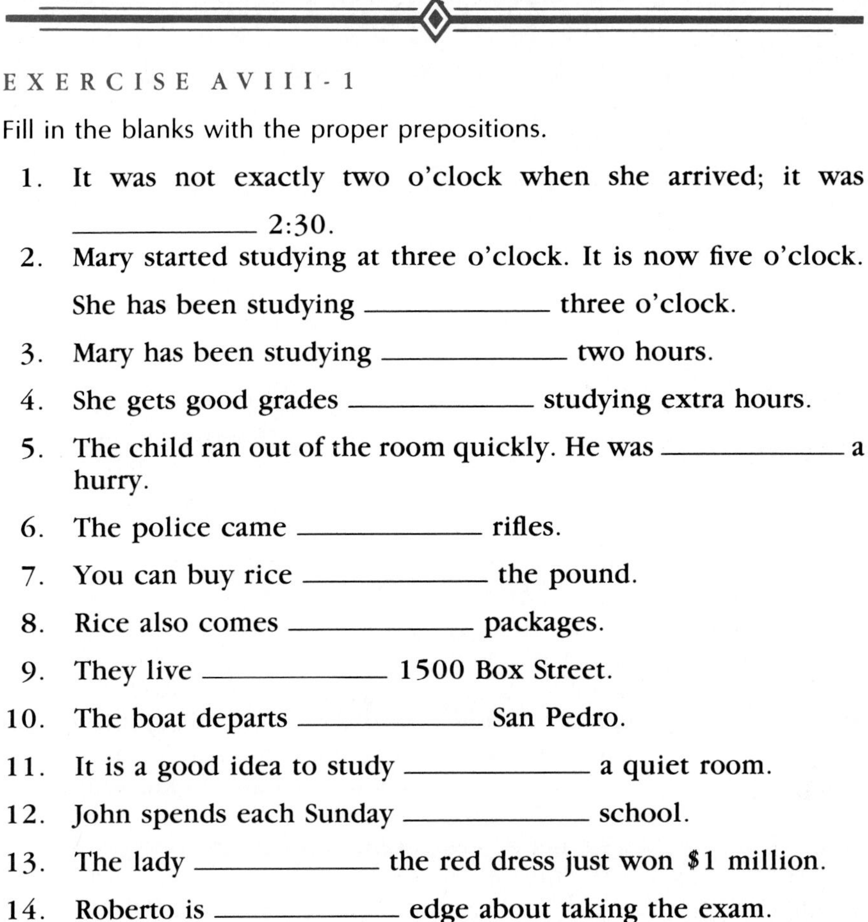

EXERCISE AVIII-1

Fill in the blanks with the proper prepositions.

1. It was not exactly two o'clock when she arrived; it was __________ 2:30.
2. Mary started studying at three o'clock. It is now five o'clock. She has been studying __________ three o'clock.
3. Mary has been studying __________ two hours.
4. She gets good grades __________ studying extra hours.
5. The child ran out of the room quickly. He was __________ a hurry.
6. The police came __________ rifles.
7. You can buy rice __________ the pound.
8. Rice also comes __________ packages.
9. They live __________ 1500 Box Street.
10. The boat departs __________ San Pedro.
11. It is a good idea to study __________ a quiet room.
12. John spends each Sunday __________ school.
13. The lady __________ the red dress just won $1 million.
14. Roberto is __________ edge about taking the exam.
15. We flew down to New Orleans __________ Mardi Gras, or "Carnival," as they call it.

Appendix IX

Verb – Preposition Combinations

account for	Nothing could *account for* his depression.
accuse . . . of	They *accused* him *of* robbing a bank.
agree on	No one could *agree on* anything.
agree with	I *agree with* the man who is speaking.
allude to	It is not polite to *allude to* someone's disability.
apologize for	The former leader said that he had nothing to *apologize for*, although he did *apologize for* running away.
apologize to	The leader did not want to *apologize to* the people.
apply for	Every June college graduates *apply for* jobs.
approve of	We do not *approve of* his behavior.
argue with	It does little good to *argue with* a judge.
argue about	A judge does not want you to *argue about* anything unless you have a good case.
arrive at	We *arrived at* our destination safely. He *arrived at* a conclusion early.
ask for	Children like to *ask* their parents *for* gifts, but they especially like to *ask for* special toys.
become of	John has disappeared; I do not know what has *become of* him.
believe in	Do you *believe in* magic?
belong to	Whom does this pet *belong to*? It *belongs to* her.
blame . . . for	Don't *blame* me *for* your problems!
blame . . . on	Don't *blame* your problems *on* me!
borrow from	He has *borrowed* enough money *from* the bank.
care for	She enjoys the time she can *care for* her nieces and nephews.

	"I *care* a great deal *for* you," said the young lover.
come from	She *came from* Honduras with her family.
compare with	How does a small car *compare with* a large car?
complain about	He is always *complaining about* something.
compliment on	*Compliment* them *on* their performance and they will all be happy.
congratulate on	They deserve to be *congratulated on* (or *for*) their performance.
consent to	The parents refused to *consent to* their son's marriage.
consist of	The solution *consists of* some strange chemicals.
convince of	I am *convinced of* his goodness.
decide between	We cannot *decide between* the two.
decide on	We have *decided on* the red vase.
delight in	My child *delights in* watching the ducks.
depend on (upon)	Do not *depend on* other people.
detract from	Such behavior *detracts from* your beauty.
dream about (of)	We are *dreaming about* going to Paris. I *dream of* it every night.
excuse . . . for	The teacher *excused* the child *for* his behavior.
explain . . . to	It is difficult to *explain* a problem *to* students who aren't curious.
happen to	Oh, I just *happened to* be in the neighborhood and thought I'd stop by.
	I didn't know such a thing could *happen to* me.
hear of	Have you ever *heard of* something like that?
	That name means nothing to me. I've never *heard of* her before.
hear about	Did you *hear about* Mary? She's getting married.
hear from	Did you get a letter from him? I have not *heard from* him at all.
insist on	The decorator *insists on* blue drapes.
invite . . . to	It would be a good idea to *invite* him *to* our party.
laugh about	We did some crazy things as children. We can *laugh about* them now.
laugh at	It's not nice to *laugh at* someone because it's not nice to mock them.
	It's nice to *laugh at* a joke, though.
laugh with	When a person laughs, it's good to *laugh with* him.
listen for	I hope the letter carrier comes soon; I'll *listen for* him until he does.
listen to	*Listen to* me! I am speaking to you!
look at	It is not wise to *look at* someone for a long time; it's called staring.
look for	My child is lost! We must *look for* her.
object to	Most people do not *object to* giving to charity.
plan on	Why don't you *plan on* staying at our place during the holidays?
praise . . . for	We have much *praise for* her.

	It is good to *praise* someone *for* a good deed.
prefer . . . to	I *prefer* red cars *to* blue cars.
provide . . . with	My parents have *provided* me *with* enough money to last for one month.
recover from	It often takes a long time to *recover from* a serious illness.
refer to	If you are *referring to* me, you should say so.
rely on	I can always *rely on* my strength.
remind . . . of	You *remind* me *of* a bear.
search for	We *searched for* the lost child for three hours, but we couldn't find her.
spend . . . on	Anna *spent* all of her money *on* a new car.
substitute for	When I was absent, William *substituted for* me.
succeed in	I have *succeeded in* discovering a cure for that disease!
talk to	When I am *talking to* you, I expect you to listen to me.
talk about	It is not nice to *talk about* people when they are not present.
thank . . . for	*Thank* you *for* the nice gift.
vote for	You should *vote for* my candidate.
wait for	Please *wait for* me! I'll be ready in a moment.
wait on	No, I will not bring you breakfast in bed. I won't *wait on* you like that.
waste . . . on	Manuel *wasted* $4,000 *on* that project.
wish for	What do you *wish for* your birthday?
work for	*We* should all *work for* the good of mankind.
	Mukesh *works for* that big company.
worry about	Parents always *worry about* their children.
wrestle with	We spent three hours *wrestling with* that problem, but we could not solve it.

EXERCISE AIX-1

Insert the proper prepositions in the blanks.

1. I just cannot make up my mind. It is difficult to decide ____________ these two movies.
2. Please do not let me down. I depend ____________ you.
3. What country do you come ____________?
4. May I borrow some money ____________ you?
5. When you offend someone, you should apologize ____________ him or her.
6. It is difficult to ask your boss ____________ a raise.
7. Whatever happened ____________ that girl you used to date?

8. You should not argue ____________ your parents.
9. Do not argue ____________ that problem; try to solve it.
10. Just listen ____________ that beautiful music. Isn't it nice?

Appendix X

Prepositions After Other Expressions

ability in	I have *ability in* math.
access to	He has *access to* valuable documents.
accustomed to	He is *accustomed to* dining at Antoine's.
afraid of	Many people are *afraid of* the dark. (*But:* I am *afraid to* go.)
agree on	The children could not *agree on* anything.
agree to	We cannot *agree to* that.
angry about	Many people are *angry about* the high cost of living.
angry with/at	You can be *angry with* or *at* someone.
authority on	Dr. Jones is an *authority on* apes.
aware of	Are you *aware of* the difficulties involved?
based on	This movie is *based on* her life.
capable of	That animal is *capable of great harm.*
certain of	I am *certain of* success.
charge of	In fact, he has *charge of* those documents.
composed of	That material is *composed of* many things.
confidence in	Have *confidence in* me!
content with	Are you *content with* your lot?
delighted with (at)	The teacher was *delighted with* the student's progress.
dependent on (upon)	The chicks are *dependent upon* help from their mother.
different from	We are very *different from* each other.
disappointed in	The boy was *disappointed in* his creation.
due to	The mistake was *due to* clerical error.
faith in	You should have *faith in* me!
familiar with	We are all *familiar with* Shakespeare, aren't we?
famous for	Colonel Jones is *famous for* his victory.

followed by	I'm being *followed by* someone.
fond of	I am very *fond of* you.
frightened by	The babysitter was *frightened by* some noise.
happy with	We are *happy with* our progress.
in charge of	John is *in charge of* food for the picnic.
in contact with	We have been *in contact with* each other.
independent of	I am *independent of* you. (This expression does not have to come after the verb *to be*.)
in favor of	I am *in favor of* reform.
influence on (over)	Her husband has great *influence on* her.
interested in	I am *interested in* your progress. I am *interested in* doing work.
involved in	Our company is *involved in* some serious affairs.
involved with	You are involved in something, but you are usually *involved with* someone.
knowledge of	He has *knowledge of* many serious things.
known for	He is *known for* his cooking.
limited to	Seating is *limited to* one hundred people for tonight's concert.
made of	Chairs are often *made of* wood.
married to	I am *married to* him.
oblivious to (of)	She is *oblivious to* the world around her.
opposed to	We are *opposed to* his candidacy.
patience with	Please try to have *patience with* children.
proud of	James was very *proud of* his brother.
reason for	I don't have a *reason for* failing.
related to	We are *related to* the Hernandez family that lives in New Jersey.
sorry about	I am very *sorry about* your loss.
sorry for	You have lost all of your money. I feel *sorry for* you.
suspicious of	We are often *suspicious of* strangers.
thrilled by (with)	I am *thrilled with* the gift.
time for	We don't have *time for* such nonsense.
tired of	I am *tired of* your complaints.

Note the differences:

I am *ashamed to* go.	I am *ashamed of* myself.
He is careful *to write* nice letters.	He is careful *about writing* nice letters.
I would be *delighted to* go.	I am *delighted about* going.
I am *glad to* see you.	I am very *glad about* the raise.
He is *sure to* go there.	I am *sure about* his going there.
We are *happy to* pass.	We are *happy about* passing.
I was *surprised to* learn the truth.	I am *surprised about* his past.
I am *pleased to* go.	I am *pleased about* the party's success.
Movies *frighten* me.	I am *frightened by* movies.

EXERCISE AX-1

Fill in the blanks with the correct prepositions.

1. After living in the United States for three years, I am accustomed ____________ the culture.
2. The police chief is in charge ____________ the force.
3. My Aunt Antonia is married ____________ a dentist.
4. Paul McCartney is known ____________ his part in the Beatles.
5. Can we agree ____________ at least one thing?
6. Would you agree ____________ these terms?
7. Please try to have patience ____________ old people.
8. Students have access ____________ the library on the weekend.
9. Professor Smith is an authority ____________ DNA.
10. My father is very proud ____________ my mother.
11. I am very interested ____________ art.
12. We have been in contact ____________ officials.
13. Are you interested ____________ dancing in the musical?
14. Most people are in favor ____________ reducing taxes.
15. I have the ability to work hard, but I have no ability ____________ typing.

Appendix XI

Two-Word Verbs

Two-word verbs are verbs that have prepositions attached to them (called *particles*). These particles help define the meaning of the verbs.

VERB	MEANING	EXAMPLE
barge in	(entered uninvited)	They *barged in* on the party.
bawl out	(reprimand orally)	She *bawled out* the boy for this wrong deed.
bear up	(endure)	He *bears up* well under pressure.
bear with	(be patient with)	You must *bear with* me; I'm just tired.
blow in	(arrive)	He *blew in* to town last week.
blow out	(extinguish)	You can only *blow out* small flames.
bound for	(heading toward)	I am *bound for* New Orleans.
bound to	(destined)	He is *bound to* get into mischief.
break away	(sever, depart)	He *broke away* from her embrace.
break in	(enter forcefully)	The thief *broke into* her house.
break off	(stop, sever)	The other country *broke off* negotiations.
brush up on	(review)	I need to *brush up on* math before taking physics.

VERB	MEANING	EXAMPLE
call away	(summon)	*Call* that dog *away* from that child!
call back	(summon to return)	*Call* your dog *back*!
call for	(request)	The young man *called for* a vote on the issue.
call off	(postpone)	They *called off* the picnic because of rain.
call on	(visit)	The fiancé *called on* the young woman every night.
call up	(telephone)	*Call* me *up* at 6:00.
carry off	(succeed)	He *carried off* the robbery superbly.
carry off	(take away)	She *carried off* the oranges before anybody noticed.
carry on	(continue)	The crew *carried on* without the captain.
cheer up	(become happy)	*Cheer up*! Things can't be that bad!
come about	(evolve)	How did this problem *come about*?
come across	(find unexpectedly)	I *came across* an interesting word in the dictionary.
come around	(convert)	He finally *came around* to my way of thinking.
come by	(acquire)	I do not know how he *came by* his money.
come down (with)	(become sick)	She *came down with* a cold just before New Year's.
come upon	(discover, surprise)	When I was walking in the forest, I *came upon* a little squirrel.
count in	(include)	You can *count* me *in* the game.
count on	(expect, depend on)	When you are in trouble, you can *count on* me.
crack up	(wreck)	He *cracked up* his new sports car.
crack up	(have a nervous breakdown)	The patient *cracked up* after too many months of pressure.
crack up	(amuse)	That comedian just *cracks* me *up*.
cross off	(eliminate)	I hope you will *cross* me *off* the list.
cross out	(erase, remove)	*Cross out* his name. He does not want to join.

VERB	MEANING	EXAMPLE
cut down	(diminish, lower)	I am typing better. I have *cut down* on the number of errors I make.
cut off	(halt, sever)	The two countries have *cut off* relationships.
cut out	(eliminate, remove)	The rich old man *cut* his only son *out* of his will.
cut out for	(designed, destined)	I guess I am not *cut out for* medicine.
die down	(diminish)	The noise *died down* before the curtain opened.
die out	(extinguish)	The fire *died out* before the firefighters got there.
draw up	(write, usually legal)	The lawyer *drew up* a contract.
dress up	(clothe nicely)	The guests decided to *dress up* for the dance.
fill in	(substitute)	The teacher *filled in* for the sick friend.
fill in	(complete a slot)	Just *fill in* your name there in that spot.
fill out	(complete, as a form)	John *filled out* the entire form incorrectly.
fill up	(load to capacity)	"*Fill* 'er *up*" is a common phrase at a gas station.
find out	(discover, learn)	I *found out* that she is not who she says she is.
get ahead	(advance)	People work hard, trying to *get ahead* in life.
get along	(manage)	The retirement folks are *getting along* okay.
get along	(be in harmony, in friendly agreement)	I *get along* with my brother quite well.
get at	(implying, suggesting)	Just what are you *getting at* anyway?
get away	(escape, flee)	We need to *get away* for a vacation.
get away with	(succeed wrongfully, escape punishment)	Too many criminals *get away with* their crimes.
get back	(return)	I think I had better *get back* home before it's late.
get back at	(avenge)	I'll *get back at* you for this!
get by	(manage)	I will *get by* with what I have; I don't need help.
get in	(make entry)	I don't know how we will *get in* this house.

VERB	MEANING	EXAMPLE
get off	(descend)	She is *getting off* the bus now.
get off	(escape with little or no punishment)	He *got off* with only one year in jail.
get on	(board)	David *gets on* the bus every day at 7:30.
get on with	(continue)	Let's *get on* with the show.
get out	(exit)	I think we had better *get out* of here.
get over	(recover)	She never did *get over* him.
get through	(survive, finish)	We *got through* that crisis without much harm done.
get to	(become)	It *got to* be a real problem.
get up	(rise)	*Get up* early, won't you!
give away	(donate, reveal)	Don't *give* my secret *away*! I *gave away* a lot of money.
give in	(surrender)	I just *gave in* to his demand.
give up	(stop, surrender)	I just *gave up* trying.
go by	(be known as)	He *goes by* the title "Le Petit Colonel."
go for	(like, attracted to)	Julio really *goes for* that girl.
go into	(discuss in detail)	We won't *go into* that now, but we will later.
go on	(continue)	Don't stop. *Go on* with your story.
go through	(repeat)	Do you have to *go through* that again?
go through with	(finish)	He wants to *go through with* his plans to marry her.
head off	(stop, catch)	It is difficult to *head off* inflation.
hold back	(restrain)	Nothing can *hold* her *back* now.
hold off	(delay)	Can you *hold off* counting until everyone's here?
hold on	(grasp)	You've got to *hold on* to what you've got.
hold out	(maintain)	"I cannot *hold out* any longer," the sick man cried.
jot down	(write quickly)	*Jot down* his address on this piece of paper.
keep back	(prevent from continuing)	"Don't crowd! *Keep back*, everyone!" ordered the man.

VERB	MEANING	EXAMPLE
keep on	(continue)	We just have to *keep on* trying.
keep up	(continue)	*Keep up* the good work.
lay off	(fire from work, stop)	He was *laid off* on Friday.
lay on	(deliver—usually words of anger or compliments)	That guy is really *laying* it *on* thick!
leave out	(omit)	We try not to *leave out* any important rules.
look after	(watch)	The woman asked her neighbor to *look after* her flowers while she was gone.
look into	(investigate)	The district attorney looked *into* the matter.
look over	(examine)	People *look* things *over* carefully before buying them.
look up	(seek—as in a book)	*Look up* that word in the dictionary.
make up	(fabricate)	The child *made up* the whole story.
make up	(reconcile)	The lovers *made up* after their fight.
mix up	(confuse)	I always get those twins *mixed up*.
pass away	(die)	The woman *passed away* at age 103.
pass out	(faint)	He *passed out* upon seeing blood.
pass up	(skip, let go)	They *passed up* the opportunity to see the star.
pick on	(torment)	Big boys often *pick on* little boys.
pick out	(select, identify)	The victim *picked out* the criminal from the line-up.
pick up	(take off the ground, and so forth)	The litterbug had to *pick up* trash for a week.
pick up	(meet for the first time and go out)	Teenagers like to go to drive-ins to *pick up* members of the opposite sex; however, *picking up* potential dates is not considered wise.
play down	(decrease significance)	The president tried to *play down* the role of the government in the situation.

VERB	MEANING	EXAMPLE
play up	(increase significance)	However, he did *play up* the role of the police.
point out	(indicate, emphasize)	Let me *point out* to you that this is very crucial.
pull off	(succeed)	He *pulled* it *off*! He *pulled off* the greatest ruse in the history of this city!
pull over	(take aside)	The police officer *pulled* the speeder *over.*
put across	(communicate—clarify)	I am trying to *put across* to you the importance of the role of the instructor in this issue.
put down	(insult, debase)	Don't *put* me *down* for not knowing that.
put down	(suppress)	The squad tried to *put down* the rioting.
put up with	(tolerate)	I don't think I can *put up with* it any longer.
run across	(meet unexpectedly)	Guess who I *ran across* at the market today?
run after	(follow)	The thief *ran after* the victim.
run into	(meet unexpectedly)	You can *run into* a person, and you can run across a person; but you cannot *run into* a word, though you can run across a word.
run off	(duplicate)	Mister Jones, will you *run off* one hundred copies for me?
run out	(deplete)	We have just *run out* of money.
run up	(increase)	She *ran up* a bill of $1,000 at the store.
show off	(display with pride)	The teenager *showed off* his new car.
show up	(match someone)	I *showed* him *up*! I also got a new sports car.
sit out	(not participate)	The player had to *sit* the game *out.*
stand by	(wait)	*Stand by* for the report.
take away	(remove)	*Take* that sugar *away*! I don't want it.
take back	(repossess)	The company *took back* the car.
take on	(absorb, obtain)	The clerk *took on* more responsibilty.

VERB	MEANING	EXAMPLE
take up	(begin)	The teacher decided to *take up* knitting.
throw away	(dispense with)	*Throw away* that awful thing.
try on	(see if it fits)	I *tried on* three suits today and none fit.
try out	(test)	Let's *try out* this rocket fuel today.
		The player *tried out* for the team.
turn down	(deny, refuse)	They *turned down* my request for a raise.
turn in	(retire for sleep)	We *turned in* at nine o'clock last night.
turn in	(surrender)	He *turned in* his gun when he *turned* himself *in*.
turn into	(become)	He has *turned into* a real Dr. Jekyll.
turn out	(attend)	Thirty thousand people *turned out* for the parade.
vote down	(defeat by ballot)	The tax increase was *voted down*.
vote into	(elect)	The woman was *voted into* office in January.
wait on	(serve)	I am not about to *wait on* you, you lazy person!
wait out	(wait patiently until the end)	The fan *waited out* the game with tears in her eyes.
wait up	(stay awake)	The nervous father *waited up* for his daughter.
wear off	(lose the effects)	The medicine *wore off* after about three hours.
wear out	(exhaust)	The two-year-old completely *wore* his parents *out*.
wind down	(unwind, relax)	After about three hours, the energetic child began to *wind down*.
wind up	(raise to a high level of excitement)	The child started to *wind up* again soon, however.
wind up	(finish)	Let's try to *wind up* at six o'clock tonight.
wind up at	(end, make the last stop)	We *wound up at* Mary's house last night.
work in (to)	(include)	I think we can *work* some of these ideas *in (to)* the design.
work out	(succeed—in order to be	I don't know if that young

VERB	MEANING	EXAMPLE
	kept on)	worker will *work out*. We might have to let him go (fire him).
work out	(resolve)	Don't worry about our problems. I am sure we can *work* them *out*.
work up	(build, augment)	They *work up* a lot of perspiration out there.
write down	(put on paper)	Why don't you *write down* your telephone number for me?
write out	(write completely)	Why don't you *write out* your proposal on official stationery?
write up	(write a description of, put into the final form)	Joan *wrote up* her proposal for the boss.

Appendix XII

Proofreading

The final draft of a composition is not complete until after it has been proofread and corrected. Proofreading involves reading over your writing to catch errors in grammar, spelling, and punctuation. The following exercise is designed to help you sharpen your proofreading skills.

EXERCISE AXII-1

Proofread each of the following paragraphs and correct errors in grammar, spelling, and punctuation. The general types of errors and the number of them are identified for all paragraphs except paragraph 10.

1. I love to arrive on campus early in morning. On my way to school I get to enjoy the sunrise, its beauty has a calming effect on me. When I turn into the campus, I know I'll alway find good parking place. After I park. I go to the cafeteria, which opens at 7:00 A.M. The coffee is fresh and the biscuits are warm. While I am drinking my coffee and eating my biscuit. I gaze out the window and watch the squirrels run among the branch of the oak trees. When I'm finished, I review my class notes for about thirty minute. Sometime I have another cup of coffee or tea. Then, at about a quarter to 8:00, I walk to class, but I'm in no hurry so I can stopping along the way and glance at the front page of the day's newspaper locates near the university center. I alway arrive in class at least five minutes early, I can get a good seat. By time lecture begins, I'm ready for busy day.

ERRORS

article misuse (5)	fragment (2)
comma splice (2)	misuse of plural form (2)
misspelling (2)	misuse of verb form (2)

2. It is heartbreaking to observe person with Parkinson's disease, which is degenerative brain disease that strikes many older people. The person with Parkinson's disease has blank expression on his face, he shows no emotional expression at all. When he moved his hands, you notice that they shake. When he stands up, he looked stiff and had trouble initiating movement. Once he starts to walking, he walks without smoothness and then had difficulty to stop. Unless the patient receives treatment. She will only get worse. Until he cannot control his movements.

ERRORS

article misuse (3)	comma splice (1)
misuse of verb tense (4)	fragment (2)
misuse of verb form (2)	

3. The brain and spinal cord are encased by protective sheaths call the meninges, which divide into three layers, each has a different name. The outer layer, which is called the dura mater. This layer is tough yet flexible, though it cannot be stretched. The middle layer is referring to as the arachnoid membrane, it is soft and spongy. The bottom layer, which call the pia mater. It actually lines the brain and contains many blood vessel that provide nutrients to brain.

ERRORS

misuse of verb form (4)	fragment (2)
comma splice (2)	misuse of plural form (1)
article misuse (1)	

4. A good place to meet people is a gourmet coffee shop. This type of places attracts people like to sit around and chat, and often people go there on a regular basis. If they see other regulars there, after a while they will start talking to them. A subtle comraderie can develops over a period of a time. If the coffee shop is crowd, someone who has seen you there before might to ask to sit at your table. This is good way to starting a conversation. Often people read newspaper while they are drink coffee, so there is alway something to talk about. Too, some coffee shop have free poetry readings. This is a good opportunity to catch up on current trend in poetry and to meet some of people. What is particularly nice for women is that they can going to a gourmet coffee shop without to worry about people bothering them, which is a very different situation from a bar. So, gourmet coffee shopes, which attracts people of similar tastes and interests. They are generally good, safe place to meet new people.

ERRORS

misuse of plural form (4)
article misuse (3)
misspelling (2)
misuse of preposition (1)
misuse of relative pronoun (1)
misuse of verb form (7)
fragment (1)
incorrect subject-verb agreement (1)

5. A cat makes better pet than dog because cat is so much cleaner than dog. Cat usually stay out of dirt and mud, and if it does to get dirty, it will lick itself until its fur is cleaning. Cat is also careful to cover up its messes. Finally, when cat eats, it is eat small bites at a time so the food does not get scatter all over the floor. Dog, on the other hand, are alway get dirty. It enjoy to roll over in the dirt, especially right after bath! And even though it does make small effort to groom itself, it never licks its coat really clean. Owner must to bathe it for that. Finally, unlike a cat, when dog eats, he gobble down his food and water in big gulps, scattering the dog food and water all over floor. I'll take nice clean cat any day!

ERRORS

article misuse (15)
incorrect subject-verb agreement (4)
misuse of verb form (7)
misspelling (1)

6. There is significant difference between *conformity* and *compliance*. When person conforms, he is doing something because other are doing it. The person is motivating by a desire to be like other people. For example; if a youngster wear black jeans because all of his friends are, then this is call conformity. *Compliance*, on the other hand, refer to a situation where person does something because he or she is asked or told to do it. Even if he or she doesn't really want to do it. If a young person wear a black jeans because someone asked him to, then this situation is refer to as compliance.

ERRORS

article misuse (4)
incorrect subject-verb agreement (3)
punctuation error (1)
misuse of verb form (3)
misuse of plural form (1)
fragment (1)

7. Why is math so difficult for many student? One answer may be in the idea of the self-fulfilling prophecy. This is when you predict that something will happen and because of expectation that it will happen, it does. Many student expect to have difficult time in math, they may not even try very hard. As a result, they end up to get low grades in math! Another way prophecy is fulfilled is that if student expect finding math hard, they may become so anxious about it that they can't learn well. The result again is poor performance.

ERRORS

misuse of plural form (3)
article misuse (3)
misuse of verb form (2)
comma splice (1)

8. Many people wears sunglasses for protection, but most young person wear them because of vanity. They want to look "cool," like Tom Cruise in *Top Gun*. These person think that they resemble brave pilot when they are wearing their sunglass. Other young person like the sunglass that worn by the "Terminator." But the terminator is cold, not cool. He coldly murder person. Sometimes woman wear sunglass to look like the actresses or beautiful models whose photos are in magazine. They believe what the designers want them to believe. They think that the sunglass will to make them appearing beautiful, too, specially if the sunglass have designer labels and cost $75!

ERRORS

incorrect subject–verb agreement (2)
misuse of verb form (3)
misuse of plural form (12)
misspelling (1)

9. There are several reason I like to live in city. The first is the excitment I find there, the city is alive with people. If you go downtown during day, sidewalk are full of people hurrying to work, to store, to restaurant. You can find people selling thing like jewely, newspaper, popcorn, and hotdog on the street corners. They are always shouting, "Hey! Buy this!" All the people rushing around makes me feel happy. As if I am part of exciting city.

ERRORS

misuse of plural form (7)
article misuse (3)
comma splice (1)
incorrect subject–verb agreement (1)
fragment (1)
misspelling (2)

10. A half-cup of beans provides good nutrients. To begin with, bean contain many important amino acids. If you eat grains, meat, or dairy products with your bean, you will end up with a full serving of protein. Moreover, this same half-cup of the beans provide the average person with ⅙ of the daily irons recommendtion. An added bonus is that the bean contain soluble fiber that makes them very filling, which is real benefit for dieters! Finally, there is another benefit to our fat-conscious society beans do not contain fat.*

---

*Information from "Baked Beans," *Consumer Reports* Jan. 1989: p. 15.

Appendix XIII

Fallacies

To support an argument it is necessary to use clear, logical reasoning. Sometimes, however, an argument may seem logical but really violates the rules of logic. If the rules of logic are distorted or violated, an illogical piece of reasoning results. This is called a *fallacy*. There are a number of common fallacies to be aware of. Note that they fall into the following four major categories.

1. FALLACIES OF FAULTY INFERENCE. Fallacies of faulty inference are errors caused by drawing the wrong conclusion from evidence. If you look at a piece of evidence and come to a conclusion, make sure that your conclusion is warranted from the evidence. If you do not, you may commit one of these fallacies.

A *hasty generalization* is a generalization that is based on insufficient data or on data that is not representative.

> I have gone to the laundromat twice on Saturday and it has been busy. The laundromat is always busy on Saturday. I will never go on Saturday again.
>
> All of the students who are getting A's and B's in Mr. Boyd's class think that Mr. Boyd is a good teacher. Therefore, Mr. Boyd must be a good teacher.

The writer has come to conclusions that are not warranted from the evidence. In the first example, two Saturdays are not enough data, and in the second example, the students getting A's and B's are not representative of the whole class. Therefore, both are hasty generalizations.

An *oversimplified generalization* is a broad, sweeping generalization.

> All Americans are rich.

Here the writer is making a wide generalization about Americans. He is oversimplifying the issue. There are, in fact, a number of poor Americans. This fallacy occurs when attempting to simplify a somewhat complex issue.

Post hoc, ergo propter hoc is the fallacy of assuming that because one event followed another, the first event is the cause of the second.

> I saw Mr. Lloyd leave the building only five minutes before the bomb exploded. I'm sure that Mr. Lloyd planted the bomb.

This is faulty reasoning because we cannot be sure that there is a cause–effect relationship between the two events. We cannot tell from the evidence that Mr. Lloyd planted the bomb.

2. FALLACIES OF CONFUSION. Fallacies of confusion are errors caused by confusing one thing with another on the basis of some resemblance. In order to understand the most common fallacy of this type, we must first understand what an analogy is.

An analogy is a common kind of comparison in which you explain an unknown item by showing its similarities to a known item. For example, in order to explain how the university is expanding, you might compare it to a cake baking and rising in an oven. Analogies are useful for explanation, but remember that they can never be used to *prove* anything. You cannot *prove* that the universe is expanding by comparing it to a cake; you can only explain the phenomenon. A common fallacy of confusion involves analogy. If the analogy is not well drawn, a false conclusion may result.

False analogy is a fallacy of confusing what is true in one case with what is true in a similar case. In this fallacy, two events or items are compared that do not have enough similarities to predict that what happened in the one case will happen in the second. Thus, the conclusion arrived at is false.

> The United States today is just like ancient Rome. The U.S. economy is unstable, there is widespread unemployment, and the people only want to be entertained. Therefore, we can expect the United States to decline and fall just like ancient Rome did.

This is a false analogy because two things are compared that also have many differences. The structure of the Roman Empire, the slave system, the high-ranking nobility have all been ignored. Besides, the entire world situation today is much different from Roman times. All of these differences make the U.S. situation so different from the Roman situation that we cannot predict what will happen. In other words, there are not enough essential similarities between the two to come to a valid conclusion.

3. FALLACIES OF IRRELEVANCE. Fallacies of irrelevance are errors in reasoning in which the writer tries to ignore or evade the issue by directing the reader's attention to something irrelevant.

Ad hominem, a Latin phrase meaning "to the man," is the fallacy of attacking a person's character or motive instead of the person's argument. Be aware, though, that sometimes a person's character or motive is relevant to the argument. For instance, in a court of law, if an attorney can establish that the witness is a habitual liar, then she would have the right to suspect the witness' testimony. However, if the attorney attacked the same witness because he had a beard or had divorced his wife, she would be committing the *ad hominem* fallacy. These items are not relevant to the case but would be diverting attention away from the main issue to the person.

Mr. Thomas will not make a good governor. He has long hair and always wears blue jeans.

Ad populum, a Latin phrase meaning "to the crowd," is the fallacy of appealing to popularity or the widespread occurrence of something. It asserts that since everyone approves, it must be right.

Buy this car. It is the most popular car in the world.

If you want to be like royalty, drink XYZ wines.

Here the obvious appeals to popularity divert attention away from asking whether the car or the wines are good.

4. **FALLACIES OF ASSUMPTION.** Fallacies of assumption are errors in which something false or unproved is assumed to be true, or taken for granted.

Begging the question is the fallacy of giving the conclusion as evidence or changing the wording to prove something.

That movie is very frightening because it is scary.

We will live forever because we have immortal souls.

In the first example, you need to prove that the movie is frightening. Perhaps you could point to the music, the acting, or the special effects. But you have used another word that means the same thing as frightening. You have said that the movie is frightening. You have come to the conclusion that the movie is frightening, and you use that conclusion as evidence. In the second example, you need to prove that we will live forever. You beg the question; that is, you do not prove it, but simply restate your conclusion.

EXERCISE AXIII-1

For each of the following statements, tell which type of fallacy is being committed.

1. I want a new Buick because all the people in my neighborhood have Buicks. ____________

2. I talked to three people in my class who are against nuclear power. I guess everybody is against it. ____________
3. It rained yesterday. I am getting a cold today. I guess rain causes colds. ____________
4. All countries in the world use military force to enforce their laws. If the United Nations wants to enforce its rulings, it should use military force. ____________
5. All Germans love beer. ____________
6. Jane is wrong about nuclear power. I know she is wrong because what she says is simply incorrect. ____________
7. John thinks we should disband the United Nations. His opinion is worthless. After all, he is a known Communist. ____________.

Index

Text Credits

Habeeb Al-Saeed, original paragraph. Used by permission of the author.

Nader Alyousha, original paragraph, "Americans Are Friendly to Strangers." Used by permission of the author.

Isaac Asimov, "There's No Way to Go But Ahead." © 1975 Field Enterprises, Inc. Courtesy of Field Newspaper Syndicate. Reprinted with permission from the November 1975 ***Reader's Digest.***

Floyd Bonner, "My Old Neighborhood." Used by permission of the author.

Jane Brody, "Three Kinds of Fatigue." Copyright © 1980 by The New York Times Company. Reprinted by permission.

Louisette Caron, "My Favorite Sights." Used by permission of the author.

Rachel Carson, from *Silent Spring* by Rachel Carson. Copyright © 1962 by Rachel L. Carson. Reprinted by permission of Houghton Mifflin Company and Frances Collin, Trustee.

K. C. Cole, "Women and Physics." Copyright © 1981 by The New York Times Company. Reprinted by permission.

Jacques Cousteau, "The Bounty of the Sea." Reprinted with the permission of The Cousteau Society © 1974.

Tammam Dandashi, "The Heat Engine" and "Two University Systems." Used by permission of the author.

Milton Friedman, "Prohibition and Drugs." Copyright 1972 by Newsweek, Inc. All Rights Reserved. Reprinted by permission of the author.

Igor Gonzalez, "Studying Math." Used by permission of the author.

Bob Greene, "How Unwritten Rules Circumscribe Our Lives." Reprinted by permission: Tribune Media Services.

Suzanne Gremillion, original paragraph. Used by permission of the author.

John P. Houston, *Motivation*. Copyright © 1985 by Macmillan Publishing Company.

Alfred Kazin, excerpt from "The Kitchen," from *A Walker in the City*, copyright 1951 and renewed 1979 by Alfred Kazin, reprinted by permission of Harcourt Brace Jovanovich, Inc.

Helen Keller, *The Story of My Life*. Excerpt from *The Story of My Life* by Helen Keller. Copyright 1902, 03, 05, by Helen Keller. Reprinted by permission of Doubleday & Company, Inc.

N. R. Klienfield, "Portraits of a Cop." Reprinted by permission of Best of the Wall Street Journal. © Dow Jones & Company, Inc. 1973. All rights reserved.

Donald Landry, original paragraph. Used by permission of the author.

Camara Laye, excerpt from *The Dark Child* by Camara Laye. Copyright © 1954 and renewal copyright © 1982 by Camara Laye. Reprinted by permission of Farrar, Straus and Giroux, Inc.

Chun Lee, original paragraph. Used by permission of the author.

Nobutaka Matsuo, two original paragraphs. Used by permission of the author.

A. Miller, E. Williams, and J. Howard, excerpted from "Bargain Basements Move Upscale." From *Newsweek* 19 Dec. and © 1988, Newsweek, Inc. All rights reserved. Reprinted by permission.

N. Scott Momaday, *The Way to Rainy Mountain*. First published in *The Reporter*, 26 January 1967. Reprinted from *The Way to Rainy Mountain*, © 1969, The University of New Mexico Press.

Pamela Moran, original paragraph. Used by permission of the author.

Barbara Mujica, "Bilingualism's Goal." Copyright © 1984 by The New York Times Company. Reprinted by permission.

From P. O'Leary, P. Walsh, and R. Ham, "Managing Solid Waste." Copyright © 1988 by Scientific American, Inc. All rights reserved.

Carlos Palacio, adapted from "Kinds of Hotels." Used by permission of the author.

Letty Cottin Pogrebin, "Words That Count." © 1988 by Letty Cottin Pogrebin. Reprinted from *Ms.* magazine, August 1988.

Verónica Porta, original paragraph. Used by permission of the author.

From *Psychology, Second Edition*, by Camille Wortman and Elizabeth F. Loftus. Copyright © 1985, 1981 by Alfred A. Knopf, Inc. Reprinted by permission of Alfred A. Knopf, Inc.

Mauricio Rodriguez, two original paragraphs. Used by permission of the author.

Carl Sagan, *Broca's Brain: Reflections on the Romance of Science*. Copyright © 1979 by Carl Sagan. All rights reserved. Reprinted by permission of the author.

Adam Smith, from *Powers of Mind* by Adam Smith. Copyright © 1975 by Adam Smith. Reprinted by permission of Random House, Inc. and International Creative Management Inc.

Anastasia Toufexis, "The Most Powerful Bond of All." Copyright 1984 Time Inc. Reprinted by permission.

Carolyn Udell, "Roaches." Used by permission of the author.

Tom Waters, excerpted from "Killer Gene." Tom Waters/© 1988 Discover Publications.

Tom Wolfe, "Columbus and the Moon." Copyright © 1979 by The New York Times Company. Reprinted by permission.

Elizabeth Wong, "The Struggle to Be an All-American Girl." Reprinted with permission from the author.

Jade Snow Wong, "Uncle Kwok" from *The Fifth Chinese Daughter*. Reprinted by permission of Curtis Brown, Ltd. Copyright © 1945, 1948, 1950 by Jade Snow Wong.

From Richard J. Wurtman and Judith J. Wurtman, "Carbohydrates and Depression." Copyright © 1989 by Scientific American, Inc. All rights reserved.

Gary D. Yanker, excerpts from "Walk Your Way to Health and Fitness." Reprinted with permission from the June 1984 Reader's Digest and the author.

Photo Credits

Page 1: Eric Liebowitz. **Page 25:** Eileen Prince. **Page 29:** Perkins School for the Blind, Watertown, Massachusetts 02172, photograph of Helen Keller and Anne Sullivan. Used by permission. **Page 68:** Eric Liebowitz. **Page 72:** Aggie Lorenzo. **Page 79:** Sona Doran. **Page 81:** Dennis Smith. **Page 118:** Sona Doran. **Page 129:** Eileen Prince. **Page 163:** Sona Doran. **Page 177:** The Bettmann Archive. **Page 189:** Eric Liebowitz. **Page 197:** Sona Doran. **Page 229:** Eric Liebowitz. **Page 233:** NASA. **Page 267:** Sona Doran. **Page 298:** Eric Liebowitz. **Page 305:** Greg Orr. **Page 313:** Sona Doran. **Page 342:** The Bettmann Archive. **Page 381:** Sona Doran. **Page 385:** © R. Visser/Greenpeace.